TAKING SIDES

Clashing Views in

United States History, Volume 1, The Colonial Period to Reconstruction

THIRTEENTH EDITION

TAKING SIDES

Clashing Views in

United States History, Volume 1, The Colonial Period to Reconstruction

THIRTEENTH EDITION

Selected, Edited, and with Introductions by

Larry Madaras
Howard Community College

and

James M. SoRelle
Baylor University

Boston Burr Ridge, IL Dubuque, IA New York San Francisco St. Louis
Bangkok Bogotá Caracas Kuala Lumpur Lisbon London Madrid Mexico City
Milan Montreal New Delhi Santiago Seoul Singapore Sydney Taipei Toronto

The McGraw·Hill Companies

McGraw-Hill Higher Education

TAKING SIDES: CLASHING VIEWS IN UNITED STATES HISTORY, VOLUME 1, THIRTEENTH EDITION

Published by McGraw-Hill, a business unit of The McGraw-Hill Companies, Inc., 1221 Avenue of the Americas, New York, NY 10020.
Taking Sides is published by the **Contemporary Learning Series** group within the McGraw-Hill Higher Education division.

1 2 3 4 5 6 7 8 9 0 DOC/DOC 0 9 8

MHID: 0-07-351533-7
ISBN: 978-0-07-351533-5
ISSN: 1091-8833

Managing Editor: *Larry Loeppke*
Production Manager: *Faye Schilling*
Senior Developmental Editor: *Jill Peter*
Editorial Assistant: *Nancy Meissner*
Production Service Assistant: *Rita Hingtgen*
Permissions Coordinator: *Leonard J. Behnke*
Senior Marketing Manager: *Julie Keck*
Marketing Communications Specialist: *Mary Klein*
Marketing Coordinator: *Alice Link*
Project Manager: *Jane Mohr*
Design Specialist: *Tara McDermott*
Cover Graphics: *Kristine Jubeck*

Compositor: ICC Macmillan Inc.
Cover Image: Library of Congress [LC-USZC4-4961]

Library of Congress Cataloging-in-Publication Data

Main entry under title:
Taking sides: clashing views in American history, volume 1, the colonial period to reconstruction/selected, edited, and with introductions by Larry Madaras and James M. SoRelle.—13th ed.

Includes bibliographical references.
1. United States—History. I. Madaras, Larry, *comp.* II. SoRelle, James M., *comp.*
973

www.mhhe.com

Preface

The success of the past 12 editions of *Taking Sides: Clashing Views in United States History* has encouraged us to remain faithful to its original objectives, methods, and format. Our aim has been to create an effective instrument to enhance classroom learning and to foster critical thinking. Historical facts presented in a vacuum are of little value to the educational process. For students, whose search for historical truth often concentrates on *when* something happened rather than on *why*, and on specific events rather than on the *significance* of those events, *Taking Sides* is designed to offer an interesting and valuable departure. The understanding that the reader arrives at based on the evidence that emerges from the clash of views encourages the reader to view history as an *interpretive* discipline, not one of rote memorization.

As in previous editions, the 16 issues and 32 essays that follow are arranged in chronological order and can be incorporated easily into any American history survey course. Each issue has an *introduction,* which sets the stage for the debate that follows in the pro and con selections and provides historical and methodological background to the problem that the issue examines. Each issue concludes with a *postscript,* which ties the readings together, briefly mentions alternative interpretations, and supplies detailed *suggestions for further reading* for the student who wishes to pursue the topics raised in the issue. Also, Internet site addresses (URLs), which should prove useful as starting points for further research, have been provided on the *Internet References* page that accompanies each unit opener. At the back of the book is a listing of all the *contributors to this volume* with a brief biographical sketch of each of the authors whose views are debated here.

Changes to this edition In this edition we have continued our efforts to maintain a balance between traditional political, diplomatic, and cultural issues and the new social history, which depicts a society that benefited from the presence of Native Americans, African Americans, women, and workers of various racial and ethnic backgrounds. With this in mind, we present six new issues: Was the Settlement of Jamestown a Fiasco? (Issue 3); Was the Salem Witchcraft Hysteria Caused by a Fear of Women? (Issue 4); Was Alexander Hamilton an Economic Genius? (Issue 7); Was John Brown an Irrational Terrorist? (Issue 13); Was Slavery the Key Issue in the Sectional Conflict Leading to the Civil War? (Issue 14); and Did Reconstruction Fail as a Result of Racism? (Issue 16). In all, there are 14 new selections.

A word to the instructor An *Instructor's Resource Guide with Test Questions* (multiple-choice and essay) is available through the publisher for the instructor using *Taking Sides* in the classroom. A general guidebook, *Using Taking Sides in the Classroom,* which discusses methods and techniques for integrating the procon approach into any classroom setting, is also available. An online version of *Using Taking Sides in the Classroom* and a correspondence service for *Taking Sides* adopters can be found at http://www.mhcls.com/usingts/.

Acknowledgments Many individuals have contributed to the successful completion of this edition. We appreciate the evaluations submitted to McGraw-Hill Contemporary Learning Series by those who have used *Taking Sides* in the classroom. Special thanks to those who responded with specific suggestions for past editions.

We are particularly indebted to Maggie Cullen, Cindy SoRelle, the late Barry Crouch, Kimberly Kellison, Virginia Kirk, Joseph and Helen Mitchell, Jean Soto, and Julie Anne Sweet, who shared their ideas for changes, pointed us toward potentially useful historical works, and provided significant editorial assistance. Lynn Wilder performed indispensable typing duties connected with this project. Ela Ciborowski, James Johnson, and Sharon Glover in the library at Howard Community College provided essential help in acquiring books and articles on interlibrary loan. Finally, we are sincerely grateful for the commitment, encouragement, and patience provided in recent years by Jill Peter, senior development editor for the *Taking Sides* series, and the entire staff of McGraw-Hill Contemporary Learning Series.

Larry Madaras
Emeritus, Howard Community College

James M. SoRelle
Baylor University

Contents In Brief

Contents

Preface v

Correlation Guide xiv

Introduction xvii

UNIT 1 COLONIAL SOCIETY 1

Issue 1. Is History True? 2

YES: Oscar Handlin, from *Truth in History* (The Belknap Press of Harvard University Press, 1979) *4*

NO: William H. McNeill, from "Mythistory, or Truth, Myth, History, and Historians," *The American Historical Review* (February 1986) *12*

Oscar Handlin insists that historical truth is absolute and knowable by historians who adopt the scientific method of research to discover factual evidence that provides both a chronology and context for their findings. William McNeill argues that historical truth is general and evolutionary and is discerned by different groups at different times and in different places in a subjective manner that has little to do with a scientifically absolute methodology.

Issue 2. Was Disease the Key Factor in the Depopulation of Native Americans in the Americas? 23

YES: Colin G. Calloway, from *New Worlds for All: Indians, Europeans, and the Remaking of Early America* (The Johns Hopkins University Press, 1997) *25*

NO: David S. Jones, from "Virgin Soils Revisited," *William & Mary Quarterly* (October 2003) *33*

Colin Calloway says that while Native Americans confronted numerous diseases in the Americas, traditional Indian healing practices failed to offer much protection from the diseases introduced by Europeans beginning in the late-fifteenth century and which decimated the indigenous peoples. David Jones recognizes the disastrous impact of European diseases on Native Americans, but he insists that Indian depopulation was also a consequence of the forces of poverty, malnutrition, environmental stress, dislocation, and social disparity.

Issue 3. Was the Settlement of Jamestown a Fiasco? 43

YES: Edmund S. Morgan, from *American Slavery, American Freedom: The Ordeal of Colonial Virginia* (W.W. Norton, 1975) *45*

NO: Karen Ordahl Kupperman, from *The Jamestown Project* (Harvard University Press, 2007) *54*

Professor Edmund S. Morgan argues that Virginia's first decade as a colony was a complete "fiasco" because the settlers were too lazy to engage in the subsistence farming necessary for their survival and failed to abandon their own and the Virginia Company's expectations of establishing extractive industries such as mining, timber, and fishing. Professor Karen Ordahl Kupperman argues that Jamestown was America's first successful

colony because in its first decade of trial and error "the ingredients for success—widespread ownership of land, control of taxation for public obligations through a representative assembly, the institution of a normal society through the inclusion of women, and development of a product that could be marketed profitably to sustain the economy—were beginning to be put in place by 1618 and were in full operation by 1620, when the next successful colony, Plymouth, was planted."

Issue 4. Was the Salem Witchcraft Hysteria Caused by a Fear of Women? 66

YES: Carol F. Karlsen, from *The Devil in the Shape of a Woman: Witchcraft in Colonial New England* (W. W. Norton, 1987) *68*

NO: Mary Beth Norton, from *In the Devil's Snare: The Salem Witchcraft Crisis of 1692* (Alfred A. Knopf, 2002) *78*

Carol Karlsen contends that the belief that woman was evil existed implicitly at the core of Puritan culture and explains why alleged witches, as threats to the desired order of society, were generally seen as women. Mary Beth Norton associates the events in Salem to borderland disputes with Native Americans and the French in northern New England, which led residents of Salem and Essex County to conflate attacks by Indians with assaults by witches to explain the problems confronting Massachusetts Bay Colony in the late seventeenth century.

UNIT 2 REVOLUTION AND THE NEW NATION 89

Issue 5. Did the American Revolution Produce a Christian Nation? 90

YES: Nathan O. Hatch, from "The Democratization of Christianity and the Character of American Politics," in Mark A. Noll, ed., *Religion and American Politics* (Oxford University Press, 1990) *92*

NO: Jon Butler, from "Why Revolutionary America Wasn't a 'Christian Nation'," in James H. Hutson, ed., *Religion and the New Republic: Faith in the Founding of America* (Rowman and Littlefield, 2000) *102*

Nathan Hatch argues that by eroding traditional appeals to authority and expanding the number of people who believed they were competent to think for themselves about freedom, equality, and representation, the American Revolution led to an expansion of evangelical Christianity that reinforced the democratic impulses of the new society. Jon Butler insists that men and women seldom referred to America as a "Christian nation" between 1760 and 1790 and that even though Christianity was important, most Americans opposed a Christian national identity enforced by law or governmental action.

Issue 6. Were the Founding Fathers Democratic Reformers? 112

YES: John P. Roche, from "The Founding Fathers: A Reform Caucus in Action," *American Political Science Review* (December 1961) *114*

NO: Howard Zinn, from *A People's History of the United States* (Harper Collins, 1999) *126*

Political scientist John P. Roche asserts that the Founding Fathers were not only revolutionaries but also superb democratic politicians who created

a constitution that supported the needs of the nation and at the same time was acceptable to the people. According to radical historian Howard Zinn, the Founding Fathers were an elite group of northern money interests and southern slaveholders who used Shay's Rebellion in Massachusetts as a pretext to create a strong central government, which protected the property rights of the rich to the exclusion of slaves, Indians, and non-property-holding whites.

Issue 7. Was Alexander Hamilton an Economic Genius? 139

YES: John Steele Gordon, from *An Empire of Wealth: The Epic History of American Economic Power* (Harper Collins, 2004) *141*

NO: Carey Roberts, from "Alexander Hamilton and the 1790s Economy: A Reappraisal," in Douglas Ambrose and Robert W. T. Martin, eds., *The Many Faces of Alexander Hamilton: The Life and Legacy of America's Most Elusive Founding Father* (New York University Press, 2006) *150*

Historian John Steele Gordon claims that Hamilton's policies for funding and assuming the debts of the confederation and state governments and for establishing a privately controlled Bank of the United States laid the foundation for the rich and powerful national economy we enjoy today. Professor Carey Roberts argues that in the 1790s Hamilton's financial policies undermined popular faith in the Federalist Party, diminished confidence in the federal government.

Issue 8. Was James Madison an Effective Wartime President? 164

YES: Drew R. McCoy, from *The Last of the Fathers: James Madison and the Republican Legacy* (Cambridge University Press, 1989) *166*

NO: Donald R. Hickey, from *The War of 1812: A Forgotten Conflict* (University of Illinois Press, 1989) *174*

Drew McCoy argues that James Madison was a man of integrity and virtue who exercised patience and restraint as commander-in-chief and who displayed great bravery in confronting both his domestic detractors and the nation's military foes during the War of 1812. Donald Hickey contends that Madison failed to provide the bold and vigorous leadership that was essential to a successful prosecution of the War of 1812 by tolerating incompetence among his generals and cabinet officers and by failing to secure vital legislation from Congress.

Issue 9. Did the Election of 1828 Represent a Democratic Revolt of the People? 185

YES: Sean Wilentz, from *The Rise of American Democracy: Jefferson to Lincoln* (Norton, 2005) *187*

NO: Richard P. McCormick, from "New Perspectives on Jacksonian Politics," *The American Historical Review* (January 1960) *196*

Bancroft Prize winner Sean Wilentz argues that in spite of its vulgarities and slanders, the 1828 election campaign "produced a valediction on the faction-ridden jumble of the Era of Bad Feelings and announced the rough arrival of two district national coalitions." Professor Richard P. McCormick believes that voting statistics demonstrate that a genuine political revolution

did not take place until the presidential election of 1840, when fairly well-balanced political parties had been organized in virtually every state.

Issue 10. Did the Industrial Revolution Provide More Economic Opportunities for Women in the 1830s? 209

YES: Thomas Dublin, from "Women, Work, and Protest in the Early Lowell Mills: 'The Oppressing Hand of Avarice Would Enslave Us'," *Labor History* (Winter 1975) *211*

NO: Gerda Lerner, from "The Lady and the Mill Girl: Changes in the Status of Women in the Age of Jackson," *American Studies* (Spring 1969) *224*

Professor Thomas Dublin argues that the women who worked in the Lowell mills in the 1830s were a close-knit community who developed bonds of mutual dependence in both their boarding houses and the factory. According to Professor Gerda Lerner, while Jacksonian democracy provided political and economic opportunities for men, both the "lady" and the "mill girl" were equally disenfranchised and isolated from vital centers of economic opportunity.

UNIT 3 ANTEBELLUM AMERICA 239

Issue 11. Did Slavery Destroy the Black Family? 240

YES: Wilma A. Dunaway, from *The African-American Family in Slavery and Emancipation* (Cambridge University Press, 2003) *242*

NO: Eugene D. Genovese, from *Roll, Jordan, Roll: The World the Slaves Made* (Random House, 1974) *255*

Professor Wilma A. Dunaway believes that modern historians have exaggerated the amount of control slaves exercised over their lives and underplayed the cruelty of the slave experience—family separations, nutritional deficiencies, sexual exploitation and physical abuse that occurred on the majority of small plantations. Professor Genovese argues that slaves developed their own system of family and cultural values within the Southern paternalistic and pre-capitalistic slave society.

Issue 12. Was the Mexican War an Exercise in American Imperialism? 267

YES: Ramón Eduardo Ruiz, from "Manifest Destiny and the Mexican War," in Howard H. Quint, Milton Cantor, and Dean Albertson, eds., *Main Problems in American History,* 5th ed. (Dorsey Press, 1988) *269*

NO: Norman A. Graebner, from "The Mexican War: A Study in Causation," *Pacific Historical Review* (August 1980) *277*

Professor of history Ramón Eduardo Ruiz argues that for the purpose of conquering Mexico's northern territories, the United States waged an aggressive war against Mexico from which Mexico never recovered. Professor of diplomatic history Norman A. Graebner argues that President James Polk pursued an aggressive policy that he believed would force Mexico to sell New Mexico and California to the United States and to recognize the annexation of Texas without starting a war.

Issue 13. Was John Brown an Irrational Terrorist? 288

YES: **C. Vann Woodward,** from *The Burden of Southern History,* 3d ed. (Louisiana State University Press, 1993) *290*

NO: **David S. Reynolds,** from *John Brown, Abolitionist: The Man Who Killed Slavery, Sparked the Civil War, and Seeded Civil Rights* (Alfred A. Knopf, 2005) *298*

C. Vann Woodward depicts John Brown as a fanatic who committed wholesale murder in Kansas in 1856 and whose ill-fated assault on Harpers Ferry, Virginia, in 1859 was an irrational act of treason against the United States. David S. Reynolds portrays John Brown as a deeply religious, yet deeply flawed, humanitarian reformer who employed violent means in Kansas and in the raid at Harpers Ferry against proslavery outrages at a time when the United States had failed to live up to its most cherished ideal of human equality.

UNIT 4 CONFLICT AND RESOLUTION 309

Issue 14. Was Slavery the Key Issue in the Sectional Conflict Leading to the Civil War? 310

YES: **Charles B. Dew,** from *Apostles of Disunion: Southern Secession Commissioners and the Causes of the Civil War* (University of Virginia Press, 2001) *312*

NO: **Joel H. Silbey,** from *The Partisan Imperative: The Dynamics of American Politics Before the Civil War* (Oxford University Press, 1985) *320*

Charles B. Dew uses the speeches and public letters of 41 white southerners who, as commissioners in 1860 and 1861, attempted to secure support for secession by appealing to their audiences' commitment to the preservation of slavery and the doctrine of white supremacy. Joel H. Silbey argues that historians have overemphasized the sectional conflict over slavery and have neglected to analyze local ethnocultural issues among the events leading to the Civil War.

Issue 15. Did Abraham Lincoln Free the Slaves? 330

YES: **Stephen B. Oates,** from *Abraham Lincoln: The Man Behind the Myths* (Harper & Row, 1984) *332*

NO: **Vincent Harding,** from *There Is a River: The Black Struggle for Freedom in America* (Harcourt Brace Jovanovich, 1981) *341*

Stephen B. Oates argues that Abraham Lincoln, in his capacity as president of the United States, was the individual most responsible for sanctioning an unprecedented use of military power against state institutions in the form of the Emancipation Proclamation, which further encouraged slaves to abandon the farms and plantations of their rebel masters. Vincent Harding credits slaves themselves for engaging in a dramatic movement of self-liberation while Abraham Lincoln initially refused to declare the destruction of slavery as a war aim and then issued the Emancipation Proclamation, which failed to free any slaves in areas over which he had any authority.

Issue 16. Did Reconstruction Fail as a Result of Racism? 352

YES: **George M. Fredrickson,** from *The Black Image in the White Mind: The Debate on Afro-American Character and Destiny, 1817–1914* (Harper & Row, 1971) *354*

NO: **Heather Cox Richardson,** from *The Death of Reconstruction: Race, Labor, and Politics in the Post-Civil War North, 1865–1901* (Harvard University Press, 2001) *362*

George M. Fredrickson concludes that racism, in the form of the doctrine of white supremacy, colored the thinking not only of southern whites but of most white northerners as well and produced only half-hearted efforts by the Radical Republicans in the postwar period to sustain a commitment to black equality. Heather Cox Richardson argues that the failure of Radical Reconstruction was primarily a consequence of a national commitment to a free-labor ideology that opposed an expanding central government that legislated rights to African Americans that other citizens had acquired through hard work.

Contributors 373

Correlation Guide

The *Taking Sides* series presents current issues in a debate-style format designed to stimulate student interest and develop critical thinking skills. Each issue is thoughtfully framed with an issue summary, an issue introduction, and a postscript. The pro and con essays—selected for their liveliness and substance—represent the arguments of leading scholars and commentators in their fields.

Taking Sides: Clashing Views in United States History, Volume 1: The Colonial Period to Reconstruction, 13/e is an easy-to-use reader that presents issues on important topics such as *colonial society, revolution and the new nation, antebellum America,* and *conflict/resolution.* For more information on *Taking Sides* and other *McGraw-Hill Contemporary Learning Series* titles, visit www.mhcls.com.

This convenient guide matches the issues in **Taking Sides: United States History, Volume 1, 13/e** with the corresponding chapters in one of our best-selling McGraw-Hill History textbooks by Davidson et al.

Taking Sides: United States History, Volume 1, 13/e	Nation of Nations: A Narrative History of the American Republic, Volume 1: To 1877, 6/e by Davidson et al.
Issue 1: Is History True?	**Chapter 1:** The First Civilizations of North America
Issue 2: Was Disease the Key Factor in the Depopulation of Native Americans?	**Chapter 1:** The First Civilizations of North America
Issue 3: Was the Jamestown Settlement a Fiasco?	**Chapter 2:** Old Worlds, New Worlds (1400–1600) **Chapter 3:** Colonization and Conflict in the South (1600–1750)
Issue 4: Was the Salem Witchcraft Hysteria Caused by a Fear of Women?	**Chapter 4:** Colonization and Conflict in the North (1600–1700)
Issue 5: Did the American Revolution Produce a Christian Nation?	**Chapter 8:** Crisis and Constitution (1776–1789) **Chapter 9:** The Early Republic (1789–1824)
Issue 6: Were the Founding Fathers Democratic Reformers?	**Chapter 11:** The Rise of Democracy (1824–1840)
Issue 7: Was Alexander Hamilton an Economic Genius?	**Chapter 8:** Crisis and Constitution (1776–1789) **Chapter 9:** The Early Republic (1789–1824)
Issue 8: Was James Madison an Effective Wartime President?	**Chapter 8:** Crisis and Constitution (1776–1789) **Chapter 9:** The Early Republic (1789–1824)
Issue 9: Did the Election of 1828 Represent a Democratic Revolt of the People?	**Chapter 11:** The Rise of Democracy (1824–1840)
Issue 10: Did the Industrial Revolution Provide More Opportunities for Women in the 1830s?	**Chapter 14:** Western Expansion and the Rise of Slavery (1820–1850)

Taking Sides: United States History, Volume 1, 13/e	Nation of Nations: A Narrative History of the American Republic, Volume 1: To 1877, 6/e by Davidson et al.
Issue 11: Did Slavery Destroy the Black Family?	**Chapter 13:** The Old South (1820–1860)
Issue 12: Was the Mexican War an Exercise in American Imperialism?	**Chapter 14:** Western Expansion and the Rise of Slavery (1820–1850)
Issue 13: Was John Brown an Irrational Terrorist?	**Chapter 15:** The Union Broken (1850–1861)
Issue 14: Was Slavery the Key Issue in the Sectional Conflict Leading to the Civil War?	**Chapter 15:** The Union Broken (1850–1861)
Issue 15: Did Abraham Lincoln Free the Slaves?	**Chapter 15:** The Union Broken (1850–1861) **Chapter 16:** Total War and the Republic (1861–1865) **Chapter 17:** Reconstructing the Union (1865–1877)
Issue 16: Did Reconstruction Fail as a Result of Racism?	**Chapter 17:** Reconstructing the Union (1865–1877)

Introduction

The Study of History

Larry Madaras
James M. SoRelle

In a pluralistic society such as ours, the study of history is bound to be a complex process. How an event is interpreted depends not only on the existing evidence but also on the perspective of the interpreter. Consequently, understanding history presupposes the evaluation of information, a task that often leads to conflicting conclusions. An understanding of history, then, requires the acceptance of the idea of historical relativism. Relativism means that redefinition of our past is always possible and desirable. History shifts, changes, and grows with new and different evidence and interpretations. As is the case with the law and even with medicine, beliefs that were unquestioned 100 or 200 years ago have been discredited or discarded since.

Relativism, then, encourages revisionism. There is a maxim that "the past must remain useful to the present." Historian Carl Becker argued that every generation should examine history for itself, thus ensuring constant scrutiny of our collective experience through new perspectives. History, consequently, does not remain static, in part because historians cannot avoid being influenced by the times in which they live. Almost all historians commit themselves to revising the views of other historians, synthesizing theories into macro-interpretations, or revising the revisionists.

Schools of Thought

Three predominant schools of thought have emerged in American history since the first graduate seminars in history were given at The Johns Hopkins University in Baltimore in the 1870s. The *progressive* school dominated the professional field in the first half of the twentieth century. Influenced by the reform currents of Populism, progressivism, and the New Deal, these historians explored the social and economic forces that energized America. The progressive scholars tended to view the past in terms of conflicts between groups, and they sympathized with the underdog.

The post–World War II period witnessed the emergence of a new group of historians who viewed the conflict thesis as overly simplistic. Writing against the backdrop of the Cold War, these *neoconservative,* or *consensus,* historians argued that Americans possess a shared set of values and that the areas of agreement within our nation's basic democratic and capitalistic framework are more important than the areas of disagreement.

In the 1960s, however, the civil rights movement, women's liberation, and the student rebellion (with its condemnation of the war in Vietnam) fragmented the consensus of values upon which historians and social scientists of the 1950s had centered their interpretations. This turmoil set the stage for the emergence of another group of scholars. *New Left* historians began to reinterpret the past once again. They emphasized the significance of conflict in American history, and they resurrected interest in those groups ignored by the consensus school. In addition, New Left historians critiqued the expansionist policies of the United States and emphasized the difficulties confronted by Native Americans, African Americans, women, and urban workers in gaining full citizenship status.

Progressive, consensus, and New Left history is still being written. The most recent generation of scholars, however, focuses upon social history. Their primary concern is to discover what the lives of "ordinary Americans" were really like. These new social historians employ previously overlooked court and church documents, house deeds and tax records, letters and diaries, photographs, and census data to reconstruct the everyday lives of average Americans. Some employ new methodologies, such as quantification (enhanced by advancing computer technology) and oral history, whereas others borrow from the disciplines of political science, economics, sociology, anthropology, and psychology for their historical investigations.

The proliferation of historical approaches, which are reflected in the issues debated in this book, has had mixed results. On the one hand, historians have become so specialized in their respective time periods and methodological styles that it is difficult to synthesize the recent scholarship into a comprehensive text for the general reader. On the other hand, historians know more about the American past than at any other time in history. They dare to ask new questions or ones that previously were considered to be germane only to scholars in other social sciences. Although there is little agreement about the answers to these questions, the methods employed and issues explored make the "new history" a very exciting field to study.

Issue 1 discusses the key element of historical truth and the extent to which historians, applying the technique of empirical research, can determine exactly what happened in the past. Oscar Handlin insists that the truth of past events is absolute and knowable if pursued by historians employing the scientific method of research. William McNeill, however, argues that the absolute truth about human behavior is unattainable because historians do not have all the facts at their disposal and because they tend to organize their evidence and make intellectual choices based on subjective judgments. Consequently, historians' interpretations may be challenged by others who approach the evidence from a different point of view.

The topics that follow represent a variety of perspectives and approaches. Each of these controversial issues can be studied for its individual importance to our nation's history. Taken as a group, they interact with one another to illustrate larger historical themes. When grouped thematically, the issues reveal continuing motifs in the development of American history.

The New Social History

Some of the most innovative historical research over the last 40 years reflects the interests of the new social historians. The work of several representatives of this group who treat the issues of race, gender, and class appears in this volume. For example, in Issue 2, Colin Calloway and David Jones discuss the impact of the encounters between Europeans and Native Americans. Calloway says that although Native Americans confronted numerous diseases in the Americas, traditional Indian healing practices failed to offer much protection from the diseases introduced by Europeans beginning in the late-fifteenth century, which decimated the indigenous peoples. Jones recognizes the disastrous impact of European diseases on Native Americans, but he insists that Indian depopulation also was a consequence of the forces of poverty, malnutrition, environmental stress, dislocation, and social disparity.

The English efforts to establish a permanent colony at Jamestown beginning in 1607 are addressed in Issue 3. Edmund S. Morgan emphasizes the difficulties involved in that project and is critical of the settlers' unwillingness to abandon the Virginia Company's goals of establishing extractive industries such as mining, timber, and fishing when their own physical preservation required their attention to subsistence farming. Karen Ordahl Kupperman believes that Morgan overlooks the fact that by 1618 the Jamestown settlers had achieved the main ingredients for success through a program of widespread land ownership, the creation of representative government, and the development of a marketable cash crop—tobacco—to sustain the colony.

The impact of the institution of slavery on the African American family is explored in Issue 11. Focusing on harsh realities of the antebellum plantation system in the South, Wilma Dunaway criticizes those historians who have insisted that slaves succeeded in exercising a significant amount of control over their own lives, including the realm of family relations. Eugene Genovese, one of Dunaway's targets, argues that slaves developed their own system of family and cultural values within the southern paternalistic and pre-capitalist slave society.

Two issues explore the field of women's history. Study of the Salem witch trials has produced several quite imaginative scholarly explanations for this episode in New England's history. In Issue 4, Carol F. Karlsen analyzes the relationship between the Salem witchcraft hysteria of 1692 and Puritan attitudes toward women. The belief that women were inherently evil, Karlsen concludes, operated at the core of Puritan culture. Such attitudes made it easy to blame women for disruptions in New England society. Mary Beth Norton, on the other hand, associates the events in Salem to borderland disputes with Native Americans and the French in northern New England, which led residents of Salem and Essex County to conflate attacks by Indians with assaults by witches to explain the problems confronting Massachusetts Bay Colony in the late-seventeenth century.

Issue 10 addresses the economic opportunities available to women in the 1830s. Thomas Dublin examines the labor opportunities for women in the Lowell, Massachusetts, textile mills and concludes that they benefited from the mutually dependent society that they created within their living quarters and the factories. Gerda Lerner counters this more optimistic view of women's status by concluding that most women in Jacksonian America were disfranchised and isolated from vital centers of economic opportunity.

Revolution, Religion, and Reform in the New Nation

The impact of the American Revolution on religion is considered in Issue 5. Nathan Hatch insists that the American Revolution led to an expansion of evangelical Christianity that reinforced the democratic impulses of the new nation. Jon Butler counters with the argument that, although Christianity was important, most Americans opposed a Christian national identity enforced by law of governmental action.

The major and most controversial reform effort in the pre–Civil War period was the movement to abolish slavery. Issue 13 examines the terrorist activities carried out by John Brown and his followers. C. Vann Woodward depicts John Brown as a fanatic who committed wholesale murder in Kansas in 1856 and whose ill-fated assault on Harpers Ferry, Virginia, in 1859, though admired by his fellow abolitionists and many northern intellectuals, was an irrational act of treason against the United States. David S. Reynolds portrays John Brown as a deeply religious, yet deeply flawed, humanitarian reformer who employed violent means in Kansas and in the raid at Harpers Ferry in opposition to proslavery outrages at a time when the United States had failed to live up to its most cherished ideal of human equality.

War, Leadership, and Resolution

As a nation committed to peace, the United States has faced some of its sternest tests in times of war. Such conflicts inevitably have challenged the leadership abilities of the commanders-in-chief, the commitment of the nation to involve itself in war, and the ideals of the republic founded on democratic principles. Several issues in this volume address the response to war and its aftermath. In Issue 8, Drew McCoy and Donald Hickey evaluate the wartime leadership of James Madison in the War of 1812. McCoy argues that James Madison was a man of integrity and virtue who exercised patience and restraint as commander-in-chief and who displayed great bravery in confronting both his domestic detractors and the nation's military foes during the War of 1812. Hickey, in contrast, claims that Madison failed to provide bold and vigorous leadership during the conflict.

Four issues cover topics relating to the Civil War and its consequences. In Issue 14, Charles B. Dew and Joel H. Silbey debate the causes of the Civil War. Dew employs the words of white southerners whose job it was to promote the cause of secession following Abraham Lincoln's election by appealing to their audiences' commitment to the preservation of slavery and the doctrine of white supremacy. Joel Silbey argues that historians have paid too much attention to the sectional conflict over slavery and have neglected to analyze ethnocultural factors as keys to the Civil War.

But what kind of conflict was the American Civil War? During the war, the end of slavery became a Union goal. To what extent was Abraham Lincoln responsible for freeing the slaves? In Issue 15, Stephen B. Oates argues that Abraham Lincoln was the individual most responsible for sanctioning an unprecedented use of military power against state institutions in the form of the Emancipation Proclamation, which further encouraged slaves to abandon the farms and plantations of their rebel masters. Vincent Harding, however, defends the position that slaves were the agents of their own freedom, while Lincoln was reluctant to make emancipation a war issue.

With the end of slavery, one of the most controversial questions confronting those responsible for reconstructing the nation following the war involved the future of African Americans. Perhaps no other period of American history has been subjected to more myths than has this postwar era. Even though most scholars today recognize that Reconstruction did not achieve its most enlightened economic and social goals, they differ in their explanations about the source of this failure. In Issue 16, George M. Fredrickson concludes that racism, in the form of the doctrine of white supremacy, colored the thinking not only of southern whites but of most white northerners as well and produced only half-hearted efforts by the Radical Republicans in the postwar period to sustain a commitment to black equality. Heather Cox Richardson, on the other hand, argues that the failure of Radical Reconstruction was primarily a consequence of a national commitment to a free-labor ideology that opposed an expanding central government that legislated rights to African Americans that other citizens had acquired through hard work.

Politics in America

The American people gave legitimacy to their revolution through the establishment of a republican form of government. The United States has operated under two constitutions: the first established the short-lived confederation from 1781 to 1789; the second was written in 1787 and remains in effect over two hundred years later. In Issue 6, John P. Roche contends that the drafters of the Constitution of the United States were democratic reformers. Howard Zinn describes the founders as members of an economic elite who desired a stronger central government to protect their property rights.

Alexander Hamilton was one of the most significant leaders of the early national period. Issue 7 explores Hamilton's skills as the primary architect of the nation's economic policies. John Steele Gordon views Hamilton as the person most responsible for the powerful national economy we enjoy today. Carey Roberts, however, argues that Hamilton's economic policies diminished people's confidence in the Federalist Party and its leadership.

According to the Constitution, an election is held every four years to choose a president. Political scientists have designated those elections, which mark a significant change in the distribution of power, as "key" or "realigning" elections. In Issue 9, Sean Wilentz concludes that the presidential election of 1828 marked a significant victory for the democratization of American society. Richard McCormick, however, believes that a genuine political revolution did not occur until the presidential election of 1840.

Comparative History: America in a Global Perspective

The role of American history within the larger framework of world history is central to the discussion presented in one of the issues in this volume. A discussion of early nineteenth-century foreign policy in Issue 12 concerns both U.S. diplomatic relations with the rest of the world and America's self-perception within the world of nations. Did the U.S. government conceive of its power as continental, hemispheric, or worldwide? And what were the consequences of these attitudes? Ramón Eduardo Ruiz argues that the United States waged a racist and imperialistic war against Mexico for the purpose of conquering what became the American Southwest. Norman A. Graebner contends that President James K. Polk pursued an aggressive (but not imperialistic) policy that would force Mexico to recognize the U.S. annexation of Texas and to sell New Mexico and California to its northern neighbor without starting a war.

Conclusion

The process of historical study should rely more on thinking than on memorizing data. Once the basics of who, what, when, and where are determined, historical thinking shifts to a higher gear. Analysis, comparison and contrast, evaluation, and explanation take command. These skills not only increase our knowledge of the past but also provide general tools for the comprehension of all the topics about which human beings think.

The diversity of a pluralistic society, however, creates some obstacles to comprehending the past. The spectrum of differing opinions on any particular subject eliminates the possibility of quick and easy answers. In the final analysis, conclusions often are built through a synthesis of several different interpretations, but, even then, they may be partial and tentative.

The study of history in a pluralistic society allows each citizen the opportunity to reach independent conclusions about the past. Since most, if not all, historical issues affect the present and future, understanding the past becomes essential to social progress. Many of today's problems have a direct connection with the past. Additionally, other contemporary issues may lack obvious direct antecedents, but historical investigation can provide illuminating analogies. At first, it may appear confusing to read and to think about opposing historical views, but the survival of our democratic society depends on such critical thinking by acute and discerning minds.

Internet References . . .

Virginia's Indians, Past and Present

Drawn from collections at James Madison University, under the Internet School Library Media Center, this site provides links to historical information, lesson plans, and bibliographies as well as links to tribal home pages.

http://falcon.jmu.edu/~ramsoyil/vaindians.htm

Virtual Jamestown

The Virtual Jamestown Archive, developed to coincide with the four hundredth anniversary of the settlement's founding, provides a digital research, learning, and teaching tool to explore the legacy of the Jamestown experiment.

http://virtualjamestown.org/

Salem Witch Trials Documentary Archive

This collection at the University of Virginia provides access to documents and links to archives relating to the Salem witchcraft trials.

http://etext.virginia.edu/salem/witchcraft/

UNIT 1

Colonial Society

Colonial settlement in British North America took place in the context of regional conditions that varied in time and place. The ethnic identity of the European colonists affected their relations with Native Americans and Africans, as well as with each other. Many of the attitudes, ideals, and institutions that emerged from the colonial experience served the early settlers well and are still emulated today.

- Is History True?
- Was Disease the Key Factor in the Depopulation of Native Americans in the Americas?
- Was the Settlement of Jamestown a Fiasco?
- Was the Salem Witchcraft Hysteria Caused by a Fear of Women?

ISSUE 1

Is History True?

YES: Oscar Handlin, from *Truth in History* (The Belknap Press of Harvard University Press, 1979)

NO: William H. McNeill, from "Mythistory, or Truth, Myth, History, and Historians," *The American Historical Review* (February 1986)

ISSUE SUMMARY

YES: Oscar Handlin insists that historical truth is absolute and knowable by historians who adopt the scientific method of research to discover factual evidence that provides both a chronology and context for their findings.

NO: William McNeill argues that historical truth is general and evolutionary and is discerned by different groups at different times and in different places in a subjective manner that has little to do with a scientifically absolute methodology.

The basic premise of this volume of readings is that the study of history is a complex process that combines historical facts and the historian's interpretation of those facts. Underlying this premise is the assumption that the historian is committed to employing evidence that advances an accurate, truthful picture of the past. Unfortunately, the historical profession in the last several years has been held up to close public scrutiny as a result of charges that a few scholars, some quite prominent, have been careless in their research methods, cited sources that do not exist, and reached conclusions that were not borne out by the facts. The result has been soiled or ruined reputations and the revocation of degrees, book awards, and tenure. Certainly, this is not the end to which most historians aspire, and the failures of a few should not cast a net of suspicion on the manner in which the vast majority of historians practice their craft.

In reflecting upon her role as a historian, the late Barbara Tuchman commented, "To write history so as to enthrall the reader and make the subject as captivating and exciting to him as it is to me has been my goal. . . . A prerequisite . . . is to be enthralled one's self and to feel a compulsion to communicate the magic." For Tuchman, it was the historian's responsibility to the reader to conduct thorough research on a particular topic, sort through the mass of facts to determine what was essential and what was not, and to formulate what remained into a dramatic narrative. Tuchman and most practicing historians also agree with the nineteenth-century German historian Leopold von Ranke that the task of the historian is to discover what really happened. In most instances, however, historians write about events at which they were not present. According to Tuchman, "We can never be certain that we have recaptured [the past] as it really was. But the least we can do is to stay within the evidence."

David Hackett Fischer has written about the difficulties confronting historians as they attempt to report a truthful past, and he is particularly critical of what he terms the "absurd and pernicious doctrine" of historical relativism as it developed in the United States in the 1930s under the direction of Charles Beard and Carl Becker. Becker's suggestion that each historian will write a history based upon his or her own values or the climate of opinion in a particular generation strikes Fischer as a slippery slope leading to the loss of historical accuracy. In conclusion, Fischer writes, "The factual errors which academic historians make today are rarely deliberate. The real danger is not that a scholar will delude his readers, but that he will delude himself."

The selections that follow explore the topic of historical truth. In the late 1970s, Oscar Handlin, like Fischer, became extremely concerned about the impact of the historical and cultural relativism of postmodern and deconstructionist approaches to the study of history. For Handlin, historical truth is absolute and knowable if pursued by the historian adopting the scientific method of research. The value of history, he believes, lies in the capacity to advance toward the truth by locating discrete events, phenomena, and expressions in the historical record.

In contrast, William McNeill recognizes a very thin line between fact and fiction. He claims that historians distinguish between the truth of their conclusions and the myth of those conclusions they reject. The result is what he terms "mythistory." Moreover, the arrangement of historical facts involves subjective judgments and intellectual choices that have little to do with the scientific method. Historical truth, McNeill proposes, is evolutionary, not absolute.

YES 

Oscar Handlin

The Uses of History

Why resist the temptation to be relevant? The question nags historians in 1978 as it does other scholars. The world is turning; it needs knowledge; and possession of learning carries an obligation to attempt to shape events. Every crisis lends weight to the plea: transform the library from an ivory tower into a fortress armed to make peace (or war), to end (or extend) social inequality, to alter (or preserve) the existing economic system. The thought boosts the ego, as it has ever since Francis Bacon's suggestion that knowledge is power. Perhaps authority really does lie in command of the contents of books!

In the 1960s the plea became an order, sometimes earnest, sometimes surly, always insistent. Tell us what we need to know—straight answers. Thus, students to teachers, readers to authors. The penalties for refusal ranged from mere unpopularity to organized boycotts and angry confrontations—in a few cases even to burning manuscripts and research notes. Fear added to the inducements for pleasing the audience, whether in the classroom or on the printed page.

To aim to please is a blunder, however. Sincere as the supplicants generally are, it is not knowledge they wish. Having already reached their conclusions, they seek only reassuring confirmation as they prepare to act. They already know that a unilateral act of will could stop wars, that the United States is racist, and that capitalism condemns the masses to poverty. The history of American foreign policy, of the failure of post-Civil War Reconstruction, and of industrial development would only clutter the mind with disturbing ambiguities and complexities.

At best, the usable past demanded of history consists of the data to flesh out a formula. We must do something about the war, the cities, pollution, poverty, and population. Our moral sense, group interest, and political affiliation define the goals; let the historian join the other social scientists in telling us how to reach them. At worst, the demand made of the past is for a credible myth that will identify the forces of good and evil and inspire those who fight with slogans or fire on one side of the barricades or the other.

The effort to meet either demand will frustrate the historian true to his or her craft. Those nimble enough to catch the swings of the market in the classroom or in print necessarily leave behind interior standards of what is important and drop by the wayside the burden of scrupulous investigation and rigorous judgment. Demands for relevance distort the story of ethnicity as they corrupt the historical novel.

From *Truth in History* by Oscar Handlin (The Belknap Press of Harvard University Press, 1979).

Whoever yields, forgoes the opportunity to do what scholars are best qualified to do. Those who chase from one disaster to another lose sight of the long-term trend; busy with the bandaids, they have no time to treat the patient's illness. The family did not originate yesterday, or the city, or addiction to narcotics; a student might well pick up some thoughts on those subjects by shifting his sights from the 1970s to Hellenistic society.

Above all, obsession with the events of the moment prevents the historian from exercising the faculty of empathy, the faculty of describing how people, like us, but different, felt and behaved as they did in times and places similar to, but different, from our own. The writer or teacher interested only in passing judgment on the good guys and the bad will never know what it meant to be an Irish peasant during a famine, or the landlord; an Alabama slave in the 1850s, or the master; a soldier at Antietam, or a general.

The uses of history arise neither from its relevance nor from its help in preparing for careers—nor from its availability as a subject which teachers pass on to students who become teachers and in turn teach others to teach.

Nevertheless, again and again former pupils who come back for reunions after twenty-five years or more spontaneously testify to the utility of what they had learned at college in the various pursuits to which life's journey had taken them. Probing usually reveals not bits of information, not a general interpretation, but a vague sense that those old transactions of classroom and library had somehow expanded their knowledge of self. The discipline of history had located them in time and space and had thereby helped them know themselves, not as physicians or attorneys or bureaucrats or executives, but as persons.

These reassuring comments leave in suspense the question of why study of the past should thus help the individuals understand himself or herself. How do those who learn this subject catch a glimpse of the process of which they are part, discover places in it?

Not by relevance, in the competition for which the other, more pliable, social sciences can always outbid history. Nor by the power of myth, in the peddling of which the advantage lies with novelists. To turn accurate knowledge to those ends is, as C. S. Peirce noted, "like running a steam engine by burning diamonds."

The use of history lies in its capacity for advancing the approach to truth.

The historian's vocation depends on this minimal operational article of faith: Truth is absolute; it is as absolute as the world is real. It does not exist because individuals wish it to anymore than the world exists for their convenience. Although observers have more or less partial views of the truth, its actuality is unrelated to the desires or the particular angles of vision of the viewers. Truth is knowable and will out if earnestly pursued; and science is the procedure or set of procedures for approximating it.

What is truth? Mighty above all things, it resides in the small pieces which together form the record.

History is not the past, any more than biology is life, or physics, matter. History is the distillation of evidence surviving from the past. Where there is no evidence, there is no history. Much of the past is not knowable in this way, and about those areas the historian must learn to confess ignorance.

No one can relive the past; but everyone can seek truth in the record. Simple, durable discoveries await the explorer. So chronology—the sequential order of events reaching back beyond time's horizon—informs the viewer of the long distance traversed and of the immutable course of occurrences: no reversal of a step taken; no after ever before. The historian cannot soar with the anthropologists, who swoop across all time and space. Give or take a thousand years, it is all one to them in pronouncements about whether irrigation systems succeeded or followed despotisms, or in linking technology, population, food, and climatic changes. In the end they pick what they need to prop up theory. The discipline of dates rails off the historian and guards against such perilous plunges. No abstraction, no general interpretation, no wish or preference can challenge chronology's dominion, unless among those peoples who, lacking a sense of time, lack also a sense of history. And whoever learns to know the tyranny of the passing hours, the irrecoverable nature of days passed, learns also the vanity of all aspirations to halt the clock or slow its speed, of all irridentisms, all efforts to recapture, turn back, redeem the moments gone by.

Another use of history is in teaching about vocabulary, the basic component of human communication. Words, singularly elusive, sometimes flutter out of reach, hide in mists of ambiguity, or lodge themselves among inaccessible logical structures, yet form the very stuff of evidence. The historian captures the little syllabic clusters only by knowing who inscribed or spoke them—a feat made possible by understanding the minds and hearts and hands of the men and women for whom they once had meaning. Words released by comprehension wing their messages across the centuries. A use of history is to instruct in the reading of a word, in the comprehension of speakers, writers different from the listener, viewer.

And context. Every survival bespeaks a context. Who graved or wrote or built did so for the eyes of others. Each line or shape denotes a relation to people, things, or concepts—knowable. The identities of sender and recipient explain the content of the letter; the mode of transmission explains the developing idea, the passions of employers and laborers, the organization of the factory. A use of history is its aid in locating discrete events, phenomena, and expressions in their universes.

The limits of those universes were often subjects of dispute. Early in the nineteenth century Henry Thomas Buckle complained, in terms still applicable decades thereafter, of "the singular spectacle of one historian being ignorant of political economy; another knowing nothing of law; another nothing of ecclesiastical affairs and changes of opinion; another neglecting the philosophy of statistics, another physical science," so that those important pursuits, being cultivated, "some by one man, and some by another, have been isolated rather than united," with no disposition to concentrate them upon history. He thus echoed Gibbon's earlier injunction to value all facts. A Montesquieu, "from the meanest of them, will draw conclusions unknown to ordinary men" and arrive at "philosophical history."

On the other hand, a distinguished scholar fifty years later pooh-poohed the very idea that there might be a relation among the Gothic style, feudalism, and scholasticism, or a link between the Baroque and Jesuitism. Nevertheless, the dominant thrust of twentieth-century historians has been toward recognition of the broader contexts; in a variety of fashions they have searched for a totality denominated civilization, culture, or spirit of an epoch, and which they have hoped would permit examination of enlightening linkages and reciprocal relations. Even those who deny that history is a single discipline and assert that it is only "congeries of related disciplines" would, no doubt, expect each branch to look beyond its own borders.

In the final analysis, all the uses of history depend upon the integrity of the record, without which there could be no counting of time, no reading of words, no perception of the context, no utility of the subject. No concern could be deeper than assaults upon the record, upon the very idea of a record.

Although history is an ancient discipline, it rests upon foundations laid in the seventeenth century, when a century of blood shed in religious and dynastic warfare persuaded those who wrote and read history to accept a vital difference in tolerance between facts and interpretation. The text of a charter or statute was subject to proof of authenticity and validity, whatever the meanings lawyers or theologians imparted to its terms. The correct date, the precise phrasing, the seal were facts which might present difficulties of verification, but which, nevertheless, admitted of answers that were right or wrong. On the other hand, discussion of opinions and meanings often called for tolerance among diverse points of view, tolerance possible so long as disputants distinguished interpretation from the fact, from the thing in itself. Scholars could disagree on large matters of interpretation; they had a common interest in agreeing on the small ones of fact which provided them grounds of peaceful discourse.

From that seminal insight developed the scientific mechanisms that enabled historians to separate fact from opinion. From that basis came the Enlightenment achievements which recognized the worth of objectivity and asserted the possibility of reconstructing the whole record of the human past.

True, historians as well as philosophers often thereafter worried about the problems of bias and perspective; and some despaired of attaining the ideal of ultimate objectivity. None were ever totally free of bias, not even those like Ranke who most specifically insisted on the integrity of the fact which he struggled to make the foundation of a truly universal body of knowledge. But, however fallible the individual scholar, the historian's task, Wilhelm von Humboldt explained, was "to present what actually happened." It may have been a dream to imagine that history would become a science meaningful to all people, everywhere. If so, it was a noble dream.

By contrast, historians in the 1970s and increasingly other scientists regarded the fact itself as malleable. As the distinction between fact and interpretation faded, all became faction—a combination of fact and fiction. The passive acceptance of that illegitimate genre—whatever mixes with fiction ceases to be fact—revealed the erosion of scholarly commitment. More and more often, the factual elements in an account were instrumental to the purpose the author-manipulator wished them to serve. It followed that different writers addressing different readers for different purposes could arrange matters as convenient. In the end, the primacy of the fact vanished and only the authority of the author, the receptivity of the audience, and the purpose intended remained.

Whence came this desertion, this rejection of allegiance to the fact?

Chroniclers of the past always suffered from external pressure to make their findings relevant, that is, to demonstrate or deny the wisdom, correctness, or appropriateness of current policies. They resisted out of dedication to maintaining the integrity of the record; and long succeeded in doing so. In the 1970s, however, the pressures toward falsification became more compelling than ever before.

Although the full fruits of the change appeared only in that decade, its origins reached back a half-century. It was one of Stalin's most impressive achievements to have converted Marxism from its nineteenth-century scientific base to an instrument of state purpose, and it was not by coincidence that history was the first discipline to suffer in the process. The Soviet Union did more than impose an official party line on interpretations of Trotsky's role in the revolution of 1917; it actually expunged the name Trotsky from the record, so that the fact of the commissar's existence disappeared. What started in the domain of history led in time to Lysenko's invasion of the natural sciences. The Nazis, once in power, burned the nonconforming books; and after 1945 the assault spread to all countries subject to totalitarian control. Those developments were neither surprising nor difficult to comprehend; they followed from the nature of the regimes which fostered them.

More surprising, more difficult to comprehend, was the acquiescence by the scholars of free societies in the attack on history, first, insofar as it affected colleagues less fortunately situated, then as it insinuated itself in their own ranks. External and internal circumstances were responsible.

In a sensate society the commercial standards of the media governed the dissemination of information. Since whatever sold was news, the salient consideration was one of attracting attention; factual accuracy receded to the remote background. An affluent and indulgent society also mistook flaccid permissiveness for tolerance. Everything went because nothing was worth defending, and the legitimate right to err became the disastrous obliteration of the difference between error and truth.

Difficult critical issues tempted the weak-minded to tailor fact to convenience. In the United States, but also in other parts of the world, the spread of a kind of tribalism demanded a history unique to and written for the specifications of particular groups. Since knowledge was relative to the knowers, it was subject to manipulation to suit their convenience. The process by which blacks, white ethnics, and women alone were conceded the capability of understanding and writing their own histories wiped out the line between truth and myth.

That much was comprehensible; these forces operated outside the academy walls and were not subject to very much control. More important, more susceptible to control, and less explicable was the betrayal by the intellectuals of their own group interests and the subsequent loss of the will to resist. A variety of elements contributed to this most recent *trahison des clercs.* Exaggerated concern with the problems of bias and objectivity drove some earnest scholars to despair. Perhaps they reacted against the excessive claims of the nineteenth century, perhaps against the inability of historians, any more than other scholars, to withstand the pressures of nationalism in the early decades of the twentieth century. In any case, not a few followed the deceptive path from acknowledgment that no person was entirely free of prejudice or capable of attaining a totally objective view of the past to the conclusion that all efforts to do so were vain and that, in the end, the past was entirely a recreation emanating from the mind of the historian. Support from this point of view came from the philosophers Benedetto Croce in Italy and, later, R. G. Collingwood in England. Support also came from a misreading of anthropological relativism, which drew from the undeniable circumstances that different cultures evolved differently, the erroneous conclusion that judgments among them were impossible.

Perhaps playfully, perhaps seriously, Carl L. Becker suggested that the historical fact was in someone's mind or it was nowhere, because it was "not the past event," only a symbol which enabled later writers to recreate it imaginatively. His charmingly put illustrations deceived many a reader unaware that serious thinkers since Bayle and Hume had wrestled with the problem. "No one could ever object to the factual truth that Caesar defeated Pompey; and whatever the principles one wishes to use in dispute, one will find nothing less questionable than this proposition—Caesar and Pompey existed and were not just simple modification of the minds of those who wrote their lives"—thus Bayle.

The starting point in Becker's wandering toward relativism, as for others among his contemporaries, was the desire to be useful in solving "the everlasting riddle of human experience." Less subtle successors attacked neutrality "toward the main issues of life" and demanded that society organize all its forces in support of its ideals. "Total war, whether it be hot or cold, enlists everyone and calls upon everyone to assume his part. The historian is no freer from this obligation than the physicists." Those too timid to go the whole way suggested that there might be two kinds of history, variously defined: one, for instance, to treat the positive side of slavery to nurture black pride; another, the negative, to support claims for compensation.

Historians who caved in to pressure and ordered the past to please the present neglected the future, the needs of which would certainly change and in unpredictable ways. Scholarship could no more provide the future than the present with faith, justification, self-confidence, or sense of purpose unless it first preserved the record, intact and inviolable.

History does not recreate the past. The historian does not recapture the bygone event. No amount of imagination will enable the scholar to describe exactly what happened to Caesar in the Senate or to decide whether

Mrs. Williams actually lost two hundred pounds by an act of faith. History deals only with evidence from the past, with the residues of bygone events. But it can pass judgment upon documentation and upon observers' reports of what they thought they saw.

Disregarding these constraints, Becker concluded that, since objectivity was a dream, everyman could be his own historian and contrive his own view of the past, valid for himself, if for no one else. He thus breached the line between interpretation, which was subjective and pliable, and fact, which was not.

Internal specialization allowed historians to slip farther in the same direction. The knowledge explosion after 1900 made specialization an essential, unavoidable circumstance of every form of scholarly endeavor. No individual could presume to competence in more than a sector of the whole field; and the scope of the manageable sector steadily shrank. One result was the dissolution of common standards; each area created its own criteria and claimed immunity from the criticism of outsiders. The occupants of each little island fortress sustained the illusion that the dangers to one would not apply to others. Lines of communication, even within a single faculty or department, broke down so that, increasingly, specialists in one area depended upon the common mass media for knowledge about what transpired in another.

The dangers inherent in these trends became critical as scholarship lost its autonomy. Increasingly reliance on support from external sources—whether governments or foundations—circumscribed the freedom of researchers and writers to choose their own subjects and to arrive at their own conclusions. More generally, the loss of autonomy involved a state of mind which regarded the fruits of scholarship as dependent and instrumental—that is, not as worthy of pursuit for their own sake, not for the extent to which they brought the inquirer closer to the truth, but for other, extrinsic reasons. Ever more often, scholars justified their activity by its external results—peace, training for citizenship, economic development, cure of illness, and the like—in other words, by its usefulness. The choice of topics revealed the extent to which emphasis had shifted from the subject and its relation to the truth to its instrumental utility measured by reference to some external standard.

The plea from utility was dangerous. In the 1930s it blinded well-intentioned social scientists and historians to the excesses of totalitarianism. It was inevitable in creating the omelette of a great social experiment that the shells of a few eggs of truth would be broken, so the argument ran. So, too, in the avid desire for peace, in the praiseworthy wish to avoid a second world war, Charles A. Beard abandoned all effort at factual accuracy. Yet the errors to which the plea for utility led in the past have not prevented others from proceeding along the same treacherous path in pursuit of no less worthy, but equally deceptive utilitarian goals.

Finally, the reluctance to insist upon the worth of truth for its own sake stemmed from a decline of faith by intellectuals in their own role as intellectuals. Not many have, in any conscious or deliberate sense, foresworn their allegiance to the pursuit of truth and the life of the spirit. But power tempted them as it tempts other men and women. The twentieth-century intellectual had unparalleled access to those who actually wielded political or military influence. And few could resist the temptation of being listened to by presidents and ministers, of seeing ideas translated into action. Moreover, a more subtle, more insidious temptation nested in the possibility that possession of knowledge may itself become a significant source of power. The idea that a name on the letterhead of an activist organization or in the endorsement of a political advertisement might advance some worthy cause gives a heady feeling of sudden consequence to the no-longer-humble professor. Most important of all is the consciousness that knowledge can indeed do good, that it is a usable commodity, not only capable of bringing fame to its possessor but actually capable of causing beneficent changes in the external world.

All too few scholars are conscious that in reducing truth to an instrument, even an instrument for doing good, they necessarily blunt its edge and expose themselves to the danger of its misuse. For, when truth ceases to be an end in itself and becomes but a means toward an end, it also becomes malleable and manageable and is in danger of losing its character—not necessarily, not inevitably, but seriously. There may be ways of avoiding the extreme choices of the ivory tower and the marketplace, but they are far from easy and call for extreme caution.

In 1679 Jacques Bossuet wrote for his pupil the Dauphin, heir apparent to the throne of France, a discourse on universal history. Here certainly was an opportunity to influence the mind of the future monarch of Europe's most powerful kingdom. Bossuet understood that the greatest service he could render was to tell, not what would be pleasant to hear, but the truth about the past, detached and whole, so that in later years his pupil could make what use he wished of it.

Therein Bossuet reverted to an ancient tradition. The first law for the historian, Cicero had written, "is never to dare utter an untruth and the second, never to suppress anything true." And, earlier still, Polybius had noted that no one was exempt from mistakes made out of ignorance. But "deliberate misstatements in the interest of country or of friends or for favour" reduced the scholar to the level of those who gained "their living by their pens" and weighed "everything by the standard of profit."

In sum, the use of history is to learn from the study of it and not to carry preconceived notions or external objectives into it.

The times, it may be, will remain hostile to the enterprise of truth. There have been such periods in the past. Historians would do well to regard the example of those clerks in the Dark Ages who knew the worth of the task. By retiring from an alien world to a hidden monastic refuge, now and again one of them at least was able to maintain a true record, a chronicle that survived the destructive passage of armies and the erosion of doctrinal disputes and informed the future of what had transpired in their day. That task is ever worthy. Scholars should ponder its significance.

William H. McNeill

NO

Mythistory, or Truth, Myth, History, and Historians

Myth and history are close kin inasmuch as both explain how things got to be the way they are by telling some sort of story. But our common parlance reckons myth to be false while history is, or aspires to be, true. Accordingly, a historian who rejects someone else's conclusions calls them mythical, while claiming that his own views are true. But what seems true to one historian will seem false to another, so one historian's truth becomes another's myth, even at the moment of utterance.

A century and more ago, when history was first established as an academic discipline, our predecessors recognized this dilemma and believed they had a remedy. Scientific source criticism would get the facts straight, whereupon a conscientious and careful historian needed only to arrange the facts into a readable narrative to produce genuinely scientific history. And science, of course, like the stars above, was true and eternal, as Newton and Laplace had demonstrated to the satisfaction of all reasonable persons everywhere.

Yet, in practice, revisionism continued to prevail within the newly constituted historical profession, as it had since the time of Herodotus. For a generation or two, this continued volatility could be attributed to scholarly success in discovering new facts by diligent work in the archives; but early in this century thoughtful historians began to realize that the arrangement of facts to make a history involved subjective judgments and intellectual choices that had little or nothing to do with source criticism, scientific or otherwise.

In reacting against an almost mechanical vision of scientific method, it is easy to underestimate actual achievements. For the ideal of scientific history did allow our predecessors to put some forms of bias behind them. In particular, academic historians of the nineteenth century came close to transcending older religious controversies. Protestant and Catholic histories of post-Reformation Europe ceased to be separate and distinct traditions of learning—a transformation nicely illustrated in the Anglo-American world by the career of Lord Acton, a Roman Catholic who became Regius Professor of History at Cambridge and editor of the first *Cambridge Modern History.* This was a great accomplishment. So was the accumulation of an enormous fund of exact and reliable data through painstaking source criticism that allowed the writing of history in the western world to assume a new depth, scope, range, and precision

From *The American Historical Review,* vol. 91, no. 1, February 1986, pp. 1–10.

as compared to anything possible in earlier times. No heir of that scholarly tradition should scoff at the faith of our predecessors, which inspired so much toiling in archives.

Yet the limits of scientific history were far more constricting than its devotees believed. Facts that could be established beyond all reasonable doubt remained trivial in the sense that they did not, in and of themselves, give meaning or intelligibility to the record of the past. A catalogue of undoubted and indubitable information, even if arranged chronologically, remains a catalogue. To become a history, facts have to be put together into a pattern that is understandable and credible; and when that has been achieved, the resulting portrait of the past may become useful as well—a font of practical wisdom upon which people may draw when making decisions and taking action.

Pattern recognition of the sort historians engage in is the chef d'oeuvre of human intelligence. It is achieved by paying selective attention to the total input of stimuli that perpetually swarm in upon our consciousness. Only by leaving things out, that is, relegating them to the status of background noise deserving only to be disregarded, can what matters most in a given situation become recognizable. Suitable action follows. Here is the great secret of human power over nature and over ourselves as well. Pattern recognition is what natural scientists are up to; it is what historians have always done, whether they knew it or not.

Only some facts matter for any given pattern. Otherwise, useless clutter will obscure what we are after: perceptible relationships among important facts. That and that alone constitutes an intelligible pattern, giving meaning to the world, whether it be the world of physics and chemistry or the world of interacting human groups through time, which historians take as their special domain. Natural scientists are ruthless in selecting aspects of available sensory inputs to pay attention to, disregarding all else. They call their patterns theories and inherit most of them from predecessors. But, as we now know, even Newton's truths needed adjustment. Natural science is neither eternal nor universal; it is instead historical and evolutionary, because scientists accept a new theory only when the new embraces a wider range of phenomena or achieves a more elegant explanation of (selectively observed) facts than its predecessor was able to do.

No comparably firm consensus prevails among historians. Yet we need not despair. The great and obvious difference between natural scientists and historians is the greater complexity of the behavior historians seek to understand. The principal source of historical complexity lies in the fact that human beings react both to the natural world and to one another chiefly through the mediation of symbols. This means, among other things, that any theory about human life, if widely believed, will alter actual behavior, usually by inducing people to act as if the theory were true. Ideas and ideals thus become self-validating within remarkably elastic limits. An extraordinary behavioral motility results. Resort to symbols, in effect, loosened up the connection between external reality and human responses, freeing us from instinct by setting us adrift on a sea of uncertainty. Human beings thereby acquired a new capacity to err, but also to change, adapt, and learn new ways of doing things. Innumerable errors, corrected by experience, eventually made us lords of creation as no other species on earth has ever been before.

The price of this achievement is the elastic, inexact character of truth, and especially of truths about human conduct. What a particular group of persons understands, believes, and acts upon, even if quite absurd to outsiders, may nonetheless cement social relations and allow the members of the group to act together and accomplish feats otherwise impossible. Moreover, membership in such a group and participation in its sufferings and triumphs give meaning and value to individual human lives. Any other sort of life is not worth living, for we are social creatures. As such we need to share truths with one another, and not just truths about atoms, stars, and molecules but about human relations and the people around us.

Shared truths that provide a sanction for common effort have obvious survival value. Without such social cement no group can long preserve itself. Yet to outsiders, truths of this kind are likely to seem myths, save in those (relatively rare) cases when the outsider is susceptible to conversion and finds a welcome within the particular group in question.

The historic record available to us consists of an unending appearance and dissolution of human groups, each united by its own beliefs, ideals, and traditions. Sects, religions, tribes, and states, from ancient Sumer and Pharaonic Egypt to modern times, have based their cohesion upon shared truths—truths that differed from time to time and place to place with a rich and reckless variety. Today the human community remains divided among an enormous number of different groups, each espousing its own version of truth about itself and about those excluded from its fellowship. Everything suggests that this sort of social and ideological fragmentation will continue indefinitely.

Where, in such a maelstrom of conflicting opinions, can we hope to locate historical truth? Where indeed?

Before modern communications thrust familiarity with the variety of human idea-systems upon our consciousness, this question was not particularly acute. Individuals nearly always grew up in relatively isolated communities to a more or less homogeneous world view. Important questions had been settled long ago by prophets and sages, so there was little reason to challenge or modify traditional wisdom. Indeed there were strong positive restraints upon any would-be innovator who threatened to upset the inherited consensus.

To be sure, climates of opinion fluctuated, but changes came surreptitiously, usually disguised as commentary upon old texts and purporting merely to explicate the original meanings. Flexibility was considerable, as the modern practice of the U.S. Supreme Court should convince us; but in this traditional ordering of intellect, all the same, outsiders who did not share the prevailing orthodoxy were shunned and disregarded when they could not be converted. Our predecessors' faith in a scientific method that would make written history absolutely and universally true was no more than a recent example of such a belief system. Those who embraced it felt no need to pay attention to ignoramuses who had not accepted the truths of "modern science." Like other true believers, they were therefore spared the task of taking others' viewpoints seriously or wondering about the limits of their own vision of historical truth.

But we are denied the luxury of such parochialism. We must reckon with multiplex, competing faiths—secular as well as transcendental, revolutionary as well as traditional—that resound amongst us. In addition, partially autonomous professional idea-systems have proliferated in the past century or so. Those most important to historians are the so-called social sciences—anthropology, sociology, political science, psychology, and economics—together with the newer disciplines of ecology and semeiology. But law, theology, and philosophy also pervade the field of knowledge with which historians may be expected to deal. On top of all this, innumerable individual authors, each with his own assortment of ideas and assumptions, compete for attention. Choice is everywhere; dissent turns into cacaphonous confusion; my truth dissolves into your myth even before I can put words on paper.

The liberal faith, of course, holds that in a free marketplace of ideas, Truth will eventually prevail. I am not ready to abandon that faith, however dismaying our present confusion may be. The liberal experiment, after all, is only about two hundred and fifty years old, and on the appropriate world-historical time scale that is too soon to be sure. Still, confusion is undoubted. Whether the resulting uncertainty will be bearable for large numbers of people in difficult times ahead is a question worth asking. Iranian Muslims, Russian communists, and American sectarians (religious and otherwise) all exhibit symptoms of acute distress in face of moral uncertainties, generated by exposure to competing truths. Clearly, the will to believe is as strong today as at any time in the past; and true believers nearly always wish to create a community of the faithful, so as to be able to live more comfortably, insulated from troublesome dissent.

The prevailing response to an increasingly cosmopolitan confusion has been intensified personal attachment, first to national and then to subnational groups, each with its own distinct ideals and practices. As one would expect, the historical profession faithfully reflected and helped to forward these shifts of sentiment. Thus, the founding fathers of the American Historical Association and their immediate successors were intent on facilitating the consolidation of a new American nation by writing national history in a WASPish mold, while also claiming affiliation with a tradition of Western civilization that ran back through modern and medieval Europe to the ancient Greeks and Hebrews. This version of our past was very widely repudiated in the 1960s, but iconoclastic revisionists felt no need to replace what they attacked with any architectonic vision of their own. Instead, scholarly energy concentrated on discovering the history of various segments of the population that had been left out or ill-treated by older historians: most notably women, blacks, and other ethnic minorities within the United States and the ex-colonial peoples of the world beyond the national borders.

Such activity conformed to our traditional professional role of helping to define collective identities in ambiguous situations. Consciousness of a common past, after all, is a powerful supplement to other ways of defining who "we" are. An oral tradition, sometimes almost undifferentiated from the practical wisdom embodied in language itself, is all people need in a stable social universe where in-group boundaries are self-evident. But with civilization, ambiguities multipled, and formal written history became useful in defining "us" versus "them." At first, the central ambiguity ran between rulers and ruled. Alien conquerors who lived on taxes collected from their subjects were at best a necessary evil when looked at from the bottom of civilized society. Yet in some situations, especially when confronting natural disaster or external attack, a case could be made for commonality, even between taxpayers and tax consumers. At any rate, histories began as king lists, royal genealogies, and boasts of divine favor—obvious ways of consolidating rulers' morale and asserting their legitimacy vis-à-vis their subjects. . . .

All human groups like to be flattered. Historians are therefore under perpetual temptation to conform to expectation by portraying the people they write about as they wish to be. A mingling of truth and falsehood, blending history with ideology, results. Historians are likely to select facts to show that we—whoever "we" may be—conform to our cherished principles: that we are free with Herodotus, or saved with Augustine, or oppressed with Marx, as the case may be. Grubby details indicating that the group fell short of its ideals can be skated over or omitted entirely. The result is mythical: the past as we want it to be, safely simplified into a contest between good guys and bad guys, "us" and "them." Most national history and most group history is of this kind, though the intensity of chiaroscuro varies greatly, and sometimes an historian turns traitor to the group he studies by setting out to unmask its pretensions. Groups struggling toward self-consciousness and groups whose accustomed status seems threatened are likely to demand (and get) vivid, simplified portraits of their admirable virtues and undeserved sufferings. Groups accustomed to power and surer of their internal cohesion can afford to accept more subtly modulated portraits of their successes and failures in bringing practice into conformity with principles.

Historians respond to this sort of market by expressing varying degrees of commitment to, and detachment from, the causes they chronicle and by infusing varying degrees of emotional intensity into their pages through particular choices of words. Truth, persuasiveness, intelligibility rest far more on this level of the historians' art than on source criticism. But, as I said at the beginning, one person's truth is another's myth, and the fact that a group of people accepts a given version of the past does not make that version any truer for outsiders.

Yet we cannot afford to reject collective self-flattery as silly, contemptible error. Myths are, after all, often self-validating. A nation or any other human group that knows how to behave in crisis situations because it has inherited a heroic historiographical tradition that tells how ancestors resisted their enemies successfully is more likely to act together effectively than a group lacking such a tradition. Great Britain's conduct in 1940 shows how world politics can be redirected by such a heritage. Flattering historiography does more than assist a given group to survive by affecting the balance of power among warring peoples, for an appropriately idealized version of the past may also allow a group of human beings to come closer to living up to its noblest ideals. What is can move toward what ought to be, given collective commitment to a flattering self-image. The American civil rights movement of the fifties and sixties illustrates this phenomenon amongst us.

These collective manifestations are of very great importance. Belief in the virtue and righteousness of one's cause is a necessary sort of self-delusion for human beings, singly and collectively. A corrosive version of history that emphasizes all the recurrent discrepancies between ideal and reality in a given group's behavior makes it harder for members of the group in question to act cohesively and in good conscience. That sort of history is very costly indeed. No group can afford it for long.

On the other hand, myths may mislead disastrously. A portrait of the past that denigrates others and praises the ideals and practice of a given group naively and without restraint can distort a people's image of outsiders so that foreign relations begin to consist of nothing but nasty surprises. Confidence in one's own high principles and good intentions may simply provoke others to resist duly accredited missionaries of the true faith, whatever that faith may be. Both the United States and the Soviet Union have encountered their share of this sort of surprise and disappointment ever since 1917, when Wilson and Lenin proclaimed their respective recipes for curing the world's ills. In more extreme cases, mythical, self-flattering versions of the past may push a people toward suicidal behavior, as Hitler's last days may remind us.

More generally, it is obvious that mythical, self-flattering versions of rival groups' pasts simply serve to intensify their capacity for conflict. With the recent quantum jump in the destructive power of weaponry, hardening of group cohesion at the sovereign state level clearly threatens the survival of humanity; while, within national borders, the civic order experiences new strains when sub-national groups acquire a historiography replete with oppressors living next door and, perchance, still enjoying the fruits of past injustices.

The great historians have always responded to these difficulties by expanding their sympathies beyond narrow in-group boundaries. Herodotus set out to award a due meed of glory both to Hellenes and to the barbarians; Ranke inquired into what really happened to Protestant and Catholic, Latin and German nations alike. And other pioneers of our profession have likewise expanded the range of their sympathies and sensibilities beyond previously recognized limits without ever entirely escaping, or even wishing to escape, from the sort of partisanship involved in accepting the general assumptions and beliefs of a particular time and place.

Where to fix one's loyalties is the supreme question of human life and is especially acute in a cosmopolitan age like ours when choices abound. Belonging to a tightly knit group makes life worth living by giving individuals something beyond the self to serve and to rely on for personal guidance, companionship, and aid. But the stronger such bonds, the sharper the break with the rest of humanity. Group solidarity is always maintained, at least partly, by exporting psychic frictions across the frontiers, projecting animosities onto an outside foe in order to enhance collective cohesion within the group itself. Indeed, something to fear, hate, and attack is probably necessary for the full expression of human emotions; and ever since animal predators ceased to threaten, human beings have feared, hated, and fought one another.

Historians, by helping to define "us" and "them," play a considerable part in focusing love and hate, the two principal cements of collective behavior known to humanity. But myth making for rival groups has become a dangerous game in the atomic age, and we may well ask whether there is any alternative open to us.

In principle the answer is obvious. Humanity entire possesses a commonality which historians may hope to understand just as firmly as they can comprehend what unites any lesser group. Instead of enhancing conflicts, as parochial historiography inevitably does, an intelligible world history might be expected to diminish the lethality of group encounters by cultivating a sense of individual identification with the triumphs and tribulations of humanity as a whole. This, indeed, strikes me as the moral duty of the historical profession in our time. We need to develop an ecumenical history, with plenty of room for human diversity in all its complexity.

Yet a wise historian will not denigrate intense attachment to small groups. That is essential to personal happiness. In all civilized societies, a tangle of overlapping social groupings lays claim to human loyalties. Any one person may therefore be expected to have multiple commitments and plural public identities, up to and including membership in the human race and the wider DNA community of life on planet Earth. What we need to do as historians and as human beings is to recognize this complexity and balance our loyalties so that no one group will be able to command total commitment. Only so can we hope to make the world safer for all the different human groups that now exist and may come into existence.

The historical profession has, however, shied away from an ecumenical view of the human adventure. Professional career patterns reward specialization; and in all the well-trodden fields, where pervasive consensus on important matters has already been achieved, research and innovation necessarily concentrate upon minutiae. Residual faith that truth somehow resides in original documents confirms this direction of our energies. An easy and commonly unexamined corollary is the assumption that world history is too vague and too general to be true, that is, accurate to the sources. Truth, according to this view, is only attainable on a tiny scale when the diligent historian succeeds in exhausting the relevant documents before they exhaust the historian. But as my previous remarks have made clear, this does not strike me as a valid view of historical method. On the contrary, I call it naive and erroneous.

All truths are general. All truths abstract from the available assortment of data simply by using words, which in their very nature generalize so as to bring order to the incessantly fluctuating flow of messages in and messages out that constitutes human consciousness. Total reproduction of experience is impossible and undesirable. It would merely perpetuate the confusion we seek to escape. Historiography that aspires to get closer and closer to the documents—all the documents and nothing but the documents—is merely moving closer and closer to incoherence, chaos, and meaninglessness. That is a dead end for sure. No society will long support a profession that produces arcane trivia and calls it truth.

Fortunately for the profession, historians' practice has been better than their epistemology. Instead of replicating confusion by paraphrasing the totality of relevant and available documents, we have used our sources to discern, support, and reinforce group identities at national, transnational, and subnational levels and, once in a while, to attack or pick apart a group identity to which a school of revisionists has taken a scunner.

If we can now realize that our practice already shows how truths may be discerned at different levels of generality with equal precision simply because different patterns emerge on different time-space scales, then, perhaps, repugnance for world history might diminish and a juster proportion between parochial and ecumenical historiography might begin to emerge. It is our professional duty to move toward ecumenicity, however real the risks may seem to timid and unenterprising minds.

With a more rigorous and reflective epistemology, we might also attain a better historiographical balance between Truth, truths, and myth. Eternal and universal Truth about human behavior is an unattainable goal, however delectable as an ideal. Truths are what historians achieve when they bend their minds as critically and carefully as they can to the task of making their account of public affairs credible as well as intelligible to an audience that shares enough of their particular outlook and assumptions to accept what they say. The result might best be called mythistory perhaps (though I do not expect the term to catch on in professional circles), for the same words that constitute truth for some are, and always will be, myth for others, who inherit or embrace different assumptions and organizing concepts about the world.

This does not mean that there is no difference between one mythistory and another. Some clearly are more adequate to the facts than others. Some embrace more time and space and make sense of a wider variety of human behavior than others. And some, undoubtedly, offer a less treacherous basis for collective action than others. I actually believe that historians' truths, like those of scientists, evolve across the generations, so that versions of the past acceptable today are superior in scope, range, and accuracy to versions available in earlier times. But such evolution is slow, and observable only on an extended time scale, owing to the self-validating character of myth. Effective common action can rest on quite fantastic beliefs. *Credo quia absurdum* may even become a criterion for group membership, requiring initiates to surrender their critical faculties as a sign of full commitment to the common cause. Many sects have prospered on this principle and have served their members well for many generations while doing so.

But faiths, absurd or not, also face a long-run test of survival in a world where not everyone accepts anyone set of beliefs and where human beings must interact with external objects and nonhuman forms of life, as well as with one another. Such "foreign relations" impose limits on what any group of people can safely believe and act on, since actions that fail to secure expected and desired results are always costly and often disastrous. Beliefs that mislead action are likely to be amended; too stubborn an adherence to a faith that encourages or demands hurtful behavior is likely to lead to the disintegration and disappearance of any group that refuses to learn from experience.

Thus one may, as an act of faith, believe that our historiographical myth making and myth breaking is bound to cumulate across time, propagating mythistories that fit experience better and allow human survival more often, sustaining in-groups in ways that are less destructive to themselves and to their neighbors than was once the case or is the case today. If so, ever-evolving mythistories will indeed become truer and more adequate to public life, emphasizing the really important aspects of human encounters and omitting irrelevant background noise more efficiently so that men and women will know how to act more wisely than is possible for us today.

This is not a groundless hope. Future historians are unlikely to leave out blacks and women from any future mythistory of the United States, and we are unlikely to exclude Asians, Africans, and Amerindians from any future mythistory of the world. One hundred years ago this was not so. The scope and range of historiography has widened, and that change looks as irreversible to me as the widening of physics that occurred when Einstein's equations proved capable of explaining phenomena that Newton's could not.

It is far less clear whether in widening the range of our sensibilities and taking a broader range of phenomena into account we also see deeper into the reality we seek to understand. But we may. Anyone who reads historians of the sixteenth and seventeenth centuries and those of our own time will notice a new awareness of social process that we have attained. As one who shares that awareness, I find it impossible not to believe that it represents an advance on older notions that focused attention exclusively, or almost exclusively, on human intentions and individual actions, subject only to God or to a no less inscrutable Fortune, while leaving out the social and material context within which individual actions took place simply because that context was assumed to be uniform and unchanging.

Still, what seems wise and true to me seems irrelevant obfuscation to others. Only time can settle the issue, presumably by outmoding my ideas and my critics' as well. Unalterable and eternal Truth remains like the Kingdom of Heaven, an eschatological hope. Mythistory is what we actually have—a useful instrument for piloting human groups in their encounters with one another and with the natural environment.

To be a truth-seeking mythographer is therefore a high and serious calling, for what a group of people knows and believes about the past channels expectations and affects the decisions on which their lives, their fortunes, and their sacred honor all depend. Formal written histories are not the only shapers of a people's notions about the past; but they are sporadically powerful, since even the most abstract and academic historiographical ideas do trickle down to the level of the commonplace, if they fit both what a people want to hear and what a people need to know well enough to be useful.

As members of society and sharers in the historical process, historians can only expect to be heard if they say what the people around them want to hear—in some degree. They can only be useful if they also tell the people some things they are reluctant to hear—in some degree. Piloting between this Scylla and Charybdis is the art of the serious historian, helping the group he or she addresses and celebrates to survive and prosper in a treacherous and changing world by knowing more about itself and others.

Academic historians have pursued that art with extraordinary energy and considerable success during the past century. May our heirs and successors persevere and do even better!

POSTSCRIPT

Is History True?

Closely associated to the question of historical truth is the matter of historical objectivity. Frequently, we hear people begin statements with the phrase "History tells us . . ." or "History shows that . . . ," followed by a conclusion that reflects the speaker or writer's point of view. In fact, history does not directly tell or show us anything. That is the job of historians, and as William McNeill argues, much of what historians tell us, despite their best intentions, often represents a blending of historical evidence and myth.

Is there such a thing as a truly objective history? Historian Paul Conkin agrees with McNeill that objectivity is possible only if the meaning of that term is sharply restricted and is not used as a synonym for certain truth. History, Conkin writes, "is a story about the past; it is not the past itself. . . . Whether one draws a history from the guidance of memory or of monuments, it cannot exactly mirror some directly experienced past nor the feelings and perceptions of people in the past." He concludes, "In this sense, much of history is a stab into partial darkness, a matter of informed but inconclusive conjecture. . . . Obviously, in such areas of interpretation, there is no one demonstrably correct 'explanation,' but very often competing, equally unfalsifiable, theories. Here, on issues that endlessly fascinate the historian, the controversies rage, and no one expects, short of a great wealth of unexpected evidence, to find a conclusive answer. An undesired, abstractive precision of the subject might so narrow it as to permit more conclusive evidence. But this would spoil all the fun." For more discussion on this and other topics related to the study of history, see Paul K. Conkin and Roland N. Stromberg, *The Heritage and Challenge of History* (Dodd, Mead & Company, 1971).

The most thorough discussion of historical objectivity in the United States is Peter Novick, *That Noble Dream: The 'Objectivity Question' and the American Historical Profession* (Cambridge University Press, 1988), which draws its title from Charles A. Beard's article in the *American Historical Review* (October 1935) in which Beard reinforced the views expressed in his 1933 presidential address to the American Historical Association. [See "Written History as an Act of Faith," *American Historical Review* (January 1934).] Novick's thorough analysis generated a great deal of attention, the results of which can be followed in James T. Kloppenberg, "Objectivity and Historicism: A Century of American Historical Writing," *American Historical Review* (October 1989), Thomas L. Haskell, "Objectivity Is Not Neutrality: Rhetoric vs. Practice in Peter Novick's *That Noble Dream*," *History & Theory* (1990), and the scholarly forum "Peter Novick's *That Noble Dream:* The Objectivity Question and the Future of the Historical Profession," *American Historical Review* (June 1991). A critique of recent historical writing that closely follows the concerns expressed by Handlin can be found in Keith Windschuttle, *The Killing of History: How Literary Critics and Social Theorists Are Murdering Our Past* (The Free Press, 1996).

Readers interested in this subject will also find the analyses in Barbara W. Tuchman, *Practicing History: Selected Essays* (Alfred A. Knopf, 1981) and David Hackett Fischer, *Historians' Fallacies: Toward a Logic of Historical Thought* (Harper & Row, 1970) to be quite stimulating. Earlier, though equally rewarding, volumes include Harvey Wish, *The American Historian: A Social-Intellectual History of the Writing of the American Past* (Oxford University Press, 1960); John Higham, with Leonard Krieger and Felix Gilbert, *History: The Development of Historical Studies in the United States* (Prentice-Hall, 1965); and Marcus Cunliffe and Robin Winks, eds., *Pastmasters: Some Essays on American Historians* (Harper & Row, 1969).

ISSUE 2

Was Disease the Key Factor in the Depopulation of Native Americans in the Americas?

YES: Colin G. Calloway, from *New Worlds for All: Indians, Europeans, and the Remaking of Early America* (The Johns Hopkins University Press, 1997)

NO: David S. Jones, from "Virgin Soils Revisited," *William & Mary Quarterly* (October 2003)

ISSUE SUMMARY

YES: Colin Calloway says that while Native Americans confronted numerous diseases in the Americas, traditional Indian healing practices failed to offer much protection from the diseases introduced by Europeans beginning in the late-fifteenth century and which decimated the indigenous peoples.

NO: David Jones recognizes the disastrous impact of European diseases on Native Americans, but he insists that Indian depopulation was also a consequence of the forces of poverty, malnutrition, environmental stress, dislocation, and social disparity.

On October 12, 1492, Christopher Columbus, a Genoese mariner sailing under the flag and patronage of the Spanish monarchy, made landfall on a tropical Caribbean island, which he subsequently named San Salvador. This action established for Columbus the fame of having discovered the New World and, by extension, America. Of course, this "discovery" was all very ironic since Columbus and his crew members were not looking for a new world but, instead, a very old one—the much-fabled Orient. By sailing westward instead of eastward, Columbus was certain that he would find a shorter route to China. He did not anticipate that the land mass of the Americas would prevent him from reaching his goal or that his "failure" would guarantee his fame for centuries thereafter.

Moreover, Columbus's encounter with indigenous peoples whom he named "Indians" (*los indios*) presented further proof that Europeans had not discovered America. These "Indians" were descendants of the first people who migrated from Asia at least 30,000 years earlier and fanned out in a southeasterly direction until they populated much of North and South America. By the time Columbus arrived, Native Americans numbered approximately 40 million, 3 million of whom resided in the continental region north of Mexico.

Columbus's arrival (and return on three separate occasions between 1494 and 1502) possessed enormous implications not only for the future development of the United States but also for the Western Hemisphere as a whole, as well as for Europe and Africa. Relations between Native Americans and Europeans were marred by the difficulties that arose from people of very different cultures encountering each other for the first time. These encounters led to inaccurate perceptions, misunderstandings, and failed expectations. While at first the American Indians deified the explorers, experience soon taught them to do otherwise. European opinion ran the gamut from admiration to contempt; for example, some European poets and painters expressed admiration for the Noble Savage, while other Europeans accepted as a rationalization for military aggression the sentiment that "the only good savage is a dead one."

William Bradford's account of the Pilgrims' arrival at Cape Cod describes the insecurity the new migrants felt as they disembarked on American soil. "[T]hey had now no friends to welcome them nor inns to entertain or refresh their weatherbeaten bodies; no houses or much less towns to repair to, to seek for succor. . . . Besides, what could they see but a hideous and deserted wilderness, full of wild beasts and wild men. . . . If they looked behind them there was the mighty ocean which they had passed and was not a main bar and gulf to separate them from all the civil parts of the world." Historical hindsight, however, suggests that if anyone should have expressed fears about the unfolding encounter in the Western Hemisphere, it would be the Native Americans since their numbers declined by as much as 95 percent in the first century following Columbus's arrival. While some of this decline can be attributed to violent encounters with Europeans, there seems to have been a more hostile (and far less visible) force at work. As historian William McNeill has suggested, the main weapon that overwhelmed indigenous peoples in the Americas was the Europeans' breath!

The following essays explore the role played by disease in the depopulation of Native Americans in the Western Hemisphere. Colin G. Calloway makes clear that Indian doctors possessed a sophisticated knowledge of the healing power of plants that they shared with Europeans, but these curatives were insufficient in providing protection against the variety of new diseases introduced into the Americas by European explorers and settlers. The "Columbian exchange" included epidemics that decimated indigenous tribes.

Physician David S. Jones recognizes the consequences of the introduction of European diseases among Native Americans, but he contends that there were other factors at work that explain the drastic loss of life among American Indians. For example, poverty, malnutrition, environmental stress, dislocation, and social disparity exacerbated the conditions within which infectious diseases could spread in such dramatic proportions.

YES 

Colin G. Calloway

New Worlds for All: Indians, Europeans, and the Remaking of Early America

Healing and Disease

North American Indians did not inhabit a disease-free paradise prior to European invasion. The great epidemic diseases and crowd infections that ravaged Europe and Asia—smallpox, diphtheria, measles, bubonic and pneumonic plague, cholera, influenza, typhus, dysentery, yellow fever—were unknown in America. Indian peoples faced other, less devastating, problems. Bioarchaeological studies reveal evidence of malnutrition and anemia resulting from dietary stress, high levels of fetal and neonatal death and infant mortality, parasitic intestinal infections, dental problems, respiratory infections, spina bifida, osteomyelitis, nonpulmonary tuberculosis, and syphilis. Indian people also suffered their share of aches and pains, breaks and bruises, digestive upsets, arthritis, wounds, and snakebites. To deal with these things, Indian doctors employed a rich knowledge of the healing properties of plants and what today we would call therapeutic medicine. They combined knowledge of anatomy and medicinal botany with curative rituals and ceremonies.

Traditional Native American and contemporary Western ways of healing are not necessarily in conflict, and are often complementary, as evidenced when Navajo medicine men and Navajo oral traditions helped investigators from the Indian Health Service and the Centers for Disease Control identify deer mice as the source of the "mystery illness" that struck the Southwest in 1993. So too in early America, European and Indian cures could work together. Contrary to the popular modern stereotype that all Indians were and are attuned to plant life, all Europeans totally out of touch with nature, many early explorers and colonists possessed an extensive knowledge of plants and their properties, knowledge that modern urban Americans have lost. Europeans in the seventeenth century generally believed that for every sickness there were natural plant remedies, if one only knew where to find them. Indian healers, many of them women, knew where to find them, and Europeans were receptive to the cures they could provide. . . .

Unfortunately, traditional Indian cures offered little protection against the new diseases that swept the land after Europeans arrived in North America. Separated from the Old World for thousands of years, the peoples of America escaped great epidemics like the Black Death, which killed perhaps a third of the population in fourteenth-century Europe. But they were living on borrowed time. Lack of exposure to bubonic plague, smallpox, and measles allowed Indian peoples no opportunity to build up immunological resistance to such diseases. From the moment Europeans set foot in America, hundreds of thousands of Indian people were doomed to die in one of the greatest biological catastrophes in human history.

Imported diseases accompanied Spanish conquistadors into Central and South America at the beginning of the sixteenth century, wreaking havoc among the great civilizations of Mexico, Peru, and Yucatán, and facilitating their conquest by the invaders. It was not long before the unseen killers were at work among the Indian populations of North America.

Established and well-traveled trade routes helped spread disease. Indians who came into contact with Europeans and their germs often contaminated peoples farther inland who had not yet seen a European; they in turn passed the disease on to more distant neighbors. It is likely that most Indian people who were struck down by European diseases like smallpox died without ever laying eyes on a European. In tracing the course of imported plagues among Indian populations in colonial America, many scholars describe them not as epidemics but as pandemics, meaning that the same disease occurred virtually everywhere.

As many as 350,000 people lived in Florida when the Spaniards first arrived, but the populations of the Calusa, Timucua, and other tribes plummeted after contact. Calusas who canoed to Cuba to trade may have brought smallpox back to the Florida mainland as early as the 1520s. When Hernando de Soto invaded the Southeast in 1539, the Spaniards found that disease had preceded them. In the Carolina upcountry, they found large towns abandoned and overgrown with grass where, said the Indians, "there had been a pest in the land two years before." In 1585, Sir Francis Drake's English crew, returning from plundering Spanish ships in the Cape Verde Islands, brought a disease that was probably typhus to the Caribbean and Florida. Indians around St. Augustine died in great numbers, "and said amongste themselves, it was the Inglisshe God that made them die so faste." The population collapse continued in the seventeenth century. Governor Diego de Rebolledo reported in 1657 that the Guale and Timucua Indians were few "because they have been wiped out with the sickness of the plague and smallpox which have overtaken them in past years." Two years later the new governor of Florida said 10,000 Indians had died in a measles epidemic. According to one scholar, the Timucuans numbered as many as 150,000 people before contact; by the end of the seventeenth century, their population had been cut by 98 percent. The Apalachee Indians of northern Florida numbered 25,000–30,000 in the early seventeenth century; by the end of the century, less than 8,000 survived. Two and a half centuries after contact with the Spaniards, all of Florida's original Indian people were gone.

The pattern repeated itself elsewhere. In 1585, the English established a colony at Roanoke Island in Virginia. Almost immediately, local Indians began to fall ill and die. "The disease was so strange to them," wrote Thomas Hariot, "that they neither knew what it was, nor how to cure it." Across the continent, Pueblo Indians in New Mexico may have suffered from a huge smallpox epidemic that spread as far south as Chile and across much of North America in 1519–24. When they first encountered Europeans in 1539, the Pueblos numbered at least 130,000 and inhabited between 110 and 150 pueblos. By 1706, New Mexico's Pueblo population had dropped to 6,440 people in 18 pueblos. When de Soto's Spaniards passed through the area now known as Arkansas in 1541–43, the region was densely populated. Thousands of people lived in large towns, cultivating extensive cornfields along rich river valleys. One hundred thirty years later, these thriving communities were gone, victims of disease and possibly drought. When French explorers arrived in the mid-seventeenth century, they found Caddoes, Osages, and Quapaws living on the peripheries of the region, but central Arkansas was empty. Epidemic diseases continued their devastation. In 1698, Frenchmen found less than one hundred men in the Quapaw villages after a recent smallpox epidemic killed most of the people. "In the village are nothing but graves," the French chronicler reported.

Indian peoples in eastern Canada who had been in contact with French fur traders and fishermen since early in the sixteenth century experienced the deadly repercussions of such commerce. Jesuit Father Pierre Biard, working among the Micmacs and Maliseets of Nova Scotia in 1616, heard the Indians "complain that since the French mingle and carry on trade with them they are dying fast, and the population is thinning out. For they assert that before this association and intercourse all their countries were very populous and they tell how one by one different coasts, according as they traffic with us, have been reduced more by disease."

Deadly pestilence swept the coast of New England in 1616–17. Indians "died in heapes," and the Massachusett Indians around Plymouth Bay were virtually exterminated. As reported by Governor William Bradford, the Pilgrims found cleared fields and good soil, but few people, the Indians "being dead & abundantly wasted in the late great mortalitiy which fell in all these parts about three years over before the coming of the English, wherin thousands of them dyed, they not being able to burie one another; their sculs and bones were found in many places lying still above ground, where their houses & dwellings had been; a very sad spectacle to behold."

Smallpox was a fact of life—or death—for most of human history. An airborne disease, normally communicated by droplets or dust particles, it enters through the respiratory tract. People can become infected simply by breathing. Not surprisingly, it spread like wildfire through Indian populations. However, because early chroniclers sometimes confused smallpox with other diseases and because the contagions came so quickly, it is difficult to discern which disease was doing the killing at any particular time. By the seventeenth century, smallpox in Europe was a childhood disease: most adults, having been infected as children, had acquired lifelong immunity and were not contagious. The long transatlantic crossings further reduced the chances that European crews could transmit the disease to America. Not until children crossed the Atlantic did smallpox, and the other lethal childhood diseases that plagued Europe, take hold on Native American populations. The Spanish brought children to the Caribbean early, but not until the beginning of the seventeenth century did Dutch and English colonists bring their families to New York and New England. The arrival of sick European children sentenced thousands of Indian people to death.

Smallpox struck New England in 1633, devastating Indian communities on the Merrimack and Connecticut Rivers. Bradford reported how "it pleased God to visite these Indeans with a great sickness, and such a mortalitie that of a 1000 above 900, and a halfe of them dyed, and many of them did rott above ground for want of buriall." The epidemic reduced the Pequots in southern Connecticut from perhaps as many as thirteen thousand people to only three thousand, setting the stage for their defeat by the English in 1637, and it may have reduced the Mohawks in eastern New York from almost eight thousand to less than three thousand. Such mortality rates were not unusual when virulent new diseases cut through previously unexposed populations. Indians from the Hudson River told Adriaen Van der Donck in 1656 "that before the smallpox broke out amongst them, they were ten times as numerous as they are now." John Lawson estimated that in 1701 there was "not the sixth Savage living within two hundred Miles of all our Settlements, as there were fifty Years ago." A recent smallpox epidemic in the Carolina upcountry had "destroy'd whole towns."

At the beginning of the seventeenth century, the Huron Indians numbered as many as 30,000–40,000 people, living in perhaps twenty-eight villages on the northern shores of the Great Lakes in southern Ontario. The French identified them as crucial to their plans for North American empire. The Hurons were the key to extensive trade networks reaching far beyond the Great Lakes, and their villages could also serve as 'jumping-off points" for Jesuit missionary enterprises among more distant tribes. French traders and missionaries arrived in Huronia, and it was not long before the new diseases were reaping a grim harvest among the Hurons. Their longhouses were transformed into death traps. The smallpox epidemic that ravaged New England in 1633 reached Huronia in 1634. Smallpox or measles was thinning Huron numbers in 1635–36. A Huron elder, blaming the epidemic on the Jesuits, said, "The plague has entered every lodge in the village, and has so reduced my family that today there are but two of us left, and who can say whether we two will survive." Influenza struck in 1636–37. Smallpox returned in 1639. Huron population was scythed in half between 1634 and 1640. In 1648–49, famine and the attacks of the Iroquois completed the deadly work the diseases had begun. The Hurons scattered, most of the survivors being absorbed by other tribes.

Smallpox continued throughout the eighteenth century. It killed half the Cherokees in 1738 and returned in 1760; the Catawbas of South Carolina lost half their number to the epidemic of 1759. In 1763, the British doled out blankets from the smallpox hospital at Fort Pitt to visiting Indians; smallpox erupted among the tribes of the Ohio Valley soon thereafter. Outbreaks of smallpox were reported among Indian populations in New Mexico in 1719,

1733, 1738, 1747, and 1749; in Texas recurrently between 1674 and 1802; and in California, where Indian neophytes congregated in Spanish mission villages made easy targets for new crowd-killing diseases.

The massive smallpox epidemic that ravaged western North America between 1779 and 1783 illustrates the speed with which the disease could spread its tentacles throughout Indian country. The epidemic seems to have broken out in Mexico, and it afflicted Indian peoples in Peru and Guatemala. Spreading north to Spanish settlements like San Antonio and Santa Fe, it was picked up by Indians who visited the area to trade for horses. It was then quickly transmitted north and west, through the Rockies and across the plains, slaughtering as it went. It spread into the Canadian forests, killed as many as 90 percent of the Chipewyans in the central subarctic, and by 1783 was killing Cree Indians around Hudson Bay.

Abundant sources of fish and other marine resources supported dense populations on the Northwest Coast before European maritime traders and explorers brought smallpox in the late eighteenth century. When English explorer George Vancouver sailed into Puget Sound in 1793, he met Indian people with pockmarked faces and found human skulls and bones scattered along the beach, a grim reminder of the ravages of an earlier epidemic. These northwestern populations declined dramatically over the next century.

Smallpox was probably the number-one killer of Indian people, but it was by no means the only fatal disease. Epidemics of measles, influenza, bubonic plague, diphtheria, typhus, scarlet fever, yellow fever, and other unidentified diseases also took their toll. Alcoholism added to the list of killer diseases imported from Europe. "A person who resides among them may easily observe the frightful decrease of their numbers from one period of ten years to another," said John Heckewelder, lamenting the impact of alcohol. "Our vices have destroyed them more than our swords."

Recurring epidemics allowed Indian populations no opportunity to bounce back from earlier losses. They cut down economic productivity, generating hunger and famine, which rendered those who survived one disease more vulnerable to affliction by the next. New diseases combined with falling birth rates, escalating warfare, alcoholism, and general social upheaval to turn Indian America into a graveyard. Decreased fecundity hindered population recovery. Nantucket, off the coast of Massachusetts, was once described as "an island full of Indians" and is estimated to have had a population of about 3,000 in the mid-seventeenth century. By 1763, there were 348 people. An epidemic of yellow fever that year left only twenty survivors. Some 3,000 Indians inhabited Martha's Vineyard in 1642; 313 survived in 1764. Mohawk population continued to decline to little more than 600 by the time of the Revolution. At the western door of the Iroquois confederacy, Seneca population remained stable, but this was largely because they adopted captives and immigrants from other communities ravaged by war and disease. The Illinois Indians of the Great Lakes region numbered more than ten thousand people in 1670; by 1800, no more than five hundred survived. On the banks of the Missouri in present-day Nebraska, the Omaha Indians numbered more than three thousand in the late 1700s; cholera and smallpox cut their population to less than three hundred by 1802. In years when Indian peoples needed all their resources to deal with Europeans and to cope with a world that was changing around them, their numbers were being steadily eroded by disease.

Survivors, many of them disfigured by pockmarks, faced the future bereft of loved ones and without the wisdom of elders to guide them. Societies woven together by ties of kinship and clan were tom apart. After disease struck Martha's Vineyard in 1645–46, one survivor lamented that all the elders who had taught and guided the people were dead, "and their wisdome is buried with them." In 1710, Indians near Charleston, South Carolina, told a settler they had forgotten most of their traditions because "their Old Men are dead." In some cases, power struggles followed the deaths of traditional leaders. Old certainties no longer applied, and long-established patterns of behavior must sometimes have seemed irrelevant. The impact of such losses on Indian minds and souls is incalculable.

Traditional healing practices proved powerless against the onslaught. Fasting, taking a sweat bath, and plunging into an icy river—a common Indian remedy for many ailments—aggravated rather than alleviated the effects of smallpox. Just as some Europeans looked to Indian skills and practices to deal with snakebites and ailments native to North America, so some Indian people looked to Europeans to provide relief from European sicknesses. Some believed that European witchcraft caused the new diseases; so it made sense to combat them with European power and medicine. Others, with their loved ones dying around them, were willing to try anything. Many Hurons accepted baptism from Jesuit priests, regarding it as a curative ritual and hoping it could save their children.

Despite instances of genocide and germ warfare against Indian populations, Europeans frequently provided what help and comfort they could. Dead Indians were of no value to European missionaries seeking converts, European merchants seeking customers, or European ministers seeking allies. Hearing that Massasoit "their friend was sick and near unto death," Governor William Bradford and the Plymouth colonists "sente him such comfortable things as gave him great contente, and was a means of his recovery." French nuns ministered to sick Indians in seventeenth-century Quebec. Most Spanish missions in eighteenth-century California had dispensaries, medical supplies, and medical books, and some padres displayed genuine concern for the health of their mission populations. The state of medical knowledge was still rudimentary in the eighteenth century, but Europeans, motivated by self-interest as much as humanitarian concern, shared with Indians what medical advances there were. British Indian superintendent Sir William Johnson had the Mohawks inoculated against smallpox, and some Indians were vaccinated after Edward Jenner developed the cowpox vaccine in 1796. Many Indian people overcame their suspicion of the white man's medicine to accept the protection it could offer against the white man's diseases.

Nevertheless, the protection was too little and too late to stop demographic disaster. Not all Indian populations suffered 75 percent or 90 percent mortality rates—indeed, in some areas of the country Indian populations were on the rise in the eighteenth century—but the result was a world newly emptied of Indian inhabitants. Europeans arriving in Indian country in the wake of one or more epidemics made inaccurate estimates of precontact Indian population size on the basis of head counts of survivors. Seeing remnant populations, they gained a distorted impression of the size and sophistication of the societies that had once existed—and that distorted impression entered the history books. America, many believed, was an "empty wilderness," a "virgin land." If the country was empty, that was a recent development; it was depopulated rather than unpopulated. The new world of opportunity, which "free lands" opened for Europeans in North America, was in itself a by-product of European invasion.

Historians working to revise the old view of the European settlement of America as a story of progress and triumph have rightly stressed the biological cataclysm that followed European "discovery." But epidemic diseases also plagued European societies and shattered European families. France suffered epidemics and famine with appalling regularity throughout the seventeenth and eighteenth centuries. Recurrent outbreaks of plague devastated overcrowded London in the seventeenth century, sometimes, as in 1625, killing 25 percent of the population. In 1665, London experienced the horror of the Great Plague, which did not end until the Fire of London destroyed much of the city the following year. European immigrants to America did not entirely escape Old World diseases, and they succumbed to some new ones. Malaria wreaked havoc among Spanish expeditions in the sixteenth century. Early settlers at Jamestown, Virginia, suffered high death rates in unfamiliar environments. In 1740, Ephraim and Elizabeth Hartwell of Concord, Massachusetts, watched helplessly as all five of their young children died of the "throat distemper" that ravaged New England. Boston suffered recurrent outbreaks of smallpox in the seventeenth and eighteenth centuries. Yellow fever, imported from the Tropics, killed one out of every ten people in Philadelphia, then the capital of the United States, in 1793. But with less crowded communities, more sanitary conditions, improved diet, and greater economic opportunities, most colonists enjoyed a healthier life and longer life expectancy in their new world than did their contemporaries in Europe.

Though scholars disagree widely in their estimates, it is likely that in what is today the United States, Indian population stood at somewhere between 5 million and 10 million in 1492. By 1800, the figure had fallen to around 600,000. By contrast, the European population of the English colonies in America doubled every twenty-five years in the late eighteenth century. The first U.S. census in 1790 counted a total population of 3.9 million people. By 1800, North America had just under 5 million whites and about 1 million blacks. As James Axtell points out, the Indian people who survived in the eastern United States were being engulfed in a sea of white and black faces. The demographic complexion of the new world created by the interaction of Europeans, Indians, and Africans was very different in 1800 from what it had been three centuries before.

Nevertheless, the American population of 1800 combined Indian and European healing practices. Indians and Europeans alike employed "folk remedies" as well as doctors to cure diseases and injuries. The British lagged behind the Spaniards in establishing hospitals in the New World: Cortez built the first hospital in Mexico City for Indian and Spanish poor in 1521, and by the end of the seventeenth century, there were more than one hundred fifty hospitals in New Spain. In contrast, the first general hospital to care for the sick poor in the British colonies was established in Philadelphia in 1752; Massachusetts General Hospital, not until 1811. The first medical school was established at the University of Pennsylvania in 1765; Harvard Medical School, not until 1783. For most of the eighteenth century, American physicians who wanted a medical education had to go to Europe. With few trained physicians and few medical facilities available, people in rural and small-town communities turned in times of sickness to family, neighbors, clergymen, skilled women, and local healers. In many areas of the country, itinerant Indian physicians remained common well into the twentieth century, providing health care for America's poor, whether Indian, white, or black. Many Indian people preserved their belief in the efficacy of traditional medicine—both herbal and spiritual—even as they benefited from European medicine as practiced by white doctors. False Face societies and curing rituals continued among the Iroquois long after many Iroquois had embraced Christianity. Medicine was power, and Indian people needed to draw on all the power available to them as they struggled to survive in the disease-ridden land that was their new world.

David S. Jones

Virgin Soils Revisited

The decimation of American Indian populations that followed European arrival in the Americas was one of the most shocking demographic events of the last millennium. Indian populations declined by as much as 95 percent in the first century after the arrival of Christopher Columbus, prompting one historian to conclude that "early America was a catastrophea—a horror story, not an epic." This collapse established the foundation for the subsequent social and political developments of American history. Since the earliest encounters of colonization, colonists and their descendants have struggled to explain how and why depopulation occurred. They have debated the role of race, politics, and even genocide. All have concluded that infectious diseases, introduced by Europeans and Africans, played a decisive role. American Indians suffered terrible mortality from smallpox, measles, tuberculosis, and many other diseases. Their susceptibility led to American Indian decline even as European populations thrived.

Discussions of the epidemiological vulnerability of American Indians rose to prominence with the work of William McNeill and Alfred W. Crosby in the 1970s. Both argued that the depopulation of the Americas was the inevitable result of contact between disease-experienced Old World populations and the "virgin" populations of the Americas. As Crosby defined them in 1976, "Virgin soil epidemics are those in which the populations at risk have had no previous contact with the diseases that strike them and are therefore immunologically almost defenseless." His theory provided a powerful explanation for the outcomes of encounter between Europeans and indigenous groups, not just in the Americas but throughout the world. Since Crosby's analysis of virgin soil epidemics appeared in the *William and Mary Quarterly,* countless writers have cited his definition and attributed the devastation of American Indian populations to their immunologic inadequacy. As argued in Jared Diamond's Pulitzer Prize-winning *Guns, Germs, and Steel,* "The main killers were Old World germs to which Indians had never been exposed, and against which they therefore had neither immune nor genetic resistance." Such assertions, which apply the intuitive appeal of natural selection to the demographic history of the Americas, dominate academic and popular discussions of depopulation.

Even as Crosby's model of virgin soil epidemics remains a central theme of the historiography of the Americas, it has been misunderstood and misrepresented. Crosby actually downplayed the "genetic weakness hypothesis" and instead emphasized the many environmental factors that might have contributed to American Indian susceptibility to Old World diseases, including lack of childhood exposure, malnutrition, and the social chaos generated by European colonization. Subsequent historians, however, have often reduced the complexity of Crosby's model to vague claims that American Indians had "no immunity" to the new epidemics. These claims obscure crucial distinctions between different mechanisms that might have left American Indians vulnerable. Did American Indians lack specific genes that made Europeans and Africans, after generations of natural selection, more resistant to smallpox and tuberculosis? Did they lack antibodies that their Eurasian counterparts acquired during childhood exposure to endemic infections? Were their immune systems compromised by the malnutrition, exhaustion, and stress created by European colonization? These different explanations, blurred within simple claims of no immunity, have very different implications for our understanding of what was responsible for this demographic catastrophe.

It is now possible to revisit the theory of virgin soil epidemics and reassess the many possible causes of American Indian susceptibility to European pathogens. The confusion can be untangled by surveying and resynthesizing diverse research about Indian depopulation. A review of the literature of colonization shows the prevalence of simplistic assertions of no immunity and their possible ideological appeals. It also demonstrates the importance of defining the specific claims contained within the theory of virgin soil epidemics and evaluating each of them separately. Recent immunological research has clarified the different mechanisms that can compromise human immunity. Parallel work by biological anthropologists, archaeologists, and historians has elucidated the details of the mortality of specific Indian populations. Taken together, this work suggests that although Indians' lack of prior exposure might have left them vulnerable to European pathogens, the specific contribution of such genetic or developmental factors is probably unknowable. In contrast, the analyses clearly show that the fates of individual populations depended on contingent factors of their physical, economic, social, and political environments. It could well be that the epidemics among American Indians, despite their unusual severity, were caused by the same forces of poverty, social stress, and environmental vulnerability that cause epidemics in all other times and places. These new understandings of the mechanisms of depopulation require historians to be extremely careful in their writing about American Indian epidemics. If they attribute depopulation to irresistible genetic and microbial forces, they risk being interpreted as supporting racial theories of historical development. Instead, they must acknowledge the ways in which multiple factors, especially social forces and human agency, shaped the epidemics of encounter and colonization. . . .

Taken as a whole, recent immunological research offers many clues about the state of Indian immunity. American Indians could certainly mount immune responses to European pathogens. Perhaps their "naïveté" left them without protective genes, making them incrementally susceptible. Perhaps their homogeneity left them vulnerable to adaptable pathogens. Research about these questions continues on the cutting edge of immunology. It is possible that definitive evidence of demographically significant resistance genes will emerge. The historical experiment, however, has run its course. European and American populations mixed for over five hundred years before scientists could study them adequately. The opportunity for further research on first contact populations remains remote. As a result, the state of virgin immunity will forever remain contested. This leaves the literature on genetics and immunity promising, but unsatisfying. Genetic arguments of population-wide vulnerability must therefore be made with great caution. Other immunological mechanisms remain plausible, but problematic. Initial lack of adaptive immunity likely left American Indian societies vulnerable to certain pathogens, but certainly not to all of them, and adaptive immunity does not seem to have been relevant for the dominant causes of mortality in developing societies.

Furthermore, the mechanisms of adaptive immunity, along with the impact of simultaneous and successive synergistic infections, emphasize the importance of the disease environment, and not only the population itself, in shaping a population's susceptibility to infection. Other features of the environment, defined broadly, also have profound effects on immunity. A population's physical, social, economic, and political environments all interact to create patterns of vulnerability, regardless of its genetic substrate.

Such vulnerabilities have long been recognized. Even as observers began asserting racial arguments of disease susceptibility in the nineteenth century, they saw that a wide range of social factors created susceptibility to epidemic disease. After studying an outbreak of measles among the indigenous populations of Fiji in 1875, W. Squire concluded, "We need invoke no special susceptibility of race or peculiarity of constitution to explain the great mortality." He blamed social conditions, especially "want of nourishment and care." In 1909, anthropologist Aleš Hrdlička reached a similar conclusion about American Indians: "Doubtless much of what now appears to be greater racial susceptibility is a result of other conditions." Sherburne Cook came to believe that disease amongst indigenous populations worldwide "acted essentially as the outlet through which many other factors found expression."

Malnutrition provides the most obvious, and prevalent, demonstration of the links between social conditions, environmental conditions, and disease. In addition to causing deficiency diseases, such as rickets and pellagra, malnutrition increases susceptibility to infection. Some vitamin deficiencies cause skin breakdown, eroding the first barrier of defense against infection. Protein deficiencies impair both cellular and humoral responses. Malnutrition during infancy and childhood has particularly devastating effects on subsequent immune function. Certain diseases have more specific connections to nutrition. Malnutrition, especially vitamin A deficiency, increases mortality from measles. Malnourished children are more likely to die from chicken pox. Such interactions create "a vicious circle. Each episode of infection increases the need for calories and protein and at the same time causes anorexia; both of these aggravate the nutritional deficiency, making the patient even more susceptible to infection." Understanding these relationships, scientists have realized that malnutrition "is the most common cause of secondary immunodeficiency in the world."

Historians have thoroughly documented the impact of malnutrition on disease susceptibility. Such connections have clear importance for American Indians, who faced both disease and social disorder following European colonization. As Cronon describes, villages disrupted by disease and social breakdown "often missed key phases in their annual subsistence cycles—the corn planting, say, or the fall hunt and so were weakened when the next infection arrived." This would have been particularly damaging for the many populations that eked out only a precarious subsistence before European arrival. Although some writers have described American Indians living in bountiful harmony with their environment, archaeologists and physical anthropologists have shown that many groups were terribly malnourished. The accomplishments of the Mayan civilization might have been undone by climate change, crop failures, and famine. Disease, malnutrition, and violence made Mesoamerican cities as unhealthful as their medieval European counterparts, with life expectancies of 21 to 26 years. The Arikaras had life expectancies as low as 13.2 years. Careful study of skeletal remains has found widespread evidence of nutritional deficiencies, with health conditions worsening in the years before contact with Europeans. Baseline malnutrition, especially in the large agricultural societies in Mexico and the Andes, left American Indians vulnerable—at the outset—to European diseases. When the conditions of colonization disrupted subsistence, the situation only grew worse.

Malnutrition may be the most obvious factor, but it was only one of many. Environmental historians have shown how physical environments can leave populations susceptible to disease. Lowland Ecuadorians, weakened by endemic parasites and intestinal diseases, were more vulnerable to European infections than their highland compatriots. After Spanish arrival in Mexico, a "plague of sheep" destroyed Mexican agricultural lands and left Mexicans susceptible to famine and disease. Colonization introduced a host of damaging changes in New England. Deforestation led to wider temperature swings and more severe flooding. Livestock overran Indian crops and required pastures and fences, leading to frequent conflict and widespread seizure of Indian land. Europeans also introduced pests, including blights, insects, and rats. All of these changes fueled rapid soil erosion and undermined the subsistence of surviving Indian populations. More dramatic environmental events also wreaked havoc. Drought, earthquakes, and volcanic eruptions undermined resistance to disease in Ecuador in the 1690s. A devastating hurricane struck Fiji in 1875, exacerbating the measles outbreak there. As one observer commented, "Certainly for the last 16 years there has been experienced no such weather, and nothing could be more fatal to a diseased Fijian than exposure to it."

Historians and anthropologists have also documented many cases in which the varied outcomes of specific populations depended on specific social environments. The Lamanai Mayas, heavily colonized by the Spanish regime, had higher mortality than the more isolated Tipu Mayas. While much of Peru suffered severely, the region of Huamanga lost only 20 percent of its population between 1532 and 1570, the result of "a high birth rate, the relative immunity of remote high-altitude areas to disease, shrewd politics, and good luck." The Pueblos suffered when "the endemic problems of drought and famine were superimposed upon the economic disruption caused by the Spanish drain on food and labor." Severe outbreaks of smallpox and erysipelas in Peru from 1800 to 1805 reflected a combination of drought, crop failures, famines, mining failures, and economic collapse. The introduction of specific epidemics reflected specific historical events. Dauril Alden and Joseph Miller traced outbreaks of smallpox from West African droughts, through the middle passage of the slave trade, to Brazil. Measles raced down the political hierarchy in Fiji in 1875 as a series of conferences carried news of a treaty with the British empire, along with the virus, from the royal family to regional and local leaders throughout the island. Local variability and contingency led Linda Newson to conclude that "levels of decline and demographic trends were influenced by the size, distribution, and character of populations, especially their settlement patterns, social organization, and levels of subsistence." Even in the late twentieth century, specific social factors left isolated indigenous populations vulnerable to European pathogens. Magdalena Hurtado, who has witnessed first-contact epidemics in South America, emphasizes the adverse consequences of "sedentism, poverty, and poor access to health care."

Studies of North American tribes in the nineteenth and twentieth centuries have found similar local variability. Geographer Jody Decker shows how a single epidemic among the northern Plains tribes had disparate effects, "even for contiguous Native groups," depending on "population densities, transmission rates, immunity, subsistence patterns, seasonality and geographic location." Drought and famine left the Hopis particularly susceptible to an epidemic in 1780. The Mandans suffered severely from smallpox in 1837: famine since the previous winter had left them malnourished, and cold, rainy weather confined them to their crowded lodges. When smallpox struck, they had both high levels of exposure and low levels of resistance. As Clyde Dollar concludes, "It is no wonder the death rate reached such tragically high levels." Once North American tribes came under the care of the federal governments in the United States and Canada, they often suffered from malnutrition and poor sanitation. Mary-Ellen Kelm, who has studied the fates of the Indians of British Columbia, concludes that "poor Aboriginal health was not inevitable"; instead, it was the product of specific government policies.

Comparative studies have particular power for demonstrating the local specificity of depopulation. Stephen Kunitz has shown that Hawaiians suffered more severely than Samoans, a consequence of different patterns of land seizure by colonizing Europeans. The Navajo did better than the neighboring Hopi because their pastoral lifestyle adapted more easily to the challenges imposed by American settlers. In these cases similar indigenous populations encountered similar colonizers, with very different outcomes: "The kind of colonial contact that occurred was of enormous importance." Kunitz's cases demonstrate that "diseases rarely act as independent forces but instead are shaped by the different contexts in which they occur."

Paralleling this work, some historians have begun to provide integrated analyses of the many factors that shaped demographic outcomes. Any factor that causes mental or physical stress—displacement, warfare, drought, destruction of crops, soil depletion, overwork, slavery, malnutrition, social and economic chaos—can increase susceptibility to disease. These same social and environmental factors also decrease fertility, preventing a population from replacing its losses. The magnitude of mortality depended on characteristics of precontact American Indian populations (size, density, social structure, nutritional status) and on the patterns of European colonization (frequency and magnitude of contact, invasiveness of the European colonial regime). As anthropologist Clark Spencer Larsen argues, scholars must "move away from monocausal explanations of population change to reach a broad-based understanding of decline and extinction of Native American groups after 1492."

The final evidence of the influence of social and physical environments on disease susceptibility comes from their ability to generate remarkable mortality among even the supposedly disease-experienced Old World populations. Karen Kupperman has documented the synergy of malnutrition, deficiency diseases, and despair at Jamestown, where 80 percent of the colonists died between 1607 and 1625. Smallpox mortality, nearly 40 percent among Union soldiers during the Civil War, reflected living conditions and not inherent lack of innate or adaptive immunity. Mortality among soldiers infected with measles, which exceeded 20 percent during the United States Civil War, reached 40 percent during the siege of Paris in the Franco-Prussian War. Poverty and social disruption continue to shape the distribution of disease, generating enormous global disparities with tuberculosis, HIV, and all other diseases.

Is it possible to quantify the variability, to delineate the relative contribution of potential genetic, developmental, environmental, and social variables? Detailed studies have documented "considerable regional variability" in American Indian responses to European arrival. Many American Indian groups declined for a century and then began to recover. Some, such as the natives of the Bahamas, declined to extinction. Others, such as the Navajo, experienced steady population growth after European arrival. More precise data exist for select groups. Newson, for instance, has compiled data about die-off ratios, the proportion of those who died to those who survived. While die-off ratios were as high as 58:1 along the Peruvian coast, they were lower (3.4:1) in the Peruvian highlands. In Mexico they varied between 47.8:1 and 6.6:1, again depending on elevation. They ranged from 5.1:1 in Chiapas to 24:1 in Honduras and 40:1 in Nicaragua. Mortality rates from European diseases among South Pacific islanders ranged between 3 percent and 25 percent for measles, and 2.5 percent to 25 percent for influenza. Such variability among relatively homogeneous populations, with die-off ratios differing by an order of magnitude, most likely reflects the contingency of social variables. But most of these numbers are, admittedly, enormous: a 4:1 die-off ratio indicates that 75 percent died. Why did so many populations suffer such high baseline mortality? Does this reflect a shared genetic vulnerability, whose final intensity was shaped by social variables? Or does it reflect a shared social experience, of pre-existing nutritional stress exacerbated by the widespread chaos of encounter and colonization? Both positions are defensible.

The variability of outcomes reflected in the different fates of different Indian populations provides powerful evidence against the inevitability of mortality. It undermines popular claims, made most influentially by Henry Dobyns, that American Indians suffered universal mortality from infectious diseases. Noble David Cook, for instance, argues that the vulnerability was so general that Indians died equally whatever the colonial context, "no matter which European territory was involved, regardless of the location of the region. It seemed to make no difference what type of colonial regime was created." Such assertions, which reduce the depopulation of the Americas to an inevitable encounter between powerful diseases and vulnerable peoples, do not match the contingency of the archaeological and historical records. These, instead, tell a story of populations made vulnerable.

One could argue that the differences in American and European disease environments, the nutritional status of precontact Americans, and the disruptions of colonization created conditions in which disease could only thrive. Only a time traveler equipped with a supply of vaccines could have altered the demographic outcomes. But it is also possible that outcomes might have been different. Suppose Chinese explorers, if they did reach the Americas, had introduced Eurasian diseases in the 1420s, leaving American populations two generations to recover before facing European colonization. Suppose smallpox struck Tenochtitlan after Cortés's initial retreat and not during his subsequent siege of the city. An epidemic then might have been better tolerated than during the siege. Or suppose that the epidemics of 1616–1617 and 1633–1634 struck New England tribes during the nutritionally bountiful summers and not during the starving times of winter (or perhaps it was because of those starving times that the epidemics tended to appear in winters). The historic record of epidemic after epidemic suggests that high mortality must have been a likely consequence of encounter. But it does not mean that mortality was the inevitable result of inherent immunological vulnerability.

Consider an analogous case, the global distribution of HIV/AIDS. From the earliest years of the epidemic, HIV has exhibited striking disparities in morbidity and mortality. Its prevalence varies between sub-Saharan Africa and developed countries and between different populations within developed countries. Few scientists or historians would argue that these disparities between African and Europeans or between urban minorities and suburban whites exist because the afflicted populations have no immunity to HIV. Instead, the social contingency of HIV on a local and global scale has long been recognized. We should be just as cautious before asserting that no immunity led to the devastation of the American Indians.

Historians and medical scientists need to reassess their casual deployment of deterministic models of depopulation. The historic record demonstrates that we cannot understand the impact of European diseases on the Americas merely by focusing on Indians' lack of immunity. It is certainly true that epidemics devastated American Indian populations. It is also likely that genetic mechanisms of disease susceptibility exist: they influence the susceptibility of

American Indians—and everyone else—to infectious disease. What remains in doubt is the relative contributions of social, cultural, environmental, and genetic forces. Even when immunologists demonstrate that a wide variety of genes contribute to susceptibility to infectious disease, it will likely remain unknown how these factors played out among American Indians in past centuries. Demographic data, meanwhile, provide convincing evidence of the strong impact of social contingency on human disease. This uncertainty leaves the door open for the debates to be shaped by ideology.

Although unprecedented in their widespread severity, virgin soil epidemics may have arisen from nothing more unique than the familiar forces of poverty, malnutrition, environmental stress, dislocation, and social disparity that cause epidemics among all other populations. Whenever historians describe the depopulation of the Americas that followed European arrival, they should acknowledge the complexity, the subtlety, and the contingency of the process. They need to replace homogeneous and ambiguous claims of no immunity with heterogeneous analyses that situate the mortality of the epidemics in specific social and environmental contexts. Only then can they overcome the widespread public and academic appeal of immunologic determinism and do justice to the crucial events of the encounter between Europeans and Americans.

POSTSCRIPT

Was Disease the Key Factor in the Depopulation of Native Americans in the Americas?

The so-called "Columbian Exchange" involved a reciprocal trade in plants and animals, human beings, and ideas, as well as diseases. With regard to the exchange of diseases, this was not a one-way street. For example, the introduction of destructive microorganisms produced epidemic diseases (smallpox, tuberculosis, measles, typhoid, and syphilis) that decimated human populations on both sides of the Atlantic. On a more positive note, Europeans brought food stuffs such as wheat and potatoes to the New World and carried home maize, beans, and manioc. Native Americans benefited from horses and other farm animals introduced from Europe, but these were offset by the efforts of the Europeans to enslave and kill the indigenous peoples whom they encountered. The best study of these various by-products of European exploration is Alfred W. Crosby, *The Columbian Exchange: Biological and Cultural Consequences of 1492* (Greenwood Press, 1973). Crosby's conclusions are largely shared by William H. McNeill, *Plagues and Peoples* (Doubleday, 1977) and Jared Diamond, *Guns, Germs, and Steel: The Fates of Human Societies* (W. W. Norton, 1997).

The effects of the encounters between Europeans and Native Americans is explored in Gary B. Nash, *Red, White & Black: The Peoples of Early North America*, 3d ed. (Prentice Hall, 1992) and three works by James Axtell, *The European and the Indian: Essays in the Ethnohistory of Colonial North America* (Oxford University Press, 1981), *The Invasion Within: The Contest of Cultures in Colonial North America* (Oxford University Press, 1985), and *Beyond 1492: Encounters in Colonial North America* (Oxford University Press, 1992). Francis Jennings, *The Invasion of America: Indians, Colonialism, and the Cant of Conquest* (University of North Carolina Press, 1975) and David E. Stannard, *American Holocaust: Columbus and the Conquest of the New World* (Oxford University Press, 1992), which accuses Europeans and white Americans of conducting a full-blown campaign of genocide against native peoples in the Americas, offer two of the harshest critiques of European dealings with American Indians. The relationship between disease and environmental conditions is explored in William Cronon, *Changes in the Land: Indians, Colonists, and the Ecology of New England* (Hill & Wang, 1983), Karen Ordahl Kupperman, *Indians and English: Facing Off in Early America* (Cornell University Press, 2000), and Russell Thornton, *American Indian Holocaust and Survival: A Population History Since 1492* (University of Oklahoma Press, 1987). Alvin M. Josephy Jr. examines the pre-Columbian Native Americans in *America in 1492: The World of the Indian Peoples Before the Arrival of Columbus* (Alfred A. Knopf, 1992).

The era of European exploration during the fifteenth, sixteenth, and seventeenth centuries is covered in J. H. Parry, *The Age of Reconnaissance: Discovery, Exploration, and Settlement, 1450 to 1650* (Praeger, 1963). Samuel Eliot Morison, *The European Discovery of America: The Northern Voyages* (Oxford University Press, 1971), David Beers Quinn, *England and the Discovery of America, 1481-1620* (Harper & Row, 1974), Wallace Notestein, *The English People on the Eve of Colonization, 1603-1630* (Harper & Brothers, 1954), Charles Gibson, *Spain in America* (Harper & Row, 1966), and W. J. Eccles, *France in America* (Harper & Row, 1972) all discuss European contacts in North America.

ISSUE 3

Was the Settlement of Jamestown a Fiasco?

YES: Edmund S. Morgan, from *American Slavery, American Freedom: The Ordeal of Colonial Virginia* (W.W. Norton, 1975)

NO: Karen Ordahl Kupperman, from *The Jamestown Project* (Harvard University Press, 2007)

ISSUE SUMMARY

YES: Professor Edmund S. Morgan argues that Virginia's first decade as a colony was a complete "fiasco" because the settlers were too lazy to engage in the subsistence farming necessary for their survival and failed to abandon their own and the Virginia Company's expectations of establishing extractive industries such as mining, timber, and fishing.

NO: Professor Karen Ordahl Kupperman argues that Jamestown was America's first successful colony because in its first decade of trial and error "the ingredients for success—widespread ownership of land, control of taxation for public obligations through a representative assembly, the institution of a normal society through the inclusion of women, and development of a product that could be marketed profitably to sustain the economy—were beginning to be put in place by 1618 and were in full operation by 1620, when the next successful colony, Plymouth, was planted."

Until the 1970s American history textbooks ignored the seventeenth century once the colonies were founded. The new social history that has incorporated ordinary people—not just elite white males, but common white males, females, African Americans, women, and Indians—has added a whole new dimension to the colonial period. Racial, class, gender, and sectional differences emerge, and for the first time historians clearly distinguished the seventeenth and eighteenth centuries.

In the 1990s archeologists have pointed colonial history in a new and exciting direction. Working with teams of forensic scientists, nuclear physicists, and archeologists, recent digs have pinpointed the exact locations of St. Mary's City, Maryland, and Jamestown, Virginia. William Kelso, chief archeologist of the Association for the Preservation of Virginia Antiquities since 1993, has published his findings in *Jamestown: The Buried Truth* (University of Virginia Press, 2006). Encouraged by clues long embedded in a Spanish map of 1608, Kelso and his team have located not only the earliest fort, but also unearthed armaments, trash, food, and remains of devoured horses, cats, dogs, and rats, which speak of the starving time. The remains of mats and beads indicate the trade between Indians and the settlers. Through techniques of imaging and facial reconstruction of surviving skeletons, we know more about the aches and pains and diseases these settlers suffered unnecessarily if penicillin, Excedrin, or even a good dentist had been available. Kelso may have exaggerated in arguing that democracy was born at Jamestown, but the work of the archeologist sheds a whole new light on history.

The first permanent English settlement was established in the Chesapeake Bay region in 1607. They were latecomers in colonizing the new world. Earlier voyages by John Cabot in 1497 and 1498 around Canada were not followed up in the same way the Spaniards had established colonies in Latin America. Before Jamestown there were notable failures at colonization in Newfoundland and Roanoke, the lost colony.

The Virginia colony had a very shaky start. The Jamestown settlement, which the 105 colonists (39 died at sea) had established in May 1607, bartered with the Indians for corn, but even Captain John Smith could not trade for enough food or force the settlers to stop arguing among themselves and plant crops. Only 38 of the original settlers survived until January 1608 when a fresh supply of food and 120 new settlers arrived from England. Still the experiences of the first year did not prevent the "starving time" of the winter of 1609–1610 when several of the inhabitants resorted to eating their deceased family members.

The Virginia colony might have collapsed except for two reasons. First was the fact that the stock holding company continued to send over people to replace those who died. Mortality rates were higher in the New World than in England because of the hot climates and concomitant rampant diseases, so few lived past the age of 45. Combined with late marriages, the population growth was low. Only sustained immigration from England prevented the colony from collapsing in its first 15 years. Second, the development of the cash crop of tobacco improved its trade relations and prevented an economic breakdown.

In the first selection, Edmond Morgan is highly critical of the first settlers of Virginia. Others have pointed out that the earliest immigrants came from the "gentlemen" class and lacked the farming skills necessary for survival. But Morgan puts as much of the blame on the policies of the Virginia company and the London government as he does on the settlers. Even after the "starving time," the survivors and the new immigrants continued to pursue extraction industries such as gold, silver, iron mining, fishing, and lumber and silk binding at the expense of subsistence agriculture.

In the second selection, Karen Ordahl Kupperman disagrees with the negative view of early Virginia. Jamestown, she argues, was America's first successful colony because in its first decade of trial and error the ingredients for success—widespread ownership of land, development of a cash crop, establishing a representative assembly, setting up permanent families—were beginning to be put into place in 1618 and became a model for the next successful colony—Plymouth in 1620.

YES 

Edmund S. Morgan

The Jamestown Fiasco

The first wave of Englishmen reached Virginia at Cape Henry, the southern headland at the opening of Chesapeake Bay, on April 26, 1607. The same day their troubles began. The Indians of the Cape Henry region (the Chesapeakes), when they found a party of twenty or thirty strangers walking about on their territory, drove them back to the ships they came on. It was not the last Indian victory, but it was no more effective than later ones. In spite of troubles, the English were there to stay. They spent until May 14 exploring Virginia's broad waters and then chose a site that fitted the formula Hakluyt had prescribed. The place which they named Jamestown, on the James (formerly Powhatan) River, was inland from the capes about sixty miles, ample distance for warning of a Spanish invasion by sea. It was situated on a peninsula, making it easily defensible by land; and the river was navigable by oceangoing ships for another seventy-five miles into the interior, thus giving access to other tribes in case the local Indians should prove as unfriendly as the Chesapeakes.

Captain Christopher Newport had landed the settlers in time to plant something for a harvest that year if they put their minds to it. After a week, in which they built a fort for protection, Newport and twenty-one others took a small boat and headed up the river on a diplomatic and reconnoitering mission, while the settlers behind set about the crucial business of planting corn. Newport paused at various Indian villages along the way and assured the people, as best he could, of the friendship of the English and of his readiness to assist them against their enemies. Newport gathered correctly from his attempted conversations that one man, Powhatan, ruled the whole area above Jamestown, as far as the falls at the present site of Richmond. His enemies, the Monacans, lived above the falls (where they might be difficult to reach if Powhatan proved unfriendly). Newport also surmised, incorrectly, that the Chesapeake Indians who had attacked him at Cape Henry were not under Powhatan's dominion. He accordingly tried to make an alliance against the Chesapeakes and Monacans with a local chief whom he mistook for Powhatan. At the same time, he planted a cross with the name of King James on it (to establish English dominion) and tried to explain to the somewhat bewildered and justifiably suspicious owners of the country that one arm of the cross was Powhatan, the other himself, and that the fastening of them together signified the league between them.

If the Indians understood, they were apparently unimpressed, for three days later, returning to Jamestown, Newport found that two hundred of Powhatan's warriors had attacked the fort the day before and had only been prevented from destroying it by fire from the ships. The settlers had been engaged in planting and had not yet unpacked their guns from the cases in which they were shipped. That was a mistake they were not likely to repeat. But for the next ten years they seem to have made nearly every possible mistake and some that seem almost impossible. It would take a book longer than this to recount them all, and the story has already been told many times. But if we are to understand the heritage of these ten disastrous years for later Virginia history, we should look at a few of the more puzzling episodes and then try to fathom the forces behind them.

Skip over the first couple of years, when it was easy for Englishmen to make mistakes in the strange new world to which they had come, and look at Jamestown in the winter of 1609–10. It is three planting seasons since the colony began. The settlers have fallen into an uneasy truce with the Indians, punctuated by guerrilla raids on both sides, but they have had plenty of time in which they could have grown crops. They have obtained corn from the Indians and supplies from England. They have firearms. Game abounds in the woods; and Virginia's rivers are filled with sturgeon in the summer and covered with geese and ducks in the winter. There are five hundred people in the colony now. And they are starving. They scour the woods listlessly for nuts, roots, and berries. And they offer the only authentic examples of cannibalism witnessed in Virginia. One provident man chops up his wife and salts down the pieces. Others dig up graves to eat the corpses. By spring only sixty are left alive.

Another scene, a year later, in the spring of 1611. The settlers have been reinforced with more men and supplies from England. The preceding winter has not been as gruesome as the one before, thanks in part to corn obtained from the Indians. But the colony still is not growing its own corn. The governor, Lord De la Warr, weakened by the winter, has returned to England for his health. His replacement, Sir Thomas Dale, reaches Jamestown in May, a time when all hands could have been used in planting. Dale finds nothing planted except "some few seeds put into a private garden or two." And the people he finds at "their daily and usuall workes, bowling in the streetes."

It is evident that the settlers, failing to plant for themselves, depend heavily on the Indians for food. The Indians can finish then off at any time simply by leaving the area. And the Indians know it One of them tells the English flatly that "we can plant any where . . . and we know that you cannot live if you want [i.e., lack] our harvest, and that reliefe we bring you." If the English drive out the Indians, they will starve. . . .

It is not easy to make sense out of the behavior displayed in these episodes. How to explain the suicidal impulse that led the hungry English to destroy the corn that might have fed them and to commit atrocities upon the people who grew it? And how to account for the seeming unwillingness or incapacity of the English to feed themselves? Although they had invaded Indian territory and quarreled with the owners, the difficulty of obtaining land was not great. The Indians were no match for English weapons. Moreover, since the Indians could afford to give up the land around Jamestown as well as Henrico without seriously endangering their own economy, they made no concerted effort to drive the English out. Although Indian attacks may have prevented the English from getting a crop into the ground in time for a harvest in the fall of 1607, the occasional Indian raids thereafter cannot explain the English failure to grow food in succeeding years. How, then, can we account for it?

The answer that comes first to mind is the poor organization and direction of the colony. The government prescribed by the charter placed full powers in a council appointed by the king, with a president elected by the other members. The president had virtually no authority of his own; and while the council lasted, the members spent most of their time bickering and intriguing against one another and especially against the one man who had the experience and the assurance to take command. The names of the councillors had been kept secret (even from themselves) in a locked box, until the ships carrying the first settlers arrived in Virginia. By that time a bumptious young man named John Smith had made himself unpopular with Captain Christopher Newport (in command until their arrival) and with most of the other gentlemen of consequence aboard. When they opened the box, they were appalled to find Smith's name on the list of councillors. But during the next two years Smith's confidence in himself and his willingness to act while others talked overcame most of the handicaps imposed by the feeble frame of government. It was Smith who kept the colony going during those years. But in doing so he dealt more decisively with the Indians than with his own quarreling countrymen, and he gave an initial turn to the colony's Indian relations that was not quite what the company had intended. . . .

In their relations to the Indians, as in their rule of the settlers, the new governing officers of the colony were ruthless. The guerrilla raids that the two races conducted against each other became increasingly hideous, especially on the part of the English. Indians coming to Jamestown with food were treated as spies. Gates had them seized and killed "for a Terrour to the Reste to cawse them to desiste from their subtell practyses." Gates showed his own subtle practices by enticing the Indians at Kecoughtan (Point Comfort) to watch a display of dancing and drumming by one of his men and then "espyeinge a fitteinge oportunety fell in upon them putt fyve to the sworde wownded many others some of them beinge after fownde in the woods with Sutche extreordinary Lardge and mortall wownds that itt seemed strange they Cold flye so far." It is possible that the rank and file of settlers aggravated the bad relations with the Indians by unauthorized attacks, but unauthorized fraternization seems to have bothered the governors more. The atrocities committed against the queen of the Paspaheghs, though apparently demanded by the men, were the work of the governing officers, as were the atrocities committed against the Englishmen who fled to live with the Indians.

John Smith had not had his way in wishing to reduce the Indians to slavery, or something like it, on the Spanish model. But the policy of his successors, though perhaps not with company approval made Virginia look far more like the Hispaniola of Las Casas that it did when Smith was in charge.

And the company and the colony had few benefits to show for all the rigor. At the end of ten years, in spite of the military discipline of work gangs, the colonists were still not growing enough to feed themselves and were still begging, bullying, and buying corn from the Indians whose lands they scorched so deliberately. We cannot, it seems, blame the colony's failures on lax discipline and diffusion of authority. Failures continued and atrocities multiplied after authority was made absolute and concentrated in one man.

Another explanation, often advanced, for Virginia's early troubles, and especially for its failure to feed itself, is the collective organization of labor in the colony. All the settlers were expected to work together in a single community effort, to produce both the food and the exports that would make the company rich. Those who held shares would ultimately get part of the profits, but meanwhile the incentives of private enterprise were lacking. The work a man did bore no direct relation to his reward. The laggard would receive as large a share in the end as the man who worked hard.

The communal production of food seems to have been somewhat modified after the reorganization of 1609 by the assignment of small amounts of land to individuals for private gardens. It is not clear who received such allotments, perhaps only those who came at their own expense. Men who came at company expense may have been expected to continue working exclusively for the common stock until their seven-year terms expired. At any rate, in 1614, the year when the first shipment of company men concluded their service, Governor Dale apparently assigned private allotments to them and to other independent "farmers." Each man got three acres, or twelve acres if he had a family. He was responsible for growing his own food plus two and a half barrels of corn annually for the company as a supply for newcomers to tide them over the first year. And henceforth each "farmer" would work for the company only one month a year.

By this time Gates and Dale had succeeded in planting settlements at several points along the James as high up as Henrico, just below the falls. The many close-spaced tributary rivers and creeks made it possible to throw up a palisade between two of them to make a small fortified peninsula. Within the space thus enclosed by water on three sides and palisaded on the fourth, the settlers could build their houses, dig their gardens, and pasture their cattle. It was within these enclaves that Dale parceled out private allotments. Dignified by hopeful names like "Rochdale Hundred" or "Bermuda City," they were affirmations of an expectation that would linger for a century, that Virginia was about to become the site of thriving cities and towns. In point of fact, the new "cities" scarcely matched in size the tiny villages from which Powhatan's people threatened them. And the "farmers" who huddled together on the allotments assigned to them proved incapable of supporting themselves or the colony with adequate supplies of food.

At first it seemed to sympathetic observers that they would. Ralph Hamor, in an account of the colony published in 1615, wrote, "When our people were fedde out of the common store and laboured jointly in the manuring of the ground and planting corne, glad was that man that could slippe from his labour, nay the most honest of them in a generall businesse, would not take so much faithfull and true paines in a weeke, as now he will doe in a day, neither cared they for the increase, presuming that howsoever their harvest prospered, the generall store must maintain them, by which meanes we reaped not so much corne from the labours of 30 men, as three men have done for themselves."

According to John Rolfe, a settler who had married John Smith's fair Pocahontas, the switch to private enterprise transformed the colony's food deficit instantly to a surplus: instead of the settlers seeking corn from the Indians, the Indians sought it from them. If so, the situation did not last long. Governor Samuel Argall, who took charge at the end of May, 1617, bought 600 bushels from the Indians that fall, "which did greatly relieve the whole Colonie." And when Governor George Yeardley relieved Argall in April, 1619, he found the colony "in a great scarcity for want of corn" and made immediate preparations to seek it from the Indians. If, then, the colony's failure to grow food arose from its communal organization of production, the failure was not overcome by the switch to private enterprise.

Still another explanation for the improvidence of Virginia's pioneers is one that John Smith often emphasized, namely, the character of the immigrants. They were certainly an odd assortment, for the most conspicuous group among them was an extraordinary number of gentlemen. Virginia, as a patriotic enterprise, had excited the imagination of England's nobility and gentry. The shareholders included 32 present or future earls, 4 countesses, and 3 viscounts (all members of the nobility) as well as hundreds of lesser gentlemen, some of them perhaps retainers of the larger men. Not all were content to risk only their money. Of the 105 settlers who started the colony, 36 could be classified as gentlemen. In the first "supply" of 120 additional settlers, 28 were gentlemen, and in the second supply of 70, again 28 were gentlemen. These numbers gave Virginia's population about six times as large a proportion of gentlemen as England had.

Gentlemen, by definition, had no manual skill, nor could they be expected to work at ordinary labor. They were supposed to be useful for "the force of knowledge, the exercise of counsell"; but to have ninety-odd wise men offering advice while a couple of hundred did the work was inauspicious, especially when the wise men included "many unruly gallants packed thether by their friends to escape il destinies" at home.

What was worse, the gentlemen were apparently accompanied by the personal attendants that gentlemen thought necessary to make life bearable even in England. The colony's laborers "were for most part footmen, and such as they that were Adventurers brought to attend them, or such as they could perswade to goe with them, that never did know what a dayes worke was." Smith complained that he could never get any real work from more than thirty out of two hundred, and he later argued that of all the people sent to Virginia, a hundred good laborers "would have done more than a thousand of those that went." Samuel Argall and John Rolfe also argued that while a few gentlemen would have been useful to serve as military leaders, "to have more to wait and play than worke, or more commanders and officers than industrious labourers was not so necessarie."

The company may actually have had little choice in allowing gentlemen and their servants to make so large a number of their settlers. The gentlemen were paying their own way, and the company perhaps could not afford to deny them. But even if unencumbered by these volunteers, the colony might have foundered on the kind of settlers that the company itself did want to send. What the company wanted for Virginia was a variety of craftsmen. Richard Hakluyt had made up a list for Walter Raleigh that suggests the degree of specialization contemplated in an infant settlement: Hakluyt wanted both carpenters and joiners, tallow chandlers and wax chandlers, bowstave preparers and bowyers, fletchers and arrowhead makers, men to rough-hew pikestaffs and other men to finish them. In 1610 and again in 1611 the Virginia Company published lists of the kind of workers it wanted. Some were for building, making tools, and other jobs needed to keep the settlers alive, but the purpose of staying alive would be to see just what Virginia was good for and then start sending the goods back to England. Everybody hoped for gold and silver and jewels, so the colony needed refiners and mineral men. But they might have to settle for iron, so send men with all the skills needed to smelt it. The silk grass that Hariot described might produce something like silk, and there were native mulberry trees for growing worms, so send silk dressers. Sturgeon swam in the rivers, so send men who knew how to make caviar. And so on. Since not all the needed skills for Virginia's potential products were to be found in England, the company sought them abroad: glassmakers from Italy, millwrights from Holland, pitch boilers from Poland, vine dressers and saltmakers from France. The settlers of Virginia were expected to create a more complex, more varied economy than England itself possessed. As an extension of England, the colony would impart its variety and health to the mother country.

If the company had succeeded in filling the early ships for Virginia with as great a variety of specialized craftsmen as it wanted, the results might conceivably have been worse than they were. We have already noticed the effect of specialization in England itself, where the division of labor had become a source not of efficiency but of idleness. In Virginia the effect was magnified. Among the skilled men who started the settlement in 1607 were four carpenters, two bricklayers, one mason (apparently a higher skill than bricklaying), a blacksmith, a tailor, and a barber. The first "supply" in 1608 had six tailors, two goldsmiths, two refiners, two apothecaries, a blacksmith, a gunner (i.e., gunsmith?), a cooper, a tobacco pipe maker, a jeweler, and a perfumer. There were doubtless others, and being skilled they expected to be paid and fed for doing the kind of work for which they had been hired. Some were obviously useful. But others may have found themselves without means to use their special talents. If they were conscientious, the jeweler may have spent some time looking for jewels, the goldsmiths for gold, the perfumer for something to make perfume with. But when the search proved futile, it did not follow that they should or would exercise their skilled hands at any other tasks. It was not suitable for a perfumer or a jeweler or a goldsmith to put his hand to the hoe. Rather, they could join the gentlemen in genteel loafing while a handful of ordinary laborers worked at the ordinary labor of growing and gathering food.

The laborers could be required to work at whatever they were told to; but they were, by all accounts, too few and too feeble. The company may have rounded them up as it did in 1609 when it appealed to the mayor of London to rid the city of its "swarme of unnecessary inmates" by sending to Virginia any who were destitute and lying in the streets.

The company, then, partly by choice, partly by necessity, sent to the colony an oversupply of men who were not prepared to tackle the work essential to settling in a wilderness. In choosing prospective Virginians, the company did not look for men who would be particularly qualified to keep themselves alive in a new land. The company never considered the problem of staying alive in Virginia to be a serious one. And why should they have? England's swarming population had had ample experience in moving to new areas and staying alive. The people who drifted north and west into the pasture-farming areas got along, and the lands there were marginal, far poorer than those that awaited the settlers of tidewater Virginia. Though there may have been some farmers among the early settlers, no one for whom an occupation is given was listed as a husbandman or yeoman. And though thirty husbandmen were included in the 1611 list of men wanted, few came. As late as 1620 the colony reported "a great scarcity, or none at all" of "husbandmen truely bred," by which was meant farmers from the arable regions. In spite of the experience at Roanoke and in spite of the repeated starving times at Jamestown, the company simply did not envisage the provision of food as a serious problem. They sent some food supplies with every ship but never enough to last more than a few months. After that people should be able to do for themselves.

The colonists were apparently expected to live from the land like England's woodland and pasture people, who gave only small amounts of time to their small garden plots, cattle, and sheep and spent the rest in spinning, weaving, mining, handicrafts, and loafing. Virginians would spend their time on the more varied commodities of the New World. To enable them to live in this manner, the company sent cattle, swine, and sheep: and when Dale assigned them private plots of land, the plots were small, in keeping with the expectation that they would not spend much time at farming. The company never intended the colony to supply England with grain and did not even expect that agricultural products might be its principal exports. They did want to give sugar, silk, and wine a try, but most of the skills they sought showed an expectation of setting up extractive industries such as iron mining, smelting, saltmaking, pitch making, and glassmaking. The major part of the colonists' work time was supposed to be devoted to processing the promised riches of the land for export; and with the establishment of martial law the company had the means of seeing that they put their shoulders to the task.

Unfortunately, the persons charged with directing the motley work force had a problem, quite apart from the overload of gentlemen and specialized craftsmen they had to contend with. During the early years of the colony they could find no riches to extract. They sent back some cedar wood, but lumber was too bulky a product to bear the cost of such long transportation to market. Sassafras was available in such quantities that the market for it quickly collapsed. The refiners found no gold or silver or even enough iron to be worth mining. Silk grass and silk proved to be a will-o'-the-wisp.

The result was a situation that taxed the patience both of the leaders and of the men they supervised. They had all come to Virginia with high expectations.

Those who came as servants of the company had seven years in which to make their employers rich. After that they would be free to make themselves rich. But with no prospect of riches in sight for anybody, it was difficult to keep them even at the simple tasks required for staying alive or to find anything else for them to do.

The predicament of those in charge is reflected in the hours of work they prescribed for the colonists, which contrast sharply with those specified in the English Statute of Artificers. There was no point in demanding dawn-to-dusk toil unless there was work worth doing. When John Smith demanded that men work or starve, how much work did he demand? By his own account, "4 hours each day was spent in worke, the rest in pastimes and merry exercise." The governors who took charge after the reorganization of 1609 were equally modest in their demands. William Strachey, who was present, described the work program under Gates and De la Warr in the summer of 1610:

> It is to be understood that such as labor are not yet so taxed but that easily they perform the same and ever by ten of the clock they have done their morning's work: at what time they have their allowances [of food] set out ready for them, and until it be three of the clock again they take their own pleasure, and afterward, with the sunset, their day's labor is finished.

The Virginia Company offered much the same account of this period. According to a tract issued late in 1610, "the setled times of working (to effect all themselves, or the Adventurers neede desire) [require] no more pains then from sixe of clocke in the morning untill ten and from two of the clocke in the afternoone till foure." The long lunch period described here was spelled out in the *Lawes Divine, Morall and Martiall.* If we calculate the total hours demanded of the work gangs between the various beatings of the drum, they come to roughly five to eight hours a day in summer and three to six hours in winter. And it is not to be supposed that these hours refer only to work done in the fields and that the men were expected to work at other tasks like building houses during the remainder of the day. The *Laws* indicate that at the appointed hours every laborer was to repair to his work "and every crafts man to his occupation, Smiths, Joyners, Carpenters, Brick makers, etc." Nor did military training occupy the time not spent in working. The *Laws* provided for different groups to train at different times and to be exempt from work during the training days. Although colonists and historians alike have condemned the *Laws* as harsh, and with reason, the working hours that the code prescribed sound astonishingly short to modern ears. They certainly fell way below those demanded at the time in English law; and they seem utterly irrational in a chronically starving community.

To have grown enough corn to feed the colony would have required only a fraction of the brief working time specified, yet it was not grown. Even in their free time men shunned the simple planting tasks that sufficed for the Indians. And the very fact that the Indians did grow corn may be one more reason why the colonists did not. For the Indians presented a challenge that Englishmen were not prepared to meet, a challenge to their image of themselves, to their self-esteem, to their conviction of their own superiority over foreigners, and especially over barbarous foreigners like the Irish and the Indians.

If you were a colonist, you knew that your technology was superior to the Indians'. You knew that you were civilized, and they were savages. It was evident in your firearms, your clothing, your housing, your government, your religion. The Indians were supposed to be overcome with admiration and to join you in extracting riches from the country. But your superior technology had proved insufficient to extract anything. The Indians, keeping to themselves, laughed at your superior methods and lived from the land more abundantly and with less labor than you did. They even furnished you with the food that you somehow did not get around to growing enough of yourselves. To be thus condescended to by heathen savages was intolerable. And when your own people started deserting in order to live with them, it was too much. If it came to that, the whole enterprise of Virginia would be over. So you killed the Indians, tortured them, burned their villages, burned their cornfields. It proved your superiority in spite of your failures. And you gave similar treatment to any of your own people who succumbed to the savage way of life. But you still did not grow much corn. That was not what you had come to Virginia for.

By the time the colony was ten years old and an almost total loss to the men who had invested their lives and fortunes in it, only one ray of hope had appeared. It had been known, from the Roanoke experience, that the Indians grew and smoked a kind of tobacco; and tobacco grown in the Spanish West Indies was already being imported into England, where it sold at eighteen shillings a pound. Virginia tobacco had proved, like everything else, a disappointment; but one of the settlers, John Rolfe, tried some seeds of the West Indian variety, and the result was much better. The colonists stopped bowling in the streets and planted tobacco in them—and everywhere else that they could find open land. In 1617, ten years after the first landing at Jamestown, they shipped their first cargo to England. It was not up to Spanish tobacco, but it sold at three shillings a pound.

To the members of the company it was proof that they had been right in their estimate of the colony's potential. But the proof was bitter. Tobacco had at first been accepted as a medicine, good for a great variety of ailments. But what gave it its high price was the fact that people had started smoking it for fun. Used this way it was considered harmful and faintly immoral. People smoked it in taverns and brothels. Was Virginia to supplement England's economy and redeem her rogues by pandering to a new vice? The answer, of course, was yes. But the men who ran the Virginia Company, still aiming at ends of a higher nature, were not yet ready to take yes for an answer.

Karen Ordahl Kupperman

The Jamestown Project

Introduction: Creation Myths

In May 1607 a party of just over a hundred men and boys landed on the James River in Virginia and planted the colony they named Jamestown in honor of the English king. The little colony struggled through a horrible first decade in which it barely held on before the settlers began to find their footing on the path that would lead to stability and, eventually, success. Jamestown has always occupied an equivocal position in American history. It is celebrated as the first permanent English settlement in the territory that would become the United States. These colonists planted the tiny seed from which would grow a powerful nation where all the world's people would mingle.

And yet Jamestown makes us uncomfortable. The portrait of it that has come down to us depicts greedy, grasping colonists in America and their arrogant backers in England. The settlement's first years were marked by belligerent intrusions on the Chesapeake Algonquians which manifested mainly the ignorance of the English. Within Jamestown, life degenerated into a shambles of death and despair. When John Rolfe finally developed a marketable crop—tobacco—the colonists exploited the land and one another in the scramble for profits. Ultimately they would institute slavery for imported Africans in their insatiable search for profits. This is the creation story from hell.

Americans prefer to think of Plymouth colony in New England as our true foundation. This 1620 settlement, also composed of just over a hundred people, was a puritan foundation; about half of the settlers were separatists, that is, puritans who considered the Church of England so hopelessly corrupt that they separated themselves from it completely. By contrast, the puritans who settled Massachusetts Bay a decade later remained nominally within the established church. The Pilgrims at Plymouth, in our agreed-upon national story, are portrayed as the direct opposites of the Jamestown group. They were humble people who wanted only a place to worship God as they saw fit, and they lived on terms of amity with one another and with the neighboring Indians, relationships memorialized in the First Thanksgiving. They occupied family farms and were content with self-sufficiency. These are the forebears we prefer to acknowledge.

The good origins versus bad origins dichotomy is a false one based on a whole series of faulty premises. *The Jamestown Project* reconstructs America's origin story by placing the Virginia colony within its true context. By examining the maelstrom of previous plans and experiences that converged on the James, we can see the genuine accomplishment that emerged from the apparent wreckage wrought by the planters, and the efforts of the rank and file who largely brought it about.

In fact, through a decade's trial and error, Jamestown's ordinary settlers and their backers in England figured out what it would take to make an English colony work. This was an enormous accomplishment achieved in a very short period of time, a breakthrough that none of the other contemporaneous ventures was able to make. The ingredients for success—widespread ownership of land, control of taxation for public obligations through a representative assembly, the institution of a normal society through the inclusion of women, and development of a product that could be marketed profitably to sustain the economy—were beginning to be put in place by 1618 and were in full operation by 1620, when the next successful colony, Plymouth, was planted. Thus the Pilgrims were able to be relatively successful (after a disastrous first year) because they had studied Jamestown's record and had learned its lessons. Jamestown was not just the earliest English colony to survive; its true priority lies in its inventing the archetype of English colonization. All other successful English colonies followed the Jamestown model.

England was a laggard in overseas ventures. By 1606, when the Virginia Company was organized and plans for the colony were laid, English merchants in collaboration with political leaders had begun to establish a role for their nation in the newly opening trades around the Atlantic, the Mediterranean, and in the East. In these endeavors they were attempting to emulate, and often intrude on, the Spanish and Portuguese, united under the Spanish crown since 1580, who were the pioneers in creating the connections and bases through which trading operations were carried on.

New Spain was almost a century old when Jamestown was founded, and French traders had established firm partnerships with Indian nations in the fur trade along the St. Lawrence to the north. Spanish ships had scouted Chesapeake Bay repeatedly before concluding that the region would not repay the effort required to sustain settlement. The Spanish had planted St. Augustine on the Florida coast, and this, not Jamestown, was actually the first permanent European colony within the future United States; it was settled in 1565, almost half a century before Jamestown. And Santa Fe in New Mexico was founded shortly after Jamestown.

By 1607 English fishermen had been visiting the Newfoundland Banks and the New England coast for a century or more, and they built temporary settlements there, but no permanent English presence existed. In the last decades of the sixteenth century, a time when England and Spain were at war, English ships participated enthusiastically in privateering—licensed piracy against Spanish fleets traveling from the Caribbean to Seville. In the 1580s Sir Walter Ralegh's colony at Roanoke, within the Outer Banks of North Carolina, was initially designed to serve as a base for those patriotic privateers.

The first group of settlers sent to Roanoke in 1585 conformed to the classic model: a group of young men under military authority. Their governor was Captain Ralph Lane. As always with such a design, Lane found the settlers, whom he characterized as the "wylde menn of myne owene nacione," hard to control and motivate. By the end of the colony's first winter, relationships with the coastal Carolina Algonquians, on whom they depended for food, had broken down completely. They deserted the site early the next summer, and Lane scorned the whole enterprise, writing that "the discovery of a good mine by the goodnesse of God, or a passage to the Southsea, or someway to it, and nothing els can bring this country in request to be inhabited by our nation."

Ralegh and his associates did not give up on Roanoke. In fact, they were the first to try the successful model. In 1587 they sent a new colony composed of families under civil government, and each family was promised a large estate to own in the new land. They were intended to settle on Chesapeake Bay near where Jamestown would eventually be planted; the Lane colony's explorations had convinced them that this would be a better location from which good commodities could be produced. But this plan had no lasting influence, for the colony was abandoned, and the planters became famous as the Lost Colonists of Roanoke. Ralegh, meanwhile, was overwhelmed by other commitments and, ultimately, by loss of his favored status at court. So although Roanoke's failure only temporarily dampened English enthusiasm for establishing American colonies, Jamestown had to learn its lessons anew.

England's late entry into the American sweepstakes spawned myriad ventures. The stark dichotomy of Jamestown and Plymouth would have been unintelligible to contemporaries. Virginia was one of many attempts, now largely forgotten, all up and down the coast as far north as the Arctic Circle and south into the Caribbean, floated by English promoters in the last years of Queen Elizabeth's reign and the early years under James I, who succeeded her in 1603. But colonization was expensive and had to be financed by private enterprise. In the absence of any sure source of return on that investment, America took last place in most promoters' minds, after endeavors in the Mediterranean, Africa, and the East, where profits were much more certain. The voyages actually sent out were a fraction of the number of schemes proposed by that class of people who became known as "projectors"—those who made a career out of spinning projects.

English venturers were very conscious of being newcomers in all these places where they sought a foothold, and the keynote of their activities was improvisation. Everywhere they went, they necessarily employed trial and error—and error often predominated. Promoters laid plans, but the ordinary people who carried them out, often very young men and women, were the ones who had to deal with realities on the ground and who ultimately founded a successful colony. Many involved in early-seventeenth-century America—Indians, Europeans, and Africans—had had experience of other Atlantic and Mediterranean regions before they came together on the James River. Often their experience was as captives, or as individuals left behind when the ships on which they had arrived departed hurriedly in the face of dangers ranging from armed resistance to violent Atlantic storms. Those who could improvise were the ones who survived. And the knowledge of transatlantic others gained from these people informed planning and responses on all sides when Europeans attempted to create bases in America. All players brought vast experience, some relevant and some irrelevant, to the changed situations that European ventures created; and they drew on this experience, for good or ill, when confronted by the necessity of making choices.

When James I came to the throne and inaugurated a policy of reconciliation with Spain that ended the lucrative privateering war, prominent policy makers and merchants decided that they would try to sustain a permanent foundation across the Atlantic in the form of a Chesapeake colony. England's being a latecomer meant that its colonists had to take the parts of North America that were left, the places that other countries had rejected as less promising for the kinds of rich products that made the expensive project of colonization worthwhile. Backers knew that the region was not the best choice for the goals they had in mind; at about the same time Jamestown was founded, other companies attempted to plant colonies in Guiana, on various islands in the Caribbean, and in Newfoundland, as well as a colony in Maine. Other locations had been tried in the last decades of the sixteenth century in addition to Roanoke. Jamestown did not stand out in people's minds as a uniquely important venture, as we might expect it to have done.

Jamestown's site, on a peninsula jutting out into the James River some fifty miles upstream from Chesapeake Bay, was chosen with defense against Spanish attack in mind. As far as the Spanish were concerned, the colony was within their territory. They had attacked and eliminated an earlier French settlement on the southern coast. Although Spain and England were officially at peace in 1607, no one expected it to last, and the Virginia Company believed that its little plantation would be a natural target. Although planners were concerned about the response of the Indians on whom they would intrude, their main fear lay in the rivalry with Spain.

The Spanish did make constant efforts to find out what was going on in Jamestown—much of the surviving information available today in actually in Spanish correspondence—and several times seriously considered mounting an attack. Expectations of such an assault also contributed to the composition of the early contingents and plans for governing them. Like Roanoke's backers, the Virginia Company assumed that a group of young men under the command of high-ranking governors was the structure that would work best in the uncertain world of American ventures. After all, such an arrangement would most closely resemble the English society from which they came. But these hierarchical arrangements did not survive the transatlantic passage well, primarily because the colony could not replicate the social relationships on which they traditionally rested. Just as Roanoke's governor, Ralph Lane, found dealing with English savages his biggest problem, ultimately the company deemed brute force under martial law necessary to keep the Jamestown colonists in line.

It was the Chesapeake Algonquians who allowed Jamestown to become established as well as it did at the outset. The land on which the English settled belonged to the Paspahegh tribe, and the Paspaheghs, not surprisingly, deemed their presence unwelcome. Slowly the newcomers came to understand that many polities around Chesapeake Bay were under the influence of one great overlord, whom they came to know as Powhatan. The colonists called him an emperor, the closest European equivalent, but Powhatan was actually his title; eventually they were told that his given name was Wahunsenacawh. His daughter, whom we know by her nickname Pocahontas, became a principal intermediary between the cultures. Later the English learned two given names for her: Amonute and Matoaka.

Wahunsenacawh knew a great deal about Europeans in 1607. The Indians had seen many transatlantic voyagers over the course of the preceding century and understood well their strengths and weaknesses, and their aspirations and fears. They knew that Europeans, because they were so vulnerable, tended to overreact when they felt threatened, so American leaders had developed a series of strategies for handling them. Not only had these people encountered many ships that had sailed in and out of the bay in the sixteenth century, but also at least one man, Paquiquineo, had lived in Spanish colonies and even in Spain for a decade before returning in 1570 to his home at Paspahegh, the site of Jamestown. There is no question that the ramshackle Jamestown colony would have been cut off had the Indians decided to eliminate it. During the early years the men were dependent on the region's native people for their food supply, and relationships with the hard-pressed Indians grew increasingly tense, replicating the pattern at Roanoke.

The problems in the early years at Jamestown stemmed from actors on all sides drawing inappropriate lessons from previous encounters. Wahunsenacawh and his advisers did not foresee the eventual growth of the colony; they assumed that it would always be easy to manipulate this motley group, and that the little settlement could serve as a valuable source of tools, weapons, and other European manufactured goods. For their part, Jamestown's leaders, who were increasingly drawn from men with military experience in Europe's religious wars, believed that they could construct a society by enforcing sufficiently strict discipline, as they had done with English troops abroad. In the event, they were all wrong. Instead, the outcome grew from the trial-and-error efforts of the many ordinary people, most lost to the records, who found a way to build a society.

Only by examining the experience of all these people from around the Atlantic can we understand how and why Jamestown, however imperfectly, managed to hold on until it found the formula for recreating a successful version of English society abroad. Once that formula was devised, then all other colonies, beginning with Plymouth, had a much easier time of it and gained stability much more quickly. Jamestown's contribution was to develop the model for a true English colony, one that would actually work in America. This plan evolved out of the welter of failed experiments, false starts, and blind violence that characterized these early years. No one could say in 1607 how to make an English plantation in America function or even why investment in such a project was worthwhile. In the space of about a decade, some people, mainly those actually in Virginia, figured out what it would take and how to raise the revenue necessary to sustain English backers' interest. The results continued to be messy, and many people suffered. But the outlines of a genuinely American society, with all its virtues and defects, first emerged along the James.

So, why does Virginia look so bad? One reason was its site, which proved to be a very poor choice for promoting the well-being of the people who tried to live there. The period during which both Roanoke and Jamestown were founded was a time of environmental crisis that made establishing thriving settlements even more difficult than it should have been. Alonso Suárez de Toledo urged Spain's King Philip II not to worry about other Europeans trying to settle on North America's east coast: "What would happen to foreigners there who must bring their subsistence from a great distance to an inhospitable coast? The land itself would wage war on them." Jamestown was notoriously unhealthy, and the colonists made it more unwholesome by the way they operated their little society. The Spanish never attacked them, and their relationships with Chesapeake area Indians were crucial to the life of the settlement.

Another reason for Jamestown's bad reputation lies in the nature of the records, which consist largely of complaints, special pleading, and excuses sent by colonists back to their patrons in England. Most of the surviving records, not surprisingly, were produced by leaders on both sides of the Atlantic. The migrants had been sent over with notoriously unrealizable goals: to find a good source of wealth, preferably precious metals, or a passage to the Pacific and the riches of Asia. Prominent men in the colony, faced with the problem of explaining why they were not sending back the rich products investors demanded, or why they had not found the passage to the Pacific, could not speak the simple truth: that getting started is extremely difficult, and they would need support for many years just to become established before any valuable products could be expected. Investors in the seventeenth century looked to the next quarterly report as much as those in the twenty-first, and they had the choice of many other potential ventures from which the returns were more secure. Had they known that Virginia would absorb money over many years with no profit, the colony would have been abandoned at the outset—as so many others were. From the company's point of view, the colony was nothing but a drain on its resources, eating up huge amounts of money in supplies and new settlers without ever repaying the backers' investment, much less returning a profit.

The colonists, for their part, desperately wrote letter after letter explaining that colonization was hard, that they had to get set up before they could become self-sustaining, and that they needed support while they did that. Once they were established, then there would be time to make the efforts required to find a source of profit; but it was foolish and counterproductive to pressure them to do it at the beginning. One unspoken message ran through all these reports: Please do not abandon us. Unable to tell the truth in the early struggling years—or even to be sure what the truth was—colonial leaders blamed one another, and especially the rank and file, who were characterized in much of the correspondence as "the scum of the earth." Elites did not know how to organize and motivate them for the necessary work; they simply blamed the men for not acting as they wanted them to. Difficulties in controlling the colonists exacerbated the worsening relationship between the settlers and the Indians on whom they depended, though the leaders blamed the Indians on whom they had intruded for not supporting the colony with food as they wished.

But these same records, if we read beyond the surface noise of complaint and charge and countercharge, demonstrate that some people on the ground were drawing on the Atlantic and Mediterranean experience many had brought to the colony and were improvising relationships with the people and the land that finally achieved a measure of stability and growth in the colony. Often it was just this sort of improvisation, undertaken by ordinary people, that made elites nervous brought forth their accusations of malfeasance. Whereas many of the leaders whose vitriol figures so prominently in the records left the Chesapeake to promote and participate in other ventures after a few years, ordinary colonists were the ones who set about the task of building families and family farms. The other ventures attempted in the first decade of the seventeenth century all failed. The truly remarkable thing about Jamestown is that it somehow survived through years of hardship and discouragement until a few settlers finally embarked on the course to success at the end of the 1610s. This book is an examination of the various kinds of experiences and backgrounds that came together in the Jamestown project to make this improbable survival—and the evolution of the successful archetype—possible. . . .

Underneath the flurry of charges and countercharges, and with new kinds of evidence becoming available, one can see signs that normal patterns were increasingly possible as colonists made lives for themselves. Archaeological investigation has demonstrated that the colonists really were engaged in the kinds of diversified production that the company kept calling for, and that this engagement actually intensified after company control ended. As Ralph Hamor had testified, a genuine town was begun to the east of the fort in about 1618; a trained surveyor laid out twelve-acre lots for "James Cittie" in the early 1620s, and settlers were soon moving out beyond the confines of the city to the island's eastern end. Moreover, they had started building in brick. All the leading colonists lived clustered together in the "New Town." Archaeologists have uncovered signs of extensive mercantile activity and have excavated the workshop of gunsmith John Jackson, who took pity on Richard Frethorne in Jamestown. Foundations of shops specializing in pottery making, brewing, and apothecary work have also been unearthed. Governor Wyatt and George Sandys fostered the beginning of some industries; the great period of varied production on the island occurred after 1625 and continued through the 1630s. John Harvey, who arrived in 1623 after three years in Guiana and became governor in 1628, particularly pushed for such development.

Moreover, documentary excavations have discovered records of genuine communities composed of families growing up away from Jemestown—near the mouth of the James River and upriver close to the falls, and on the Eastern

Shore, where Thomas Savage had taken up residence and established a family. These communities, like contemporary Plymouth in New England, increasingly resembled English country villages. The census ordered in 1624 as part of the royal investigation revealed that the planters who had been in America the longest were most likely to have families. Although the planned college never materialized, Bernard Symmes, one of the separatist puritans in Virginia, endowed the first free school in English America in 1634.

As we draw conclusions about the nature of Virginia's founding years, Bernard Symmes presents a challenge to received wisdom. It is a shock to learn that that the first English commitment to provide free education was in Virginia. Moreover, the Virginia Company's great planned effort to carry Christianity to the Indians, with contributions from many people on both sides of the Atlantic, was unique. Nothing on that scale was thought of again until the creation of formal organizations such as the Society for the Propagation of the Gospel at the end of the seventeenth century.

Because attention then focused on the revocation of the Virginia Company's charter and charges against the leadership, the first lesson of the great attack of 1622—that Chesapeake Algonquians might welcome an English presence for the "book of the world" but would resist attempts to introduce the "book of the spirit"—was lost, as it had been with the sixteenth-century Jesuit mission and Don Luis/Paquiquineo's rejection of Christianity. Instead colonists drew conclusions about the Indians' fundamental nature and foresaw a future of separation more than convergence.

The colonists' level of engagement in economic pursuits, together with their growing ability to produce a marketable tobacco crop, also led to the 1622 rupture as the Chesapeake Algonquians came to understand how threatening a fully established and expanding English presence would be to their traditional life and its necessary land base. It would have been extremely difficult to predict in 1617 that the colony would grow so dramatically in the coming years. Thus it was not their stupidity and fecklessness but the beginnings of colonists' success that led Opechancanough to try to extirpate them. The 1630s saw a massive English migration into the Chesapeake, overwhelming Indian attempts to control the terms of relationships.

The Chesapeake remained a dangerous place for newcomers, and many died in their first few years, the seasoning period. Those who survived to finish their terms of servitude joined or helped to establish the communities growing up along the James or on the Eastern Shore. Some men who had been able to establish themselves early on added incrementally to their acreage by paying servants' passage over; in gaining the fifty-acre headright for each servant, they laid the foundation for future large plantations. But in these decades most farms were a few hundred acres or less. For the fortunate ones who survived the early years and were able to marry, the opportunity to have a farm of their own represented realization of an American dream.

It was Captain John Smith who, most prominently among his contemporaries, drew the true lessons of the Jamestown experience. After he left Virginia he spent the rest of his life, except for a brief trip to New England in 1614, at home writing about colonization. New England, then called Norembega, had been deemed a hostile environment after the failure of the Sagadahoc colony in the frozen winter of 1607. Smith coined the name "New England," one of the great propaganda strokes in American history, to bolster his contention that the northern environment was healthier for English bodies and more conducive to English life than the Chesapeake. He wrote several books about his and others' American experiences and in 1624, as the government was investigating the Virginia Company, he expanded on all he had written in his great work, *The Generall Historie of Virginia, New-England and the Summer Isles*. This was the first book that analyzed the whole record of English colonization in America and drew its lessons; in its conclusion he lamented his own inability to convince investors of the right way to proceed. He wrote that American ventures had been "my children, for they have beene my Wife, my Hawks, Hounds, my Cards, my Dice, and in totall, my best content."

Smith died at the age of fifty-one in 1631. In his last years he published two smaller books. One was his autobiography, where he told the story of his early life and Turkish captivity for the first time and brought the *Generall Historie* up to date. Then in his final year, as the huge fleet for Massachusetts Bay was gathering, he wrote a more philosophical book, *Advertisements For the unexperienced Planters of New-England, or any-where*. In this book he reiterated a case he had been making for some time: that fishing, the economic base on which New England was to be founded, was far more secure than illusory searches for gold or a passage to Asia—or a nonessential product like tobacco. America needed people who were not afraid to get their hands dirty. "Let not the meanness of the word fish distaste you." He maintained that the sea was as rich as the great silver mine at Potosí, and the fish stocks, unlike mines, were a renewable resource.

Although his book was addressed to Massachusetts Bay's founders—and there is some evidence that they read his books—his plan was drawn from analysis of Virginia's record, especially the revised program after 1618. His central theme, the sum of all experience thus far, was that colonization succeeded only where each family had a stake in the outcome and where merchants rather than aristocrats did the planning. He counseled New England's leaders "not to stand too much upon the letting, setting, or selling those wild Countries, nor impose too much upon the commonalty . . . for present gain." Rather, they should weld colonists to the project by giving each man as much land as he could reasonably manage for "him and his heires for ever."

All colonization projects, whether in Ireland or in America, had grappled with the fundamental question of how policy makers could motivate and control populations of migrants. Virginia's early history, especially as it was formulated out of the complaints and unrealistic claims on all sides, has been deemed a dismal tale of failure. Even the most severe martial law could not force colonists to thrive and lead productive lives. But, as John Smith explained to this readers, the Jamestown experience had produced a fundamental understanding about human psychology. Devolution—transfer of control to America—and fostering initiative on colonists' own account were the answer to all those questions about how to motivate people and create new societies. The key to building English societies abroad, however messy and incomplete, was discovered in Virginia and all successful colonies henceforth followed its model.

POSTSCRIPT

Was the Settlement of Jamestown a Fiasco?

Professor Edmund S. Morgan is the preeminent colonial American historian who has trained three generations of scholars at Yale University. Now in his eighties, Morgan is still a productive scholar writing books and review essays for the *New York Review of Books* on the latest output of scholarship in the field. For a convenient compilation of Morgan's essays, see *The Genuine Article: a Historian Looks at Early America* (Norton, 2004).

Morgan's chapter on the "Jamestown Fiasco" is important for several reasons. First of all, he rejects the New England model of colonization as being typical. Earlier generations of colonial historians wrote a lot about the Puritans because they kept extensive written legal and church records as well as diaries—all of which provided historians with an abundance of traditional historical sources. Morgan anticipated the framework of Jack P. Greene, *Pursuits of Happiness: the Social Development of Early Modern British Colonies and the Formation of American Culture* (University of North Carolina Press, 1988) and others who see the Chesapeake settlements (and not New England) as typical of the expansionist policies of the British Empire in Ireland and the West Indies. He also implies that the original colonists were trying to imitate the Spaniards to the extent that they hoped to extract mineral wealth from the colonists for export such as iron ore, salt making, glass making, silk making, and pitch. Unfortunately these resources were not available in the original Virginia settlements.

Professor Morgan also dispatches the romantic view that many historians attributed to the colonists. He discusses in other parts of his book the "guerilla warfare" that existed between the first European settlers and the Indians. Though earlier historians have focused on the hardships of the first Virginians and the starving time of the winter of 1609–1610 that led to cannibalism, Morgan blames the colonists themselves for their plight. The colonists did not take advantage of the abundance of fish and game in Virginia nor did they plant enough grain and corn to feed themselves. Why this occurred was partly due to the social background of the earliest settlers—too many "gentlemen" and not enough farmers. But Morgan extends his argument even further. The colonists modeled themselves after their English kin and hoped to set up small industries producing exports with agriculture as only a minor part of the economy. As previously mentioned, the mineral resources did not exist. Ironically Virginia became a productive colony in later decades when tobacco became the export of salvation.

Kupperman's analysis of *The Jamestown Project* is much more upbeat than Morgan's account. As an author of numerous works on seventeenth-century

America, she places Jamestown within the context of a half century of Atlantic ventures into Newfoundland, Ireland, the lost colony of Roanoke, and the sustained contacts with Islamic states in the Mediterranean and the Ottoman Empire. Within this international context, Kupperman pronounces the Jamestown colony a success. Despite the earlier struggles with diseases and food shortages, which she attributes more to the unfriendly forces of nature rather than the lazy and unskilled backgrounds of the early immigrants, Kupperman sees the ability to survive, the creation of a workable governmental structure, and the development of tobacco as an exportable cash crop as a model for the other colonies that followed.

Kupperman is correct in arguing that some of the lessons from *The Virginia Project* were adopted by the settlers in Plymouth and Massachusetts Bay colonies. For one thing, these settlers came as families and established sizeable towns from their very beginnings. They also farmed and fished and avoided the starving time.

But it can be argued that the wrong lessons were learned in relations with the Indians. Constant raids on both sides led to an all-out war with the Powhatans in Virginia in 1624, which nearly wiped out the colony. In Plymouth, relations soon deteriorated after "the first happy thanksgiving" dinner. In Massachusetts Bay, the Pequot War of the 1630s decimated the tribe, whose survivors were sold into slavery. By the 1670s, Bacon's Rebellion in Virginia and King Phillip's War in Massachusetts set the model of Indian–white relations for the next two centuries.

Professor Edmund S. Morgan's *American Slavery, American Freedom: The Ordeal of Colonial Virginia* (Norton, 1975) remains the classic text on seventeenth-century Virginia even 30 years after it was first published. Recently, four books on Jamestown have been written that supplement but do not necessarily replace Morgan's narrative. In 1994, William M. Kelso, director of archeology for the Jamestown Rediscovery Project, oversaw the unearthing of the original Jamestown site. Not only was the palisade uncovered, which surrounded the village, but also included were 700,000 artifacts of human skeletons, dogs, armor, tools, and even a fancy silver "ear picker." In *Jamestown the Buried Truth* (University of Virginia Press, 2006) Kelso states his belief that the seeds of democracy lay not at Plymouth Rock, but are buried at Jamestown.

The merger between anthropology and history has caused historians to take a more sympathetic view of the early colonists' world view and lifestyle than does Professor Morgan. See the works of James Horn, *A Land as God Made It: Jamestown and the Birth of America* (Basic Books, 2005); Benjamin Wooley, *Savage Kingdom: The True Story of Jamestown, 1607 and the Settlement of America* (Harper Collins, 2006); and Karen Ordahl Kupperman, *The Jamestown Project* (Belknap Press, Harvard University Press, 2007). Two books that cover the non-white and gender perspectives are Helen C. Rountree, *Pocahontas, Powhatan and Opechancanough: Three Indian Lives Changed by Jamestown* (University of Virginia Press, 2006), and Tim Hashaw, *The Birth of Black America: The First African Americans and the Pursuit of Freedom at Jamestown* (Carroll & Graf Publishers, 2007).

Two readable biographies of Jamestown's most flamboyant and important leader are Dorothy and Thomas Hoobler, *Captain John Smith: Jamestown and the Birth of the American Dream* (John Wiley & Sons, 2006) and the older but student-friendly *American Genesis: Captain John Smith and the Founding of Virginia* (Little, Brown and Company, 1975) written by Alden T. Vaughan for the Library of American biography series whose analysis remains poignant today: "In John Smith," says Vaughan, "young America found a prototype of itself; bold, energetic, and optimistic; at the same time, brash, intolerant, overly proud of its achievements and overly solicitous of approval. Such a symbol fit with ease the boundless land, so laden with riches, and the aggressive settlers who conquered it." Unlike most swashbucklers, Smith was a prolific writer. James Horn has compiled 1300 pages of *Captain John Smith: Writings with Other Narratives of Roanoke, Jamestown and the First English Settlement of America* (Library of America, 2007) and a shorter edition of the writings of *Captain John Smith*, edited by Karen Ordahl Kupperman (University of North Carolina Press, 1988).

Three review essays are indispensable for students who are willing to tackle the latest scholarship. See Edmund S. Morgan and Marie Morgan, "Our Shaky Beginnings," *The New York Review of Books* (April 26, 2007); Alan Taylor, "The Other Founding," *The New York Republic* (September 24, 2007); Jill Lepore, "Our Town," *The New Yorker* (April 2, 2007). The above essays were written by colonial scholars. Two generalists, James West Davidson and Mark Hamilton Lyle, have used "Serving Time in Virginia: The Perspectives of Evidence in Social History," to illustrate *After the Fact: the Art of Historical Detection* (Alfred A. Knopf, 1982).

ISSUE 4

Was the Salem Witchcraft Hysteria Caused by a Fear of Women?

YES: Carol F. Karlsen, from *The Devil in the Shape of a Woman: Witchcraft in Colonial New England* (W.W. Norton, 1987)

NO: Mary Beth Norton, from *In the Devil's Snare: The Salem Witchcraft Crisis of 1692* (Alfred A. Knopf, 2002)

ISSUE SUMMARY

YES: Carol Karlsen contends that the belief that woman was evil existed implicitly at the core of Puritan culture and explains why alleged witches, as threats to the desired order of society, were generally seen as women.

NO: Mary Beth Norton associates the events in Salem to borderland disputes with Native Americans and the French in northern New England, which led residents of Salem and Essex County to conflate attacks by Indians with assaults by witches to explain the problems confronting Massachusetts Bay Colony in the late seventeenth century.

Although an interest in the occult, including witchcraft and devil worship, exists in modern society, for most of us the images of witches are confined to our television and movie screens or perhaps to the theatrical stage where a Shakespearean tragedy is being performed. We can watch the annual presentation of *The Wizard of Oz* and reruns of *Bewitched* or hear the cries of "Bubble, bubble, toil and trouble" in a scene from *Macbeth,* with as little concern for the safety of our souls as we exhibit when black-garbed, broomstick-toting children appear on our doorsteps at Halloween. But such was not always the case.

Prehistoric paintings on the walls of caves throughout Europe, from Spain to Russia, reveal that witchcraft was of immediate and serious concern to many of our ancestors. The most intense eruptions in the long history of witchcraft, however, appeared during the sixteenth and seventeenth centuries. In the British North American colonies, there were over 100 witchcraft trials in seventeenth-century New England alone, and 40 percent of those accused were executed. For most Americans the events that began in the kitchen of the Reverend Samuel Parris in Salem, Massachusetts, in 1692 are the most notorious.

A group of young girls, with the assistance of Parris's West Indian slave, Tituba, were attempting to see into the future by "reading" messages in the white of a raw egg they had suspended in a glass. The tragic results of this seemingly innocent diversion scandalized the Salem community and reverberated all the way to Boston. One of the participants insisted she saw the specter of a coffin in the egg white, and soon after, the girls began to display the hysterical symptoms of the possessed. Following intense interrogation by adults, Tituba, Sarah Good, and Sarah Osborne were accused of practicing magic and were arrested. Subsequently, Tituba confessed her guilt and acknowledged the existence of other witches but refused to name them. Accusations spread as paranoia enveloped the community. Between May and September 1692 hundreds of people were arrested. Nineteen were convicted and hanged (not burned at the stake, as is often assumed), and another, a man who refused to admit either guilt or innocence, was pressed to death under heavy weights. Finally, Sir William Phips, the new royal governor of the colony, halted court proceedings against the accused (which included his wife), and in May 1693, he ordered the release of those who were still in jail.

Throughout history, witchcraft accusations have tended to follow certain patterns, most of which were duplicated in Salem. Usually, they occurred during periods of political turmoil, economic dislocation, or social stress. In Salem, a political impasse between English authorities and the Massachusetts Bay Colony, economic tensions between commercial and agricultural interests, and disagreements between Salem Town and Salem Village all formed the backdrop to the legal drama of 1692. In addition, the events in Salem fit the traditional pattern that those accused were almost always women. To what extent did sexism play the central role in the Salem witchcraft hysteria of 1692? Are there other equally valid explanations that place little or no weight on the gender of the accused?

In the selections that follow, Carol F. Karlsen and Mary Beth Norton offer two varying interpretations that seek to explain the events in Salem 300 years ago. For Karlsen, gender is the key factor. Negative views of women as the embodiment of evil were deeply imbedded in the Puritan (and European) world view. But through most of the seventeenth century, according to Karlsen, New Englanders avoided explicit connections between women and witchcraft. Nevertheless, the attitudes that depicted witches as women remained self-evident truths and sprang to the surface in 1692. Norton relates the events in Salem to a fear of Native Americans produced by crises on New England's northeastern frontier during King Philip's War (1675–1676) and King William's War (1689–1697). The difficulty in defeating their enemies in these conflicts, she argues, led residents of Salem and Essex County, some of whom were refugees from these wars, to conclude that Native Americans and witches had joined forces to wreak havoc in Massachusetts.

YES 

Carol F. Karlsen

The Devil in the Shape of a Woman: Witchcraft in Colonial New England

Handmaidens of the Lord

There is a curious paradox that students of New England witchcraft encounter. The characteristics of the New England witch—demographic, economic, religious, and sexual—emerge from *patterns* found in accusations and in the life histories of the accused; they are not visible in the content of individual accusations or in the ministerial literature. No colonist ever explicitly said why he or she saw witches as women, or particularly as older women. No one explained why some older women were suspect while others were not, why certain sins were signs of witchcraft when committed by women but not when committed by men, or why specific behaviors associated with women aroused witchcraft fears while specific behaviors associated with men did not. Indeed, New Englanders did not openly discuss most of their widely shared assumptions about women-as-witches.

This cultural silence becomes even more puzzling when we consider that many of these assumptions had once been quite openly talked about in the European witchcraft tradition. In the late fifteenth and early sixteenth centuries especially, defenders of the Christian faith spelled out in elaborate detail why they believed women rather than men were likely to join Satan's forces. The reasons they gave are not very different from those evident in the patterns the New England sources reveal. This presses upon us a question of some consequence: why had once-explicit beliefs about women's proclivity to witchcraft become implicit in their New England setting?

We can probe this question by following the lead of the anthropologist Mary Douglas and other scholars who have explored the social construction of knowledge. In Douglas's analysis, human societies relegate certain information to the category of self-evident truths. Ideas that are treated as self-evident, "as too true to warrant discussion," constitute a society's implicit knowledge. At one time explicit, implicit ideas have not simply been forgotten, but have been "actively thrust out of the way" because they conflict with ideas deemed more suitable to the social order. But the conflict is more apparent than real. In the "elusive exchange" between implicit and explicit knowledge, the implicit is "obliquely affirmed" and the society is shielded from challenges to its world view. The implicit resides in a society's symbols, rituals, and myths, which simultaneously describe, reflect, and mask that world view. To understand these processes, implicit and explicit knowledge must be examined together and in the context of their social environment.

In colonial New England, the many connections between "women" and "witchcraft" were implicitly understood. In Europe, several generations before, the connections had still been explicit. Over time, these established "truths" about women's sinfulness had increasingly come into conflict with other ideas about women—ideas latent in Christian thought but brought to the fore by the Reformation and the political, economic, and social transformations that accompanied it. For the Puritans who emigrated to New England in the early seventeenth century, once-explicit assumptions about why witches were women were already self-evident.

The swiftly changing conditions of early settlement left it uncertain at first whether, or how, witchcraft would serve the goals of New England society. Though men in positions of authority believed that certain women were working against the new colonies' interests, others did not see these women as witches. By the late 1640s, however, New Englanders embraced a witchcraft belief system as integral to their social order. Over the course of the seventeenth century, Puritan rituals, symbols, and myths perpetuated the belief that women posed ever-present dangers to human society, but the newer, post-Reformation ideas about women forced colonists to shrink from explicitly justifying this belief. They therefore continued to assume the complex of ideas about women-as-witches as self-evident truths. . . .

Seventeenth-century Puritan writings on women and family life reveal that the sexual hierarchy was at stake for them also, but with this difference: knowledge that detailed, explained, and justified the denigration of women had come into conflict with newer views of women. Though still vital, the old truths had been thrust from sight by the new.

The fundamental tenet of European witchcraft—that women were innately more evil than men—did not fit with other ideas Puritans brought with them to their new world. This tenet was still as necessary to Puritans as it had been for their Catholic predecessors, but it was incompatible with the emphasis Puritanism placed on the priesthood of all believers, on the importance of marriage and family relations, and on the status of women within those relations.

Puritanism took shape in late sixteenth- and early seventeenth-century England amidst a heated controversy over the nature of women, the value of marriage, and the propriety of women's social roles. The dominant attitude toward women in the popular press and on stage did not differ very much from the views of Catholic witch-hunters except that overall it was less virulent, delivered as often in the form of mockery as invective. According to this opinion, women were evil, whorish, deceitful, extravagant, angry, vengeful, and, of course, insubordinate and proud. Women "are altogether a lumpe of pride," one author maintained in 1609—"a masse of pride, even altogether made of pride, and nothing else but pride, pride." Considering the nature of women, marriage was at best man's folly; at worst, it was the cause of his destruction.

The problem, as some writers of this school had it, was women's increasing independence, impudence, "masculine" dress, and "masculine" ways. The presence of women in the streets and shops of the new commercial centers was merely symptomatic of their newly found "forwardness" and desire for "liberties." But more than likely it was not so much women's increasing independence in the wake of commercial development that troubled these commentators; rather it was the increasing visibility of women within their traditional but increasingly commercialized occupations. Solutions to the problem, when offered, echoed a 1547 London proclamation that enjoined husbands to "keep their wives in their houses."

Other writers argued that women were equal if not superior to men, called for recognition of the abuse women suffered under men's tyranny, and intimated that society would be better served if economic power resided in women's hands—but their voices were few and barely heard. More often, defenders of women simply took exception to the worst of the misogynists' charges and recounted the contributions women made to the welfare of their families and their society. The most serious challenge to prevailing opinion, however, came from a group of men who shared some of the concerns and goals of women's most avid detractors. Most of these men were Protestant ministers, and they entered the debate indirectly, through their sermons and publications on domestic relations. Though not primarily interested in bettering women's position in society, they found certain transformations in attitudes toward women essential to their own social vision. Among them, it was the Puritan divines—in both old and New England—who mounted the most cogent, most sustained, and most enduring attack on the contemporary wisdom concerning women's inherent evil.

From the publication of Robert Cleaver's *A Godly Form of Householde Governement* in 1598 until at least the appearance of John Cotton's *A Meet Help* in 1699, a number of Puritan ministers did battle with "Misogynists, such as cry out against all women." If they were not unanimous on every point, most of them agreed with John Cotton that women were not "a necessary Evil," but "a necessary good." For justification of this belief, they turned to the Scriptures, to the story of the Creation. God in his infinite wisdom, John Robinson contended, had created woman from man and for man, when he "could find none fit and good enough for the man . . . amongst all the good creatures which he had made." He had made woman *from* man's rib, Samuel Willard noted, "Partly that all might derive Originally from One; Partly that she might be the more Dear and Precious to him, and Beloved by him as a piece of himself." He had made her *for* "man's conveniency and comfort," Cotton said, to be a helpmeet in all his spiritual and secular endeavors and "a most sweet and intimate companion." It followed from both the means and purposes of God's Creation that women and men were "joynt Heirs of salvation," that marriage was an honorable, even ideal state, and that women who fulfilled the purposes of their creation deserved to be praised, not vilified by godly men. In 1598, Cleaver called men foolish who detested women and marriage. For Cotton, a century later, such men were "a sort of Blasphemers."

What had happened? Why did Puritans (along with their reforming brethren) insist on a shift in attitude that would by the nineteenth century result in a full reversal of a number of sixteenth-century notions about the "innate" qualities of men and women? We can begin to answer this question by considering a few elements critical in bringing about the transformation.

The Puritan challenge to the authority of church and state covered many issues, but one point not in dispute was the necessity of authority itself. Puritans were as disturbed by the lack of order in their society as were their enemies and were as fully committed to the principle of hierarchy. Though Puritanism developed during the period of upheaval that followed the breakup of the feudal order, Puritans were nevertheless determined to smother the sources of upheaval. Like other propertied Englishmen, Puritan men worried especially about masterlessness—insubordination in women, children, servants, vagabonds, beggars, and even in themselves.

Where they differed with other men of property was in their belief that existing authority was both ineffective and misplaced. "Faced with the ineffectuality of authorities in everyday life," one historian has argued, "the Puritans dramatically and emphatically denied the chain of authority in the church and enthroned conscience in its place. . . . The radical solution to social deterioration was not the strengthening of external authority. It was, rather, the internalization of authority itself." Foremost among the lessons Puritans taught was God's insistence on complete submission to divine will as expressed in the Bible and interpreted by ministers and magistrates. Outward compliance was not enough. Individuals who were fully committed to following the laws of God were *self*-controlled, needing only the Scriptures and an educated ministry to guide them on the path of right behavior. Submission to God's will had to be not only complete but voluntary. External discipline was still necessary to control the ungodly, but even they could be taught a measure of self-discipline.

The internal commitment to God's laws was to be inculcated primarily within the family, under the guidance and watchful eye of the head of the household, who conducted family prayer and instilled moral values in his dependents. It was not easy for family heads to ensure willing submission in their dependents, Puritans readily admitted. Minister John Robinson was talking specifically about children when he said that the "stubbornness, and stoutness of mind arising from natural pride . . . must . . . be broken and beaten down, . . . [the] root of actual rebellion both against God and man . . . destroyed," but his remarks reflect the larger Puritan belief in the difficulty of curbing human willfulness. For subordinates to accept their places in the hierarchical order, they must first be disciplined to accept the *sin* in their very tendency to rebel. From there, it was possible to develop enlightened consciences.

The family was also crucial as a symbol of a hierarchical society. Functioning as both "a little Church" and "a little Commonwealth," it served as a model of relationships between God and his creatures and as a model for all social relations. As husband, father, and master to wife, children, and servants, the head of the household stood in the same relationship to them as the minister did to his congregants and as the magistrate did to his subjects. Also, his relationship to them mirrored God's to him. Indeed, the authority of God was vested in him as household head, and his relationship to God was immediate: he served God directly. There was therefore no need for a priesthood to mediate between God and family heads. Other household members had immortal souls and could pray to God directly, but they served God indirectly by serving their superiors within the domestic frame. This model enhanced the position of all male heads of household and made any challenge to their authority a challenge to God's authority. It thereby more firmly tied other family members into positions of subordination.

The relationship of household heads to other family members fit within a larger Puritan world view. God had created the world, Puritans maintained, in the form of a great "Chain of Being" in which man was both above other creatures and subordinate to the Deity. God had ordained that human relationships were to be similarly patterned, with husbands superior to wives, parents to children, masters to servants, ministers to congregants, and magistrates to subjects. All, however, were subordinate to God. In each of these relations, inferiors served God by serving their superiors. While Puritans viewed the parent-child relation as a natural one, all other unequal relationships were described as voluntary, based on a covenant between the individuals concerned. God also required that family heads enter into another contractual relationship, called a "family covenant." Under this agreement, men promised to ensure obedience in all their dependents, in return for God's promise of prosperity.

Finally, the family also guided children in the right selection of their "particular callings." For the English divine William Perkins, particular callings were of two types. The first was God's call to individuals to enter into one or more of the several kinds of unequal social relations (husband/wife, parent/child, master/servant, and so on), relations that were "the essence and foundation of any society, without which the society cannot be." The second was God's call to specific kinds of employment by which individuals earned their livelihoods. In each case, God did the calling, but children had to endeavor to know what God had in mind for them, and parents were responsible to see that their charges made appropriate choices. Once chosen, callings were to be attended to conscientiously, not for honor or material reward but in the service of God. What Perkins did not say was that for Puritans the second sort of calling did not apply to females. Woman was called for only one employment, the work of a wife. . . .

As the old idea of woman as a necessary evil was gradually transformed into the idea of woman as a necessary good, the fear and hostility that men felt toward women remained. The old view of woman was suppressed, but it made its presence known in the many faults and tensions that riddled Puritan formulations on woman. Though largely unspoken, the old assumptions modified the seemingly more enlightened knowledge Puritans imparted. The new discourse, "first uttered out of the pulpit," was in fact dedicated to affirming the beliefs of the old, but in ways that would better serve male interests in a society that was itself being transformed.

The belief that woman was evil continued to reside in the myth at the core of Puritan culture—the biblical tale of human origins. Really two myths in one, it is the story of Creation in the Garden of Eden and the story of Adam and Eve's fall from grace. Our concern is mostly with the latter, but the two tales are nonetheless interdependent—the joys of Paradise making comprehensible the agonies of Paradise lost.

In their version of human origins, the Puritan clergy were more ambiguous than usual about when they were discussing "man, male and female," and when they were discussing men only. Despite its many contradictions, this creation myth allowed the Puritans to establish their two most cherished truths: hierarchy and order. Even before the Fall, they maintained, God had designated woman as both inferior to and destined to serve man—though her original inferiority was based "in innocency" and without "grief." Woman's initial identity was not—like man's—as a separate individual, but as a wife in relation to a husband. The very purpose of her creation allowed Puritans to extend the idea of her subordination *as wife* to her subordination *as woman*, in much the same manner as Anglican minister Matthew Griffiths did when he observed: "No sooner was she a Woman, but presently a Wife; so that Woman and Wife are of the same standing." So interchangeable were these terms in the minds of the clergy that they could barely conceive of woman's relationship to God except through a husband.

Woman's position in the Puritan version of Eden was analogous to that of the angels and the animals. Angels were formed before Creation as morally perfect spiritual beings. Though angels were clearly above man in the hierarchy of Creation, and though man was not to have dominion over them, God would require the angels to "minister for man." Animals were even closer to the position of woman since they too were created specifically to serve man.

The Puritan account of the Fall follows the standard Christian version in its general outlines. Discontented with their position in the hierarchical order, Adam and Eve succumbed to the Devil's temptation to eat the forbidden fruit, thus challenging God's supremacy over them and rebelling against the order of Creation. Guilty of pride, both were punished, but Eve doubly because she gave in to the temptation first, thereby causing man's downfall.

Puritan elaborations on this tale are revealing. According to Samuel Willard, Adam and Eve were both principal causes of man's fall, but there were also three instrumental causes: the serpent, the Devil, and the woman. Exonerating the serpent as a creature lacking the ability to reason, he went on to discuss the two "blamable Causes," the Devil and Eve. The events of the Fall originated with the Devil, he said, explaining that the word "Devil" was a collective term for a group of apostate angels. Filled with pride in their positions as the most noble of God's creations, discontented that they were assigned to serve "such a peasant as man," envious of what they saw as a "greater honour conferred upon him," and consumed with malice against God and man, the apostate angels sought revenge by plotting man's downfall. What motivated them was not their displeasure at their place in the hierarchical order, Willard claimed, for only God was above them. Rather it was their "supreme contempt for their employment." United by their evil intentions, they are called "Satan" in the Scriptures as a sign that they had traded their natural subjection to God for a diabolical subjection to the "Prince of Evil." In the process of accomplishing their ends, they were the first to speak falsehoods in Eden, becoming in the process blasphemers against God and murderers of the bodies and souls of men. "They seduced them . . . and thus in procuring of man's fall, they compleated their own; in making of him miserable, they made themselves Devils."

Eve's story—and her motivations—were more complex. Entering the body of the serpent, the Devil addressed himself to Eve, Willard said, suggesting to her that if she ate the fruit he offered, she would become godlike. Her senses suddenly deluded, she gave in to her lusts: "the lusts of the flesh, in giving way to carnal appetite, good for food; the lust of the eye, in entertaining the desirable aspect of the forbidden fruit, pleasant to the eyes; [and] the lusts of pride, in aspiring after more wisdom than God saw meet to endow a creature withal, to make one wise." Easily seduced, she in turn seduced Adam, thereby implicating him in her guilt. She commended the fruit, "makes offers to him, insinuates herself into him, backs all that the Serpent had said, and attracts him to joint consent with her in the great Transgression." Eve was moved not only by her sensuality but, like Satan, by pride. Her action bespoke the pride of a desire for knowledge, and by extension for God's position, rather than the resentment of her obligation to serve man.

Adam and Eve were both punished for the sin of pride, for rebelling against the order of Creation, but Eve rebelled both as part of man and as man's "other." For this reason, Willard called her both a principal and an instrumental cause of man's fall. According to Willard, when God commanded man not to eat the fruit of the tree of knowledge, "though their prohibition be expresst as given to Adam in the singular [necessarily so, as Eve had yet to be created in the chapter Willard was citing]. . . yet Eve understood it as comprehending them both." Thus she shared with Adam responsibility as a principal in the matter. "Yet, looking upon her as made for the man, and by the Creators law owing a subordination to him, so she may also be looked upon as instrumental." Elaborating on this point, Willard argued that having been created as his helpmeet, she ought to have encouraged and fortified him in that obedience which God had required of them both. Instead she became a mischief, "an occasion, yea a blamable cause of his ruin." For this, the Lord placed his "special curse" upon the female sex: "Unto the woman he said, I will greatly multiply thy sorrow and thy conception: in sorrow shalt thou bring forth children: and thy desire shall be to thy husband, and he shall rule over thee."

Part of woman's sin, then, was the seduction of man; another part was her failure to serve man. Though Willard never explicitly charged woman with having the same sinister motives as Satan, he did strengthen the association between these two instruments of man's fall by defining her as the Devil's willing agent: she acted "upon deliberation," he said, "and was voluntary in what she did."

In contrast, Adam (as distinguished from "man") lacked any motive for his sin. His role in the Fall was essentially passive. When God confronted the pair about their sin Adam defended himself by pointing the accusatory finger at his mate: "the woman which thou gavest to be with me, she gave me of the tree, and I did eat." Willard exonerated Adam by supporting his disclaimer and by describing him as an unwitting victim of his temptress wife: "Adam was not deceived, but the woman being deceived, was in the transgression." The burden of Adam's guilt was thereby lifted, and the blame placed on Eve. If "man's" sin in the Garden of Eden was pride, it was woman subsumed in man who committed it. Her male counterpart deserved a share of the punishment, but merely for allowing himself to be made "a servant of servants." Willard reinforced this point in his description of the sins that made human beings like devils. It is by now a familiar list: pride, discontent, envy, malice, lying, blasphemy, seduction, and murder. Some were explicitly Eve's, others implicitly hers; none were attributed to Adam.

Eve was the main symbol of woman-as-evil in Puritan culture. She was, in many ways, the archetypal witch. Whatever the new beliefs affirmed about women's potential goodness, the persistence of Eve as a figure in the Puritan cosmology signals the endurance of older if more covert beliefs. Women could be taught to internalize the authority of men, Puritans thought—but they knew that the sweeping denial of self they demanded of women was "too bitter a pill to be well digested," that it had to "be sweetened" before it could "be swallowed." The story of the Fall taught the lesson that female submission would not come easily—not, certainly, through a theological reformulation alone. Their continuing references to the Fall bespeak Puritan belief that the subjection of the daughters of Eve, whether religious, economic, or sexual, would have to be coerced. That was the message of Eve's punishment.

Ever fearful that women's conversion to virtuous womanhood was incomplete, ministers sometimes resorted to more vivid images of physical and psychological coercion. They warned the Puritan husband that he should not "bee satisfied that hee hath robed his wife of her virginitie, but in that hee hath possession and use of her will." Women tempted to abandon their chastity, and therefore their God, were told to resolve "that if ever these Other Lords do after this Obtain any thing from you, it shall be by the Violence of a Rape." For women who had yet to learn the necessity of subjection came the ever-present threat of additional punishment: "Christ will sorely revenge the rebellion of evill wives." Though the clergy protested again and again that the position of wives was different from that of servants, when they tried to picture what husbands' position would be like if the power relations within marriage were reversed, they envisioned men kept as vassals or enchained as slaves.

Ministers described this reversal of the sexual order as a complete perversion of the laws of God and the laws of nature. The most frequently employed symbols of female usurpers were perversions of those other beings destined to serve man: angels and animals. For woman to be "a man-kinde woman or a masterly wife" conjured up images of fallen angels, demons, and monsters, distortions of nature in every respect.

The tensions within the new ideology suggest that Puritans could no more resolve the ambivalence in their feelings than they could the contradictions in their thought. There was a deep and fundamental split in the Puritan psyche where women were concerned: their two conflicting sets of beliefs about women coexisted, albeit precariously, one on a conscious level, the other layers beneath. If woman was good—if she was chaste, submissive, deferential—then who was this creature whose image so frequently, if so fleetingly, passed through the mind and who so regularly controlled the night? Who was this female figure who was so clearly what woman was not? The ministers were not the only ones who lived with this tension, of course. The dual view of women affected everyone, male and female alike. Still, as the primary arbiters of culture in an age when God still reigned supreme, the clergy played the crucial role not only in creating the virtuous wife but in perpetuating belief in her malevolent predecessor.

In colonial New England, the intensity of this psychic tension is best seen in the writings of Cotton Mather—perhaps simply because he wrote so much, perhaps because his own ambivalence was so extreme.

In 1692, Mather published his lengthiest treatise on womanhood, *Ornaments for the Daughters of Zion.* His purpose, as he stated in his preface, was "to advocate virtue among those who can not forget their Ornaments and to promote a fear of God in the female sex." He was concerned both with women's behavior and with their relationship to God. He devoted much of his attention to the celebration of individual women, mostly biblical figures, whose lives were distinguished by quiet piety and godly ways. He presented them as models for New England women to emulate.

That same year, Mather completed *Wonders of the Invisible World,* his major justification for the Salem witchcraft trials and executions. Mather's focus here was on the behavior of witches and their relationships with the Devil—particularly women's complicity in Satan's attempts to overthrow the churches of New England. The book featured the witchcraft testimony presented against five of the accused at Salem, four of whom were women.

The nearly simultaneous publication of these two mirror-image works was not, it would seem, merely coincidental. Though Mather's witchcraft book does not explicitly address the reason why most of his subjects are women, his witches are nonetheless embodiments of peculiarly female forms of evil. Proud, discontented, envious, and malicious, they stood in direct contrast to the embodiments of female good in *Ornaments,* all of whom fully accepted the place God had chosen for them and regarded a willing and joyous submission to his will as the ultimate expression of their faith. Unable to ignore the profound uneasiness these two diametrically opposed views generated, Mather, like other New Englanders, relegated the still-powerful belief in women's evil to witches, on whom his fear and hatred could be unleashed. He was thereby freed to lavish praise on virtuous women—women who repressed the "witch" in themselves. Though his resolution allowed him to preserve man's superior position in the universe, Mather's heavy reliance in *Ornaments* on figures of Eve reveals how very delicate the balance was.

Mather's resolution was also his culture's. In the late sixteenth and seventeenth centuries, Puritans and other like-minded Protestants were engaged in the task of transforming an ideology, formulating beliefs that would better serve them in a world in which many of the old hierarchies and truths were no longer useful or plausible. They devised a new conception of man which, though drawn from the old, increasingly conceived him as an individual in relation to his God and his neighbors. It was a formulation that better fit the new economic order. The new man required a new woman: not an individual like himself, but a being who made possible his mobility, his accumulation of property, his sense of self-importance, and his subjection to new masters. By defining women as capable and worthy of the helpmeet role, the Puritan authorities offered a powerful inducement for women to embrace it. But they also recognized that the task they had set for themselves was a difficult one. If women were to repress their own needs, their own goals, their own interests—and identify with the needs, goals, and interests of the men in their families—then the impulse to speak and act on their own behalf had to be stifled.

As the witchcraft trials and executions show, only force could ensure such a sweeping denial of self. New England witches were women who resisted the new truths, either symbolically or in fact. In doing so, they were visible—and profoundly disturbing—reminders of the potential resistance in all women.

Puritans' witchcraft beliefs are finally inseparable from their ideas about women and from their larger religious world view. The witch was both the negative model by which the virtuous woman was defined and the focus for Puritan explanations of the problem of evil. In both respects, Puritan culture resembles other cultures with witchcraft beliefs: the witch image sets off in stark relief the most cherished values of these societies. A central element in these cosmologies, witches explain the presence of not only illness, death, and personal misfortune, but of attitudes and behavior antithetical to the culture's moral universe.

For Puritans, hierarchy and order were the most cherished values. People who did not accept their place in the social order were the very embodiments of evil. Disorderly women posed a greater threat than disorderly men because the male/female relation provided the very model of and for all hierarchical relations, and because Puritans hoped that the subordination of women to men would ensure men's stake in maintaining those relations. Many years ago the anthropologist Monica Hunter Wilson said that witchcraft beliefs were "the standardized nightmare of a group, and . . . the comparative analysis of such nightmares . . .one of the keys to the understanding of society." New England's nightmare was what the historian Natalie Zemon Davis has called "women on top": women as the willing agents of the Prince of Evil in his effort to topple the whole hierarchical system.

Mary Beth Norton

In the Devil's Snare: The Salem Witchcraft Crisis of 1692

New Witch-Land

What really happened at Salem in 1692? Why were so many people charged with witchcraft? And why were so many of the defendants convicted and hanged? Such questions still haunt Americans at the beginning of the twenty-first century. Numerous responses to those inquiries have been proposed over the years, yet . . . too many of the answers have failed to take into account the specific late-seventeenth-century context in which the witchcraft crisis occurred. In particular, historians have not fully recognized how two quite distinct phenomena combined to help create the crisis, and how examining the chain of events within a chronological framework can reveal the key patterns.

The foundation of the witchcraft crisis lay in Puritan New Englanders' singular worldview, one they had inherited from the first settlers of Massachusetts Bay more than sixty years earlier. That worldview taught them that they were a chosen people, charged with bringing God's message to a heathen land previously ruled by the devil. And in that adopted homeland God spoke to them repeatedly through his providences—that is, through the small and large events of their daily lives. Remarkable signs in the sky (comets, the aurora borealis), natural catastrophes (hurricanes, droughts), smallpox epidemics, the sudden deaths of children or spouses, unexpected good fortune: all carried messages from God to his people, if only they could interpret the meanings properly. New England's Puritans, even in the third generation, believed themselves to be surrounded by an invisible world of spirits as well as by a natural world of palpable objects. Both worlds communicated God's messages, because both operated under his direction. Satan, whom they understood to be (as Samuel Willard put it in a sermon in late May 1692) "the power of the air," leader of the "evil angels," played a major role in the invisible world. Yet because the devil was one of God's creatures even though he had revolted against divine authority, Puritans knew that Satan could do no more than God allowed. To believe otherwise would be to deny God's omnipotence.

Then in the last quarter of the seventeenth century, two successive, devastating wars on the northeastern frontier, King Philip's War and King William's War—or the First and Second Indian Wars—together wreaked havoc with what had been prosperous settlements along the coast northeast of Massachusetts. The continued and seemingly unstoppable successes of the Indians and their French allies called into question New Englanders' ability to sustain the northern outposts that contributed significantly to the prosperity of their economy through the production of fish and timber. That their Wabanaki enemies were Catholic (or at least aligned with French Catholics) made matters worse, suggesting that the settlers' own Protestantism might not be destined for the triumph they had long assumed to be inevitable.

The First Indian War, though extremely costly, ended with a victory in southern New England in late summer 1676 and with a standoff in the northeast in spring 1678. When hostilities began again "to the eastward" a decade later, the precarious nature of the earlier truce became evident to all. Nevertheless, the colonists at first anticipated renewed success in the second war. Yet those expectations were not met. New Englanders instead suffered repeated, serious losses of men and women, houses, livestock, and shipping. In the aftermath of each devastating defeat, they attributed their failures not to mistakes by their military and political leaders but rather to God's providence. He had, they concluded, visited these afflictions upon them as chastisements for their many sins of omission and commission. They had developed similar interpretations of the causes of earlier setbacks, but the consequences of those beliefs never extended far beyond the walls of their meetinghouses, primarily affecting their religious attitudes. This time, however, something was different.

In early 1692, several children and teenage girls began having fits of a sort previously recorded elsewhere in old and New England. The wartime context could well have influenced the onset of those fits—that the afflicted first accused an Indian of tormenting them certainly suggests as much—but more important than such plausible, if not wholly provable, origins was the long-term impact of the young women's charges in the context of Puritan New Englanders' belief system. Since Puritans insisted that the devil could do nothing without God's permission, they logically decided that God bore the ultimate responsibility for the witches' malefic activities. As the Reverend Deodat Lawson instructed his former parishioners in Salem Village on March 24, 1691/2, "The LORD doth terrible things amongst us, by lengthening the Chain of the Roaring Lyon, in an Extraordinary manner; so that the Devil is come down in great wrath." God, who was "Righteous & Holy," would not afflict them "without a Cause, and that Cause is always Just." What was the Lord saying to them? They needed to ask themselves, for "these malicious operations of Satan, are the sorest afflictions [that] can befal a person or people."

So too had God brought about their losses in the war, especially through providential actions during the 1690 campaigns against targets in New France. . . . [I]n November 1690 Governor Simon Bradstreet attributed the failure of Sir William Phips's Quebec expedition to "the awfull Frowne of God." The contrary winds that halted the ships' progress at the mouth of the St. Lawrence, Bradstreet declared, showed "the providence of God, appearing against us." Additional "particular providences" to the same effect included "the loss of so many of our friends sent out in the Expedition, in and at their return by the contagion of the small Pox, Fevers and other killing distempers," amounting perhaps to two hundred men. Likewise, when Fitz-John Winthrop reflected on the disasters that had befallen his attempt to lead colonial militia against Montreal that same year, he concluded that the "Devine hand that governs the world, and pointes out the sorrowes and succes of all mankinde" had caused the plan to collapse. To God's "good pleasure in this matter, as in all things," he told the governor and council of Connecticut, "we must submit, remembering that not one hayre of our heades fall to the ground without Gods appointments."

The Lord, in short, was simultaneously punishing New England in two different ways—through the Second Indian War on the northeastern frontier and through the operations of witchcraft in Essex County. . . . [T]he assaults from the visible and invisible worlds became closely entwined in New Englanders' minds. Those connections permeated the witchcraft examinations and trials, as revealed by repeated spectral sightings of the "black man," whom the afflicted described as resembling an Indian; and in the threats that the witches and the devil—just as the Wabanakis had—would "tear to pieces" or "knock in the head" those who opposed them. The links evident in legal proceedings are underscored by events elsewhere as well: the attack by apparitions on Gloucester in midsummer; Joseph Ring's repeated encounters with the spectral demonic militia; Mary Toothaker's pact with the "tawny" devil, who protected her for a time from his Wabanaki minions; Mercy Short's visions of meetings attended by both Indian sachems and witches; and Cotton Mather's later history of the war, which repeatedly described the Wabanakis as "devilish."

Joshua Scottow's "Narrative of the Planting of the Massachusetts Colony," written shortly after the end of the witchcraft crisis, also tied the two themes inextricably together. Scottow, a longtime resident of Black Point who had earlier referred to several Wabanaki sachems as "Satan's Emissaries," presented the Wabanakis' attacks and those of the witches as related phenomena, both instigated by God. "These wicked Cannibals," he explained to his readers, are "Gods Sword, and have been so for many years together." But the "Cruel Cannibals, Scalping and Fleaing of our Bodies, burning us as Sacrifices," only killed their material selves, he observed, while "the Devourer out of the Bottomless Pit," the "Do-evil," threatened their very souls. God, he asserted, "calls us, now being Alarmed by these Spirits," to assess our spiritual estates. Pointing out that those "upon whom this Great Wrath is fallen . . . are chiefly the members of our Churches, or their Hearers and Dependants," and furthermore that the witches observed diabolic sacraments, he predicted that "*New England* will be called, new Witch-land." Had the settlers not misbehaved, Satan would never have gained such an advantage over them, and they would never have experienced so many accusations, convictions, executions, and even "some Accused among our Rulers in Commonwealth and Churches." The combined assaults, Scottow contended, should rouse New Englanders from "our Læthal Lethargy" and return their churches to *"the good Old Way we have walked in."*

Accordingly, had the Second Indian War on the northeastern frontier somehow been avoided, the Essex County witchcraft crisis of 1692 would not have occurred. This is not to say that the war "caused" the witchcraft crisis, but rather that the conflict created the conditions that allowed the crisis to develop as rapidly and extensively as it did. In its early stages (that is, prior to mid-April 1692), the episode that originated in Salem Village resembled several other witchcraft incidents in seventeenth-century New England. Although the afflictions of Abigail Williams and Betty Parris were unusual, they were by no means unique, nor were adults' initial reactions to those afflictions unprecedented. But the girls' fits occurred in a supercharged atmosphere marked by ongoing conflict within Salem Village itself and, even more important, by the broader conflict on New England's northeastern borders. The afflictions that began in the Salem Village parsonage, after all, did not stop there. . . . Instead, the sufferings soon spread to other households, especially to those inhabited by youthful refugees from the frontier wars (Mercy Lewis, Susannah Sheldon, Sarah Churchwell) and by others with close ties to the frontier (Mary Walcott). All the afflicted joined in accusing others of bewitching them.

Under normal circumstances, New England's magistrates displayed a notable skepticism when confronting witchcraft charges. The judges believed in the existence of witches, but understood that providing legally acceptable proof of guilt in specific cases could be extremely difficult. In 1692, though, circumstances were not normal. . . . Bay Colony magistrates had good reason to find a witch conspiracy plausible in 1692. *It must always be remembered that the judges of the Court of Oyer and Terminer were the very men who led the colony both politically and militarily.*

William Stoughton, the chief judge, had unaccountably failed to effect a key hostage exchange at Casco in the fall of 1688, thus bungling possibly the last chance to avert the bloodshed that followed.

John Hathorne and Jonathan Corwin had most likely caused the devastating losses of Fort Loyal and Falmouth, and so all of Maine north of Wells, by recommending the withdrawal of Captain Simon Willard's militiamen on May 15, 1690, without provision for replacements. All councilors at the time (among them a near majority of the 1692 judges) were also implicated in that decision, with its catastrophic consequences.

Samuel Sewall and Stoughton (again) had committed Massachusetts' resources to the failed expedition against Montreal.

On that campaign, Fitz-John Winthrop, brother of Judge Waitstill Winthrop, had led men from New York and Connecticut into an unmitigated disaster north of Albany. (Indeed, Jacob Leisler, then in control of New York, adopted precisely that view when he ordered Winthrop's arrest after the expedition collapsed.)

Sir William Phips had, it was true, taken Port Royal, but that success was more than offset by the fiasco at Quebec and its terrible aftermath of a raging smallpox epidemic and seemingly endless indebtedness.

The colony's leading merchants—among them Sewall and Bartholomew Gedney, and presumably Peter Sergeant and John Richards as well—had promoted and encouraged the catastrophic attempt on Quebec, perhaps as much for anticipated profits from plunder as for the colony's welfare.

Gedney and Nathaniel Saltonstall both held senior positions in the Essex County militia, and Winthrop served as the major general of the colony's militia and was ultimately responsible for all its operations.

If the devil was operating in their world with impunity—if God for his own inscrutable reasons had "lengthened the chain" that usually limited Satan's active malevolence against mankind, to adopt Lawson's memorable phrase—then the Massachusetts leaders' lack of success in combating the Indians could be explained without reference to their own failings. If God had providentially caused the wartime disasters and he had also unleashed the devil on Massachusetts, then they bore no responsibility for the current state of affairs.

Thus first the Essex justices and then all the members of the court proved receptive to charges they would otherwise have most likely dismissed. In traditional witchcraft cases, neighbors alleged difficult-to-prove malefic activities by a vengeful witch at some point in the past. Judges, mindful of the rules of English law requiring two witnesses to a capital crime, had rarely convicted—and even more rarely agreed to execute—people accused solely of such offenses. But the Essex County cases appeared to be dramatically different. The initial accusations came from young girls, then later from teenagers and older women, whose terrible sufferings seemed obvious to all who beheld them. (For that reason, the 1692 indictments most often focused on the tortures endured by the afflicted during suspects' examinations, because many witnesses could attest to the severity of the fits and the painful nature of the sufferings thereby inflicted. Indeed, later members of the grand jury had themselves probably witnessed the torments of the complainants during examinations.)

By their own lights, the magistrates—first John Hathorne and Jonathan Corwin, then the other judges of the Court of Oyer and Terminer—did the best they could to properly assess the evidence against the accused and to apply the advice given in such English treatises as Michael Dalton's *The Countrey Justice* and Richard Bernard's *Guide to Grand-Jury Men*. Although bystanders from mid-January on pitied the afflicted children and unhesitatingly accepted the reality of their torments, not until such older accusers as Betty Hubbard, Ann Carr Putnam, and Sarah Vibber joined the group of complainants did crucial legal steps proceed. But the judges had too much personally at stake in the outcome. They quickly became invested in believing in the reputed witches' guilt, in large part because they needed to believe that they themselves were *not* guilty of causing New England's current woes. Simon Bradstreet alluded to such an interpretation in his November 1690 letter. The governor informed the colony's London agents that upon reading the dismal narrative he was enclosing of the Quebec debacle, "some may charge as matter of blame upon these or those Instruments Imployed in the conduct of that Affayre." Bradstreet, though, declined to do so, placing the responsibility instead (as was already indicated) on "the providence of God, appearing against us."

Even before mid-April, most of the people of Salem Village and environs found the sufferings of the afflicted completely credible. When the accusations moved from the confines of the Parris, Putnam, and Griggs households to various makeshift courtrooms, the examining magistrates—Hathorne and Corwin, joined occasionally by Sewall, Gedney, Thomas Danforth, and others—too did not question the truth of the charges they were hearing. Not only did they, like all their contemporaries, believe in the existence of witches, witchcraft, and the devil, they also, like seventeenth-century judges in general, commonly dealt only with defendants who had committed the offenses with which they were charged. And so, assuming the guilt of those they questioned, they sought to elicit the expected confessions that played a ritual role in most New England legal proceedings. With the exception of Tituba and the little girl Dorcas Good, they failed miserably until they encountered Abigail Hobbs.

Then the young teenager, a Maine refugee, made the crucial connection explicit. After Abigail proclaimed in the Salem Village meetinghouse at her April 19 examination that the devil had recruited her in Maine four years earlier—just prior to the resumption of hostilities—Essex County residents first fully perceived the challenge they faced in the visible and invisible worlds combined. Not only were their menfolk being drawn off to the frontier to fight an elusive and often victorious enemy, witches in their midst had allied themselves spectrally with the Wabanakis. The younger Ann Putnam—mouthing opinions that could only have come from Mercy Lewis—revealed that George Burroughs, former pastor of the Village and longtime Falmouth resident, had admitted bewitching the soldiers during Andros's winter expedition of 1688–1689, the very campaign that, in its failure to engage the enemy, had set the pattern for future blunders throughout the war.

Other afflicted accusers, especially those with ties to the frontier, then started to identify as witches men like John Alden and John Floyd, whose actions during the war suggested that they had joined Burroughs in an alliance with malevolent spirits. And given the logic that lay behind such charges, it was not surprising that the accusers also identified councilors and wealthy merchants as among the demonic conspirators. Even though most such names were never publicly recorded, several contemporary accounts reported the allegations. Far from being inexplicable, accusations of the colony's leaders and their spouses—as Sir William Phips seems to have understood altogether too well—were possibly the most obvious of all. Residents of the northeastern frontier believed their region's leaders had betrayed them, and they readily conflated visible traitors with invisible attackers. Indeed, Mercy Short and Samuel Wardwell did just that when they described spectral meetings attended by both Indians and witches. Although neither named the witches they saw at those meetings, by identifying the Wabanaki attendees as sachems, they implied that the witch-representatives had equivalent stature in colonial society. Wabanaki leaders would certainly have negotiated only with men of their own rank, not with the stereotypical elderly female practitioners of the malefic arts.

As the nature of the conspiracy against New England described by the afflicted accusers became clear, ordinary Essex folk started to tell each other stories about those among them whom they had long believed to be witches, and about people whose recent activities—perhaps fortune-telling (like Samuel Wardwell), experimenting with countermagic (like Martha Emerson), or drunken mutterings (like Thomas Farrar Sr.)—had aroused their suspicions. The large number of people identified as witches in 1692, in short, provides historians today with an oral snapshot of prevailing gossip.

Imagine a camera pointed at Essex County in 1692 that captured not visual images but rather aural ones. The crisis revealed the gossip about witchcraft that spread through the towns and villages of Essex County over the period from mid-April through mid-September 1692. Some of that gossip would have existed at any time, and some was generated by the crisis. But it is preserved today only through a special lens, one provided by the willingness of Massachusetts judges to entertain in court (and thus to record for posterity) the charges about which the common folk were talking. . . .

The charges were validated too by those who followed Abigail Hobbs in choosing to confess to being witches. Because confessors, having admitted an alliance with the devil, were not allowed to swear in court to the truth of their statements, the significance of their role in leading to convictions and executions has been overlooked by historians relying solely on written records. But, as such contemporaries as Cotton Mather, Deodat Lawson, and Thomas Brattle revealed, confessors' oral, unsworn testimony played a major role at most of the trials. After all, the English legal authorities consulted by the judges insisted that although the best proof of guilt in witchcraft prosecutions was a confession by the guilty party, the next-best proof was a confession from another witch, naming the suspect as a fellow supporter of the devil.

Although it is impossible to know exactly what such early confessors as Deliverance Hobbs, Mary Warren, Margaret Jacobs, and Sarah Churchwell said during the trials, their initial statements, augmented by the later, more detailed revelations elicited by the judges in repeated interviews in the Salem prison, offer at least an approximation of what must have been their official testimony. And in Andover in August and September many confessors—notably Mary Lacey Jr., Richard Carrier, the Post-Bridges daughters, and Samuel Wardwell—participated actively in the examinations of those whom they had named as witches, urging them to confess as well. By then, as other scholars have pointed out, it had become clear to the accused that confessors were not being tried. Accordingly, self-interest, deference to authority or age, and physical or psychological coercion combined to cause many Andover residents to confess a guilt that they were later to deny. But their subsequent retractions could not retroactively alter the confirming impact of their confessions at the time they were initially given.

Before the magistrates achieved much success in extracting confessions from examinees, the witches' specters had already started to confess freely to the afflicted female Villagers. After the apparition of George Burroughs told Ann Putnam Jr. on April 20 that he had killed his first two wives, fifteen other specters obligingly offered confessions to the children and young women who were serving as conduits between the visible and invisible worlds. Some of those confessions consisted of identifying themselves as witches or admitting having recruited additional malefic practitioners, while others detailed murders going back to the 1680s. Significantly, almost all such confessions were offered between late April and early June, or before the justices encountered the willing Andover confessors after mid-July. At a time when the justices could not extract confessions, in short, the afflicted filled in as their surrogates. Once the justices achieved success, the specters ceased to speak to the afflicted and instead the witches spoke "in bodily form" during their examinations. The timing thus underscored the complementary relationship between the magistrates in the visible world and their young female counterparts in the invisible one.

In other ways as well the accusers took on "official" duties in the invisible world. They solved crimes, disclosing who had committed murders both recently and in years past. They spied on the enemy, warning their fellow settlers of the militant witch conspiracy by reporting the musters of the spectral militias and by describing the nature of the meetings the conspirators attended. (If only the vulnerable outposts of Salmon Falls and Falmouth had received similar timely warnings of Wabanaki assaults!) By their adamant refusal to join the witches and their revelations about the conspiracy, they were defending New England against some of the most powerful enemies the region had ever faced. In fact, one might contend that the youthful female "magistrates" were defending New England far more effectively than had their male counterparts in the visible world during the previous few years.

That young women, especially servants such as Betty Hubbard and Mercy Lewis, would dare to assume those "public duties" was extraordinarily audacious, but nevertheless it accorded with the role they played throughout the crisis. From at least late February on, the afflicted served as intermediaries with the spirits in the invisible world, at the same time as they worked to establish their distance from the devil and his minions. Their repeated torments and the conversations in which they constantly said "no" to the requests that they sign Satan's book constituted the proof that, although they communicated with the malevolent spirits in the invisible world, they were not a part of it. Yet they remained potentially vulnerable to the charge that they had become *too* close to Satan, as was indicated, for example, in the Nurse family's attempts to implicate Abigail Williams in devilish doings because she conversed too easily with him. Over and over again the afflicted had to deny involvement with the witches in order to maintain their own credibility. By the late summer such critics as Robert Pike had begun to suggest that the accusers might themselves be complicit in the attack on New England: this reveals how fine a line they had been walking from the very beginning.

In the end, the fact that the afflicted girls and a few older women (especially Ann Carr Putnam and Sarah Vibber) had provided so much of the courtroom testimony caused the rapid collapse of support for the prosecutions. What had initially seemed the most compelling evidence—the torments the children and young women endured in the sight of many witnesses, and their testimony as to the identification of their spectral torturers—disintegrated once too many observers began to believe that Satan could assume the shape of an innocent person. The identifications then became the utterly untrustworthy "devil's testimony," and although few as yet charged them with dissembling (that would come later), Thomas Brattle called them decisively "these blind, nonsensical girls." The trials' eventual critics focused on the young female accusers, ignoring all the maleficium witnesses and the older confessors who had also testified against those who had been convicted and hanged. The critics understood at some level that the most effective way to attack the trials was to attack the core group of accusers. When they and their charges had been successfully discredited, support for the prosecutions melted away.

POSTSCRIPT

Was the Salem Witchcraft Hysteria Caused by a Fear of Women?

After 1692, a few witches were tried in the British North American colonies: in Virginia (1706), North Carolina (1712), and Rhode Island (1728). The last execution for witchcraft in England occurred in 1712 and in Scotland in 1727. On the Continent, royal edicts put an end to such persecutions before the close of the seventeenth century. Documentary evidence of seventeenth-century witchcraft can be examined in Paul Boyer and Stephen Nissenbaum's *Witchcraft in Salem Village* (Wadsworth, 1972) and George L. Burr, ed., *Narratives of the Witchcraft Cases, 1648–1706* (Charles Scribner's Sons, 1914). For an older comparative study, see George L. Kittridge, *Witchcraft in Old and New England* (Harvard University Press, 1929).

The Salem witch trials represent one of the most thoroughly studied episodes in American history. Several scholars have concluded that the enthusiasm for learning more about the Salem witches and their accusers far outweighs the importance of the event; yet essays and books continue to roll off the presses. As suggested in the introduction to this issue, the selections by Karlsen and Norton summarize but two of the many interpretations of the incident at Salem. Those interested in pursuing this topic further should examine Marion Starkey's *The Devil in Massachusetts: A Modern Enquiry into the Salem Witch Trials* (Knopf, 1949), which blames the episode on the lies told by the accusers. An intriguing alternative is Chadwick Hansen's *Witchcraft at Salem* (George Braziller, 1969), in which the author insists that several Salem residents did practice black magic, thereby heightening the fears of their neighbors. Paul Boyer and Stephen Nissenbaum, in *Salem Possessed: The Social Origins of Witchcraft* (Harvard University Press, 1974), emphasize the conflicts between the residents of Salem Town and Salem Village. More recently, Laurie Winn Carlson in *A Fever in Salem* (Ivan R. Dee, 1999) has postulated that the spectral visions described by accusers and accused in Salem were the product of physical and neurological symptoms produced by an unrecognized epidemic of encephalitis. John Putnam Demos's *Entertaining Satan: Witchcraft and the Culture of Early New England* (Oxford University Press, 1982) applies theories and insights from the fields of psychology, sociology, and anthropology to explore the influence of witchcraft throughout New England. Also of value is Demos's earlier essay, "Underlying Themes in the Witchcraft of Seventeenth-Century New England," *American Historical Review* (June 1970). More recent studies include Larry Gragg, *The Salem Witch Crisis* (Praeger, 1992), and Bernard Rosenthal, *Salem Story: Reading the Witch Trials of 1692* (Cambridge University Press, 1993). For additional discussion of the relationship between women and witchcraft, see Elizabeth Reis, *Damned*

Women: Sinners and Witches in Puritan New England (Cornell University Press, 1997) and Elaine G. Breslaw, *Tituba, Reluctant Witch of Salem: Devilish Indians and Puritan Fantasies* (New York University Press, 1995).

Carol Karlsen's work reflects a growing interest in the status of colonial American women. Students in American history classes have for generations read of the founding of the colonies in British North America, their political and economic development, and the colonists' struggle for independence without ever being confronted by a female protagonist. Only in the last three decades have discussions of the role of women in the development of American society made their appearance in standard textbooks. Consequently, it is useful to explore the status of women in colonial America. Surveys of American women's history that address the colonial period include June Sochen, *Herstory: A Woman's View of American History* (Alfred Publishing Company, 1974) and Nancy Woloch, *Women and the American Experience* (Alfred A. Knopf, 1984). The idea that colonial American women enjoyed a higher status than their European counterparts is supported in Richard B. Morris, *Studies in the History of American Law* (2d ed.; Octagon Books, 1964), Roger Thompson, *Women in Stuart England and America: A Comparative Study* (Routledge & Kegan, 1974), and Page Smith, *Daughters of the Promised Land: Women in American History* (Little, Brown, 1977). For a contrary view, see Lyle Koehler, *A Search for Power: The "Weaker Sex" in Seventeenth-Century New England* (University of Illinois Press, 1980). Laurel Thatcher Ulrich's *Good Wives: Image and Reality in the Lives of Women in Northern New England, 1650–1750* (Alfred A. Knopf, 1980) describes a variety of roles performed by married women.

Women in the age of the American Revolution are the focus of Linda Grant DePauw and Conover Hunt, *"Remember the Ladies": Women in America, 1750–1815* (Viking Press, 1976), Mary Beth Norton, *Liberty's Daughters: The Revolutionary Experience of American Women, 1750–1800* (Little, Brown, 1980), Linda Kerber, *Women of the Republic: Intellect and Ideology in Revolutionary America* (University of North Carolina Press, 1980), and Joy Day Buel and Richard Buel, Jr., *The Way of Duty: A Woman and Her Family in Revolutionary America* (W. W. Norton, 1984).

Internet References . . .

Virtual Marching Tour of the American Revolution

Sponsored by the Independence Hall Association in Philadelphia, this site is a promising work in progress. Its goal is to provide information about Revolutionary times through text and images.

http://www.ushistory.org/march/

The Constitution of the United States

Sponsored by the national Archives and Records Administration, this site presents a wealth of information on the U.S. Constitution. From here you can link to the biographies of the 55 delegates to the Constitutional Convention, take an in-depth look at the convention and the ratification process, and read a transcription of the complete text of the Constitution, including high-resolution images of each page of the document.

http://www.nara.gov/exhall/charters/constitution/conmain.html

Alexander Hamilton: The Man Who Made Modern America

Sponsored by the New York Historical Society, this site includes a virtual tour of the Hamilton traveling exhibition and links to documents and databases relating to Hamilton.

http://alexanderhamiltonexhibition.org/

Andrew Jackson: "Champion of the Kingly Commons"

Collection of the Jacksonian era, including discussion of the myth and image of Andrew Jackson and his times.

http://xroads.virginia.edu/~CAP/jackson.html

UNIT 2

Revolution and the New Nation

The American Revolution led to independence from England and to the establishment of a new nation. As the United States matured, its people and leaders struggled to implement fully the ideals that had sparked the Revolution. What had been abstractions before the formation of the new government had to be applied and refined in day-to-day practice. The nature of post-revolutionary America, government stability, the transition of power against the backdrop of political factionalism, the extension of democracy, and the international role of the new United States had to be worked out.

ISSUE 5

Did the American Revolution Produce a Christian Nation?

YES: Nathan O. Hatch, from "The Democratization of Christianity and the Character of American Politics," in Mark A. Noll, ed., *Religion and American Politics* (Oxford University Press, 1990)

NO: Jon Butler, from "Why Revolutionary America Wasn't a 'Christian Nation'," in James H. Hutson, ed., *Religion and the New Republic: Faith in the Founding of America* (Rowman and Littlefield, 2000)

ISSUE SUMMARY

YES: Nathan Hatch argues that by eroding traditional appeals to authority and expanding the number of people who believed they were competent to think for themselves about freedom, equality, and representation, the American Revolution led to an expansion of evangelical Christianity that reinforced the democratic impulses of the new society.

NO: Jon Butler insists that men and women seldom referred to America as a "Christian nation" between 1760 and 1790 and that even though Christianity was important, most Americans opposed a Christian national identity enforced by law or governmental action.

Although generations of American schoolchildren have been taught that the British colonies in North America were founded by persons fleeing religious persecution in England, the truth is that many of those early settlers were motivated by other factors, some of which had little to do with theological preferences. To be sure, the Pilgrims and Puritans of New England sought to escape the proscriptions established by the Church of England. Many New Englanders, however, did not adhere to the precepts of Calvinism and, therefore, were viewed as outsiders. The Quakers who populated Pennsylvania were mostly fugitives from New England, where they had been victims of religious persecution. But to apply religious motivations to the earliest settlers of Virginia, South Carolina, or Georgia is to engage in a serious misreading of the historical record. Even in New England the religious mission of (the first governor of Massachusetts Bay Colony) John Winthrop's "city upon a hill" began to erode as the colonial settlements matured and stabilized.

Although religion was a central element in the lives of the seventeenth- and eighteenth-century Europeans who migrated to the New World, proliferation of religious sects and denominations, emphasis upon material gain in all parts of the colonies, and the predominance of reason over emotion that is associated with the Deists of the Enlightenment period all contributed to a gradual but obvious movement of the colonists away from the church and clerical authority. William Bradford (the second governor of Plymouth Colony), for example, expressed grave concern that many Plymouth residents were following a path of perfidy, and William Penn (founder of Pennsylvania) was certain that the "holy experiment" of the Quakers had failed. Colonial clergy, fearful that a fall from grace was in progress, issued calls for a revival of religious fervor. The spirit of revivalism that spread through the colonies in the 1730s and 1740s, therefore, was an answer to these clerical prayers.

The episode known as the First Great Awakening coincided with the Pietistic movement in Europe and England and was carried forward by dynamic preachers such as Gilbert Tennant, Theodore Frelinghuysen, and George Whitefield. They promoted a religion of the heart, not of the head, in order to produce a spiritual rebirth. These revivals, most historians agree, reinvigorated American Protestantism. Many new congregations were organized as a result of irremediable schisms between "Old Lights" and "New Lights." Skepticism about the desirability of an educated clergy sparked a strong strain of anti-intellectualism. Also, the emphasis on conversion was a message to which virtually everyone could respond, regardless of age, sex, or social status. For some historians, the implications of the Great Awakening extended beyond the religious sphere into the realm of politics and were incorporated into the American Revolution. To what extent was the cause of religion, especially Protestant Christianity, advanced by the revolutionary era? Did the United States become a Christian nation in the wake of the Revolution?

In the following selections, Nathan O. Hatch points out that the most dynamic popular movements in the new republic were religious in nature. The American Revolution, he argues, broke down traditional appeals to authority, and the democratization of American society went hand-in-hand with the expansion of Protestant Christianity. Ordinary people, not elites, took the lead in applying the new political ideals of freedom and equality to evangelical Christian commitments to popular sovereignty.

Jon Butler recognizes that throughout the eighteenth century the British North American colonies established governmentally supported religion, but he sees this as a product of the colonists' weak adherence to Christianity in that only about 20 percent of the colonists were church members. After the Revolution, Butler says that most states reduced or withdrew their involvement with religion. This process culminated with the ratification of the First Amendment prohibiting government activity in religion generally.

Nathan O. Hatch

The Democratization of Christianity and the Character of American Politics

This essay will argue that at the very inception of the American republic the most dynamic popular movements were expressly religious. However powerful working-class organizations became in cities such as New York and Baltimore, their presence cannot compare with the phenomenal growth, and collective elán, of Methodists, Baptists, Christians, Millerites, and Mormons. It was lay preachers in the early republic who became the most effective agents in constructing new frames of reference for people living through a profoundly transitional age. Religious leaders from the rank and file were phenomenally successful in reaching out to marginal people, in promoting self-education and sheltering participants from the indoctrination of elite orthodoxies, in binding people together in supportive community, and in identifying the aspirations of common people with the will of God.

The vitality of these religious ideologies and mass movements has had a considerable long-term effect upon the character and limits of American politics. Churches, after all, came to serve as competing universes of discourse and action. And the political implications of mass movements that were democratic and religious at the same time are far more profound than merely predisposing members to vote Federalist or Republican, Democrat or Whig. As mass popular movements, churches came to be places in which fundamental political assumptions were forged: ideas about the meaning of America, the priority of the individual conscience, the values of localism, direct democracy, and individualism, and the necessity of dynamic communication, predicated on the identification of speaker or author with an audience.

This paper will suggest that to understand the democratization of American society, one must look at what happened to Protestant Christianity in the years 1780–1830. In an age when people expected almost everything from religion (and churches) and almost nothing from politics (and the state), the popular churches are essential to comprehending the enduring shape of American democracy. . . .

The American Revolution is the single most crucial event in American history. The generation overshadowed by it and its counterpart in France stands at the fault line that separates an older world, premised on standards of deference, patronage, and ordered succession, from a newer one to which we are attuned since it continues to shape our values. The American Revolution and the beliefs flowing from it created a cultural ferment over the meaning of freedom, a debate that brought to the fore crucial issues of authority, organization, and leadership.

Above all, the Revolution dramatically expanded the circle of people who considered themselves capable of thinking for themselves about issues of freedom, equality, sovereignty, and representation; and it eroded traditional appeals to the authority of tradition, station, and education. Ordinary people moved towards these new horizons as they gained access to a powerful new vocabulary, a rhetoric of liberty that would not have occurred to people were it not for the Revolution. In time, the well-being of ordinary people edged closer to the center of what it means to be American, public opinion came to assume normative significance, and leaders could not survive who would not, to use Patrick Henry's phrase, "bow with utmost deference to the majesty of the people." The correct solution to any important problem, political, legal, or religious, would have to appear as the people's choice.

The profoundly transitional age between 1776 and 1830 left the same kind of indelible imprint upon the structures of American Christianity as it did upon those of American political life. Only land, Robert Wiebe has noted, could compete with Christianity as the pulse of a new democratic society. The age of the democratic revolutions unfolded with awesome moment for people in every social rank. Amidst such acute uncertainty, many humble Christians in America began to redeem a dual legacy. They yoked together strenuous demands for revivals, in the name of Whitefield, and calls for the expansion of popular sovereignty, in the name of the Revolution. It is the linking of these equally potent traditions that sent American Christianity cascading in so many creative directions in the early republic. Church authorities had few resources to restrain these movements fed by the passions of ordinary people. American Methodism, for example, under the tutelage of Francis Asbury, veered sharply from the course of British Methodism from the time of Wesley's death until the end of the Napoleonic Wars. The heavy, centralizing hand of Jabez Bunting kept England's potent evangelical tradition firmly grounded in traditional notions of authority and leadership. After 1800, the leaders of British Methodism were able to bar the eccentric American revivalist Lorenzo Dow from contaminating their meetings. In America, however, Dow took the camp meeting circuit by storm despite periodic censure from bishops and presiding elders. Given his effectiveness and popular support, they were unable to mount a direct challenge to his authority.

A diverse array of evangelical firebrands went about the task of movement-building in the generation after the Revolution. While they were intent on bringing evangelical conversion to the mass of ordinary Americans, rarely could they divorce that message from contagious new vocabularies and impulses that swept through American popular cultures in an era of democratic revolution: an appeal to class as the fundamental problem of society, a refusal to recognize the cultural authority of elites, a disdain for the supposed lessons of history and tradition, a call for reform using the rhetoric of the Revolution, a commitment to turn the press into a sword of democracy, and an ardent faith in the future of the American republic.

At the same time, Americans who espoused evangelical and egalitarian convictions, in whatever combination, were left free to experiment with abandon, unopposed by civil or religious authority. Within a few years of Jefferson's election in 1800, it became anachronistic to speak of dissent in America—as if there were still a commonly recognized center against which new or emerging groups had to define themselves. There was little to restrain a variety of new groups from vying to establish their identity as a counterestablishment. The fundamental history of this period, in fact, may be a story of things left out, as Roland Berthoff has recently suggested. Churches and religious movements after 1800 operated in a climate in which ecclesiastical establishments had withered, in which the federal government had almost no internal functions—a "midget institution in a giant land"—and in which a rampant migration of people continued to snap old networks of personal authority. American churches did not face the kind of external social and political pressures which in Great Britain often forced Christianity and liberty to march in opposite directions. Such isolation made it possible for religious "outsiders" to see their own destiny as part and parcel of the meaning of America itself. If the earth did belong to the living, as President Jefferson claimed, why should the successful newcomer defer to the claims of education, status, and longevity.

The reality of a nonrestrictive environment permitted an unexpected and often explosive conjunction of evangelical fervor and popular sovereignty. It was this engine that greatly accelerated the process of Christianization with America popular culture, allowing indigenous expressions of faith to take hold among ordinary people, both white and black. This expansion of evangelical Christianity did not proceed primarily from the nimble response of religious elites meeting the challenge before them. Rather, Christianity was effectively reshaped by ordinary people who molded it in their own image and threw themselves into expanding its influence. Increasingly assertive common people wanted their leaders unpretentious, their doctrines self-evident and down-to-earth, their music lively and singable, their churches in local hands. It was this upsurge of democratic hope that characterized so many religious cultures in the early republic and brought Baptists, Methodists, Disciples, and a host of other insurgent groups to the fore. The rise of evangelical Christianity in the early republic is, in some measure, a story of the success of common people in shaping the culture after their own priorities rather than the priorities outlined by gentlemen, such as the Founding Fathers. A style of religious leadership that the public had deemed "untutored" and "irregular" as late as the First Great Awakening became overwhelmingly successful, even normative, in the first decades of the new nation.

It is easy to miss the profoundly democratic character of the early republic's insurgent religious movements. The Methodists, after all, retained power in a structured hierarchy under the control of bishops; the Mormons reverted to rule by a single religious prophet and revelator; and groups such as the Disciples of Christ, despite professed democratic structures, came to be controlled by powerful individuals such as Alexander Campbell, who had little patience with dissent. As ecclesiastical structures, these movements often turned out to be less democratic than the congregational structure of the New England Standing Order.

The democratization of Christianity, then, has less to do with the specifics of polity and governance and more with the very incarnation of the church into popular culture. In at least three respects the popular religious movements of the early republic articulated a profoundly democratic spirit. First, they denied the age-old distinction that set the clergy apart as a separate order of men and they refused to defer to learned theologians and received orthodoxies. All were democratic or populist in the way their instinctively associated virtue with ordinary people rather than with elites, exalted the vernacular in word and song as the hallowed channel for communicating with and about God, and freely turned over the reigns of power. These groups also shared with the Jeffersonian Republicans an overt rejection of the past as a repository of wisdom. By redefining leadership itself, these movements were instrumental in shattering the centuries-old affinity between Christianity and the norms of high culture. They reconstructed the foundations of religion fully in keeping with the values and priorities of ordinary people.

Second, these movements empowered ordinary people by taking their deepest spiritual impulses at face value rather than subjecting them to the scrutiny of orthodox doctrine and the frowns of respectable clergymen. In the last two decades of the century, preachers from a wide range of new religious movements openly fanned the flames of religious ecstasy. Rejecting in 1775 the Yankee Calvinism of his youth, Henry Alline found that his soul was transported with divine love, "ravished with a divine ecstasy beyond any doubts or fears, or thoughts of being then deceived." What had been defined as "enthusiasm" increasingly became advocated from the pulpit as an essential part of Christianity. Such a shift in emphasis, accompanied by rousing gospel singing rather than formal church music, reflected the success of common people in defining for themselves the nature of faith. In addition, an unprecedented wave of religious leaders in the last quarter of the century expressed their own openness to a variety of signs and wonders—in short, an admission of increased supernatural involvement in everyday life. Scores of preachers' journals, from Methodists and Baptists, from North and South, from white and black, indicated a ready acceptance to interpret dreams and visions as inspired by God, normal manifestations of divine guidance and instruction. "I know the word of God is our infallible guide, and by it we are to try all our dreams and feelings," conceded the Methodist stalwart Freeborn Garrettson. But, he added, "I also know, that both sleeping and waking, things of a divine nature have been revealed to me." Those volatile aspects of popular religion, long held in check by the church, came to be recognized and encouraged from the pulpit. It is no wonder that a dismayed writer in the *Connecticut Evangelical Magazine* countered in 1805: "No person is warranted from the word of God to publish to the world the discoveries of heaven or hell which he supposes he has had in a dream, or trance, or vision."

The early republic was also a democratic moment in a third sense. Religious outsiders were flushed with confidence about their prospects and had little sense of their own limitations. They dreamed that a new age of religious and social harmony would spring up naturally out of their own efforts to overthrow coercive and authoritarian structures. This upsurge of democratic hope, this passion for equality, led to a welter of diverse and competing forms, many of them structured in highly undemocratic ways. The Methodists under Francis Asbury, for instance, used authoritarian means to build a church that would not be a respecter of persons. This church faced the curious paradox of gaining phenomenal influence among laypersons with whom it would not share ecclesiastical authority. Similarly, the Mormons used a virtual religious dictatorship as the means to return power to illiterate men. Yet, despite these authoritarian structures, the fundamental impetus of these movements was to make Christianity a liberating force, giving people the right to think and act for themselves rather than being forced to rely upon the mediations of an educated elite. The most fascinating religious story of the early republic is the signal achievements of these and other populist religious leaders, outsiders who brought to bear the full force of democratic persuasions upon American culture.

The wave of popular religious movements that broke upon the United States in the half-century after independence did more to Christianize American society than anything before or since. Nothing makes that point clearer than the growth of Methodists and Baptists as mass movements among white and black Americans. Starting from scratch just prior to the Revolution, the Methodists in America grew at a rate that terrified other denominations, reaching a quarter of a million members by 1820 and doubling again by 1830. Baptist membership multiplied tenfold in the three decades after the Revolution, the number of churches increasing from 500 to over 2500. The black church in America was born amidst the crusading vigor of these movements and quickly assumed its own distinct character and broad appeal among people of color. By the middle of the ninteenth century, Methodist and Baptist churches had splintered into more different denominational forms than one cares to remember. Yet together these movements came to constitute nearly 70 percent of Protestant church members in the United States and two-thirds of its ministers.

This essay grows out of research on five distinct traditions or mass movements that came to the fore early in the nineteenth century: the Christian movement, the Methodists, the Baptists, the black churches, and the Mormons. Each was led by young men of relentless energy who went about movement-building as self-conscious outsiders. They shared an ethic of unrelenting labor, a passion for expansion, a hostility to orthodox belief and style, a zeal for religious reconstruction, and a systematic plan to labor on behalf of their ideals. However diverse their theologies and church organizations, they were able to offer common people, especially the poor, compelling visions of individual self-respect and collective self-confidence. . . .

In passing, it is instructive to suggest at least four reasons that historians have failed to explore the dynamics of popular religion in this era. First, during the last three decades the quickened interest in religion as a cultural force emerged within a broader historiographical tendency to downplay the social impact of the Revolution. Second, historians have interpreted the Second Great

Awakening as an attempt by traditional religious elites to impose social order upon a disordered and secularized society—revivalism as an attempt to salvage Protestant solidarity. A third reason is that church historians from the more popular denominations have had reasons to sanitize their own histories. Modern church historians have chosen to focus on those dimensions of their own heritage that point to cultural enrichment, institutional cohesion, and intellectual respectability. William Warren Sweet, for instance, was committed to a vision of Methodists and Baptists as bearers of civilization to the uncouth and unretrained society of the frontier. Churches were instruments of order, education, and moral discipline.

A fourth reason that popular religious movements remain unexplored is surprising given the deep commitment by a new generation of social historians to understand the lives of common people in the age of capitalist transformation. While considerable attention has been focused on the changing nature of markets, on the decline of independent artisans and farmers and the rise of the American working class, surprisingly little energy has gone into exploring the dynamics of insurgent religious movements. This neglect stems both from the neo-Marxist preoccupation with the formation of social classes and the assumption that religion is generally a conservative force and a pernicious one. What these studies fail to take into account is that, for better or worse, the most dynamic popular movements in the early republic were expressly religious. . . .

An additional benefit of piecing together the story of these democratic religious movements is new insight into crucial questions about how America became a liberal society, individualistic, competitive, and market driven. In an age when most ordinary Americans expected almost nothing from government institutions and almost everything from religious ones, popular religious ideologies were perhaps the most important bellwethers of shifting worldviews. The passion for equality that came to the fore in these years decisively rejected the past as a repository of wisdom. Far from looking backward and clinging to an older moral economy, insurgent religious leaders espoused convictions that were essentially modern and individualistic. These persuasions defied elite privilege and vested interests, and anticipated the dawn of a millennial age of equality and justice. Yet, to achieve these visions of the common good, they espoused means inseparable from the individual pursuit of one's own spiritual and temporal well-being. They assumed that the leveling of aristocracy, root and branch, in all areas of human endeavor would naturally draw people together in harmony and equality. In this way, religious movements fervent about preserving the supernatural in everyday life had the ironic effect of accelerating the breakup of traditional society and the advent of a social order given over to competition, self-expression, and free enterprise. In this moment of fervent democratic aspiration, insurgent religious leaders had no way to foresee that their own assault upon mediating structures could lead to a society in which grasping entrepreneurs could erect new forms of tyranny in religious, political, or economic institutions. The individualization of conscience, which they so greatly prized, moved them to see the very hand of providence in a social order of free and independent persons with interests to promote. Nothing better shows this process than the tumultuous career of John Leland, a career illustrating dramatically the ties in the early republic between popular religion, democratic politics, and liberal individualism.

In 1814 Leland was one of the most popular and controversial Baptists in America. He was most famous as a protagonist of religious freedom. As a leader among Virginia Baptists in the 1780s, Leland had been influential in petitioning the legislature on behalf of Jefferson's bill for religious freedom and for the bill to end the incorporation of the Protestant Episcopal Church. There is strong evidence that James Madison personally sought his support for the federal constitution, which Leland had first opposed. At the same time, Leland also marshalled Baptist opposition to slavery in Virginia. After returning to New England in 1791, he became the outstanding proponent of religious freedom as preacher, lecturer, and publicist and served two terms in the Massachusetts legislature representing the town of Cheshire.

On a national level Leland was best known for the 1,235-pound "Mammoth Cheese" he had presented to President Thomas Jefferson. In New York and Baltimore crowds flocked to see this phenomenal creation, molded in a cider press supposedly from the milk of 900 cows and bearing the motto "Rebellion to tyrants is obedience to God." Leland made the presentation to Mr. Jefferson at the White House on New Year's Day 1802 as a token of esteem from the staunchly republican citizens of Cheshire. Two days later, at the president's invitation, he preached before both houses of Congress on the text "And behold a greater than Solomon is here." One congressman who heard that sermon, Manasseh Cutler, a Massachusetts Federalist and Congregationalist clergyman, had few kind words to say about Leland's politics or his religion, dismissing "the cheesemonger" as a "poor ignorant, illiterate, clownish creature." "Such a farrago, bawled with stunning voice, horrid tone, frightful grimaces, and extravagant gestures, I believe, was never heard by any decent auditory before. . . . Such an outrage upon religion, the Sabbath, and common decency, was extremely painful to every sober, thinking person present."

Leland's political notoriety has often masked the fact that fundamentally he was a preacher and itinerant evangelist. In 1824 he confessed that he had preached 8,000 times, had baptized over 1,300 persons, had known almost 1,000 Baptist preachers, and had traveled an equivalent of three times round the world. Given Leland's stature and connections, it is not at all surprising that he attended the Baptists' first Triennial Convention in Philadelphia and preached at William Staughton's church the night before the first session. That sermon sounded a sharp alarm for Baptists who were hungry for respectability. Even before any decision had been made about forming a missions organization, Leland warned against the danger of "Israel" insisting on having a king so that they could be like other nations: "like the people now-a-days; they form societies, and they must have a president and two or three vice-presidents, to be like their neighbors around them." After Baptists joined the Protestant quest for voluntary association, Leland stepped up his attacks upon missionary agencies and the clerical elites that stood behind them. For the next decade and a half, he went on the offensive against the organizational schemes and clerical professionalism at the core of American Protestant denominations. Leland ridiculed the mercenary foundation of foreign and domestic missions, the oppression of "a hierarchical clergy—despotic judiciary—[and] an aristocratic host of lawyers," the mechanical operations of theological seminaries, the tyranny of formal structures, and the burden of creedalism—"this Virgin Mary between the souls of men and the Scriptures." In a letter to John Taylor, the stalwart foe of mission activity in Kentucky, Leland confessed in 1830 that his calling had been "to watch and check *clerical hierarchy,* which assumes as many shades as a chameleon."

John Leland had every reason to take up the path of order and decorum that appealed to other Baptist leaders. Yet he seemed to come out of Revolutionary times with a different set of impulses stirring within. Rather than looking for ways to instill energy in government and to promote vigorous central policies, Leland sought at every step to restrain the accumulation of power. "I would as soon give my vote to a wolf to be a shepherd," he said in an oration celebrating American independence in 1802, "as to a man, who is always contending for the energy of government, to be a ruler." John Leland's dissent flowed out of a passion for religious liberty that exalted the individual conscience over creedal systems, local control over powerful ecclesiastical structures, and popular sensibility over the instincts of the educated and powerful. As prolific publicist, popular hymnwriter, amusing and satirical preacher, Leland strongly advocated freedom in every sphere of life. Self-reliant to an eccentric degree, Leland is fascinating and important in his own right. He also stands as an important bridge between the Revolutionary era and the quest for localism and independence that confounded Baptist history through the Jacksonian period. The importance of this story, played out on the fringes of denominational life, is not fully appreciated given its lack of coherence and the orientation of early denominational historians to celebrate the opposite, the growth of respectability and organizational coherence.

Brought up as a fervent New Light, John Leland found resources to accept, even defend, his own "rusticity of manners." Chief among these was a Jeffersonian view of conscience that championed intellectual self-reliance. In a pamphlet published in 1792 attacking the New England Standing Order, Leland explained how he came to trust his own reasoning rather than the conclusions of great men. Having once had "profound reverence" for leading civic figures, Leland discovered that in reality "not two of them agreed."...

Leland hammered out his view of conscience as he battled the state-church tradition of Virginia during the 1780s and of New England thereafter. In over thirty pamphlets and regular contributions to Phinehas Allen's staunchly Jeffersonian *Pittsfield Sun,* Leland spelled out a vision of personal autonomy that colored his personal life, his theological views, and his conception of society.

As early as 1790 Leland began to sound his clarion call that conscience should be "free from human control." His passion was to protect the "empire of conscience," the court of judgment in every human soul, from the inevitable encroachments of state-church traditions, oppressive creeds, ambitious and greedy clergymen—even from family tradition. "For a man to contend for religious liberty on the court-house green, and deny his wife, children and servants, the liberty of conscience at home, is a paradox not easily reconciled. . . . each one must give an account of himself to God." Upon returning to New England in 1791, Leland assailed the Standing Order in a pamphlet entitled *The Rights of Conscience Inalienable . . . or, The High-flying Churchman, Stripped of his Legal Robe, Appears a Yaho* (New London, 1791). With language borrowed directly from Jefferson's *Notes on the State of Virginia,* he argued that truth can stand on its own without the props of legal or creedal defense. He reiterated the theme that "religion is a matter between God and individuals." In addition to repeating his warning to parents that it was "iniquitous to bind the consciences" of children, Leland clarified his explicitly democratic view of conscience: that the so-called wise and learned were actually less capable of mediating truth than were common people. Leland dismissed the common objection that "the ignorant part of the community are not capacited to judge for themselves":

> Did many of the rulers believe in Christ when he was upon earth? Were not the learned clergy (the scribes) his most inveterate enemies? Do not great men differ as much as little men in judgment? Have not almost all lawless errors crept into the world through the means of wise men (so called)? Is not a simple man, who makes nature and reason his study, a competent judge of things? Is the Bible written (like Caligula's laws) so intricate and high, that none but the letter learned (according to the common phrase) can read it? Is not the vision written so plain that he that runs may read it?

In an 1801 sermon, *A Blow at the Root,* published in five editions in four different states from Vermont to Georgia, Leland continued to project an image of the autonomous person besieged by the coercive forces of state, creed, tradition, and clerical hierarchy. The political triumph of Jefferson, the *"Man of the People,"* convinced Leland that the "genius of America," which had been slumbering, had finally "arisen, like a lion, from the swelling of Jordon, and roared like thunder in the states, 'we will be free; we will rule ourselves; our officers shall be honorable servants, but not mean masters.'"

Leland's legacy is an exaggerated opposition to official Christianity. He articulated a twofold persuasion that operated powerfully in the hinterland of Baptist church life: an aversion to central control and a quest for self-reliance. One reason that it is so difficult to write Baptist history in the early republic is that centrifugal forces were so powerfully at work, giving free reign to regional distinctives and take-charge entrepreneurs. Whatever success cosmopolitan leaders like Richard Furman or Francis Wayland had in building central institutions, their way was dogged at very step: by serious defections to the antiformalist appeals of Alexander Campbell and, later, William Miller, by the rise of significant Antimission Baptist associations in regions as diverse as New York, Pennsylvania, Illinois, Kentucky, and North Carolina; and by the appearance of charismatic dissenters such as J. R. Graves and his Landmark Baptists. Equally important was the entrenched opposition to central authority among those who remained within the regular Baptist fold. The Triennial Convention, after all, had never represented Baptist churches themselves, but only individuals and societies willing to pay appropriate dues to the organization. After 1826 it was virtually dismembered when its champions from different regions locked horns over issues of authority and control.

John Leland is also important because of the way he turned a quest for self-reliance into a godly crusade. Like Elias Smith, James O'Kelly, Lorenzo Dow, Barton Stone, and William Miller, he fervently believed that individuals had to make a studied effort to prune away natural authorities: church, state, college, seminary, even family. Leland's message carried the combined ideological leverage of evangelical urgency and Jeffersonian promise. Choosing simple language and avoiding doctrinal refinements, he proclaimed a divine economy that was atomistic and competitive rather than wholistic and hierarchical. The triumph of liberal individualism, in this form at least, was not something imposed upon the people of America from above. They gladly championed the promise of personal autonomy as a message they could understand and a cause to which they could subscribe—in God's name no less.

Jon Butler

NO

Why Revolutionary America Wasn't a "Christian Nation"

Was America a "Christian nation" on the eve of the Revolution? Colonial law certainly would have made it appear so throughout most of the eighteenth century. Indeed, one of the great transformations of the eighteenth century centered on the renewal, not the decline, of the state church tradition in colonial America. Between 1690 and 1710 the colonial legislatures in South Carolina, North Carolina, Maryland, and New York effectively established the Church of England as the governmentally supported religion in their colonies, and the Virginia Burgesses thoroughly reworked the feeble Anglican establishment of the early seventeenth century. To the north, the old Puritan order in Massachusetts and Connecticut not only survived what contemporaries and historians have, rightly or wrongly, long described as "declension" or, put differently, the creation of a new, more diverse, more commercial, and more secular society. The state church apparatus found itself strengthened, not weakened. It became more elastic, and unlike the Anglican establishments to the south, it survived into the nineteenth century. In all, then, seven of the thirteen colonies gave legal support to a single expression of Protestant Christianity for 60 to 150 years before the Revolution.

Even where the law did not establish a single church, it usually upheld Protestant Christianity. Above all, the law punished. In colonies with church establishments, the law may have tolerated religious activity by dissenters, but it did not always do so, and it sometimes made that activity difficult. In colonies without establishments, the law customarily penalized a wide variety of settlers who may not have upheld Protestant Christianity in at least some perfunctory fashion. It openly discriminated against Catholics and Jews, denying them the right to own property or to vote, sometimes both, in different colonies. The law penalized blasphemers who spoke ill of Protestant Christianity. Long after the Salem witch trials of 1692 the law outlawed magic and witchcraft. Perhaps the situation in Pennsylvania, usually regarded as the most tolerant of all the colonies, expressed the legal situation well. Throughout the pre-Revolutionary period, Pennsylvania forced officeholders to swear to their belief in the divinity of Jesus, banned blasphemy, forbade Sunday labor, and urged all settlers to attend Christian services on the Sabbath so "looseness, irreligion, and Atheism may not creep in under the pretense of conscience."

From *Religion and the New Republic: Faith in the Founding of America*, James Hutson, ed. (Rowman and Littlefield, 2000).

The eighteenth century also witnessed an explosion of congregational expansion that substantially increased church participation and membership in ways that might give life to the laws' strictures. Fully 85 percent of the colonial congregations that existed at the beginning of the American Revolution had been formed after 1700 and no less than 60 percent of these congregations had been formed after 1740. This expansion occurred in two waves, the first between 1680 and 1710, and the second between 1740 and 1770. The expansion came primarily from two causes. The first was revivalism, meaning the growth of evangelical, born-again Christianity in its rudimentary modern sense. The second was denominational expansion, meaning the systematic provision of leadership and ministry by ever more religious organizations, often headquartered in Philadelphia (not Boston), including Quakers, Presbyterians, Baptists, German Lutheran, and German Reformed, among others.

Thus, where we think of the early seventeenth century, and especially early New England, as the preeminent period of religious activity in colonial America, the eighteenth century dwarfed that activity and expansion many times over. It contributed crucial new forms of ministry, especially revivalism, and it bolstered new models of denominational leadership central to American religion in the next two centuries.

Were we to stop here, perhaps the answer to our question "Was late eighteenth-century America a Christian nation" might be yes. But as lawyers and mathematicians know, if the law and statistics are not funny things, they are at least arguable. This is particularly true when the facts turn out to be more complicated than they seem, not merely in the courtroom but in life, and when these complications occurred long before the relationship between religion and government changed after American independence.

One complication centered on the people. Put simply, whatever the law required or demanded, and however much congregational expansion skyrocketed in the eighteenth century, the people by no means either responded or followed. Though historians do indeed argue about these things, it is all but impossible to calculate church membership at more than 20 percent of colonial adults before the American Revolution, a figure that would only decline further when the enslaved population is added, given the overwhelming failure of Christian proselytizing among the half-million Africans forcibly transported to the mainland colonies after 1680. In short, surprising as it may seem, church membership was far lower on the eve of independence—about 80 percent of adults did not belong—than it is at the end of the twentieth century, when it runs about 60 percent of adults.

Nor does computing attendance improve the situation. In fact, very few congregations recorded attendance, and when clergymen bragged about it, as Anglican ministers did in reports to the Bishop of London in 1724, their facts often seemed contradictory, to put it generously. Something seems suspicious when, for example, the minister in Virginia's Henrico Parish reported "sometimes 100 or 200 attend" but "20 is the greatest number that do [take communion] at one time," or when the minister of St. Paul's church in Narragansett, Rhode Island, reported congregations of 150 to 270 on Sundays but only 17 communicants. If these figures are accurate, these allegedly numerous listeners evinced a spiritual shyness that could have made even Puritans blush.

In this light, we might rethink the eighteenth-century colonial congregational expansion. Rather than seal the identity of the colonies as "Christian," congregational growth mainly helped to keep Christianity's head above the waters of the public indifference to Christian practice and belief that concerned Crèvecoeur and Woodmason. This in itself was no mean accomplishment, and it bore immense significance for Christianity's fate during and after the Revolution and for Christianity's expansion in the early national and antebellum periods, when techniques devised in the pre-Revolutionary era made powerful contributions to religious and social reform before the Civil War.

Ironically, perhaps, both the revivalism and proliferation of institutional formation and leadership that escalated congregational growth in the four score years before the Revolution cast the "Christian nation" question into doubt. Perhaps an oxymoron will help. We might say that, on the surface, the pre-Revolutionary "colonial nation" was nominally or even formally Christian. The law demanded adherence to a rudimentary Christianity and seven colonies established state churches. But these laws made sense precisely because actual Christian adherence in the population was relatively weak—perhaps no more so than it was in contemporary Europe, including Britain—not because attachment to Christianity was strong and overwhelming. In short, the law existed to compel Christian attachment. The law did not measure the Christian commitment of the people.

The proliferation of congregations, combined with Enlightenment doubts about coercion in religion generally, threw into doubt even the old minimal or formal pattern of Christian church establishment. In the aftermath of the Revolution, this led most states to withdraw from or greatly reduce government involvement with religion and culminated in the First Amendment to the Federal Constitution.

The remarkable proliferation of congregations between 1680 and 1770 led settlers in many places to ask the question that Charles Woodmason heard in the Carolina backcountry in the 1760s: "Whose Christianity?" The post-1680 congregational growth was not monochromatic. Instead, it introduced a religious pluralism unprecedented in Western society. Numbers alone tell part of the story. About 75 percent of all seventeenth-century churches were Congregational (in New England) or Anglican (Church of England and largely in Virginia). By the Revolution, however, Congregational and Anglican churches formed only about 35 percent of all colonial congregations. Now, 65 percent of the congregations were Presbyterian, Baptist, Quaker, German Reformed, Lutheran, Dutch Reformed, Methodist, Catholic, Moravian, Separatist-Congregational, German Baptist, Mennonite, French Protestant, Sandemanian, Jewish, and Rogerene, many of which had only been thinly visible or could not even be found in the colonies as late as 1700.

This vigorous pluralism never produced the religious antagonism and violence that characterized nineteenth- and twentieth-century America, to say nothing of the world in the 1990s. But it produced substantial tensions and arguments that unsettled familiar patterns of government aid to Christianity.

In New England, the arguments prospered during a revivalism of the 1740s and 1750s among both Congregationalists and Baptists that produced so-called "separatist" congregations of "born-again" or "revived" believers. Many arguments centered on theology, and some were inevitably personal. But many others focused on the spoils of government support for local religion or involved new government activity in religion. When a congregation split between "Old Lights" and "New Lights," who retained monies levied for Christianity's support in the town?

The arguments among the disputing Congregationalists joined those of Baptists, who generally objected to paying levies for religion at all. In turn, traditional Congregationalists turned up coercive legislation surrounding religion. In 1742, for example, the Connecticut assembly passed an "Act for Regulating Abuses and Correcting Disorders in Ecclesiastical Affairs," clearly directed against Congregational and Baptist revivalists. The act effectively banned unapproved itinerant preaching, ordered ministerial associations not to "meddle" in affairs outside their own jurisdiction, and allowed magistrates to eject nonresidents from the colony if they preached without the permission of the local clergymen and a majority of his congregation.

In Virginia, Anglicans, Presbyterians, and Baptists quickly fell out into disputes about the liberty of dissenters to preach and thereby contest the Anglicans' domination of Virginia's public religious life. As Thomas Jefferson rightly remembered the situation, the Anglican attack on Presbyterians and Baptists in the 1750s and 1760s had been preceded by efforts to curtail Quakers in the seventeenth century, "driving them from the colony by the severest penalties." (In fact, Virginia also chased Puritans from Nansemond County to Maryland in 1647–1648, which Jefferson did not know about.) In the late 1740s Virginia officials sought to inhibit the Presbyterian leader, Samuel Davies, by denying him a license to preach beyond his congregation. The Board of Trade in London, not American politicians, settled the matter, reminding Virginia's government in 1751 that "Toleration and a Free Exercise of Religion . . . should ever be held sacred in His Majesties Colonies."

Baptists received even rougher treatment because their preaching combined social, legal, and theological challenges to the Anglicans' status in Virginia. John Williams described the physical attack on "Brother Waller," a Caroline County Baptist preacher, in 1771, only five years before the Revolution. Coercion here was not mild or merely irritating but physical and violent.

> The Parson of the Parish would keep running the end of his horsewhip in [Waller's] mouth, laying his whip across the hymn book, etc. When done singing, [Waller] proceeded to prayer. In it he was violently jerked off the stage; [the parson and sheriff] caught him by the back part of his neck, beat his head against the ground, sometimes up, sometimes down, they carried him through a gate that stood some considerable distance, where a gentleman gave him . . . twenty lashes with his horsewhip.

Certainly, Anglicans had much to defend, from their social status to the political power held by their members, to their control of local and provincial government, to their power to tax, and to their church buildings, which represented the finest widespread domestic public architecture in the colony and, perhaps, in the colonies generally.

Even in places where there was no establishment, as in Pennsylvania, or where the establishment was weak, as in New York, eighteenth-century pluralism and revivalism brought difficulty rather than repose. Presbyterians who had fought Anglicans in Virginia had been well trained by their own internal disputing in the middle colonies. The arguments over revivalism produced innumerable personal confrontations in the 1740s and a fifteen-year schism in the Synod of Philadelphia from 1743 to 1758. George Whitefield caused dissension up and down the colonies as he drew listeners from clergymen jealous of his charismatic preaching. The combination of pluralism, lack of coercion, and lethargic ministerial leadership induced nominally German Lutheran and Reformed immigrants to Pennsylvania into utter spiritual indifference, the kind about which Crèvecoeur complained. Taken together, then, the specter of religious turmoil caused by pluralism, revivalism, and the bitterness engendered by government partiality in religion left the question of a colonial "Christian nation" increasingly open as the Revolution began.

A question not left open was that of church establishment. The experience of colonial religious diversity, the failures of the old religious establishments, the association of the Church of England with king and parliament, and the principles of the Declaration of Independence all encouraged many Americans to rethink the relationship between government and religion as the Revolution proceeded. The old Church of England lost most in this reevaluation. Between 1776 and 1785 the legal establishments that the Church of England had won eighty years earlier collapsed everywhere from New York to South Carolina. As this occurred, even Connecticut relieved "separates," including Episcopalians, Baptists, Quakers, "or any other Denomination," from church taxes. Only Massachusetts held out firmly, continuing to collect taxes for the local ministry. Although the new state distributed the church funds by local vote, this was majoritarianism, not democracy; it effectively funneled aid only to traditional Congregational churches except in a few towns.

The most important contest over religious identity and government occurred in Virginia. It merged growing colonial doubt about the wisdom of government involvement in religion with the narrower question of a single church establishment. The result proved dramatic. The Virginia debate stimulated a remarkable movement away from any substantial government aid for religious activity and directly shaped the religion clause in the First Amendment.

The Virginia debate, which occurred between 1779 and 1785, centered on two issue—general support for religion by aiding numerous Christian denominations and complete disestablishment. Proponents of aid to many denominations, including some Presbyterians and Patrick Henry, backed freedom of worship for all religious groups but advocated government support and tax funds for several if not all Protestant groups. In contrast, Thomas Jefferson, later supported by James Madison, offered a bill "for Establishing Religious Freedom." It prohibited tax levies for "any religious worship, place, or ministry whatsoever" and also upheld freedom of worship for all religious groups. Both sides struggled over these issues from 1779 to 1785 without any resolution.

A crucial debate during elections for the Virginia Burgesses in 1785 completely altered public opinion on the religion question. George Washington's turnaround symbolized the process. At first, Washington supported multiple establishment; he thought it was a fine idea to give government aid to several Protestant groups. But as the debate proceeded and stimulated increasing rancor, Washington turned against the proposal. Multiple establishment, Washington commented, seemed innocuous and natural, but it clearly would "rankle, and perhaps convulse the state."

As a result, in 1786 the Virginia legislature turned down Patrick Henry's bill for multiple establishment. Overwhelming opposition to it came from Baptists, Methodists, Episcopalians, and some Presbyterians. The legislature then approved by a vote of 74 to 20 Thomas Jefferson's bill "for Establishing Religious Freedom." It outlawed government aid to religion and guaranteed freedom of worship to all religions in the state, not just Protestants or even merely to Christians.

The Virginia debate renewed discussions in other states, and then with regard to the new federal government, about the relationship between America's religious identity and its relationship to government. In the states, it produced a rush of sentiment against a single establishment and against government aid to denominations generally. South Carolina's 1778 constitution had authorized government aid to several Protestant groups. But its 1790 constitution abandoned multiple establishment and guaranteed a broad freedom of worship. Multiple establishment bills failed in Georgia in 1782 and 1784, and in 1789 a new Georgia constitution eliminated multiple religious establishment entirely. The post-Revolutionary Maryland constitution permitted multiple establishment. But the Maryland assembly rejected funding for several Protestant groups by a two-to-one margin in 1785, and in 1810 a constitutional amendment eliminated multiple establishment in Maryland.

In New Hampshire, government aid to local Protestant congregations slowly collapsed, and in 1819 the legislature repealed the statute permitting the collection of local church taxes. Only Connecticut and Massachusetts held out, Connecticut until 1818 and Massachusetts until 1833; tellingly, these establishments fell in large measure because citizens of both states tired of the incessant bickering about church taxes, especially as they watched tax-supported congregations split over the doctrine of Unitarianism and lawsuits over the tax revenues belonging to the now divided congregations increase.

The First Amendment to the Federal Constitution passed in 1791 reflected this dual trend of eschewing a single church establishment and of prohibiting governmental activity in religion generally. The First Amendment prohibited a federal "establishment of religion," not merely of churches. Many commentators routinely describe the First Amendment as being about "church and state," following Jefferson in his famous 1802 letter to the Danbury Baptist Association where he backed a "wall of separation between church and state" in America. But the First Amendment banned government activity in religion generally and did not mention the narrower issue of church.

In its breadth, the First Amendment confirmed the eighteenth-century colonial American experience that religion increasingly took many forms, and complex ones, in this extraordinarily compound society. In this multifarious society, government should refrain from activity in religion. Congress specifically rejected wording that would have limited the First Amendment to narrower issues, such as prohibiting government support for a specific "religious doctrine," for "articles of faith or modes of worship," to protect only the "rights of conscience," to prohibit aid to "one religious sect or society in preference to others," or to establish a national church. All this language was deemed too narrow.

The amplitude of the First Amendment and the debates surrounding its wording help answer our question about late eighteenth-century America as a "Christian nation." It is surprising—or perhaps it is not surprising at all—how seldom, if ever, men and women referred to America as a "Christian nation" between 1760 and 1790. Indeed, such a phrase would have puzzled or even alarmed advocates of church establishment, whether traditional single establishments or more general government aid to religion or multiple denominations. When Yale president Ezra Stiles supported the continuation of Connecticut's Congregational establishment in 1783, he did so precisely because he believed Connecticut—indeed, America—was not a Christian nation. Too much atheism, too much indifference, too much heterodoxy, and too much immorality made that phrase meaningless. Indeed, for Stiles, Connecticut's church establishment had a simple attraction: it coerced men and women to support Christianity in at least some rudimentary fashion when they would otherwise ignore it. Government tax revenues could guarantee the modicum of "religion" that might keep a sinful, spiritually indifferent society afloat.

The Virginia Baptist John Leland agreed with Stiles's diagnosis of America's spiritual malaise but disputed Stiles's prescription. Leland likewise ridiculed the notion that a "Christian commonwealth" could or did exist in either Virginia or even the nation. Virginia and the nation needed saving, not praising. But unlike Stiles, Leland denied the government's right to engage the religious enterprise, and he did so on religious grounds, indeed, on specifically Christian grounds. As other Virginia opponents of general aid to religion put it in 1785, Christ "not only maintained and supported his gospel in the world for several hundred years without the aid of civil power, but against all the powers of the earth." To Leland, if not to Stiles, the contrast between early Christian practice and modern governmental aid to religion was stark and negative. If Christ did not use or want government aid, why did modern Christians?

The debate about America's religious identity and about government involvement with religion changed after passage of the Bill of Rights and the First Amendment in 1791 and especially after the 1810s. America's attraction as a field for Christian proselytizing only increased as American power and vibrancy became more obvious. The lure of the new public schools as a vehicle for Christian, or at least Protestant, instruction proved irresistible. Protestants increasingly attached providence to American purposes, especially in foreign affairs. Few heeded Lincoln's caution when, after ministers assured him that God was on the North's side in the Civil War, he replied that he was more concerned that the North was on God's side. Fewer still observed even the least caution when the federal government began to mold American Indians into "Christian nations" in the 1870s and when, to aid the effort, the War Department assigned reservations to specific denominations—Presbyterian, Methodist, Episcopal, Catholic, and even Quaker. These denominations then excluded competing missionaries, sometimes by force. They taught Christian doctrine in government-funded schools. They openly, vigorously, and sometimes violently suppressed traditional Indian religion and ceremonies, including most notoriously the Ghost Dance, a campaign capped but not ended by the massacre at Wounded Knee in South Dakota in December 1890. And they did so unashamedly for over sixty years with the support of many religious groups and Indian "reformers" from the advent of President Grant's ill-named "Peace Policy" in 1869 until 1933, when the New Deal Indian commissioner John Collier abolished these policies.

This struggle to shape America as a Christian nation after 1790 also frequently used "history" as a proselytizing instrument. Backers of such efforts rewrote a complex and often ambiguous eighteenth-century past to recast Revolutionary America as a "Christian nation," a phraseology that has appeared episodically in American history at crucial intervals down to the present.

Yet however politically useful in either the nineteenth century or in our own times, the concept of the "Christian nation" does not resonate well with the facts of eighteenth-century colonial and American history. Both before and after the American Revolution most, if not all, observers understood America as a society where Christianity was important yet not ubiquitous. In it, a partially Christian people imbibed multifarious religions—innumerable versions of Christianity plus Judaism, traditional African religious expression, native American religions, even notions of magic and occultism (to the chagrin of many). The capacity of all these religions to uplift and inspire was tempered by an often equally strong propensity to divide, anger, and demean. In the 1780s this complexity and energy increasingly prompted Americans to distrust governmental involvement in religion. At the founding of the republic they moved to protect the civil peace and spiritual renewal simultaneously by withdrawing from specific and general establishments of Christianity everywhere except Connecticut and Massachusetts, by prohibiting the federal government from "an establishment of religion," not merely an establishment of Christianity, and by requiring that the federal government never breach the "free exercise of religion." In short, although the people should or might become "Christian," such a national identity would best remain a matter of practice, not law or governmental encouragement.

This was not a unanimous construction, though unwittingly it might have been elegant. Certainly it was not easy. But it was the unique late-eighteenth-century construction that made the relationship between religion and the formation of the American republic so remarkable, so compelling, and so important. No other Western society knew it. And no other Western society ever wrote so bold, so novel, and so successful a prescription for religion's role in a nation's destiny.

POSTSCRIPT

Did the American Revolution Produce a Christian Nation?

In his book *Religion in America: Past and Present* (Prentice-Hall, 1961), Clifton E. Olmstead argues for a broader application of religious causes to the origins of the American Revolution. First, Olmstead contends that the First Great Awakening fostered a sense of community among American colonists, thus providing the unity required for an organized assault on English control. Moreover, the Awakening further weakened existing ties between colonies and Mother Country by drawing adherents of the Church of England into the evangelical denominations that expanded as a result of revivalistic Protestantism. Second, tensions were generated by the demand that an Anglican bishop be established in the colonies. Many evangelicals found in this plan evidence that the British government wanted further control over the colonies. Third, the Quebec Act, enacted by Parliament in 1774, not only angered American colonists by nullifying their claims to western lands, but also heightened religious prejudice in the colonies by granting tolerance to Roman Catholics. Fourth, ministers played a significant role in encouraging their parishioners to support the independence movement. Olmstead claims that this revolutionary movement in the colonies was defended overwhelmingly by Congregationalist, Presbyterian, Dutch Reform, and Baptist ministers. Finally, many of the revolutionaries, imbued with the American sense of mission, believed that God was ordaining their revolutionary activities.

In his famous revolutionary-era pamphlet *Common Sense*, Thomas Paine formulated a rationale for the American colonies to declare their independence from England. In one passage, Paine employed a form of geographical predestination by stressing the differences between England and America. "[E]ven the distance at which the Almighty hath placed England and America is a strong and natural proof that the authority of the one over the other was never the design of heaven." In other words, if God had wanted the colonies to remain part of the British Empire, he would not have placed such a wide expanse of ocean between them; hence, God favored American independence. While many Americans today would use the above passage to conclude that the Revolution was divinely ordained, it does not necessarily follow that the American revolutionaries conceived of their conflict with England as an opportunity to create a godly republic. They may have invoked the guidance of a Supreme Being, but seldom did these expressions emanate from a devoutly Christian faith. For a discussion of the role of Christianity in the Revolutionary era and beyond, see Mark A. Noll, Nathan O. Hatch, and George M. Marsden, *The Search for Christian America* (Crossway Books, 1983).

Further support for these views can be found in Alan Heimert, *Religion and the American Mind from the Great Awakening to the Revolution* (Cambridge University Press, 1966), Cedric B. Cowing, *The Great Awakening and the American Revolution: Colonial Thought in the Eighteenth Century* (University of Chicago, 1971), Richard Hofstadter, *America at 1750: A Social Portrait* (Knopf, 1973), Rhys Isaac, *The Transformation of Virginia, 1740–1790* (University of North Carolina Press, 1982), Ruth H. Bloch, *Visionary Republic* (Cambridge University Press, 1985), and Harry S. Stout, *The New England Soul: Preaching and Religious Culture in Colonial New England* (Oxford University Press, 1986). Alan Heimert's views have been challenged by Sidney Mead and Bernard Bailyn. Students interested in further analyses of the Great Awakening should consult Edwin Scott Gaustad, *The Great Awakening in New England* (Harper & Brothers, 1957), David S. Lovejoy, *Religious Enthusiasm and the Great Awakening* (Prentice-Hall, 1969), and Marilyn J. Westerkamp, *Triumph of the Laity: Scots-Irish Piety and the Great Awakening, 1625–1760* (Oxford University Press, 1987).

ISSUE 6

Were the Founding Fathers Democratic Reformers?

YES: John P. Roche, from "The Founding Fathers: A Reform Caucus in Action," *American Political Science Review* (December 1961)

NO: Howard Zinn, from *A People's History of the United States* (Harper Collins, 1999)

ISSUE SUMMARY

YES: Political scientist John P. Roche asserts that the Founding Fathers were not only revolutionaries but also superb democratic politicians who created a constitution that supported the needs of the nation and at the same time was acceptable to the people.

NO: According to radical historian Howard Zinn, the Founding Fathers were an elite group of northern money interests and southern slaveholders who used Shay's Rebellion in Massachusetts as a pretext to create a strong central government, which protected the property rights of the rich to the exclusion of slaves, Indians, and non-property-holding whites.

The United States possesses the oldest written constitution of any major power. The 55 men who attended the Philadelphia Convention of 1787 could scarcely have dreamed that 200 years later the nation would venerate them as the most "enlightened statesmen" of their time. James Madison, the principal architect of the document, may have argued that the Founding Fathers had created a system that might "decide forever the fate of Republican Government which we wish to last for ages," but Madison also told Thomas Jefferson in October 1787 that he did not think the document would be adopted, and if it was, it would not work.

The enlightened statesmen view of the Founding Fathers, presented by nineteenth-century historians like John Fiske, became the accepted interpretation among the general public until the Progressive Era. In 1913 Columbia University professor Charles A. Beard's *An Economic Interpretation of the Constitution of the United States* (Free Press, 1913, 1986) caused a storm of controversy because it questioned the motivations of the Founding Fathers. The

Founding Fathers supported the creation of a stronger central government, argued Beard, not for patriotic reasons but because they wanted to protect their own economic interests.

Beard's research method was fairly simple. Drawing upon a collection of old, previously unexamined treasury records in the National Archives, he discovered that a number of delegates to the Philadelphia Convention and, later, to the state ratifying conventions held substantial amounts of continental securities that would sharply increase in value if a strong national government were established. In addition to attributing economic motives to the Founding Fathers, Beard included a Marxist class conflict interpretation in his book. Those who supported the Constitution, he said, represented "personalty interests which had been adversely affected under the Articles of Confederation: money, public securities, manufactures, and trade and shipping." Those who opposed ratification of the Constitution were the small farmers and debtors.

Beard's socioeconomic conflict interpretation of the supporters and opponents of the Constitution raised another issue: How was the Constitution ratified if the majority of Americans opposed it? Beard's answer was that most Americans could not vote because they did not own property. Therefore, the entire process, from the calling of the Philadelphia Convention to the state ratifying conventions, was nonrepresentative and nondemocratic.

An economic interpretation was a product of its times. Economists, sociologists, and political scientists had been analyzing the conflicts that resulted from the Industrial Revolution, which America had been experiencing at the turn of the twentieth century. Beard joined a group of progressive historians who were interested in reforming the society in which they lived and who also shared his discontent with the old-fashioned institutional approach. The role of the new historians was to rewrite history and discover the real reason why things happened. For the progressive historians, reality consisted of uncovering the hidden social and economic conflicts within society.

In the years between the world wars, the general public held steadfastly to the enlightened statesmen view of the Founding Fathers, but Beard's thesis on the Constitution became the new orthodoxy in most college texts on American history and government. The post–World War II period witnessed the emergence of the neoconservative historians, who viewed the Beardian approach to the Constitution as overly simplistic.

In the first of the following selections, which is a good example of consensus history, John P. Roche contends that although the Founding Fathers may have been revolutionaries, they were also superb democratic politicians who framed a Constitution that supported the needs of the nation and at the same time was acceptable to the people. A good example of Beard's lasting influence can be found in the second selection in which radical historian Howard Zinn argues from the Beardian perspective. The Founding Fathers, he argues, were an elite group of northern money interests and southern slaveholders who used Shay's Rebellion in Massachusetts as a pretext to create a strong central government, which protected the property rights of the rich to the exclusion of slaves, Indians, and non-property-holding whites.

YES 

John P. Roche

The Founding Fathers: A Reform Caucus in Action

The work of the Constitutional Convention and the motives of the Founding Fathers have been analyzed under a number of different ideological auspices. To one generation of historians, the hand of God was moving in the assembly; under a later dispensation, the dialectic (at various levels of philosophical sophistication) replaced the Deity: "relationships of production" moved into the niche previously reserved for Love of Country. . . . The Framers have undergone miraculous metamorphoses: at one time acclaimed as liberals and bold social engineers, today they appear in the guise of sound Burkean conservatives, men who in our time would subscribe to *Fortune*. . . .

The "Fathers" have thus been admitted to our best circles; the revolutionary ferocity which confiscated all Tory property in reach . . . has been converted . . . into a benign dedication to "consensus" and "prescriptive rights." . . . It is not my purpose here to argue that the "Fathers" were, in fact, radical revolutionaries; that proposition has been brilliantly demonstrated. . . . My concern is with the further position that not only were they revolutionaries, but also they were democrats. Indeed, in my view, there is one fundamental truth about the Founding Fathers . . . : They were first and foremost superb democratic politicians. . . . As recent research into the nature of American politics in the 1780s confirms, they were committed (perhaps willy-nilly) to working within the democratic framework, within a universe of public approval. . . . The Philadelphia Convention was not a College of Cardinals or a council of Platonic guardians working within a manipulative, pre-democratic framework; it was a nationalist reform caucus which had to operate with great delicacy and skill in a political cosmos full of enemies to achieve the one definitive goal—popular approbation. . . .

What they did was to hammer out a pragmatic compromise which would both bolster the "national interest" and be acceptable to the people. What inspiration they got came from their collective experience as professional politicians in a democratic society. As John Dickinson put it to his fellow delegates on August 13, "Experience must be our guide. Reason may mislead us."

In this context, let us examine the problems they confronted and the solutions they evolved. The Convention has been described picturesquely as a counter-revolutionary junta and the Constitution as a coup d'état, but this

From *American Political Science Review,* vol. 55, no. 4, December 1961.

has been accomplished by withdrawing the whole history of the movement for constitutional reform from its true context. No doubt the goals of the constitutional elite were "subversive" to the existing political order, but it is overlooked that their subversion could only have succeeded if the people of the United States endorsed it by regularized procedures. . . .

I

When the Constitutionalists went forth to subvert the Confederation, they utilized the mechanisms of political legitimacy. And the roadblocks which confronted them were formidable. At the same time, they were endowed with certain potent political assets. The history of the United States from 1786 to 1790 was largely one of a masterful employment of political expertise by the Constitutionalists as against bumbling, erratic behavior by the opponents of reform. Effectively, the Constitutionalists had to induce the states, by democratic techniques of coercion, to emasculate themselves. . . . And at the risk of becoming boring, it must be reiterated that the only weapon in the Constitutionalist arsenal was an effective mobilization of public opinion.

The group which undertook this struggle was an interesting amalgam of a few dedicated nationalists with the self-interested spokesmen of various parochial bailiwicks. The Georgians, for example, wanted a strong central authority to provide military protection for their huge, underpopulated state against the Creek Confederacy; Jerseymen and Connecticuters wanted to escape from economic bondage to New York; the Virginians hoped to establish a system which would give that great state its rightful place in the councils of the republic. The dominant figures in the politics of these states therefore cooperated in the call for the Convention. In other states, the thrust towards national reform was taken up by opposition groups who added the "national interest" to their weapons system; in Pennsylvania, for instance, the group fighting to revise the Constitution of 1776 came out four-square behind the Constitutionalists, and in New York, [Alexander] Hamilton and the Schuyler [family] ambiance took the same tack against George Clinton. There was, of course, a large element of personality in the affair: there is reason to suspect that Patrick Henry's opposition to the Convention and the Constitution was founded on his conviction that Jefferson was behind both, and a close study of local politics elsewhere would surely reveal that others supported the Constitution for the simple (and politically quite sufficient) reason that the "wrong" people were against it. . . .

What distinguished the leaders of the Constitutionalist caucus from their enemies was a "Continental" approach to political, economic and military issues. To the extent that they shared an institutional base of operations, it was the Continental Congress (thirty-nine of the delegates to the Federal Convention had served in Congress), and this was hardly a locale which inspired respect for the state governments. . . . Membership in the Congress under the Articles of Confederation worked to establish a continental frame of reference, that a Congressman from Pennsylvania and one from North Carolina would share. . . . This was particularly true with respect to external affairs: the average state legislator was probably about as concerned with foreign policy than as he is today, but Congressmen were constantly forced to take the broad view of American prestige, were compelled to listen to the reports of Secretary John Jay and to the dispatches and pleas from their frustrated envoys in Britain, France and Spain. From considerations such as these, a "Continental" ideology developed which seems to have demanded a revision of our domestic institutions primarily on the ground that only by invigorating our general government could we assume our rightful place in the international arena. . . .

Note that I am not endorsing the "Critical Period" thesis; on the contrary, Merrill Jensen seems to me quite sound in his view that for most Americans, engaged as they were in self-sustaining agriculture, the "Critical Period" was not particularly critical. In fact, the great achievement of the Constitutionalists was their ultimate success in convincing the elected representatives of a majority of the white male population that change was imperative. A small group of political leaders with a Continental vision and essentially a consciousness of the United States' international impotence, provided the matrix of the movement. To their standard other leaders rallied with their own parallel ambitions. Their great assets were (1) the presence in their caucus of the one authentic American "father figure," George Washington, whose prestige was enormous; (2) the energy and talent of their leadership (in which one must include the towering intellectuals of the time, John Adams and Thomas Jefferson, despite their absence abroad), and their communications "network," which was far superior to anything on the opposition side; (3) the preemptive skill which made "their" issue The Issue and kept the locally oriented opposition permanently on the defensive; and (4) the subjective consideration that these men were spokesmen of a new and compelling credo: American nationalism, that ill-defined but nonetheless potent sense of collective purpose that emerged from the American Revolution. . . .

The Constitutionalists got the jump on the "opposition" (a collective noun: oppositions would be more correct) at the outset with the demand for a Convention. Their opponents were caught in an old political trap: they were not being asked to approve any specific program of reform, but only to endorse a meeting to discuss and recommend needed reforms. If they took a hard line at the first stage, they were put in the position of glorifying the status quo and of denying the need for any changes. Moreover, the Constitutionalists could go to the people with a persuasive argument for "fair play"—"How can you condemn reform before you know precisely what is involved?" Since the state legislatures obviously would have the final say on any proposals that might emerge from the Convention, the Constitutionalists were merely reasonable men asking for a chance. Besides, since they did not make any concrete proposals at that stage, they were in a position to capitalize on every sort of generalized discontent with the Confederation.

Perhaps because of their poor intelligence system, perhaps because of over-confidence generated by the failure of all previous efforts to alter the Articles, the opposition awoke too late to the dangers that confronted them in 1787. Not only did the Constitutionalists manage to get every state but Rhode Island . . . to appoint delegates to Philadelphia, but when the results were in, it appeared that they dominated the delegations. Given the apathy of the opposition, this was a natural phenomenon: in an ideologically nonpolarized political atmosphere those who get appointed to a special committee are likely to be the men who supported the movement for its creation. . . . Much has been made of the fact that the delegates to Philadelphia were not elected by the people; some have adduced this fact as evidence of the "undemocratic" character of the gathering. But put in the context of the time, this argument is wholly specious: the central government under the Articles was considered a creature of the component states and in all the states but Rhode Island, Connecticut and New Hampshire, members of the national Congress were chosen by the state legislatures. This was not a consequence of elitism or fear of the mob; it was a logical extension of states'-rights doctrine to guarantee that the national institution did not end run the state legislatures and make direct contact with the people.

II

With delegations safely named, the focus shifted to Philadelphia. While waiting for a quorum to assemble, James Madison got busy and drafted the so-called Randolph or Virginia Plan with the aid of the Virginia delegation. This was a political master-stroke. Its consequence was that once business got under way, the framework of discussion was established on Madison's terms. There was no interminable argument over agenda; instead the delegates took the Virginia Resolutions—"just for purposes of discussion"—as their point of departure. And along with Madison's proposals, many of which were buried in the course of the summer, went his major premise: a new start on a Constitution rather than piecemeal amendment. . . .

Standard treatments of the Convention divide the delegates into "nationalists" and "states'-righters" with various improvised shadings ("moderate nationalists," etc.), but these are a posteriori categories which obfuscate more than they clarify. What is striking to one who analyzes the Convention as a case-study in democratic politics is the lack of clear-cut ideological divisions in the Convention. Indeed, I submit that the evidence—Madison's Notes, the correspondence of the delegates, and debates on ratification—indicates that this was a remarkably homogeneous body on the ideological level. [Robert] Yates and [John] Lansing [of New York], who favored the New Jersey Plan] . . . left in disgust on July 10. . . . Luther Martin, Maryland's bibulous narcissist, left on September 4 in a huff when he discovered that others did not share his self-esteem; others went home for personal reasons. But the hard core of delegates accepted a grinding regimen throughout the attrition of a Philadelphia summer precisely because they shared the Constitutionalist goal.

Basic differences of opinion emerged, of course, but these were not ideological; they were structural. If the so-called "states'-rights" group had not accepted the fundamental purposes of the Convention, they could simply have pulled out and by doing so have aborted the whole enterprise. Instead of bolting, they returned day after day to argue and to compromise. An interesting symbol of this basic homogeneity was the initial agreement on secrecy: these professional politicians did not want to become prisoners of publicity; they wanted to retain that freedom of maneuver which is only possible when men are not forced to take public stands in the preliminary stages of negotiation. There was no legal means of binding the tongues of the delegates: at any stage in the game a delegate with basic principled objections to the emerging project could have taken the stump (as Luther Martin did after his exit) and denounced the convention to the skies. Yet . . . the delegates generally observed the injunction. Secrecy is certainly uncharacteristic of any assembly marked by strong ideological polarization. . . .

Commentators on the Constitution who have read *The Federalist* in lieu of reading the actual debates have credited the Fathers with the invention of a sublime concept called "Federalism." . . . Federalism, as the theory is generally defined, was an improvisation which was later promoted into a political theory. Experts on "federalism" should take to heart the advice of David Hume, who warned . . . "there is no subject in which we must proceed with more caution than in [history], lest we assign causes which never existed and reduce what is merely contingent to stable and universal principles." In any event, the final balance in the Constitution between the states and the nation must have come as a great disappointment to Madison. . . .

It is indeed astonishing how those who have glibly designated James Madison the "father" of Federalism have overlooked the solid body of fact which indicates that he shared Hamilton's quest for a unitary central government. To be specific, they have avoided examining the clear import of the Madison-Virginia Plan, and have disregarded Madison's dogged inch-by-inch retreat from the bastions of centralization. The Virginia Plan envisioned a unitary national government effectively freed from and dominant over the states. The lower house of the national legislature was to be elected directly by the people of the states with membership proportional to population. The upper house was to be selected by the lower and the two chambers would elect the executive and choose the judges. The national legislature was to be empowered to disallow the acts of state legislatures, and the central government was vested, in addition to the powers of the nation under which the Articles of Confederation, with plenary authority wherever ". . . the separate States are incompetent or in which the harmony of the United States may be interrupted by the exercise of individual legislation." Finally, just to lock the door against state intrusion, the national Congress was to be given the power to use military force on recalcitrant states. This was Madison's "model" of an ideal national government, though it later received little publicity in *The Federalist.*

The interesting thing was the reaction of the Convention to this militant program for a strong autonomous central government. Some delegates were startled, some obviously leery of so comprehensive a project of reform, but nobody set off any fireworks and nobody walked out. Moreover, in the two weeks that followed, the Virginia Plan received substantial endorsement *en principe;* the initial temper of the gathering can be deduced from the approval "without debate or dissent," on May 31, of the Sixth Resolution which granted Congress the authority to disallow state legislation ". . . contravening in its opinion the Articles of Union." Indeed, an amendment was included to bar states from contravening national treaties.

The Virginia Plan may therefore be considered, in ideological terms, as the delegates' Utopia, but as the discussions continued and became more specific, many of those present began to have second thoughts. . . . They were practical politicians in a democratic society, and no matter what their private dreams might be, they had to take home an acceptable package and defend it—and their own political futures—against predictable attack. On June 14 the breaking point between dream and reality took place. Apparently realizing that under the Virginia Plan, Massachusetts, Virginia and Pennsylvania could virtually dominate the national government—and probably appreciating that to sell this program to "the folks back home" would be impossible—the delegates from the small states dug in their heels and demanded time for a consideration of alternatives. . . .

Now the process of accommodation was put into action smoothly—and wisely, given the character and strength of the doubters. Madison had the votes, but this was one of those situations where the enforcement of mechanical majoritarianism could easily have destroyed the objectives of the majority: the Constitutionalists were in quest of a qualitative as well as a quantitative consensus; . . . it was a political imperative if they were to attain ratification.

III

According to the standard script, at this point the "states'-rights" group intervened in force behind the New Jersey Plan, which has been characteristically portrayed as a revision to the status quo under the Articles of Confederation with but minor modifications. A careful examination of the evidence indicates that only in a marginal sense is this an accurate description. It is true that the New Jersey Plan put the states back into the institutional picture, but one could argue that to do so was a recognition of political reality rather than an affirmation of states'-rights. A serious case can be made that the advocates of the New Jersey Plan, far from being ideological addicts of states'-rights, intended to substitute for the Virginia Plan a system which would both retain strong national power and have a chance of adoption in the states. The leading spokesman for the project asserted quite clearly that his views were based more on counsels of expediency than on principle. . . . In his preliminary speech on June 9, Paterson had stated ". . . to the public mind we must accommodate ourselves," and in his notes for this and his later effort as well, the emphasis is the same. The structure of government under the Articles should be retained:

> 2. Because it accords with the Sentiments of the People
>
>> [Proof:] 1. Coms. [Commissions from state legislatures defining the jurisdiction of the delegates]
>> 2. News-papers—Political Barometer. Jersey never would have sent Delegates under the first [Virginia] Plan—
>
> Not here to sport Opinions of my own. Wt. [What] can be done. A little practicable Virtue preferrable to Theory.

This was a defense of political acumen, not of states'-rights. . . .

In other words, the advocates of the New Jersey Plan concentrated their fire on what they held to be the political liabilities of the Virginia Plan—which were matters of institutional structure—rather than on the proposed scope of national authority. Indeed, the Supremacy Clause of the Constitution first saw the light of day in Paterson's Sixth Resolution; the New Jersey Plan contemplated the use of military force to secure compliance with national law; and finally Paterson made clear his view that under either the Virginia or the New Jersey systems, the general government would ". . . act on individuals and not on states." From the states'-rights viewpoint, this was heresy: the fundament of that doctrine was the proposition that any central government had as its constituents the states, not the people, and could only reach the people through the agency of the state government.

Paterson then reopened the agenda of the Convention, but he did so within a distinctly naturalist framework. Paterson's position was one of favoring a strong central government in principle, but opposing one which in fact put the big states in the saddle.

How attached would the Virginians have been to their reform principles if Virginia were to disappear as a component geographical unit (the largest) for representational purposes? Up to this point, the Virginians had been in the happy position of supporting high ideals with that inner confidence born of knowledge that the "public interest" they endorsed would nourish their private interest. Worse, they had shown little willingness to compromise. Now the delegates from the small states announced that they were unprepared to be offered up as sacrificial victims to a "national interest" which reflected Virginia's parochial ambition. Caustic Charles Pinckney was not far off when he remarked sardonically that ". . . the whole [conflict] comes to this: Give N. Jersey an equal vote, and she will dismiss her scruples, and concur in the Natil. system." What he rather unfairly did not add was that the Jersey delegates were not free agents who could adhere to their private convictions; they had to take back, sponsor and risk their reputations on the reforms approved by the Convention—and in New Jersey, not in Virginia. . . .

IV

On Tuesday morning, June 19, . . . James Madison led off with a long, carefully reasoned speech analyzing the New Jersey Plan which, while intellectually vigorous in its criticisms, was quite conciliatory in mood. "The great difficulty," he observed, "lies in the affair of Representation; and if this could be adjusted, all others would be surmountable." (As events were to demonstrate, this diagnosis was correct.) When he finished, a vote was taken on whether to continue with the Virginia Plan as the nucleus for a new constitution: seven states voted "Yes"; New York, New Jersey, and Delaware voted "No"; and Maryland, whose position often depended on which delegates happened to be on the floor, divided. Paterson, it seems, lost decisively; yet in a fundamental sense he and his allies had achieved their purpose: from that day onward, it could never be forgotten that the state governments loomed ominously in the background. . . . Moreover, nobody bolted the convention: Paterson and his colleagues took their defeat in stride and set to work to modify the Virginia Plan, particularly with respect to its provisions on representation in the national legislature. Indeed, they won an immediate rhetorical bonus; when Oliver Ellsworth of Connecticut rose to move that the word "national" be expunged from the Third Virginia Resolution ("Resolved that a national Government ought to be established consisting of a supreme Legislative, Executive and Judiciary"), Randolph agreed and the motion passed unanimously. The process of compromise had begun.

For the next two weeks, the delegates circled around the problem of legislative representation. The Connecticut delegation appears to have evolved a possible compromise quite early in the debates, but the Virginians and particularly Madison (unaware that he would later be acclaimed as the prophet of "federalism") fought obdurately against providing for equal representation of states in the second chamber. . . . On July 2, the ice began to break when through a number of fortuitous events—and one that seems deliberate—the majority against equality of representation was converted into a dead tie. The Convention had reached the stage where it was "ripe" for a solution (presumably all the therapeutic speeches had been made), and the South Carolinians proposed a committee. Madison and James Wilson wanted none of it, but with only Pennsylvania dissenting, the body voted to establish a working party on the problem of representation.

The members of this committee, one from each state, were elected by the delegates—and a very interesting committee it was. Despite the fact that the Virginia Plan had held majority support up to that date, neither Madison nor Randolph was selected (Mason was the Virginian) and Baldwin of Georgia, whose shift in position had resulted in the tie, was chosen. From the composition, it was clear that this was not to be a "fighting" committee: the emphasis in membership was on what might be described as "second-level political entrepreneurs." On the basis of the discussions up to that time, only Luther Martin of Maryland could be described as a "bitter-ender." Admittedly, some divination enters into this sort of analysis, but one does get a sense of the mood of the delegates from these choices—including the interesting selection of Benjamin Franklin, despite his age and intellectual wobbliness, over the brilliant and incisive Wilson or the sharp, polemical Gouverneur Morris, to represent Pennsylvania. His passion for conciliation was more valuable at this juncture than Wilson's logical genius, or Morris' acerbic wit. . . .

It would be tedious to continue a blow-by-blow analysis of the work of the delegates; the critical fight was over representation of the states and once the Connecticut Compromise was adopted on July 17, the Convention was over the hump. Madison, James Wilson, and Gouverneur Morris of New York (who was there representing Pennsylvania!) fought the compromise all the way in a last-ditch effort to get a unitary state with parliamentary supremacy. But their allies deserted them. . . . Moreover, once the compromise had carried (by five states to four, with one state divided), its advocates threw themselves vigorously into the job of strengthening the general government's substantive powers—as might have been predicted, indeed, from Paterson's early statements. It nourishes an increased respect for Madison's devotion to the art of politics, to realize that this dogged fighter could sit down six months later and prepare essays for *The Federalist* in contradiction to his basic convictions about the true course the Convention should have taken.

V

Two tricky issues will serve to illustrate the later process of accommodation. The first was the institutional position of the Executive. Madison argued for an executive chosen by the National Legislature and on May 29 this had been adopted with a provision that after his seven-year term was concluded, the chief magistrate should not be eligible for reelection. In late July this was reopened and for a week the matter was argued from several different points of view. . . . One group felt that the states should have a hand in the process; another small but influential circle urged direct election by the people. There were a number of proposals: election by the people, election by state governors, by electors chosen by state legislatures, by the National legislature, . . . and there was some resemblance to three-dimensional chess in the dispute because of the presence of two other variables, length of tenure and reeligibility. Finally, after opening, reopening, and re-reopening the debate, the thorny problem was consigned to a committee for resolution.

The Brearley Committee on Postponed Matters was a superb aggregation of talent and its compromise on the Executive was a masterpiece of political improvisation. (The Electoral College, its creation, however, had little in its favor as an institution—as the delegates well appreciated.) The point of departure for all discussion about the presidency in the Convention was that in immediate terms, the problem was non-existent; in other words, everybody present knew that under any system devised, George Washington would be President. Thus they were dealing in the future tense and to a body of working politicians the merits of the Brearley proposal were obvious: everybody got a piece of cake. (Or to put it more academically, each viewpoint could leave the Convention and argue to its constituents that it had really won the day.) First, the state legislatures had the right to determine the mode of selection of the electors; second, the small states received a bonus in the Electoral College in the form of a guaranteed minimum of three votes while the big states got acceptance of the principle of proportional power; third, if the state legislatures agreed (as six did in the first presidential election), the people could be involved directly in the choice of electors; and finally, if no candidate received a majority in the College, the right of decision passed to the National Legislature with each state exercising equal strength. (In the Brearley recommendation, the election went to the Senate, but a motion from the floor substituted the House; this was accepted on the ground that the Senate already had enough authority over the executive in its treaty and appointment powers.)

This compromise was almost too good to be true, and the Framers snapped it up with little debate or controversy. No one seemed to think well of the College as an institution; indeed, what evidence there is suggests that there was an assumption that once Washington had finished his tenure as President, the electors would cease to produce majorities and the chief executive would usually be chosen in the House. George Mason observed casually that the selection would be made in the House nineteen times in twenty and no one seriously disputed this point. The vital aspect of the Electoral College was that it got the Convention over the hurdle and protected everybody's interests. . . .

In short, the Framers did not in their wisdom endow the United States with a College of Cardinals—the Electoral College was neither an exercise in applied Platonism nor an experiment in indirect government based on elitist distrust of the masses. It was merely a jerry-rigged improvisation which has subsequently been endowed with a high theoretical content. . . .

The second issue on which some substantial practical bargaining took place was slavery. The morality of slavery was, by design, not at issue; but in its other concrete aspects, slavery colored the arguments over taxation, commerce, and representation. The "Three-Fifths Compromise," that three-fifths of the slaves would be counted both for representation and for purposes of direct taxation (which was drawn from the past—it was a formula of Madison's utilized by Congress in 1783 to establish the basis of state contributions to the Confederation treasury) had allayed some Northern fears about Southern over-representation. . . . The Southerners, on the other hand, were afraid that Congressional control over commerce would lead to the exclusion of slaves or to their excessive taxation as imports. Moreover, the Southerners were disturbed over "navigation acts," i.e., tariffs or special legislation providing, for example, that exports be carried only in American ships; as a section depending upon exports, they wanted protection from the potential voracity of their commercial brethren of the Eastern states. To achieve this end, Mason and others urged that the Constitution include a proviso that navigation and commercial laws should require a two-thirds vote in Congress.

These problems came to a head in late August and, as usual were handed to a committee in the hope that, in Gouverneur Morris' words, ". . . these things may form a bargain among the Northern and Southern states." The Committee reported its measures of reconciliation on August 25, and on August 29 the package was wrapped up and delivered. What occurred can best be described in George Mason's dour version (he anticipated Calhoun in his conviction that permitting navigation acts to pass by majority vote would put the South in economic bondage to the North—it was mainly on this ground that he refused to sign the Constitution):

> The Constitution as agreed to till a fortnight before the Convention rose was such a one as he would have set his hand and heart to. . . . [Until that time] The 3 New England States were constantly with us in all questions . . . so that it was these three States with the 5 Southern ones against Pennsylvania, Jersey and Delaware. With respect to the importation of slaves, [decision-making] was left to Congress. This disturbed the two Southernmost States who knew that Congress would immediately suppress the importation of slaves. Those two States therefore struck up a bargain with the three New England States. If they would join to admit slaves for some years, the two Southern-most States would join in changing the

> clause which required the 2/3 of the Legislature in any vote [on navigation acts]. It was done.

On the floor of the Convention there was a virtual love-feast on this happy occasion. Charles Pinckney of South Carolina attempted to overturn the committee's decision, when the compromise was reported to the Convention, by insisting that the South needed protection from the imperialism of the Northern states. But his Southern colleagues were not prepared to rock the boat and General C. C. Pinckney arose to spread oil on the suddenly ruffled waters; he admitted that:

> It was in the true interest of the S[outhern] States to have no regulation of commerce; but considering the loss brought on the commerce of the Eastern States by the Revolution, their liberal conduct towards the views of South Carolina [on the regulation of the slave trade] and the interests the weak Southn. States had in being united with the strong Eastern states, he thought it proper that no fetters should be imposed on the power of making commercial regulations; and that his constituents, though prejudiced against the Eastern States, would be reconciled to this liberality. He had himself prejudices against the Eastern States before he came here, but would acknowledge that he had found them as liberal and candid as any men whatever.

Pierce Butler took the same tack, essentially arguing that he was not too happy about the possible consequences, but that a deal was a deal. . . .

VI

Drawing on their vast collective political experience, utilizing every weapon in the politician's arsenal, looking constantly over their shoulders at their constituents, the delegates put together a Constitution. It was a makeshift affair; some sticky issues (for example, the qualification of voters) they ducked entirely; others they mastered with that ancient instrument of political sagacity, studied ambiguity (for example, citizenship), and some they just overlooked. In this last category, I suspect, fell the matter of the power of the federal courts to determine the constitutionality of acts of Congress. When the judicial article was formulated (Article III of the Constitution), deliberations were still in the stage where the legislature was endowed with broad power under the Randolph formulation, authority which by its own terms was scarcely amenable to judicial review. In essence, courts could hardly determine when ". . . the separate States are incompetent or . . . the harmony of the United States may be interrupted"; the National Legislature, as critics pointed out, was free to define its own jurisdiction. Later the definition of legislative authority was changed into the form we know, a series of stipulated powers, but the delegates never seriously reexamined the jurisdiction of the judiciary under this new limited formulation. All arguments on the intention of the Framers in this matter are thus deductive and a posteriori, though some obviously make more sense than others.

The Framers were busy and distinguished men, anxious to get back to their families, their positions, and their constituents. . . . They were trying to do an important job, and do it in such a fashion that their handiwork would be acceptable to very diverse constituencies. No one was rhapsodic about the final document, but it was a beginning, a move in the right direction, and one they had reason to believe the people would endorse. In addition, since they had modified the impossible amendment provisions of the Articles . . . to one demanding approval by only three-quarters of the states, they seemed confident that gaps in the fabric which experience would reveal could be rewoven without undue difficulty.

So with a neat phrase introduced by Benjamin Franklin (but devised by Gouverneur Morris) which made their decision sound unanimous, and an inspired benediction by the Old Doctor urging doubters to doubt their own infallibility, the Constitution was accepted and signed. Curiously, Edmund Randolph, who had played so vital a role throughout, refused to sign, as did his fellow Virginian George Mason and Elbridge Gerry of Massachusetts. Randolph's behavior was eccentric; . . . the best explanation seems to be that he was afraid that the Constitution would prove to be a liability in Virginia politics, where Patrick Henry was burning up the countryside with impassioned denunciations. Presumably, Randolph wanted to check the temper of the populace before he risked his reputation, and perhaps his job, in a fight with both Henry and Richard Henry Lee. Events lend some justification to this speculation: after much temporizing . . . Randolph endorsed ratification in Virginia and ended up getting the best of both worlds. . . .

The Constitution, then, was an apotheosis of "constitutionalism," a triumph of architectonic genius; it was a patchwork sewn together under the pressure of both time and events by a group of extremely talented democratic politicians. They refused to attempt the establishment of a strong, centralized sovereignty on the principle of legislative supremacy for the excellent reason that the people would not accept it. They risked their political fortunes by opposing the established doctrines of state sovereignty because they were convinced that the existing system was leading to national impotence and probably foreign domination. For two years, they worked to get a convention established. For over three months, in what must have seemed to the faithful participants an endless process of give-and-take, they reasoned, cajoled, threatened, and bargained amongst themselves. The result was a Constitution which the people, in fact, by democratic processes, did accept, and a new and far better national government was established. . . .

To conclude, the Constitution was neither a victory for abstract theory nor a great practical success. Well over half a million men had to die on the battlefields of the Civil War before certain constitutional principles could be defined—a baleful consideration which is somehow overlooked in our customary tributes to the farsighted genius of the Framers and to the supposed American talent for "constitutionalism." The Constitution was, however, a vivid demonstration of effective democratic political action, and of the forging of a national elite which literally persuaded its countrymen to hoist themselves by their own boot straps.

Howard Zinn

A People's History of the United States

To many Americans over the years, the Constitution drawn up in 1787 has seemed a work of genius put together by wise, humane men who created a legal framework for democracy and equality. This view is stated, a bit extravagantly, by the historian George Bancroft, writing in the early nineteenth century:

> The Constitution establishes nothing that interferes with equality and individuality. It knows nothing of differences by descent, or opinions, of favored classes, or legalized religion, or the political power of property. It leaves the individual alongside of the individual. . . . As the sea is made up of drops, American society is composed of separate, free, and constantly moving atoms, ever in reciprocal action . . . so that the institutions and laws of the country rise out of the masses of individual thought which, like the waters of the ocean, are rolling evermore.

Another view of the Constitution was put forward early in the twentieth century by the historian Charles Beard (arousing anger and indignation, including a denunciatory editorial in the *New York Times*). He wrote in his book *An Economic Interpretation of the Constitution:*

> Inasmuch as the primary object of a government, beyond the mere repression of physical violence, is the making of the rules which determine the property relations of members of society, the dominant classes whose rights are thus to be determined must perforce obtain from the government such rules as are consonant with the larger interests necessary to the continuance of their economic processes, or they must themselves control the organs of government.

In short, Beard said, the rich must, in their own interest, either control the government directly or control the laws by which government operates.

Beard applied this general idea to the Constitution, by studying the economic backgrounds and political ideas of the fifty-five men who gathered in Philadelphia in 1787 to draw up the Constitution. He found that a majority of them were lawyers by profession, that most of them were men of wealth, in land, slaves, manufacturing, or shipping, that half of them had money loaned out at interest, and that forty of the fifty-five held government bonds, according to the records of the Treasury Department.

Thus, Beard found that most of the makers of the Constitution had some direct economic interest in establishing a strong federal government: the manufacturers needed protective tariffs; the moneylenders wanted to stop the use of paper money to pay off debts; the land speculators wanted protection as they invaded Indian lands; slaveowners needed federal security against slave revolts and runaways; bondholders wanted a government able to raise money by nationwide taxation, to pay off those bonds.

Four groups, Beard noted, were not represented in the Constitutional Convention: slaves, indentured servants, women, men without property. And so the Constitution did not reflect the interests of those groups.

He wanted to make it clear that he did not think the Constitution was written merely to benefit the Founding Fathers personally, although one could not ignore the $150,000 fortune of Benjamin Franklin, the connections of Alexander Hamilton to wealthy interests through his father-in-law and brother-in-law, the great slave plantations of James Madison, the enormous landholdings of George Washington. Rather, it was to benefit the groups the Founders represented, the "economic interests they understood and felt in concrete, definite form through their own personal experience."

Not everyone at the Philadelphia Convention fitted Beard's scheme. Elbridge Gerry of Massachusetts was a holder of landed property, and yet he opposed the ratification of the Constitution. Similarly, Luther Martin of Maryland, whose ancestors had obtained large tracts of land in New Jersey, opposed ratification. But, with a few exceptions, Beard found a strong connection between wealth and support of the Constitution.

By 1787 there was not only a positive need for strong central government to protect the large economic interests, but also immediate fear of rebellion by discontented farmers. The chief event causing this fear was an uprising in the summer of 1786 in western Massachusetts, known as Shays' Rebellion.

In the western towns of Massachusetts there was resentment against the legislature in Boston. The new Constitution of 1780 had raised the property qualifications for voting. No one could hold state office without being quite wealthy. Furthermore, the legislature was refusing to issue paper money, as had been done in some other states, like Rhode Island, to make it easier for debt-ridden farmers to pay off their creditors.

Illegal conventions began to assemble in some of the western counties to organize opposition to the legislature. At one of these, a man named Plough Jogger spoke his mind:

> I have been greatly abused, have been obliged to do more than my part in the war; been loaded with class rates, town rates, province rates, Continental rates and all rates . . . been pulled and hauled by sheriffs, constables and collectors, and had my cattle sold for less than they were worth. . . .
>
> . . . The great men are going to get all we have and I think it is time for us to rise and put a stop to it, and have no more courts, nor sheriffs, nor collectors nor lawyers. . . .

The chairman of that meeting used his gavel to cut short the applause. He and others wanted to redress their grievances, but peacefully, by petition to the General Court (the legislature) in Boston.

However, before the scheduled meeting of the General Court, there were going to he court proceedings in Hampshire County, in the towns of Northampton and Springfield, to seize the cattle of farmers who hadn't paid their debts, to take away their land, now full of grain and ready for harvest. And so, veterans of the Continental army, also aggrieved because they had been treated poorly on discharge—given certificates for future redemption instead of immediate cash—began to organize the farmers into squads and companies. One of these veterans was Luke Day, who arrived the morning of court with a fife-and-drum corps, still angry with the memory of being locked up in debtors' prison in the heat of the previous summer.

The sheriff looked to the local militia to defend the court against these armed farmers. But most of the militia was with Luke Day. The sheriff did manage to gather five hundred men, and the judges put on their black silk robes, waiting for the sheriff to protect their trip to the courthouse. But there at the courthouse steps, Luke Day stood with a petition, asserting the people's constitutional right to protest the unconstitutional acts of the General Court, asking the judges to adjourn until the General Court could act on behalf of the farmers. Standing with Luke Day were fifteen hundred armed farmers. The judges adjourned.

Shortly after, at courthouses in Worcester and Athol, farmers with guns prevented the courts from meeting to take away their property, and the militia were too sympathetic to the farmers, or too outnumbered, to act. In Concord, a fifty-year-old veteran of two wars, Job Shattuck, led a caravan of carts, wagons, horses, and oxen onto the town green, while a message was sent to the judges:

> The voice of the People of this county is such that the court shall not enter this courthouse until such time as the People shall have redress of the grievances they labor under at the present.

A county convention then suggested the judges adjourn, which they did.

At Great Barrington, a militia of a thousand faced a square crowded with armed men and boys. But the militia was split in its opinion. When the chief justice suggested the militia divide, those in favor of the court's sitting to go on the right side of the road, and those against on the left, two hundred of the militia went to the right, eight hundred to the left, and the judges adjourned. Then the crowd went to the home of the chief justice, who agreed to sign a pledge that the court would not sit until the Massachusetts General Court met. The crowd went back to the square, broke open the county jail, and set free the debtors. The chief justice, a country doctor, said: "I have never heard anybody point out a better way to have their grievances redressed than the people have taken."

The governor and the political leaders of Massachusetts became alarmed. Samuel Adams, once looked on as a radical leader in Boston, now insisted people act within the law. He said "British emissaries" were stirring up the farmers. People in the town of Greenwich responded: You in Boston have the money, and we don't. And didn't you act illegally yourselves in the Revolution? The insurgents were now being called Regulators. Their emblem was a sprig of hemlock.

The problem went beyond Massachusetts. In Rhode Island, the debtors had taken over the legislature and were issuing paper money. In New Hampshire, several hundred men, in September of 1786, surrounded the legislature in Exeter, asking that taxes be returned and paper money issued; they dispersed only when military action was threatened.

Daniel Shays entered the scene in western Massachusetts. A poor farm hand when the revolution broke out, he joined the Continental army, fought at Lexington, Bunker Hill, and Saratoga, and was wounded in action. In 1780, not being paid, he resigned from the army, went home, and soon found himself in court for nonpayment of debts. He also saw what was happening to others: a sick woman, unable to pay, had her bed taken from under her.

What brought Shays fully into the situation was that on September 19, the Supreme Judicial Court of Massachusetts met in Worcester and indicted eleven leaders of the rebellion, including three of his friends, as "disorderly, riotous and seditious persons" who "unlawfully and by force of arms" prevented "the execution of justice and the laws of the commonwealth." The Supreme Judicial Court planned to meet again in Springfield a week later, and there was talk of Luke Day's being indicted.

Shays organized seven hundred armed farmers, most of them veterans of the war, and led them to Springfield. There they found a general with nine hundred soldiers and a cannon. Shays asked the general for permission to parade, which the general granted, so Shays and his men moved through the square, drums banging and fifes blowing. As they marched, their ranks grew. Some of the militia joined, and reinforcements began coming in from the countryside. The judges postponed hearings for a day, then adjourned the court.

Now the General Court, meeting in Boston, was told by Governor James Bowdoin to "vindicate the insulted dignity of government." The recent rebels against England, secure in office, were calling for law and order. Sam Adams helped draw up a Riot Act, and a resolution suspending habeas corpus, to allow the authorities to keep people in jail without trial. At the same time, the legislature moved to make some concessions to the angry farmers, saying certain old taxes could now be paid in goods instead of money.

This didn't help. In Worcester, 160 insurgents appeared at the courthouse. The sheriff read the Riot Act. The insurgents said they would disperse only if the judges did. The sheriff shouted something about hanging. Someone came up behind him and put a sprig of hemlock in his hat. The judges left.

Confrontations between farmers and militia now multiplied. The winter snows began to interfere with the trips of farmers to the courthouses. When Shays began marching a thousand men into Boston, a blizzard forced them back, and one of his men froze to death.

An army came into the field, led by General Benjamin Lincoln, on money raised by Boston merchants. In an artillery duel, three rebels were killed. One soldier stepped in front of his own artillery piece and lost both arms. The winter grew worse. The rebels were outnumbered and on the run. Shays took refuge in Vermont, and his followers began to surrender. There were a few more deaths in battle, and then sporadic, disorganized, desperate acts of violence against authority: the burning of barns, the slaughter of a general's horses. One government soldier was killed in an eerie night-time collision of two sleighs.

Captured rebels were put on trial in Northampton and six were sentenced to death. A note was left at the door of the high sheriff of Pittsfidd:

> I understand that there is a number of my countrymen condemned to die because they fought for justice. I pray have a care that you assist not in the execution of so horrid a crime, for by all that is above, he that condemns and he that executes shall share alike. . . . Prepare for death with speed, for your life or mine is short. When the woods are covered with leaves, I shall return and pay you a short visit.

Thirty-three more rebels were put on trial and six more condemned to death. Arguments took place over whether the hangings should go forward. General Lincoln urged mercy and a Commission of Clemency, but Samuel Adams said: "In monarchy the crime of treason may admit of being pardoned or lightly punished, but the man who dares rebel against the laws of a republic ought to suffer death." Several hangings followed; some of the condemned were pardoned. Shays, in Vermont, was pardoned in 1788 and returned to Massachusetts, where he died, poor and obscure, in 1825.

It was Thomas Jefferson, in France as ambassador at the time of Shays' Rebellion, who spoke of such uprisings as healthy for society. In a letter to a friend he wrote: "I hold it that a little rebellion now and then is a good thing. . . . It is a medicine necessary for the sound health of government. . . . God forbid that we should ever be twenty years without such a rebellion. . . . The tree of liberty must be refreshed from time to time with the blood of patriots and tyrants. It is its natural manure."

But Jefferson was far from the scene. The political and economic elite of the country were not so tolerant. They worried that the example might spread. A veteran of Washington's army, General Henry Knox, founded an organization of army veterans, "The Order of the Cincinnati," presumably (as one historian put it) "for the purpose of cherishing the heroic memories of the struggle in which they had taken part," but also, it seemed, to watch out for radicalism in the new country. Knox wrote to Washington in late 1786 about Shays' Rebellion, and in doing so expressed the thoughts of many of the wealthy and powerful leaders of the country:

> The people who are the insurgents have never paid any, or but very little taxes. But they see the weakness of government; they feel at once their own poverty, compared with the opulent, and their own force, and they are determined to make use of the latter, in order to remedy the former. Their creed is "That the property of the United States has been protected from the confiscations of Britain by the joint exertions of all, and therefore ought to he the common property of all. And he that attempts opposition to this creed is an enemy to equity and justice and ought to be swept from off the face of the earth."

Alexander Hamilton, aide to Washington during the war, was one of the most forceful and astute leaders of the new aristocracy. He voiced his political philosophy:

> All communities divide themselves into the few and the many. The first are the rich and well-born, the other the mass of the people. The voice of the people has been said to be the voice of God; and however generally this maxim has been quoted and believed, it is not true in fact. The people are turbulent and changing; they seldom judge or determine right. Give therefore to the first class a distinct permanent share in the government. . . . Can a democratic assembly who annually revolve in the mass of the people be supposed steadily to pursue the public good? Nothing but a permanent body can check the imprudence of democracy. . . .

At the Constitutional Convention, Hamilton suggested a President and Senate chosen for life.

The Convention did not take his suggestion. But neither did it provide for popular elections, except in the case of the House of Representatives, where the qualifications were set by the state legislatures (which required property-holding for voting in almost all the states), and excluded women, Indians, slaves. The Constitution provided for Senators to be elected by the state legislators, for the President to be elected by electors chosen by the state legislators, and for the Supreme Court to be appointed by the President.

The problem of democracy in the post-Revolutionary society was not, however, the Constitutional limitations on voting. It lay deeper, beyond the Constitution, in the division of society into rich and poor. For if some people had great wealth and great influence; if they had the land, the money, the newspapers, the church, the educational system—how could voting, however broad, cut into such power? There was still another problem: wasn't it the nature of representative government, even when most broadly based, to be conservative, to prevent tumultuous change?

It came time to ratify the Constitution, to submit to a vote in state conventions, with approval of nine of the thirteen required to ratify it. In New York, where debate over ratification was intense, a series of newspaper articles appeared, anonymously, and they tell us much about the nature of the Constitution. These articles, favoring adoption of the Constitution, were written by James Madison, Alexander Hamilton, and John Jay, and came to be known as the *Federalist Papers* (opponents of the Constitution became known as anti-Federalists).

In *Federalist Paper #10,* James Madison argued that representative government was needed to maintain peace in a society ridden by factional disputes. These disputes came from "the various and unequal distribution of property. Those who hold and those who are without property have ever formed distinct interests in society." The problem, he said, was how to control the factional struggles that came from inequalities in wealth. Minority factions could be controlled, he said, by the principle that decisions would be by vote of the majority.

So the real problem, according to Madison, was a majority faction, and here the solution was offered by the Constitution, to have "an extensive republic," that is, a large nation ranging over thirteen states, for then "it will be more difficult for all who feel it to discover their own strength, and to act in unison with each other. . . . The influence of factious leaders may kindle a flame within their particular States, but will be unable to spread a general conflagration through the other States."

Madison's argument can be seen as a sensible argument for having a government which can maintain peace and avoid continuous disorder. But is it the aim of government simply to maintain order, as a referee, between two equally matched fighters? Or is it that government has some special interest in maintaining a certain kind of order, a certain distribution of power and wealth, a distribution in which government officials are not neutral referees but participants? In that case, the disorder they might worry about is the disorder of popular rebellion against those monopolizing the society's wealth. This interpretation makes sense when one looks at the economic interests, the social backgrounds, of the makers of the Constitution.

As part of his argument for a large republic to keep the peace, James Madison tells quite clearly, in *Federalist #10*, whose peace he wants to keep: "A rage for paper money, for an abolition of debts, for an equal division of property, or for any other improper or wicked project, will be less apt to pervade the whole body of the Union than a particular member of it."

When economic interest is seen behind the political clauses of the Constitution, then the document becomes not simply the work of wise men trying to establish a decent and orderly society, but the work of certain groups trying to maintain their privileges, while giving just enough rights and liberties to enough of the people to ensure popular support.

In the new government, Madison would belong to one party (the Democrat-Republicans) along with Jefferson and Monroe. Hamilton would belong to the rival party (the Federalists) along with Washington and Adams. But both agreed—one a slaveholder from Virginia, the other a merchant from New York—on the aims of this new government they were establishing. They were anticipating the long-fundamental agreement of the two political parties in the American system. Hamilton wrote elsewhere in the *Federalist Papers* that the new Union would be able "to repress domestic faction and insurrection." He referred directly to Shays' Rebellion: "The tempestuous situation from which Massachusetts has scarcely emerged evinces that dangers of this kind are not merely speculative."

It was either Madison or Hamilton (the authorship of the individual papers is not always known) who in *Federalist Paper #63* argued the necessity of a "well-constructed Senate" as "sometimes necessary as a defense to the people against their own temporary errors and delusions" because "there are particular moments in public affairs when the people, stimulated by some irregular passion, or some illicit advantage, or misted by the artful misrepresentations of interested men, may call for measures which they themselves will afterwards be the most ready to lament and condemn." And: "In these critical moments, how salutary will be the interference of some temperate and respectable body of citizens in order to check the misguided career, and to suspend the blow meditated by the people against themselves, until reason, justice, and truth can regain their authority over the public mind?"

The Constitution was a compromise between slaveholding interests of the South and moneyed interests of the North. For the purpose of uniting the thirteen states into one great market for commerce, the northern delegates wanted laws regulating interstate commerce, and urged that such laws require only a majority of Congress to pass. The South agreed to this, in return for allowing the trade in slaves to continue for twenty years before being outlawed.

Charles Beard warned us that governments—including the government of the United States—are not neutral, that they represent the dominant economic interests, and that their constitutions are intended to serve these interests. One of his critics (Robert E. Brown, *Charles Beard and the Constitution*) raises an interesting point. Granted that the Constitution omitted the phrase "life, liberty and the pursuit of happiness," which appeared in the Declaration of Independence, and substituted "life, liberty, or property"—well, why shouldn't the Constitution protect property? As Brown says about Revolutionary America, "practically everybody was interested in the protection of property" because so many Americans owned property.

However, this is misleading. True, there were many property owners. But some people had much more than others. A few people had great amounts of property; many people had small amounts; others had none. Jackson Main found that one-third of the population in the Revolutionary period were small farmers, while only 3 percent of the population had truly large holdings and could be considered wealthy.

Still, one-third was a considerable number of people who felt they had something at stake in the stability of a new government. This was a larger base of support for government than anywhere in the world at the end of the eighteenth century. In addition, the city mechanics had an important interest in a government which would protect their work from foreign competition. As Staughton Lynd puts it: "How is it that the city workingmen all over America overwhelmingly and enthusiastically supported the United States Constitution?"

This was especially true in New York. When the ninth and tenth states had ratified the Constitution, four thousand New York City mechanics marched with floats and banners to celebrate. Bakers, blacksmiths, brewers, ship joiners and shipwrights, coopers, cartmen and tailors, all marched. What Lynd found was that these mechanics, while opposing elite rule in the colonies, were nationalist. Mechanics comprised perhaps half the New York population. Some were wealthy, some were poor, but all were better off than the ordinary laborer, the apprentice, the journeyman, and their prosperity required a government that would protect them against the British hats and shoes and other goods that were pouring into the colonies after the Revolution. As a result, the mechanics often supported wealthy conservatives at the ballot box.

The Constitution, then, illustrates the complexity of the American system: that it serves the interests of a wealthy elite, but also does enough for small property owners, for middle-income mechanics and farmers, to build a broad base of support. The slightly prosperous people who make up this base of support are buffers against the blacks, the Indians, the very poor whites. They enable the elite to keep control with a minimum of coercion, a maximum of law—all made palatable by the fanfare of patriotism and unity.

The Constitution became even more acceptable to the public at large after the first Congress, responding to criticism, passed a series of amendments known as the Bill of Rights. These amendments seemed to make the new government a guardian of people's liberties: to speak, to publish, to worship, to petition, to assemble, to be tried fairly, to be secure at home against official intrusion. It was, therefore, perfectly designed to build popular backing for the new government. What was not made clear—it was a time when the language of freedom was new and its reality untested—was the shakiness of anyone's liberty when entrusted to a government of the rich and powerful.

Indeed, the same problem existed for the other provisions of the Constitution, like the clause forbidding states to "impair the obligation of contract," or that giving Congress the power to tax the people and to appropriate money. They all sound benign and neutral until one asks: Tax who, for what? Appropriate what, for whom? To protect everyone's contracts seems like an act of fairness, of equal treatment, until one considers that contracts made between rich and poor, between employer and employee, landlord and tenant, creditor and debtor, generally favor the more powerful of the two parties. Thus, to protect these contracts is to put the great power of the government, its laws, courts, sheriffs, police, on the side of the privileged—and to do it not, as in premodern times, as an exercise of brute force against the weak but as a matter of law.

The First Amendment of the Bill of Rights shows that quality of interest hiding behind innocence. Passed in 1791 by Congress, it provided that "Congress shall make no law . . . abridging the freedom of speech, or of the press. . . ." Yet, seven years after the First Amendment became part of the Constitution, Congress passed a law very clearly abridging the freedom of speech.

This was the Sedition Act of 1798, passed under John Adams's administration, at a time when Irishmen and Frenchmen in the United States were looked on as dangerous revolutionaries because of the recent French Revolution and the Irish rebellions. The Sedition Act made it a crime to say or write anything "false, scandalous and malicious" against the government, Congress, or the President, with intent to defame them, bring them into disrepute, or excite popular hatreds against them.

This act seemed to directly violate the First Amendment. Yet, it was enforced. Ten Americans were put in prison for utterances against the government, and every member of the Supreme Court in 1798–1800, sitting as an appellate judge, held it constitutional.

There was a legal basis for this, one known to legal experts, but not to the ordinary American, who would read the First Amendment and feel confident that he or she was protected in the exercise of free speech. That basis has been explained by historian Leonard Levy. Levy points out that it was generally understood (not in the population, but in higher circles) that, despite the First Amendment, the British common law of "seditious libel" still ruled in America. This meant that while the government could not exercise "prior restraint"—that is, prevent an utterance or publication in advance—it could legally punish the speaker or writer afterward. Thus, Congress has a convenient legal basis for the laws it has enacted since that time, making certain kinds of speech a crime. And, since punishment after the fact is an excellent deterrent to the exercise of free expression, the claim of "no prior restraint" itself is destroyed. This leaves the First Amendment much less than the stone wall of protection it seems at first glance.

Are the economic provisions in the Constitution enforced just as weakly? We have an instructive example almost immediately in Washington's first administration, when Congress's power to tax and appropriate money was immediately put to use by the Secretary of the Treasury, Alexander Hamilton.

Hamilton, believing that government must ally itself with the richest elements of society to make itself strong, proposed to Congress a series of laws, which it enacted, expressing this philosophy. A Bank of the United States was set up as a partnership between the government and certain banking interests. A tariff was passed to help the manufacturers. It was agreed to pay bondholders—most of the war bonds were now concentrated in a small group of wealthy people—the full value of their bonds. Tax laws were passed to raise money for this bond redemption.

One of these tax laws was the Whiskey Tax, which especially hurt small farmers who raised grain that they converted into whiskey and then sold. In 1794 the farmers of western Pennsylvania took up arms and rebelled against the collection of this tax. Secretary of the Treasury Hamilton led the troops to put them down. We see then, in the first years of the Constitution, that some of its provisions—even those paraded most flamboyantly (like the First Amendment)—might be treated lightly. Others (like the power to tax) would be powerfully enforced.

Still, the mythology around the Founding Fathers persists. To say, as one historian (Bernard Bailyn) has done recently, that "the destruction of privilege and the creation of a political system that demanded of its leaders the responsible and humane use of power were their highest aspirations" is to ignore what really happened in the America of these Founding Fathers.

Bailyn says:

> Everyone knew the basic prescription for a wise and just government. It was so to balance the contending powers in society that no one power could overwhelm the others and, unchecked, destroy the liberties that belonged to all. The problem was how to arrange the institutions of government so that this balance could be achieved.

Were the Founding Fathers wise and just men trying to achieve a good balance? In fact, they did not want a balance, except one which kept things as they were, a balance among the dominant forces at that time. They certainly did not want an equal balance between slaves and masters, propertyless and property holders, Indians and white.

As many as half the people were not even considered by the Founding Fathers as among Bailyn's "contending powers" in society. They were not mentioned in the Declaration of Independence, they were absent in the Constitution, they were invisible in the new political democracy. They were the women of early America.

POSTSCRIPT

Were the Founding Fathers Democratic Reformers?

Roche stresses the political reasons for writing a new Constitution. In a spirited essay that reflects great admiration for the Founding Fathers as enlightened politicians, Roche describes the Constitution as "a triumph of architectonic genius; it was a patch-work sewn together under the pressure of both time and events by a group of extremely talented democratic politicians."

Roche narrates the events of the convention of 1787 with a clarity rarely seen in the writings on this period. He makes the telling point that once the dissenters left Philadelphia, the delegates were able to hammer out a new Constitution. All the Founding Fathers agreed to create a stronger national government, but differences centered around the shape the new government would take. The delegates' major concern was to create as strong a national government as possible that would be acceptable to all the states. Had the ratifying conventions rejected the new Constitution, the United States might have disintegrated into 13 separate countries.

An avowed Marxist and radical leftist, Howard Zinn is a political activist who served in a bombing squadron in the Army Air Corps in World War II, was an early member of the Student Non-Violent Coordinating Committee (SNCC), which was the most vocal civil rights group in the 1960s, and a staunch peace activist against our wars in Vietnam, Central America, and the Middle East. He believes that history should be studied and written primarily for the purpose of eliminating America's violent past and moving it in a more peaceful, equitable direction.

Zinn's *A People's History of the United States* (Harper Collins, 1999) has sold over a million copies since it was first published in 1980. His critique of the Founding Fathers draws upon the scholarship of Charles Beard's *An Economic Interpretation of the Constitution* (Free Press, 1913, 1986), which argued that the Founding Fathers were primarily interested in protecting their property rights. He believes that Shay's Rebellion, an uprising of western Massachusetts farmers who were unable to pay their taxes to the Massachusetts government, was the catalyst that inspired the men at Philadelphia in 1787 to write a new constitution. He quotes from James Madison's *Federalist Paper #10* that it will be easier to keep order in a large nation of 13 states where minority factions could be controlled by a vote of the majority. He admits that one-third of the population were small farmers, "a considerable number of people who felt that they had something at stake in the new society."

Zinn believes that there were structural difficulties with the Constitution. For example, representative government was designed to prevent tumultuous change and therefore was inherently conservative. He also argues that the major problem in American society—the division into rich and poor—transcended constitutional problems.

How does Zinn explain the support for the new government if it favored the well-to-do? "The Constitution," he says, "illustrates the complexity of the American system; that it serves the interests of a wealthy elite, but also does enough for small property owners, for middle-income mechanics and farmers, to build a broad base of support. The slightly prosperous people who make up this base of support are buffers against the blacks, the Indians, the very poor whites. They enable the elite to keep control with a minimum of coercion, a maximum of law—all made palatable by the fanfare of patriotism and unity."

The enlightened statemen's views reasserted itself during the cold war in the 1950s and 1960s with the methodological critiques of Charles Beard's *An Economic Interpretation of the Constitution* (Macmillan, 1913) by Robert E. Brown, *Charles Beard and the Constitution* (Princeton University Press, 1956) and Forrest McDonald's many works, the earliest *We the People* (University of Chicago Press, 1958), which argued that numerous interest groups in the states ratified the Constitution for a variety of political and economic reasons. The best summary of this scholarship is the widely reprinted article by Stanley Elkins and Eric McKitrick, "The Founding Fathers: Young Men of the Revolution," in Jack P. Greene, ed., *The Reinterpretation of the American Revolution 1763–1789* (Harper & Row, 1968), pp. 378–395, which argues that the Federalists were broad-minded nationalists and the less organized anti-Federalists were small-minded localists, an interpretation influenced by Cecilia Kenyon, "Men of Little Faith: the Anti-Federalists on the Nature of Representative Government," *William and Mary Quarterly* 12 (1955), pp. 3–43.

Historian Gordon S. Wood changed the focus of the debate by trying to recapture the conflicting views of politics in the eighteenth century in *The Creation of the American Republic, 1776–1787* (University of North Carolina Press, 1969), a seminal work that has replaced Beard as the starting point for scholarship on this topic. A devastating critique of the methodological fallacies of Wood and other intellectual writers on this period can be found in Ralph Lerner's "The Constitution of the Thinking Revolutionary," in Richard Beeman et al., eds., *Beyond Confederation: Origins of the Constitution and American National Identity* (University of North Carolina Press, 1987). See other essays in *Beyond Confederation* including Wood's response, "Interests and Disinterestedness in the Making of the Constitution," pp. 69–109. The bicentennial produced an explosion of scholarship by historians and law professors. For overviews, see Peter S. Onof, "Reflections on the Founding: Constitutional Historiography in Bicentennial Perspective," *William and Mary Quarterly*, 30 Ser., XLVI (1989), pp. 341–375), and Richard D. Bernstein, "Charting the Bicentennial," *Columbia Law Review*, LXXXVII (1987), 1565–1624.

In recent years the anti-Federalists have received positive evaluations from both conservatives and leftists who reject the excessive accumulation of power by the national government. See conservative Herbert J. Storing, *What the Anti-Federalists Were For* (University of Chicago Press, 1981), an influential effort to analyze anti-Federalist ideas and Alfred F. Young, "The Framers of the

Constitution and the 'Genius' of the People," *Radical History Review* (Vol. 42, 1988). Earlier, Jackson Turner Main revived the Beardian conflict interpretations between agrarian localists and cosmopolitan elitists in "The Anti-Federalists," *Critics of the Constitution, 1781–1788* (University of North Carolina Press, 1961), which has been superseded by Saul Cornell, *The Other Founders: Anti-Federalism and the Dissenting Tradition in America, 1788–1828* (University of North Carolina Press, 1999), a sympathetic and comprehensive analysis buttressed by research into the primary writings and secondary accounts of the anti-Federalists critically evaluated by the author.

Readers can gain a sense of the debates over ratification of the Constitution by reading some of the original texts. Two of the most convenient anthologies are Michael Kammen, ed., *The Origins of the American Constitution: A Documentary History* (New York, 1986) and Bernard Bailyn, ed., *The Debate on the Constitution,* 2 vols. (New York, 1993).

ISSUE 7

Was Alexander Hamilton an Economic Genius?

YES: John Steele Gordon, from *An Empire of Wealth: The Epic History of American Economic Power* (Harper Collins, 2004)

NO: Carey Roberts, from "Alexander Hamilton and the 1790s Economy: A Reappraisal," in Douglas Ambrose and Robert W. T. Martin, eds., *The Many Faces of Alexander Hamilton: The Life and Legacy of America's Most Elusive Founding Father* (New York University Press, 2006)

ISSUE SUMMARY

YES: Historian John Steele Gordon claims that Hamilton's policies for funding and assuming the debts of the confederation and state governments and for establishing a privately controlled Bank of the United States laid the foundation for the rich and powerful national economy we enjoy today.

NO: Professor Carey Roberts argues that in the 1790s Hamilton's financial policies undermined popular faith in the Federalist Party, diminished confidence in the federal government.

Alexander Hamilton remains the most enigmatic, elusive, and highly criticized of the group we call "the founding fathers." When contrasted with Jefferson, Hamilton comes off second best as arrogant, crude, and manipulative, an embezzler who was worst of all a "crypto-monarchist." Yet nationally syndicated conservative columnist George Will astutely observes: "There is an elegant memorial in Washington to Jefferson, but none to Hamilton. However, if you seek Hamilton's monument, look around. You are living in it. We honor Jefferson but live in Hamilton's country."

Hamilton grew up in very humble circumstances. Born out of wedlock in the West Indies in 1755, Hamilton was abandoned by his father at age 9, orphaned by the death of his mother at age 13, and left penniless. He and his older brother were assigned by the courts to live with a cousin who committed suicide less than a year after he had taken in the boys.

In spite of such a volatile childhood that limited his formal schooling, Hamilton was a voracious reader who taught himself French and became skilled in mathematics and economics. As a sixteen-year-old, he was employed as a clerk in the firm of Beckman and Cruger. But it was Hugh Knox, a Presbyterian minister, who recognized Hamilton's talents and changed his life forever when he collected funds to send him to the mainland for an education.

Hamilton was not only talented but also very ambitious. Washington appointed Hamilton his aide-de-camp and promoted him to the rank of lieutenant-colonel in the Continental army. He served with the general at key battles including the near disaster at Valley Forge.

Hamilton's military experiences with the financially starved Continental army, along with his service as a delegate from New York in the Confederation Congress, turned him into a staunch nationalist. He attended the Annapolis convention in 1786 to discuss the problems of interstate commerce under the Articles of Confederation, but when so few delegates showed up, he introduced a resolution for a meeting at Philadelphia the following year.

At the Constitutional Convention of 1787, Hamilton's proposal to model the new government after the British system with lifetime appointments for the president, Supreme Court, and Senate met with strong hostility. His two fellow New York delegates were even opposed to the government supported by the majority of the delegates. "But Hamilton was instrumental in convincing a hostile New York Convention to support the Constitution." *The Federalist Papers* were published in book form and became the bible of interpreting the Constitution.

The highpoint of Hamilton's career was his appointment as President George Washington's secretary of the treasury, where his proposals for funding the new government, assuming the debts of the states and establishing a Bank of the United States, created a political furor that is still being debated by historians today.

After his resignation from Washington's cabinet in 1795, Hamilton's advice was sought by Washington and he penned the president's famous farewell address. Though out of office, he dominated the cabinet of his opponent, President John Adams, but lost influence after his Federalist Party was thrown out of office. In the election of 1800, he supported Jefferson over Burr when a tie resulted in the electoral-college vote. When Hamilton labeled Burr "a dangerous man who ought not to be trusted with the reigns of government" and cost him the gubernatorial election in New York in 1804, Burr challenged Hamilton to a duel. Hamilton accepted and was mortally wounded on a field on July 11, 1804. He died a day later, bidding farewell to his wife and children.

Was Hamilton an economic genius or was he overrated in terms of his influence of the future American economy? In the first essay, historian John Steele Gordon believes that Hamilton's policies for funding and assuming the debts of the confederation and state governments, and for establishing a privately controlled Bank of the United States laid the foundation for the rich and powerful national economy we enjoy today. But Professor Carey Roberts disagrees. He argues that in the context of the 1790s, Hamilton's financial policies were politically unpopular and helped undermine popular faith in the Federalist Party. Such policies also diminished confidence in the federal government because of the increasing tax burden necessary to fund the full debt and enabled some people to increase their own wealth through political influence.

YES 

John Steele Gordon

The Hamiltonian Creation

The importance that the Washington administration, which took office on April 30, 1789, placed on dealing with the financial situation confronting the government under the new Constitution can be judged by the numbers. While the newly created State Department had five employees, the Treasury had forty.

The tasks before the Treasury were monumental. A tax system had to be created out of whole cloth and put in place. The debt left over from the Revolution had to be rationalized and funded. The customs had to be organized to collect the duties that would be the government's main source of revenue for more than a century. The public credit had to be established so that the federal government could borrow when necessary. A monetary system had to be implemented.

The last already existed, at least in theory, established by Congress under the Articles of Confederation. In what was to be his only positive contribution to the financial system of the United States, it had been devised by Thomas Jefferson.

[B]efore the Revolution, the merchants of the various colonies had kept their books in pounds, shillings, and pence, but the money in actual circulation was almost everything *but* pounds, shillings, and pence. The question of what new unit of account to adopt was nearly as complex, because the inhabitants of the various colonies "thought" in terms of so many different, often incommensurate units.

Robert Morris, who had done so much to keep the Revolution financially afloat, tried to bridge the differences by finding the lowest common divisor of the most often encountered monetary unit of each state. He calculated this to be 1,440th of a Spanish dollar. Jefferson thought this far too infinitesimal to be practical, and Morris agreed. He proposed that his unit be multiplied by one thousand and made equal to 25/36ths of a dollar. Jefferson argued instead for just using the dollar, already familiar throughout the United States, as the new monetary unit.

The origin of the word *dollar* lies in the German word for valley, *Thal*. In the fifteenth century major silver deposits had been discovered in Bohemia, in what is now the Czech Republic. In 1519 the owner of mines near the town of Joachimsthal, the Graf zu Passaun und Weisskirchen, began minting silver coins that weighed a Saxon ounce and were called thalers, literally "from the valley." These coins, new and pure, met with great acceptance from merchants, and other rulers in the Holy Roman Empire began to imitate them with their own coinage.

The Holy Roman Emperor, the Hapsburg Charles V, also adopted the thaler as the standard for his own coinage in both his Austrian and Spanish lands and his new-won, silver-rich empire in the New World. The staggering amounts of gold and silver mined in Spanish America in the sixteenth and seventeenth centuries (just between 1580 and 1626, more than eleven thousand tons of gold and silver were exported to Spain from the New World) made the thaler the standard unit of international trade for centuries. *Thaler* became *dollar* in the English language, much as *Thal*, centuries earlier, had become *dale* and *dell*. It also became the most common major coin in the British North American colonies.

Jefferson, in his "Notes on the Establishment of a Money Unit, and of a Coinage for the United States," advocated not only using the dollar but making smaller units decimal fractions of the dollar. Today this seems obvious. After all, every country in the world now has a decimal monetary system, and as Jefferson himself explained, "in all cases where we are free to choose between easy and difficult modes of operation, it is most rational to choose the easy." But Thomas Jefferson was the first to advocate such a system, and the United States, in 1786, was the first country in the world to adopt one.

Spanish dollars had often been clipped into halves, quarters, and eighths, called bits, to make small change (which is why they were often called "pieces of eight"). But Jefferson advocated coinage of a half dollar, a fifth, a tenth (for which he coined the word *dime*), a twentieth, and a hundredth of a dollar (for which he borrowed the word *cent* from Robert Morris's scheme). In 1785 Congress declared that the "monetary unit of the United States of America be one dollar." But the next year Congress, while adopting the cent, five-cent, dime, and fifty-cent coins advocated by Jefferson, decided to authorize a quarter-dollar coin rather than a twenty-cent piece.

The quarter is with us yet, now the last, distant echo of the old octal monetary system of colonial days. But other echoes held on for decades. The New York Stock Exchange still gave prices in eighths of a dollar as late as 1999. And the term *shilling* long remained in common use to mean twelve and a half cents, an eighth of a dollar, although there has never been a United States coin in that denomination. The east side of Broadway, in New York, where the less fashionable stores were located, was still called the "shilling side" as late as the 1850s, while the west side of the street was called the "dollar side."

One reason the term *shilling* held on so long, of course, was that American coinage was not adequate to the ever-growing demand for it and the old hodgepodge of foreign coins thus held on as well. The first United States coin, a copper cent bearing the brisk motto "Mind Your Business," was privately minted. The Philadelphia mint was established in 1792 but minted few coins in the early years for lack of metal with which to do so.

Robert Morris, bent on making money, turned down Washington's offer to name him as secretary of the treasury in the new government (it was a bad decision—he ended up in debtors' prison). The president then turned to one of his aides-de-camp during the Revolution, Alexander Hamilton, only in his early thirties.

Hamilton was the only one of the Founding Fathers not to be born in what is now the United States. He was born in Nevis, one of Britain's less important Leeward Island possessions. He was also the only one—besides Benjamin Franklin, who had made a large fortune on his own and an even larger reputation—not to be born to affluence. Indeed, he grew up in poverty after his feckless father—who had never married his mother—deserted the family when Hamilton was only a boy.

Living in St. Croix, now part of the U.S. Virgin Islands but then a possession of Denmark, Hamilton went to work at a trading house owned by the New York merchants Nicholas Cruger and David Beekman, when he was eleven years old. Extraordinarily competent and ferociously ambitious, Hamilton was managing the place by the time he was in his mid-teens, quite literally growing up in a counting house. Thus, of all the Founding Fathers, only Franklin had so urban and commercial a background. Even John Adams, a lawyer by profession, considered his family farm in Braintree (now Quincy), Massachusetts, to be home, not Boston.

Cruger, recognizing Hamilton's talents, helped him come to New York in 1772 and to attend King's College, now Columbia University. After the Revolution he studied law and began practicing in New York City, where he married Elizabeth Schuyler, from one of New York's most prominent families. After the Revolution he wrote a series of newspaper articles and pamphlets outlining his ideas of what was needed to create an effective federal government. In 1784 he founded the Bank of New York, the first bank in that city and the second in the country.

He attended the Constitutional Convention in Philadelphia and worked tirelessly to get the document ratified, writing two-thirds of *The Federalist Papers*. When Robert Morris took himself out of consideration, Hamilton, whom Morris called "damned sharp," was more than happy to take the job of secretary of the treasury.

He was also one of the very few competent to do so. While Americans had already distinguished themselves in many fields of endeavor, they "were not well acquainted with the most abstruse science in the world [public finance], which they never had any necessity to study."

Hamilton, a deep student of economics, understood public finance thoroughly, a fact that he would make dazzlingly clear in the next few years. But like so many of the Founding Fathers, he was also a deep student of human nature and knew that there was no more powerful motivator in the human universe than self-interest. He sought to establish a system that would both channel the individual pursuit of self-interest into developing the American economy and protect that economy from the follies that untrammeled self-interest always leads to.

Even before the Treasury Department was created on September 2, 1789, and Hamilton was confirmed by the Senate as its first secretary on September 11, Congress had passed a tax bill to give the new government the funds it needed to pay its bills. There was no argument that the main source of income was to be the tariff, but there was lengthy debate over what imports should be taxed and at what rate. Pennsylvania had had a high tariff under the old Articles to protect its nascent iron industry and wanted it maintained. The southern states, importers of iron products such as nails and hinges, wanted a low tariff on iron goods or none at all. New England rum distillers wanted a low tariff on its imports of molasses. Whiskey manufacturers in Pennsylvania and elsewhere wanted a high tariff on molasses, to stifle their main competition.

Congress finally passed the Tariff and Tonnage Acts (the latter imposed a duty of 6 cents a ton on American ships entering U.S. ports and 50 cents a ton on foreign vessels) in the summer of 1789. But, second only to slavery, the tariff would be the most contentious issue in Congress for the next hundred years. Pierce Butler of South Carolina even issued the first secession threat before the Tariff Act of 1789 made it through Congress.

With funding in place, Hamilton's most pressing problem was to deal with the federal debt. The Constitution commanded that the new federal government should assume the debts of the old one, but how that should be done was a fiercely debated question. Much of the debt had fallen into the hands of speculators who had bought it for as little as 10 percent of its face value.

On January 14, 1790, Hamilton submitted to Congress his first "Report on the Public Credit." It called for redeeming the old debt on generous terms and issuing new bonds to pay for it, backed by the revenue from the tariff. The report became public knowledge in New York City, the temporary capital, immediately, but news of it spread only slowly to other parts of the country, and New York speculators were able to snap up large quantities of the old debt at prices far below what Hamilton proposed redeeming it for.

Many were outraged that speculators should profit while those who had taken the debt at far higher prices during the Revolution should not see their money again. James Madison argued that only the original holders should have their paper redeemed at the full price and the speculators get only what they had paid for it. But this was hopelessly impractical. For one thing, determining who was the original holder would have often been impossible.

Even more important, such a move would have greatly impaired the credit of the government in the future. If the government could decide to whom along the chain of holders it owed past debts, people would be more reluctant to take future debt, and the price in terms of the interest rate demanded, therefore, would be higher. And Hamilton was anxious to establish a secure and well-funded national debt, modeled on that of Great Britain and for precisely the purposes that Great Britain had used its debt.

Many of those in the new government, unversed in public finance, did not grasp the power of a national debt, properly funded and serviced, to add to a nation's prosperity. But Hamilton grasped it fully. One of the greatest problems facing the American economy at the start of the 1790s was the lack of liquid capital, capital available for investment. Hamilton wanted to use the national debt to create a larger and more flexible money supply. Banks holding government bonds could issue banknotes backed by them. And government bonds could serve as collateral for bank loans, multiplying the available capital. He also knew they would attract still more capital from Europe.

Hamilton's program eventually passed Congress, although not without a great deal of rhetoric. Hamilton's father-in-law, a senator from New York in the new Congress, was a holder of $60,000 worth of government securities he hoped would be redeemed by Hamilton's program. It was said the opposition to the program made his hair stand "on end as if the Indians had fired at him."

Hamilton also wanted the federal government to assume the debts that had been incurred by the various states in fighting the Revolution. His main reason for doing so was to help cement the Union. Most of the state debt was held by wealthy citizens of those states. If they had a large part of their assets in federal bonds, instead of state bonds, they would be that much more interested in seeing that the Union as a whole prospered.

Those states, mostly northern, that still had substantial debt were, of course, all for Hamilton's proposal. Those that had paid off their debts were just as naturally against it. Jefferson and Madison—Virginia had paid off its debts—were adamantly opposed and had enough votes to defeat the measure. Hamilton offered a deal.

If enough votes were switched to pass his assumption bill, he would see that the new capital was located in the South. To assure Pennsylvania's cooperation, the capital would be moved from New York to Philadelphia for ten years while the new one was built. Jefferson and Madison agreed. Hamilton's program passed and was signed into law by President Washington, who was delighted at the prospect of the new capital being located on his beloved Potomac River.

The program was an immediate success, and the new bonds sold out within a few weeks. When it was clear that the revenue stream from the tariff was more than adequate to service the new debt, the bonds became sought after in Europe. In 1789 the United States had been a financial basket case, its obligations unsalable, it ability to borrow nil. By 1794 it had the highest credit rating in Europe, and some of its bonds were selling at 10 percent over par.

Talleyrand, the future French foreign minister, then in the United States to escape the Terror, explained why. The bonds, he said, were "safe and free from reverses. They have been funded in such a sound manner and the prosperity of this country is growing so rapidly that there can be no doubt of their solvency."

Talleyrand might have added that the willingness of the new federal government to take on the debt of the old, rather than repudiate it for short-term fiscal reasons or political advantage, also helped powerfully to gain the trust of investors. The ability of the federal government to borrow huge sums at affordable rates in times of emergency—such as during the Civil War and the Great Depression—has been an immense national asset. In large measure, we owe that ability to Alexander Hamilton's policies that were put in place at the dawn of the Republic. It is no small legacy.

To be sure, Hamilton, and the United States, had the good fortune to have a major European war break out in 1793, after Louis XVI was guillotined. This proved a bonanza for American foreign trade and for American shipping, which was protected from privateers by the country's neutrality. European demand for American foodstuffs and raw materials greatly increased, and the federal government's tariff revenues increased proportionately. In 1790 the

United States exported $19,666,000 worth of goods, while imports not reexported amounted to $22,461,000. By 1807 exports were $48,700,000 and imports $78,856,000. Government revenues that year were well over five times what they had been seventeen years earlier.

The other major part of Hamilton's fiscal policy was the establishment of a central bank, to be called the Bank of the United States and modeled on the Bank of England.

Hamilton expected a central bank to carry out three functions. First, it would act as a depository for government funds and facilitate the transfer of them from one part of the country to another. This was a major consideration in the primitive conditions of the young United States. Second, it would be a source of loans to the federal government and to other banks. And third, it would regulate the money supply by disciplining state-chartered banks.

The money supply was a critical problem at the time. Specie—gold and silver coins—was in very short supply. In 1790 there were only three state-chartered banks empowered to issue paper money, including Hamilton's Bank of New York, but these notes had only local circulation. Hamilton reasoned that if the Bank of the United States accepted these local notes at par, other banks would too, greatly increasing the area in which they would circulate. And if the BUS refused the notes of a particular bank, because of irregularities or excess money creation, other banks would refuse them as well, helping to keep the state banks on the straight and narrow.

Hamilton had learned not to like the idea of the government itself issuing paper money, knowing that in times of need the government would be unable to resist the temptation to solve its money problems by simply printing it. Certainly the Continental Congress had shown no restraint during the Revolution, but at least it had had the excuse of no alternative. And the history of paper money since Hamilton's day has shown him to be correct. Without exception, wherever politicians have possessed the power to print money, they have abused it, at great cost to the economic health of the country in question.

Hamilton proposed a bank with a capitalization of $10 million. That was a very large sum when one considers that the three state banks in existence had a combined capitalization of only $2 million. The government would hold 20 percent of the stock of the bank and have 20 percent of the seats on the board. The secretary of the treasury would have the right to inspect its books at any time. But the rest of the bank's stock would be privately held.

"To attach full confidence to an institution of this nature," Hamilton wrote in his "Report on a National Bank," delivered to Congress on December 14, 1790, "it appears to be an essential ingredient in its structure, that it shall be under a *private* not a *public* direction—under the guidance of *individual interest,* not of *public policy;* which would be supposed to be, and, in certain emergencies, under a feeble or too sanguine administration, would really be, liable to being too much influenced by *public necessity.*"

The bill passed Congress with little trouble, both houses splitting along sectional lines. Only one congressman from states north of Maryland voted against it and only three congressmen from states south of Maryland voted for it. Hamilton thought the deal was done.

But he had not counted on Thomas Jefferson, by now secretary of state, and James Madison, who then sat in the House of Representatives. Although Jefferson had personally enjoyed to the hilt the manifold pleasures of Paris while he had served as minister to Louis XVI under the old Articles of Confederation, nonetheless he had a deep political aversion to cities and to the commerce that thrives in them.

Nothing symbolized the vulgar, urban moneygrubbing he so despised as banks. "I have ever been the enemy of banks . . ." he wrote to John Adams in old age. "My zeal against those institutions was so warm and open at the establishment of the Bank of the U.S. that I was derided as a Maniac by the tribe of bank-mongers, who were seeking to filch from the public their swindling, and barren gains."

Jefferson, born one of the richest men in the American colonies—on his father's death he inherited more than five thousand acres of land and three hundred slaves—spent money all his life with a lordly disdain for whether he actually had any to spend. He died, as a result, deeply in debt, bankrupt in all but name. And regardless of his own aristocratic lifestyle, his vision of the future of America was a land of self-sufficient yeoman farmers, a rural utopia that had never really existed and would be utterly at odds with the American economy as it actually developed in the industrial age then just coming into being.

Jefferson and his allies Madison and Edmund Randolph, the attorney general, fought Hamilton's bank tooth and nail. They wrote opinions for President Washington saying that the bank was unconstitutional. Their arguments revolved around the so-called necessary and proper clause of the Constitution, giving Congress the power to pass laws "necessary and proper for carrying into Execution the foregoing Powers."

As the Constitution nowhere explicitly grants Congress the power to establish a bank, they argued, only if one were absolutely necessary could Congress do so. This "strict construction" of the Constitution has been part of the warp and woof of American politics ever since, although even Jefferson admitted that it appealed mostly to those out of power. The fact that the Constitution nowhere mentions the acquisition of land from a foreign state did not stop Jefferson, as president, from snatching the Louisiana Purchase when the opportunity presented itself.

Hamilton countered with a doctrine of "implied powers." He argued that if the federal government were to deal successfully with its enumerated duties, it must be supreme in deciding how to do so. "Little less than a prohibitory clause," he wrote to Washington, "can destroy the strong presumptions which result from the general aspect of the government. Nothing but demonstration should exclude the idea that the power exists." Further, he asserted that Congress had the right to decide what means were necessary and proper. "The national government like every other," he wrote, "must judge in the first instance of the proper exercise of its powers." Washington, his doubts quieted, signed the bill.

The sale of stock was a resounding success, as investors expected that the bank would prove very profitable, which it was. It also functioned exactly as Hamilton thought it would. The three state banks in existence in 1790 became twenty-nine by the turn of the century, and the United States enjoyed a more reliable money supply than most nations in Europe.

With the success of the Bank of the United States stock offering, the nascent securities markets in New York and Philadelphia had their first bull markets, in bank stocks. Philadelphia, the leading financial market in the country at that time, thanks to the location there of the headquarters of the Bank of the United States, established a real stock exchange in 1792. In New York a group of twenty-one individual brokers and three firms signed an agreement—called the Buttonwood Agreement because it was, at least according to tradition, signed beneath a buttonwood tree (today more commonly called a sycamore) outside 68 Wall Street. In it they pledged "ourselves to each other, that we will not buy or sell from this day for any person whatsoever any kind of Public Stock, at a less rate than one quarter per cent Commission on the specie value, and that we will give preference to each other in our negotiations."

The new group formed by the brokers was far more a combination in restraint of trade and price-fixing scheme than a formal organization, but it proved to be a precursor of what today is called the New York Stock Exchange.

A speculative bubble arose in New York, centered on the stock of the Bank of New York. Rumors abounded that it would be bought by the new Bank of the United States and converted to its New York branch. Numerous other banks were announced and their stock, or, often, rights to buy the stock when offered, was snapped up. The Tammany Bank announced a stock offering of 4,000 shares and received subscriptions for no fewer than 21,740 shares.

An unscrupulous speculator named William Duer was at the center of this frenzy in bank stocks. He had worked, briefly, for the Treasury, but had resigned rather than obey the rule Hamilton had put in place for bidding Treasury officials from speculating in Treasury securities. Hamilton was appalled by what was happening on Wall street. "'Tis time," he wrote on March 2, 1792, "there should be a line of separation between honest Men & knaves, between respectable Stockholders and dealers in the funds, and mere unprincipled Gamblers."

It didn't take long for Duer's complex schemes to fall apart, and he was clapped into debtors prison, from which he would not energe alive. Panic swept Wall street for the first time, and the next day twenty-five failures were reported in New York's still tiny financial community, including one of the mighty Livingston clan.

Jefferson was delighted with this turn of events. "At length," he wrote a friend, "our paper bubble is burst. The failure of Duer in New York soon brought on others, and these still more, like nine pins knocking down one another." Jefferson, who loved to calculate things, estimated the total losses at $5 million, which he thought was about the total value of all New York real estate at the time. Thus, Jefferson gleefully wrote, the panic was the same as though some natural calamity had destroyed the city.

In fact, the situation was not nearly that dire, especially as Hamilton moved swiftly to stabilize the market and ensure that the panic did not bring down basically sound institutions. He ordered the Treasury to buy its own securities to support the market, and he added further liquidity by allowing customs duties—ordinarily payable only in specie or Bank of the United States banknotes—to be paid with notes maturing in forty-five days.

The system Hamilton had envisioned and put in place over increasing opposition from Thomas Jefferson and his political allies worked exactly as Hamilton had intended. Several speculators were wiped out, but they had been playing the game with their eyes open and had no one to blame but themselves. The nascent financial institutions, however, survived. "No calamity truly *public* can happen," Hamilton wrote, "while these institutions remain sound." The panic soon passed and most brokers were able to get back on their feet quickly, thanks to Hamilton's swift action.

Unfortunately, Thomas Jefferson was a better politician than Hamilton, and a far better hater. The success of the Bank of the United States and its obvious institutional utility for both the economy and the smooth running of the government did not cause him to change his mind at all about banks. He loathed them all. The party forming around Thomas Jefferson would seize the reins of power in the election of 1800 and would not lose them for more than a generation. In that time, they would destroy Hamilton's financial regulatory system and would replace it with nothing.

As a result, the American economy, while it would grow at an astonishing rate, would be the most volatile in the Western world, subject to an unending cycle of boom and bust whose amplitude far exceeded the normal ups and downs of the business cycle. American monetary authorities would not—indeed could not—intervene decisively to abort a market panic before it spiraled out of control for another 195 years.

Thomas Jefferson, one of the most brilliant men who has ever lived, was psychologically unable to incorporate the need for a mechanism to regulate the emerging banking system or, indeed, banks at all, into his political philosophy. His legion of admirers, most of them far less intelligent than he, followed his philosophy for generations as the country and the world changed beyond recognition. As a direct result, economic disaster would be visited on the United States roughly every twenty years for more than a century.

Carey Roberts

NO

Alexander Hamilton and the 1790s Economy: A Reappraisal

Historians and political scientists commonly credit Alexander Hamilton's economic plans for revitalizing the American economy and providing the impetus for extended economic progress. Such arguments usually take for granted many of the criticisms levied against the policies of the states and Confederation during the 1780s. They further assume that the weakness of the American economy stemmed from the decentralized nature of its financial institutions, lack of specie, and burdensome problems of the Revolutionary debt.

There is little doubt that economic problems prevailed under the Articles of Confederation; however, it remains unclear how much Hamilton's policies corrected those problems. Hamilton's program of assumption and funding resulted in an overall increase in the nation's monetary base. The Bank of the United States (BUS) furthered the monetary expansion by following a pattern of fractional-reserve lending up until 1795. As a result, inflation continued to affect the economy during the early 1790s. Burdensome taxes were levied to pay off government debts at face value rather than at prevailing market values. And significant opposition formed against Federalist officials due to the perceived joining of monied interests to the federal government.

Without understanding the short-term consequences, our praise for the long-term results seems strained at best. If what is called "Hamiltonian" finance resulted in short-term problems, or even disasters, long-term success would be less likely. If long-term success could actually be attributed to Jeffersonian policies carried forward by Jacksonian Democrats, the place of Hamiltonian finance in our history would change drastically. Furthermore, even if it is determined that the American economy surged after 1791, attributing the rise to beneficial market conditions totally independent from federal politics could jeopardize Hamilton's place as a financial genius. Such is not the scope of this essay, nor is it a challenge to the dominant interpretation of Hamilton's character and financial vision. However, puzzling discrepancies present themselves when one compares the effects of the Federalist financial plan and its short-term consequences in the 1790s. Limitation of space prevents a full treatment of the period, but it is hoped that the following might serve as a prolegomena for further study.

From *The Many Faces of Alexander Hamilton: The Life and Legacy of America's Most Elusive Founding Father*, Douglas Ambrose and Robert W. T. Martin, eds. (New York University Press, 2006).

Economic Problems of the 1790s

The first decade under the new constitution was not a period of strong economic growth, nor was it free from periods of economic distress. Data are sketchy at best, and debate still rages as to whether the economy of antebellum America was rapidly expanding or mediocre. Likewise, we may never have a complete grasp on the economic condition for the period between 1789 and 1800, a problem further complicated by the loss of records, especially those of the BUS, during the War of 1812.

While the fine details of economic growth remain elusive, much can still be said about economic conditions both before and after Hamilton and Congress implemented Hamilton's plan for the national economy. A speculative crash occurred in New York City in 1792 and spread sporadically across the eastern seaboard. Steep inflation rates existed between 1791 and 1796. And while infrastructure investments bustled throughout the East and the developing West, their creation coincided with a rapid increase in bankruptcy and insolvency. Even at this early date, the cyclical activity of the American economy appeared in short booms and busts.

Several explanations could be offered for the development of an early boom-bust cycle. One might suggest business cycles are a natural element of capitalism, and as the economy modernized, cyclical fluctuations would be expected. Sheer greed on the part of speculators could have produced more services than consumers demanded, thus causing overproduction. The financial infrastructure may have remained too immature to adequately finance the needs of investors despite Hamilton's attempt to strengthen it. State governments may have improperly managed their economic situation either by refusing to cooperate with other states or by failing to sufficiently support newly chartered companies. Investors and promoters may have been unsuccessful in getting farmers and minor merchants to see how they could benefit from a vigorous—and united—national economy.

Another explanation for a business cycle emerging early in the 1790s suggests that far from stabilizing the economy, Hamilton and the Federalist Congress destabilized financial markets causing entrepreneurs to misread the market and make incorrect business decisions.

Many important entrepreneurs in the early republic also held most of the domestic debt. As the country's public credit rose, debt holders profited from debt redemption. The Bank of the United States added to the potential for increased investment by pursuing a policy of easy money until 1796. By receiving higher profits and easier credit than market conditions allowed, entrepreneurs took much greater risks with their subsequent investments. They also mistook the dramatic deflation of the late 1780s and the inflation of the early 1790s as evidence of a strengthening economy. Prices surged after ratification of the Constitution due to perceived political actions of Congress, not due to Americans being in a position to demand more goods and services. The resulting malinvestments in transportation improvements, banking, and manufacturing far exceeded market demand and resulted in the Panic of 1792 and would add to the distress in 1796. To complicate matters further, the Treasury, following Hamilton's "Report on the Mint," fixed the exchange rate of specie so that gold slightly overvalued silver. The decision instigated a classic example of Gresham's Law, where "bad" money chases out "good" money, and in this case, the country's gold supply was steadily depleted in favor of silver.

Debt Funding, Conversion, and the Bank of the United States

There is no need to regurgitate the intricacies of the financial program proposed by Alexander Hamilton while Secretary of Treasury. Yet misunderstanding Hamilton's goals and the monetary effects of his plans creates a distorted view of Hamilton's role. Hamilton was neither a defender of an aristocracy of wealth nor was he the architect of America's economic "take-off."

Alexander Hamilton laid clear plans as to what he wished to do with the Revolutionary debt. Though not a dedicated bullionist, like most economic nationalists of his day Hamilton believed the country's economic problems grew from a lack of sufficient specie in circulation. The underlying goal required augmenting existing specie by coverting federal and state government securities into a capital pool for financiers and entrepreneurs. Financiers, traders, merchants, manufacturers, and all other businessmen would benefit by having access to cheap credit while consumers would have sufficient currency with which to purchase products. Hamilton never questioned the federal government's role in providing specie, albeit to him, that role was supervisory rather than regulatory.

Hamilton publicly reasoned that the country's credit problems weakened the federal government's ability to get more specie. Low public credit also prevented private citizens from getting loans at reasonable interest rates. The economy needed a jump-start, but not by a direct infusion of specie. Entrepreneurs, who knew how to use capital to spur on economic growth, needed the specie before average citizens. Getting specie to entrepreneurs first (or at all) proved problematic given the immature state of the country's commercial credit system. Hamilton's solution involved bringing in enough specie and then using the federal government to provide a financial network to dispense capital where it was best used. The Revolutionary War debt offered the means of accomplishing both.

Influenced by the predominant view that the economy suffered from a shortage of specie, Hamilton assumed a new credit network needed something other than a finite amount of specie. To be feasible, it must grow with the needs of the people. A rigid specie standard and a credit market where all banknotes equaled specie reserves would be too tight. The best strategy must include a combination of specie, redeemable bank notes, and government securities, where all forms of money and money substitutes traded as currency. Hamilton envisioned nothing less than a sophisticated credit market that could aid investors and supply the country with much needed currency, or as he called it, "the active capital of a country."

Hamilton believed banks could issue more credit than they held in specie reserves as long as all notes were fully redeemable in specie on demand.

Like many advocates of commercial banking, Hamilton understood that a bank's depositors rarely demanded all their specie at once. At any given time, banks easily lent out more credit than they held on deposit. He did not understand, however, that the subsequent alteration in the overall purchasing power of money distorted rather than stabilized prices.

Three distinct but interrelated events came together between 1788 and 1791: funding the federal debt through the federal government, not the states; converting the old debt into new debt; and using the Bank of the United States to facilitate the acceptance of securities and bank notes as currency. Only Hamilton advocated all three from a position of high political office. Some congressmen supported him on this. But like many of the great compromises in American history, a majority probably did not exist in support of all three segments combined, only on each segment individually.

As the Philadelphia convention met and produced a new constitution, the market value of debt securities rose based on the expectation of payment. Never did the securities become worthless, but never did they actually reach par with their face value before conversion in 1790. Speculators stood to make impressive gains from buying the debt cheap in the early 1780s and selling high, as many did, in the late 1780s. Furthermore, those who kept their securities through the conversion process stood to gain even more. As late as 1789, confused debt holders did not know what to expect from Congress with regard to the debt. Their only anchor during the hectic first session of Congress was that most congressmen favored paying the debt in some manner.

Congressmen differed on whom to pay and how much. Many opponents of funding, James Madison and Thomas Jefferson excepted, knew the problem was not forsaking the initial common people and soldiers who held the debt. Rather, they saw the issue as a battle between market value on the one hand and a sizable expansion of credit, high taxation, and enlargement of the federal debt's market value, on the other. There were few if any true "repudiationists" in Congress at the time it debated funding.

Thanks to James Madison, the discrimination, or market value forces, lost. Madison, knowingly or not, sidetracked to opponents of face value funding on to questions of morality and social obligation as opposed to financial questions and taxation. By the end of the debate, discrimination meant giving original holders a portion of *face* value, illustrating how Hamilton's most vocal opponents moved toward the center. To make the opposition's position on discrimination less tenable, the difference between market value and face value shrank as the debate dragged on.

Indeed, talk of funding during the ratification process had already increased the market value of the debt and caused a wave of deflation to sweep the economy. Between 1787 and 1789 prices fell between 4 and 7 percent across the country. In Philadelphia alone, extending the dates from 1784 to 1790 shows a 20 percent deflation rate overall. By itself, deflation probably caused some market distortions, and regardless of which policy Congress followed, whether Hamilton's or an alternative, some malinvestments likely would have occurred.

Congress finally agreed to take specie from a new European loan and apply it to the national debt and the assumed value of state debts. Congress offered to exchange old securities for stock, substituting two-thirds of the principal for 6 percent stock and one-third for 6 percent deferred stock. It also paid all remaining interests and indents at 3 percent and old continental currency at 100: 1. The process of conversion both raised the market value of the debt by fully backing it with specie and turned it into usable currency. But conversion also reduced the new currency's purchasing power by infusing the economy with new specie and new notes whose value must have been slightly higher than the highest market value of old notes in the summer of 1790.

One would think conversion continued the process of deflation, but such was not the case since new notes were issued based on the face value of old notes. Because conversion exchanged notes rather than allowed the old ones to continue in circulation and because the federal government injected more notes than the total market value of the old notes, the overall supply of money increased. The resulting inflation appeared immediately as prices increased nationwide. Between 1791 and 1796, prices in Charleston increased 57 percent, Cincinnati grew by 38 percent, and Philadelphia prices rose an astonishing 98 percent. Additional foreign loans (of specie) and creating the Bank of the United States compounded the situation by further increasing the supply of specie *and* redeemable notes. Had Congress followed a policy of paying the old debt at market value, even market value over a period of months, Congress might have continued the deflation. Corresponding taxation may have softened the monetary expansion, but it was unlikely to significantly counteract its effects given the variety of products taxed and the variation of the tax burden.

It is important not to focus merely on general monetary phenomena, but to suggest monetary changes that affected individual entrepreneurs. One must be careful to keep in mind that holders of the debt purchased the bulk of it at prices far below what they were worth after 1790. Prices paid for the debt and the profits debt holders made did not reflect market demand for the debt so much as it reflected Congress's demand for its own debt. In other words, the American economy did not cause the price of securities to increase, Congress's decisions did. The subsequent rise in prices cannot be attributed to a rise in consumer spending, but to a drop in the purchasing power of government securities and BUS notes.

Far ahead of his time, Hamilton took possible inflation into account. In fact, he expected it and anticipated its effect on government securities in terms of bringing down the rate of interest. When Hamilton's proposal went to Congress, some congressmen wished to pay interest on the new stock at present rates of interest, or around 8 percent. But having more money and money substitutes available for banks to lend, the price of money dropped. Betting on interest rates to fall, Hamilton hoped to get debt holders to agree to 6 percent stock that would sell at a premium if interest rates dropped below 6 percent.

Beyond conversion and assumption, other aspects of Hamilton's plan exercised significant influence over prices. Hamilton hoped the Bank of the United States would create a commercial credit network, pool capital for investors, and strengthen the country's merchant base. But like funding and conversion, the Bank exercised an inflationary effect. It certainly increased available commercial credit to individual entrepreneurs as well as to new commercial banks chartered by various states. The bank and its branches fully redeemed its notes upon demand, but the banknotes were not fully backed by specie reserves, and notes circulated in a high proportion to specie in the vaults especially before 1796.

During the first years of the Bank's operation, it followed a course of fairly rapid credit expansion. The BUS played a substantial role in the Panic of 1792, and it may have accounted for some of the economic distress of the period up to 1796. Taking into account the Bank's proportion of notes to specie between 1792 and 1794, the Bank held about a 2:1 ratio. By January 1795, the ratio increased to 5:1 only to drop down slightly by the end of the year. The excess of fiduciary currency, or the notes issued in excess of specie reserves, likely contributed to the rise in prices from 1792 forward. New commercial banks, which pyramided their assets on top of BUS notes and stock, compounded the situation. Wisely, BUS officials changed course by late 1796, boosted their specie holdings, and the notes to specie ratio evened out to near equity by 1799–1800. Not coincidentally, 1796 marked a turning point where the Bank began loaning more capital to private investors than it did to the federal government.

Even assuming the BUS followed a conservative path, those banks whose capital came from BUS notes pursued a different course until competition from BUS branches intensified. Hamilton's consternation with state banks rested on their willingness to expand credit through fiduciary offerings at a much faster rate than the BUS. While some Federalists supported the coexistence of state banks with the Bank and its branches, Hamilton worried the inflationary tendency of the combined circulation of BUS notes and notes of state banks would wreck the fledgling commercial credit system. State banks, Hamilton thought, could not be trusted to control their credit emissions. Should the notes of state banks begin to depreciate, BUS notes might slip as well, thus jeopardizing the whole system. Hamilton must also have known other banks could curtail credit, making loans more expensive, thereby raising interest rates and detrimentally affecting the BUS.

Hamilton mistakenly saw credit as a means of stimulating investment and failed to recognize that demand for credit does not correlate to demand for the investments created with it. If credit expansion prompted investors to place that credit in things for which the economy was not strong enough to endure, then consumer demand would not be strong enough to make investments pan out. At least publicly, Hamilton insisted the opposite would occur. Investors, he claimed, would place their money in ventures sure to make a profit instead of "permanent" improvements like canals and manufacturing. Such was not the case.

A counterargument to the one given here might suggest that inflation is desirable and that deflation is to be avoided. Critics might also insist that the purpose of Hamiltonian finance, as he stated, was to raise the credit rating of the United States government and American businessmen seeking capital or credit from abroad, or to set better terms on foreign contracts. From this perspective, Hamilton was successful, thus contributing to the increase of foreign trade and the export-led expansion of the economy. If not this, then he helped lay the groundwork for institutions that used securities for a finance-led expansion of the economy.

Another way of examining Hamilton's contributions may be in order. Though many debt holders did quite well, many notable exceptions occurred that cannot be attributed to poor luck or lack of entrepreneurial wisdom. Instead, it seems that the inflationary tendencies of Hamiltonian finance produced faulty economic "signals" that misled entrepreneurs into thinking the economy was better than it actually was. Rather than analyzing what influence debt holders exerted over the formation of the new government and Hamilton's plan, a focus on how federal policies influenced their business practices reveals much about the effects of funding, conversion, and the First Bank. Such an approach would follow the one briefly outlined below concerning William Duer.

The Panic of the Early 1790s

The example of the much-maligned William Duer illustrates how economic repercussions from funding and assumption were far from positive. Duer was English by birth and, like Hamilton, spent time in the West Indies, though Duer did so only long enough to manage his father's plantation. Also like Hamilton, Duer settled in New York and married into a wealthy family. The wives of both men were even cousins. Duer briefly served in the Continental Congress but made a fortune fulfilling contracts with the Continental Army. Following the war, he speculated in real estate holdings and served on the Confederation's Treasury Board. He then became Assistant Secretary of Treasury under Hamilton in 1789 and assisted Hamilton in the creation of the Society of Useful Manufactures. Duer often used inside information to exploit the government securities market, but his misapplication—or corrupt application—of this information can account for most of his financial mistakes.

Duer lost with deflation leading up to debt conversion and with the subsequent inflation. Scholars rightly distance Hamilton from Duer with regard to their personal relationship. And Hamilton had no control over Duer's speculations. However, lack of personal involvement does not mean that repercussions from Hamilton's financial plan failed to influence Duer's decisions.

No doubt Duer's life followed that of a frontier gambler more than it did a New York aristocrat. Yet the most incredible of his speculative endeavors depended on specific actions of the federal government, either under the Articles of Confederation or under the Constitution. Two examples merit mentioning: his role in the Scioto land company and his direct influence over the Panic of 1792.

Following the Revolution, Americans started pushing the bounds of the western territory. Given the perceived shortage of specie, prospective land customers petitioned Congress in the late 1780s to accept debt certificates in the place of hard currency. Two companies led the way: the Ohio Company of Association and the Scioto Company. Duer participated in the creation of both since they were part of the same deal, though he directly influenced the Scioto Company. Land developers wished to use the companies to purchase land cheaply and sell it to needy settlers. When Congress agreed to accept specie *and* debt certificates as payment, Duer and his clients stood to make a substantial profit if the market value of the debt certificates remained low. In other words, they based their assessment of the situation on current prices in 1787 and did not expect the rapid rise in market value. In the end, the Scioto Company went broke due to mismanagement and the substantial increase of land costs as government debt values increased.

The Scioto example should not be used to discount Hamiltonian finance, which began operation after the Scioto Company became insolvent. It does, however, indicate how entrepreneurs based their decisions on the value of government securities and how changes in their value harmed some investors. Regardless of what Congress did, debt certificates would have fluctuated in value to some extent. In hindsight, Scioto investors should have known better. But how could they? There was no certainty in 1787 that Congress would even pay the national debt, and less certainty existed over whether Congress would pay the debt at face value.

Integral to Duer's association with the Scioto Company was his use of it to manage his personal speculation in government securities. In fact, the same forces that injured the land company encouraged Duer to try his hand at another form of speculation. While assistant to Hamilton, Duer counted on uncertainty about a new congressional policy: full funding of state debts. He busily purchased as much outstanding debt as possible before Congress reached a final decision in August 1790.

Afterwards, as interest rates dropped, new government debt traded at a premium. Additional stock and securities came onto the market as the Bank of the United States commenced business and supported the creation of new commercial banks. BUS shares, bank stocks, and new securities traded openly in major American cities, but no city contained as much speculative buying as New York. At the center of all this stood William Duer.

Duer participated in the selling of most forms of stocks and securities, and he worked both sides of the market. Able to control vast sums of capital, Duer bought and traded the same stock, virtually cornering the market and creating his own profits. Like other speculators in government securities, Duer commenced planning a number of important new companies ranging from banks and factories to bridges and canals. Thinking the market rise in securities knew no limit, Duer plunged everything he had into the market. He began buying on margin by taking out loans from all possible sources, including the fledgling Society for the Erection of Useful Manufacturers and wealthy New Yorkers. The activity of speculators, drawing on the extensive new credit system created by the Federalists under Alexander Hamilton, peaked in March 1792. When directors of the Bank of New York realized credit had been extended too much, their decision to stop all loans commenced a credit contraction spelling the end to William Duer's operation. By the end of March, the panic that began in New York became nationwide.

Ultimately, the federal government and Hamilton bore the greatest economic cost of the Panic of 1792. By late 1792 Hamilton and members of Congress realized projected revenue would not meet the government's demands for expenses and interest payments on the debt. The situation forced Hamilton to take out another foreign loan. The combination of economic distress and the apparent inability of the funding system and BUS to "fund" the debt without more loans elicited stern attacks from Hamilton's opponents in Congress. William B. Giles of Virginia, with the assistance of William Findley of Pennsylvania and Nathaniel Macon of North Carolina, pushed through a series of resolutions questioning Hamilton's leadership of the Treasury and accusing him of misallocation of funds.

The economy momentarily improved, but inflation rates continued to climb until 1796. At that point, the economy slipped back into a panic, albeit less severe than the one in 1792.

The question must be asked: Was William Duer representative of American entrepreneurs during the 1780s and 1790s? Certainly not, especially when considering that all American entrepreneurs did not speculate in government securities and lose all their investments in the Panic of 1792. However, Duer illustrates how expansive credit systems, like that proposed by Hamilton, cannot be sustained indefinitely and how credit booms mislead entrepreneurs and thus lay the groundwork for credit bursts. More importantly, if an insider like William Duer could not make good decisions based on the information at his disposal, how could average entrepreneurs?

Duer shows how politically generated conditions encourage speculative behavior. He based his decisions in part on the signals he received from the securities market—prices boosted by funding and assumption. And if Winifred Rothenberg is correct, debt holders were not the only people basing their decisions on market prices. Though Rothenberg's coverage covers mainly New England, it is safe to say that by the 1780s and 1790s an increasing number of Americans relied exclusively on market prices for economic decisions, prices made possible by moving away from bartering. A different policy, one that allowed for the gradual redemption of securities at market value, may have alleviated some of the extreme cases of speculation and price distortions.

Other speculators who benefited from funding and assumption followed a pattern similar to Duer's. Men like Robert Morris, Thomas Willing, James Greenleaf, Nathaniel Massie, and John Nicholson took profits made from government securities and invested them in projects the market could not sustain.

Land prices rose faster than any other investment in the inflationary climate of the early 1790s, leading numerous speculators to place investments on western expansion (or even on undeveloped land in the East). The Ohio Company, the North American Land Company, the Connecticut Land Company, and the Yazoo land claims, to name a few, began after investors wildly exaggerated the gains to be made in land development. One of the best examples fueled by inflating land prices, Washington, D.C., included several prominent debt holders like Uriah Forrest and Robert Morris, who plunged into an uncertain market and were financially ruined.

Investors thought higher land prices resulted from higher demand for property. When land prices began dropping, developers went to great lengths to get returns on their investments. William Blout, Nicholas Romayne, and John Chisholm went so far as inviting Great Britain to get Spanish holdings in North America.

The credit boom of the early 1790s also coincided with the expansion of internal improvement companies and commercial banks, whose capital was often pyramided on BUS funds, state subsidies, or mutual credit extensions. To help prospective settlers move west, or to link local eastern markets together, transportation companies quickly emerged with the assistance of state legislatures. The number of banks grew from one in 1790 to twenty in 1795. Thirty-two new navigation companies, including canals and waterways, were charted between 1790 and 1795. States granted twelve new charters in 1796, alone. Charters for bridges increased from one per year in 1791 to as many as fourteen per year in 1795, totaling forty-four between 1791 and 1796. And by 1796, there were sixteen new turnpike charters. Naturally, not all of these new companies relied on bank credit, nor did former debt holders promote them all by themselves. Some companies evolved from lucrative family holdings or from capital raised from investors. But even if some did not rely directly on credit expansion, their customers and investors often did.

New internal improvement companies faced obstacles similar to those encountered by land companies. Most investors wished to build improvements in order to expand their markets. They assumed that Federalist financial measures reinvigorated the economy and continued growth would offset the expense of linking markets together. In doing so, rural markets could be tapped to further commercial potential. Those relying exclusively on prices and available commercial credit, however, ignored the economy's weakness as well as latent hostility to their projects from farmers.

State laws required companies to have charters, which carried certain advantages such as monopoly status, state grants, and the ability to exercise eminent domain. However, charters also carried numerous restrictions that ultimately hindered profitability. And since companies often undermined the property rights of common people, rural farmers condemned the new companies for their special, political privileges. Like the land schemes, most internal improvement projects faced substantial losses. Promoters repeatedly returned to state legislatures for additional support only to be turned away by politicians weary of mounting demands and disillusioned with development schemes. In the end, national fiscal measures encouraged investment, whereas state and local policies were ignored only to the detriment of uncanny or misled investors.

Great wealth was made, as such prominent examples of John J. Astor and Stephen Girard show. But the 1790s were far from the boom time many speculators imagined. In fact, business failures, missed opportunities, and collapsed fortunes may have been the norm. Even wealth made in the decade later diminished as competition intensified and the monetary shocks wore off.

Detractors of this argument may be prepared to accept both the benefits and costs of this boom-bust cycle. The market would never have produced the transportation improvements so quickly. And in the long run, society still enjoys the fruits of the products such as better roads, canals, and a commercial banking network. All modernization efforts proceed along a bumpy path, but society ultimately benefits by laying the foundation for future stages of economic growth.

However, one must take into account that insolvent companies cannot maintain their investments. Bridges fell into disrepair, roads washed away, and canals remained unfinished. Above all, long-run benefits must take into account not only the material costs of malinvestments, but the social and political costs as well. The Federalist financial system did not solidify broad support for the federal government and Federalist Party. In fact, Hamilton's financial program failed to secure the continued support of the "monied" interests to which his opponents claimed he catered. No elite group of financiers found continued fortune at the hands of the Federalists.

Political Ramifications of Hamiltonian Finance and Federalist Policy

The political success of the Federalist Party depended upon the success of Alexander Hamilton and his financial policies. From the beginning, supporters of the Federalists counted on the new government to meet their financial interests. Three major political results proceeded from Federalist financial arrangements.

First, the economic malaise of the early 1790s undermined popular faith in the Federalist Party. As Albert Gallatin insisted in 1796, "Far from strengthening government," aspects of Hamiltonian finance "created more discontent and more uneasiness than any other measure." It is inconceivable to assume political and cultural differences alone could have instigated the first party system. It is true that issues like Jay's Treaty, for example, aggravated party feelings, as did the economic conditions of the late 1790s, for which Hamilton was not directly responsible. It is also true that the self-appointed leaders of the opposition, Madison and Jefferson, worked with Hamilton to pass key aspects of the Federalist program, including the BUS and assumption. Nevertheless, partisan attacks against Hamilton and the Federalists carried great weight as inflation intensified during the mid-1790s.

Second, confidence in the federal government shrank in light of the increasing tax burden to fund the full debt. Direct taxes, particularly that on liquor, provoked heated debate in Congress, which ultimately spilled over into the Whiskey Rebellion. However, direct taxes continued after Hamilton's departure from Philadelphia. Whether Fries's Rebellion or the Virginian assault on the carriage tax, animosities toward Federalist finance served as a conduit for even greater animosity toward the federal government.

Third, in a few cases, Hamiltonian finance enabled some people to aggrandize their wealth through political influence. John Beckley, James Monroe, and John Taylor attacked the Federalists early on for creating a privileged elite. They pointed to the large number of debt holders in Congress who passed the major elements of Hamilton's program as evidence of corruption. Examples of privilege enabled the Jeffersonians to adopt portions of the antiwealth rhetorical tradition of eighteenth-century England and extend it well into the nineteenth century.

The link between Hamiltonian finance and the business problems of the 1790s is not tenuous. Many investors profited handsomely from debt conversion and found additional resources available from new commercial banks. They had to put their new money somewhere, and, though risky, land companies and internal improvements seemed to offer the best returns. Here was the problem. Because of the new credit and steep profits from conversion, investors could afford to take advantage of pioneering companies, whereas those with limited funds were more careful with their investments. Not everyone lost, but overall, new investments in the 1790s offered disappointing results and intensified political conflict. By the late 1790s, when the Federalist leadership under John Adams began questioning financial incentives for business, or when Federalists in Congress could not pass bankruptcy protection for suffering ventures, those entrepreneurs most dependent on state aid migrated to the Republican Party.

Alexander Hamilton cannot be blamed for all of this. But the bulk of his defense of the Constitution implied that it protects and promotes the various interests of the country. Far from classical republicanism, Hamilton recognized that a government cannot deny the existence of different interest groups, nor can it seek to destroy those interests most people consider legitimate. Hoping to promote as many economic interests as possible, Hamilton constructed a financial plan from which as many people as possible got something. Entrepreneurs gained easy credit, debt holders received payment, assumption restored stability for debtor states, moral nationalists got taxes on whiskey, and politicians at least paid lip service to manufacturers and then promised farmers that grain exports would lift them to prosperity.

Entrepreneurs received mixed signals as new government securities and credit spread through the economy. The increased value of debt certificates, the lowering of interest rates, the ready availability of capital, and the expansion of banking reflected an artificial boom. The federal government was in no position to sustain the boom, and even if it were, the economy could not elevate consumer demand high enough to return investors' profits on their infrastructure improvements. At precisely the same time that Americans embraced a mature market system based on prices rather than barter, monetary shocks implemented by Alexander Hamilton and the Federalists rendered available prices insufficient to support entrepreneurial decisions.

POSTSCRIPT

Was Alexander Hamilton an Economic Genius?

Authors Gordon and Roberts are analyzing Hamilton's economic policies as secretary of the treasury from totally different perspectives. Gordon is sympathetic to the aims of Hamilton. As a staunch nationalist, Hamilton tried to establish the new nation on a firm credit basis. His funding and debt programs where the nation goes in debt to itself were designed to establish creditworthiness of the new nation in the eyes of its European trading partners. The assumption of state debts and the establishment of a Bank of the United States were also designed to increase the power of the national government over the states and to curb reckless spending. When such controls were loosened during the Jefferson and post-Jackson years when there was no strong national bank in operation, the establishment of the Federal Reserve System in 1913 was a testament to the legacy of Hamilton.

Carey Roberts is one of the few writers about Hamilton today who is critical of his economic policies. Roberts places Hamilton in the context of the political and economic environment of the 1790s. He argues, contrary to most writers, that Hamilton was concerned about the country's "lack of sufficient specie in circulation." In order to jump-start the economy, Hamilton reasoned that the specie needed to be funded to entrepreneurs and not the average citizen. The Bank of the United States was supposed to act as a check on bad investments, but in Roberts's view the Bank often encouraged reckless speculation on projects of dubious merit. His program often favored certain business interests and did little for the agricultural sector where the vast majority was employed. The resultant hostility towards Hamilton, brought on by both his arrogant attitude and unpopular fiscal program, was partially responsible for the defeat of the Federalist Party in the congressional and presidential elections of 1800.

There is some merit in both Gordon's and Roberts's assessments of Hamilton. Roberts examines in detail some of the land deals and speculations in government securities of the reckless William Duer, a former assistant secretary of the treasury under Hamilton. Gordon downplays the negative effects of Duer and others on the economy and argues that Hamilton had gotten rid of Duer who eventually died in debtors' prison and moved quickly "to stabilize the market and ensure that panic did not bring down basically sound institutions." Finally, Roberts underplays the importance of Hamilton's policies in improving foreign trade, though Gordon does admit that Hamilton and the nation had the good fortune to have a major European war break out in 1793 after Louis XVI, the king of France, lost his head.

The bibliography on Alexander Hamilton is enormous. For the best journal articles published between 1925 and 1966, see Jacob E. Cooke's *Alexander*

Hamilton: a Profile (Hill and Wang, 1967). The most recent interpretations can be found in Douglas Ambrose and Robert W. T. Martin, eds., *The Many Faces of Alexander Hamilton: the Life and Legacy of America's Most Elusive Founder* (New York University Press, 2006). The most recent and comprehensive biographies are Ron Chernow's prize-winning *Alexander Hamilton* (Penguin Press, 2004) with new information on his youth; Forrest McDonald, *Alexander Hamilton: A Biography* (W.W. Norton, 1979), which contains an excellent discussion on his career as secretary of the treasury; John C. Miller, *Alexander Hamilton: Portrait in Paradox* (Harper and Brothers, 1959); and Richard Brookhiser, *Alexander Hamilton: American* (Free Press, 1999).

Most of the recent biographies are sympathetic to the Hamilton view of the economy. See John Steele Gordon's *Hamilton's Blessing: the Extraordinary Life and Times of Our National Debt* (Walker, 1997). Stephen Knott's *Alexander Hamilton and the Persistence of Myth* (University of Kansas Press, 2002) and his article "The Hamiltonian Invention of Thomas Jefferson," in Ambrose and Martin, ed., *The Many Faces of Alexander Hamilton,* trace the changing positive and negative images of Hamilton via American historians and politicians since his death.

The first party system contains a voluminous secondary literature. Most comprehensive is Stanley Elkins and Eric McKitrick, *The Age of Federalism: the Early American Republic 1788–1800* (Oxford University Press, 1994); more readable is *Joseph Ellis, Founding Brothers: the Revolutionary Generation* (Knopf, 2000); more scholarly are several essays in Ambrose and Martin, and also in Doran Ben-Atar and Barbara B. Oberg, eds., *Federalists Reconsidered* (University Press of Virginia, 1998).

Hamilton was compulsive in publishing his essays on politics and economics. Harold C. Syrett, et al., have published 27 volumes of *The Papers of Alexander Hamilton* (Columbia University Press, 1961–1987). Among the many shorter versions of Hamilton's essays and letters are: Michael Lind, ed., *Hamilton's Republic: Readings in the American Democratic Nationalist Tradition* (Free Press, 1997); Richard B. Morris, ed., *Alexander Hamilton and the Founding of the Nation* (The Dial Press, 1957); Jo Anne Freeman, *Alexander Hamilton: Writings* (Library of America, 2001). An attempt to make Hamilton relevant today are the quotes from *Citizen Hamilton: The Wit and Wisdom of an American Founder* (Rowman and Littlefield, 2006) by Donald R. Hickey and Connie D. Clark.

ISSUE 8

Was James Madison an Effective Wartime President?

YES: Drew R. McCoy, from *The Last of the Fathers: James Madison and the Republican Legacy* (Cambridge University Press, 1989)

NO: Donald R. Hickey, from *The War of 1812: A Forgotten Conflict* (University of Illinois Press, 1989)

ISSUE SUMMARY

YES: Drew McCoy argues that James Madison was a man of integrity and virtue who exercised patience and restraint as commander-in-chief and who displayed great bravery in confronting both his domestic detractors and the nation's military foes during the War of 1812.

NO: Donald Hickey contends that Madison failed to provide the bold and vigorous leadership that was essential to a successful prosecution of the War of 1812 by tolerating incompetence among his generals and cabinet officers and by failing to secure vital legislation from Congress.

With the signing of the Treaty of Paris in 1783, the American Revolution came to an end, and the United States entered the family of nations as an independent and sovereign state. Although some diplomatic historians have insisted that the United States immediately became a major player on the world stage, clearly independence did not automatically bring into being a strong nation capable of competing effectively with the major European powers. Despite having defeated the British, the new country possessed only marginal army and naval forces and no income to support the military. Moreover, the central government under the Articles of Confederation was simply too weak to enforce wide-reaching foreign interests. John Adams, the American minister to England, shouldered most of the diplomatic burden for the United States in the years immediately following the Revolution, and Adams realized from the outset that until the United States possessed a stronger national government that it would not be able to enforce its will on other countries. A remedy for this situation, therefore, was accomplished at the Constitutional Convention.

With the French Revolution and, subsequently, the outbreak of a general European conflict culminating in the Napoleonic Wars, American leaders were forced to determine what, if any, role the United States should play in the European struggles, especially when the nations involved in those conflicts called upon the fledgling nation for assistance. President George Washington insisted upon a flexible foreign policy that would permit the United States to pursue its own interests and issued a Proclamation of Neutrality in 1793 stating that the United States should pursue "a conduct friendly and impartial toward the belligerent powers." John Adams, as president, witnessed deteriorating relations with France in the wake of the XYZ Affair but responded to his own party's call for war by concluding that such action was not in the security interests of the United States. Later, Adams viewed this decision to avoid war as the capstone of his political career.

As relations with England over American shipping and trade rights declined during the presidency of Thomas Jefferson, the United States found itself once again moving toward armed conflict with the former Mother Country. Following the 1807 attack on the American frigate *Chesapeake* by the British vessel *Leopard,* Jefferson sought to protect the national interest short of going to war by imposing economic sanctions through the Embargo Act. The measure delayed the war but also crippled American shipping interests, and when James Madison succeeded Jefferson as president in 1809, he faced several perplexing problems. After all, England's maritime practice of impressment and further harassment of American shipping on the high seas violated the United States' national honor, wreaked economic havoc in the West and South whose farmers depended upon exporting their surplus agricultural goods to Europe, and threatened the young nation's rightful claims to neutrality. When he failed to persuade the British to halt their attacks on American shipping, President Madison requested from Congress a declaration of war against Great Britain, which Congress provided on June 18, 1812.

In the essays that follow, Madison's execution of the war as commander-in-chief is evaluated. Drew McCoy summarizes the many criticisms leveled against Madison's wartime leadership but emphasizes the character traits that served the president and the nation well during the War of 1812. In the face of withering criticism at home, says McCoy, Madison demonstrated remarkable patience and avoided repressive legislation that would have undermined the civil liberties of American citizens. In addition, Madison refused to expand significantly his executive power during wartime and displayed great bravery when confronted with the British military assault on Washington, D.C.

Donald Hickey is far less enthusiastic about Madison's performance as wartime president. In fact, he believes that the general lack of attention given to the War of 1812 by scholars stems from the fact "that no great president is associated with the conflict." To his critics, Madison, like Nero, fiddled while the nation's capital burned. The president's overly cautious leadership, his inability to command influence in Congress, and his failure to appoint effective military and administrative leaders to prosecute the war seriously undermined the effort and brought the United States perilously close to defeat.

YES  **Drew R. McCoy**

The Last of the Fathers: James Madison and the Republican Legacy

The Character of the Good Statesman

In the spring of 1817, when James Madison quit public office for the last time, he behaved as if he were beginning rather than ending a career. Making the first leg of his journey home from Washington by steamboat, a novel means of approaching Montpelier, he was accompanied by a young writer from New York with an endearing blend of wit and patriotism. During their brief voyage down the Potomac River, James Kirke Paulding recalled, the elder statesman was "as playful as a child"; talking and jesting with everyone on board, he resembled "a school Boy on a long vacation." Perhaps Madison savored memories of his first journey along the Potomac, on horseback, almost fifty years before, when an eighteen-year-old youth bound for college in Princeton, New Jersey, had confronted poor roads and seemingly countless ferries. What proved to be Madison's final passage through this area was a telling measure of the changes he had witnessed in his lifetime, and no doubt the convenience and excitement of traveling by steamboat buoyed the old man's spirits. But his good cheer also surely reflected the happy condition of his country after a crisis-ridden term as chief executive that had nearly issued in disaster. As Henry Adams observed three-quarters of a century later, with a characteristic touch of irony, "few Presidents ever quitted office under circumstances so agreeable as those which surrounded Madison."

Most of Madison's countrymen in 1817 would probably have shared Adams's judgment but missed the irony. An old friend and neighbor, Francis Corbin, welcomed Madison home in words that appear to have caught the sentiments of a wider citizenry: "Long may you enjoy, in health and happiness, the well earned and truly legitimate plaudits of a grateful Country, and that sweetest of all consolations, an approving conscience." Corbin had served with Madison in the Virginia House of Delegates during the pivotal and trying years just after the Revolution. At the Richmond convention of 1788 they had joined hands to win the difficult struggle to secure the commonwealth's ratification of the Constitution. Now, in April 1817, Corbin assured Madison that his recent tenure as President was the glorious capstone to an illustrious career. "The End," he exclaimed, "has indeed crowned the Work!"

Few historians today would take seriously, much less share, Corbin's flattering assessment of his friend's eight years in the White House. Scholars generally agree that Madison achieved greatness much earlier in his career, especially in the late 1780s and early 1790s when he did more than any other individual to create and secure a republic that would, with amendments and a rather momentous interregnum in the 1860s, endure for the next two centuries. From there, convention has it, his career went into decline. Riddled with diplomatic blunders and other grievous errors of judgment, Madison's presidency was characterized by something close to colossal ineptitude in leadership, constituting a profound embarrassment to him and to the government he administered during the War of 1812. The British invasion and burning of Washington, D.C., in August 1814 and the near collapse of that government marked the appropriate nadir of a failed administration. Writing in 1938, for instance, Edward M. Burns leveled a withering blast. As chief executive, Madison "added nothing to his reputation"; in fact, his record was one "of treason to his own ideals, of humiliation and failure."

Some of Madison's biographers have tried to soften this harsh view, but with little success. Certainly Madison's popularity after the war—what Ralph Ketcham has described as "the adulation surrounding him during his last two years as President and his twenty years in retirement"—has counted for little. No one is surprised, after all, that when his contemporaries celebrated the happy conclusion of "Mr. Madison's War," some of the goodwill rubbed off on their commander in chief, no matter how hapless his leadership had been. Indeed, historians have generally portrayed this postwar euphoria among the American people as naive and shortsighted, blithely unmindful of the military and political catastrophe that had barely been averted; and Madison as president has thus been denied, for the most part, the credit and even the glory that his countrymen lavishly bestowed on him. When Madison's present-day admirers are not apologizing for his presidency, they feel compelled, at the least, to unravel the puzzle of "how such a brilliant man could become a less effective statesman as he grew older and more experienced."

This unfavorable image of Madison's presidency has obscured the depth and precise nature of his postwar popularity. When Corbin referred to the sweet comfort of "an approving conscience," he doubtless echoed the sentiments of a committee of citizens from Washington who addressed Madison on the day he left office. After elaborating the salutary consequences of the recent war, the committee's spokesman paid homage to Madison's principled leadership: "Power and national glory, Sir, have often before, been acquired by the sword; but rarely without the sacrifice of civil or political liberty." It was with reference to his use of "the sword," indeed, that Madison's presidency deserved special commendation. He had earned the profound gratitude of his fellow citizens, the committee declared, for "the vigilance" with which he had "restrained [that sword] within its proper limits," for "the energy" with which he had "directed it to its proper objects," and for "the safety" with which he had "wielded an armed force of fifty thousand men, aided by an annual disbursement of many millions, without infringing a political, civil, or religious right." Madison had led his nation through a difficult, but ultimately successful, second war for independence—and he had done so without violating its republican soul. Writing from Paris in the summer of 1817, his Republican colleague Albert Gallatin echoed Corbin's and the committee's emphasis when he observed that "few indeed have the good fortune, after such a career as yours, to carry in their retirement the entire approbation of their fellow citizens with that of their own conscience."

Such praise reminds us of the extraordinary restraint that Madison had exercised as a wartime leader. Although few Presidents have been subjected to so much personal invective and abuse, he never hinted at measures abridging freedom of speech or press, even in the face of rampant obstruction of his government's policies and countless cases of outright treason in the "eastern states" of New England. His administration pursued nothing akin to the repressive Alien and Sedition Acts of 1798—the distasteful badge of the high Federalism that, merely anticipating war, had outlawed virtually any show of opposition to the federal government and that Madison, earlier in his career, had vigorously assailed. Less than two years after the end of "Mr. Madison's War," one of his admirers proudly noted that not only a powerful foreign enemy, but violent domestic opposition as well, had been "withstood without one trial for treason, or even one prosecution for libel." As the historian Harry L. Coles has noted, this absence of repressive legislation "enabled the country quickly to unite after the war with a minimum of bitterness and resentment." And there is ample evidence that appreciation of Madison's behavior outlived the surge of postwar euphoria. Among the editors and orators who eulogized him in 1836, we find what one biographer has called "grateful memory of his unswerving protection of civil liberties" at a time when "provocations" had been "greatest for their restraint."

Just as important to his countrymen, Madison had not used the occasion of war to expand executive power or to create a vast patronage machine. "Of all the enemies to public liberty," Madison himself had written in 1795, "war is, perhaps, the most to be dreaded, because it comprises and develops the germ of every other." As "the parent of armies," of course, war encouraged "debts and taxes," which republicans recognized as "the known instruments for bringing the many under the domination of the few." But as Madison so powerfully argued, the danger was especially acute in relation to a particular branch of the government. "In war, too," he added, "the discretionary power of the Executive is extended; its influence in dealing out offices, honors, and emoluments is multiplied; and all the means of seducing the minds, are added to those of subduing the force, of the people." War always nourished the potential for corruption; in a young and experimental republic like the United States, the danger of executive usurpation was particularly ominous.

Two decades later, in quite different circumstances, Madison's adversaries could wax eloquent in describing this very danger in his own administration. In March 1814, for instance, a Federalist congressman from Massachusetts, Artemas Ward, vehemently opposed increasing the size of the federal army, imputing to Madison's regime nothing less than an intention "to change the form of Government." Lest his fellow legislators dismiss his words as "the vagaries or wanderings of a jealous, perhaps, distempered mind," Ward played upon the central themes of a republican melody that Americans had been humming for the better part of four decades. "All the Republics which have gone before us have lost their liberties," he reminded his fellow legislators, imploring them "to consider what has taken place in our time, and what they have read in the history of other times." They had seen "the Legislature of France turned out of the Hall of Liberty by a military force which it had nurtured and established." History told them "that the same was done in England in the days of Cromwell." And "however secure gentlemen may feel in their seats," they should not ignore the possibility that "they may witness the reaction of the same scenes here"; the military force they now voted to raise might indeed "ere long put an end to their existence as legislators." Above all, Ward cautioned the members of Congress, "Executive patronage and Executive influence are truly alarming."

Within a year, however, any such suspicions of Madison were exposed as unfounded, even absurd. To be sure, given Madison's modest bearing and his utter lack of military experience or ambition, the thought of him becoming a dictator on horseback is ludicrous; but we might also note that he prevented anyone else from assuming that role in the midst of an unprecedented political and military crisis. And in an age dominated by the specter of Napoleon, and in a republican political culture still very much tied to classical referents, including the danger of "Caesarism," President Madison's executive restraint confirmed his principled resistance to all temptations of power and thus drew effusive retrospective praise from his constituents, including many Federalists. An orator at a Fourth of July celebration in 1816 boldly predicted that Madison's name would "descend to posterity with that of our illustrious Washington," since "one achieved our independence, and the other sustained it." He was wrong about Madison's image in history, of course, but the linking of Madison to Washington, quite common in the postwar years and almost inconceivable today, points again to the source as well as to the extent of the adulation that surrounded him.

Although Madison's republican restraint as president and commander in chief contributed, ironically, to his later reputation as indecisive and incompetent, it earned substantial dividends in his own time. Writing from Braintree shortly after the presidential election of 1816, John Adams told Madison (who had not stood for reelection) that "such is the State of Minds here, that had Mr. Madison been candidate, he would probably have had the votes of Massachusetts and consequently of all New England." Adams was generally not one to flatter rivals for public esteem. But even if we allow for some measure of polite hyperbole in his estimation of his correspondent's popularity in the vicinity of Boston—only recently the center of intense opposition to the war against England—his statement to Jefferson a few months later confirms his sincerity. "Notwithstand[ing] a thousand Faults and blunders," Adams mused, Madison's administration had "acquired more glory, and established more Union, than all his three Predecessors, Washington Adams and Jefferson, put together." The mood captured in Adam's penetrating judgment was not always evanescent, either. Some of Madison's countrymen remembered the last two years of his presidency as the pinnacle of republican triumph, as nothing less than a golden age in which "a balmy peace" had overtaken the profound crisis of national confidence that had accompanied the tumultuous passions of war and regional partisanship. Moreover, they could attribute this happy situation, to a remarkable extent, to the diffusive influence of Madison's personal character. Writing in 1844, the Whig John Pendleton Kennedy attempted to evoke the spirit of this luminous postwar world, in which "the calm and philosophic temper of Mr. Madison, the purity of his character, the sincerity of his patriotism, and the sagacity of his intellect" had inspired "universal trust."

Kennedy's allusion to Madison's sage intellect jibes nicely with our image of him as a profound thinker. But his references to Madison's "calm and philosophic temper" and to "the purity of his character" were probably more vital to the nostalgis reverence that many Americans of the antebellum era, especially Whigs, came to feel for him and his presidency. In 1845 Charles Jared Ingersoll (a Democrat) published a multivolume "historical sketch" of the War of 1812 that assessed both Madison's leadership and his reputation. Compared to Jefferson and Washington, Ingersoll acknowledged, Madison must be judged deficient in genius and command. Yet "no mind has stamped more of its impressions on American institutions than Madison's," and his presidency was especially revealing of both his limitations and his peculiar virtues. Assuming the position of chief magistrate "bequeathed to him by his more salient predecessor with a complication of difficulties," Madison, Ingersoll averred, "went through the war meekly, as adversaries alleged shrinkingly, no doubt with anxious longing for the restoration of peace, but without ever yielding a principle to his enemies or a point to his adversaries; leaving the United States, which he found embarrassed and discredited, successful, prosperous, glorious and content." Ingersoll went on:

> A constitution which its opponents pronounced incapable of hostilities, under his administration triumphantly bore their severest brunt. Checkered by the inevitable vicissitudes of war, its trials never disturbed the composure of the commander-in-chief, always calm, consistent and conscientious, never much elated by victory or depressed by defeat, never once by the utmost emergencies of war, betrayed into a breach of the constitution. Exposed to that licentious abuse which leading men in free countries with an unshackled press cannot escape, his patience was never exhausted; nor his forbearance deprived of dignity by complaint, retort, or self-defence, but in the quiet serenity of rectitude, he waited on events with uninterrupted confidence.

American readers, of course, could hardly fail to see the appropriate analogy. Madison may not have been the equal of General Washington; no one was. But in his stoical perseverance in the face of countless setbacks, not to mention his steady adherence to principle amid alarming confusion and disorder, Madison, as a civilian commander in chief during this second war for independence, offered a display of bravery and self-command reminiscent of the heroic example set on the battlefields of the Revolution. As Ingersoll suggested, everything that went into his quiet but firm leadership—his unflappable dignity; his unwillingness to despair; his unyielding confidence in American institutions and the character of the people; and his dogged persistence—somehow overcame all of his specific failures and misjudgments. This kind of leadership may, in fact, have literally saved the republic. Modern historians remind us that a different, less happy outcome was far from inconceivable. "That government should have survived in Washington at all after August 1814 [following the successful British invasion] was itself no mean achievement," the historian J. C. A. Stagg has recently noted, "and for this Madison was largely responsible. By persisting in his duty and refusing to admit defeat, even under the most difficult circumstances, he ensured that his administration could survive the war and enjoy the benefits of peace when it came."

Ingersoll's survey of Madison's career (and his two decades of retirement, when he provided "a model for American statesmen"), culminated in the question he expected his readers in 1845 to have: "What then is the shading of this seeming strain of panegyric?" "No one has been more abused than Madison," he admitted, "but not only did it all die away, but died before he died." Although "a remnant of inveterate, respectable federalists" still denied his merits, "the great body of his countrymen" were now "unanimous in awarding him immortality." Much more than Jefferson, Madison enjoyed "undivided favour." And Ingersoll knew why: "He was no hero, not a man of genius, not remarkable for the talent of personal ascendency. But his patriotic services are parcel of the most fundamental civil, and the most renowned military grandeur of this republic, and his private life without stain or reproach."

Those who had known Madison well, especially during the War of 1812, seconded Ingersoll's contention that Madison's public conduct was best understood as the projection of an exemplary character and temperament. No better example of this common insight can be found than the testimony of Edward Coles, who was the president's private secretary for six years and hence a member of the White House family. Madison's "persevering and indefatigable efforts to prevent the war" as well as his "manner of carrying it on," Coles remarked in the 1850s, "were in perfect keeping with the character of the man, of whom it may be said that no one ever had to a greater extent, firmness, mildness, and self-possession, so happily blended in his character." A fellow Virginian by birth and a cousin of Madison's wife, Dolley, Coles's acquaintance with the Madisons went back to the 1790s, when as a child he had helped his family welcome the middle-aged congressman and his young bride for a postnuptial visit. From 1809 to 1815, Coles, now in his mid-twenties, became Madison's regular companion. Much later, when he wished to convey to his countrymen an accurate sense of his mentor's greatness, Coles made an intriguing observation—one wholly at odds with Madison's modern historical reputation—that casts fresh light on Madison and on the reverence his presence, and later his memory, frequently evoked.

Writing in 1854 to the Virginia historian Hugh Blair Grigsby, who had solicited his recollections, Coles drew extensive parallels between Madison and Washington. He noted of Madison, in this connection, that "if History do him justice, posterity will give him credit, more for the goodness of his heart, than for the strength and acquirements of his mind." Coles acknowledged Madison's intellectual brilliance, but he insisted that his impressive mind (and the fascinating conversation it produced, for which he was justly renowned) were "but decorations to set off to advantage his pure and incorruptible virtue and integrity." At first glance Coles's observation smacks of republican ritual in its celebration of Madison's disinterested commitment to the public good, long a sine qua non of the virtuous statesman; yet clearly he meant something more specific than that. A just history, he said, would show Madison to have been "the most virtuous, calm, and amiable, of men, possessed of one of the purest hearts, and best tempers with which man was ever blessed." It was Madison's peculiar temperament and the character it shaped, more than the depth of his mind or even his specific achievements, Coles believed, that entitled him to sit by Washington's side in the pantheon of classical heroes that had graced the American scene in the days of the Founding.

As his secretary, Coles had observed Madison's conduct under the kind of "trying circumstances" that indeed put character to the test. As Charles Francis Adams noted in 1841, "foreign war and domestic discored came together upon him in a manner that would have tried the nerves of the strongest man." But "amidst all the troubles and excitement attendant on a foreign war, and provoking feuds at home," Coles recalled, he had never once heard the president "utter one petulant expression, or give way for one moment to passion or despondency." It seemed that "nothing could excite or ruffle him"; no matter how vexing the provocation, he had remained "collected" and "self-possessed." Coles asserted that this rigorous self-control—a calm, deliberate steadiness of mind and behavior (again, so reminiscent of Washington)—had shaped Madison's leadership in entirely admirable ways. Without a single lapse, he told Grigsby, Madison had succeeded in abiding by his own "maxim" that "public functionaries should never display, much less act, under the influence of passion." Moreover, he had been "ever mindful of what was due from him to others, and cautious not to wound the feelings of any one." Indeed, at times during the war Coles had found the president's patience with his many critics exasperating. Besieged by deputations of citizens with advice and instructions, Madison's habit was to listen with the utmost attention, depite the tax on his valuable time and patience. Once, when Coles had pleaded with him to ignore an importunate group of delegates soliciting an interview, Madison had told his secretary, in no uncertain terms, that since these citizens had come a long distance to advise him, surely their president owed them his attention for an hour or two.

Coles's portrait of Madison's temperament and its influence on his public conduct was confirmed by other intimates. James Barbour, a major figure in both Virginia and national politics in the early nineteenth century, was also Madison's Orange County neighbor. In 1836 he eulogized his friend in terms that Coles must have appreciated, praising Madison's "private virtues, equal to, if not beyond, his public worth" and paying great attention to "the force of his character" on public life. Above all, Barbour said, Madison was distinguished "for a serenity of temper, which, under no circumstances, in public or private, did I ever see disturbed." This serene temperament was not the demeanor of a bland or dull man, however, as Barbour emphasized Madison's gentle charm and benevolence. Cheerful by nature, he frequently indulged in "a playful Attic wit," but "always without a sting"—it was, Barbour said, "the rose without the thorn." Scrupulously attentive to the needs and feelings of others, Madison had an uncanny ability to make acquaintances and visitors comfortable. "With the less intelligent of these," Barbour observed, "he seemed anxious to veil his superiority, and, by kindness and affability, to elevate them to a feeling of equality with himself"; quick to discern "the bent of their minds," he was always able to give to the conversation "a congenial direction." But what Barbour saw as most remarkable about Madison was his ability either to control or to vanquish altogether the darker side of his passionate nature, which in other men nourished the selfish motives of revenge and spite. In testimony that other acquaintances often corroborated in a similar tone of disbelief, Barbour declared that he had never heard Madison "speak ill of any one." And such extraordinary "magnanimity of character" saved him, as a public leader, "from the degradation of prostituting his high trust to the gratification of private malice," of which, indeed, he simply had "none to gratify."

Donald R. Hickey

NO

The War of 1812: A Forgotten Conflict

Introduction

The war of 1812 is probably our most obscure war. Although a great deal has been written about the conflict, the average American is only vaguely aware of why we fought or who the enemy was. Even those who know something about the contest are likely to remember only a few dramatic moments, such as the Battle of New Orleans, the burning of the nation's capital, or the writing of "The Star-Spangled Banner."

Why is this war so obscure? One reason is that no great president is associated with the conflict. Although his enemies called it "Mr. Madison's War," James Madison hardly measures up to such war leaders as Abraham Lincoln, Woodrow Wilson, or Franklin Roosevelt. Moreover, the great generals in this war—Andrew Jackson and Winfield Scott—were unable to turn the tide because each was confined to a secondary theater of operations. No one like George Washington, Ulysses Grant, or Dwight Eisenhower emerged to put his stamp on the war and to carry the nation to victory. . . .

The campaign of 1812 was both disappointing and embarrassing to Republicans. The string of defeats on the Canadian frontier had dashed all hopes for a quick and an easy victory and had exposed the administration to criticism. The war had never lost its political character, and Republican leaders had hoped that triumphs on the battlefield would disarm their critics and enhance their chances at the polls. "[A] little success," said one Republican, "would silence many who are clamerous." "[I]f our government does not look sharp," said another, "the Federalists will come in again." But except for the naval victories, there was little to cheer about, and the result was growing disillusionment with the management of the war. "Our affairs," Senator Thomas Worthington of Ohio scrawled in his diary on December 1, "is [in] a miserable way[,] defeated and disgraced[,] the revenue extravagantly expended[,] the war not man[a]ged at all."

Although voters usually rally around a wartime president, Madison fared worse in 1812 than he had in 1808. A split in the Republican party and charges of mismanagement very nearly cost him his office. In addition, the Federalists

From *The War of 1812: A Forgotten Conflict* by Donald R. Hickey (University of Illinois Press, 1989).

made significant gains in the congressional and state elections. Although the Republicans retained control over the national government and a majority of the state governments, the election results showed that many questioned not only the administration's handling of the war but the wisdom of the war itself.

The presidential campaign opened in February of 1812 when Republicans in the Virginia legislature nominated electors committed to Madison. In the ensuing months Republican caucuses in seven other states followed suit. The regular Republicans in Congress added their endorsement in May of 1812. At a widely publicized meeting (which most people considered the official Republican caucus), eighty-three members of Congress promised to support Madison for the presidency and seventy-one-year-old John Langdon of New Hampshire for the vice presidency. (Langdon declined because of age, which necessitated substituting Elbridge Gerry of Massachusetts.) Nine other members of Congress later added their endorsements, so Madison ended up with the avowed support of about two-thirds of the Republican membership. Most Republican congressmen from New York and other northern states, however, withheld their support because they preferred a northern candidate.

Shortly after the Washington caucus, Republicans in the New York state legislature met to nominate their own candidate. The favorite was De Witt Clinton, the mayor of New York City. Known as the "Magnus Apollo," Clinton was a handsome, popular, and talented statesman from a family long active in politics. Although some New Yorkers were fearful of splitting the party, Clinton won the legislature's endorsement when congressmen returning from Washington brought stories of growing disillusionment with Madison and letters from Postmaster General Gideon Granger urging support for a northern candidate.

Clinton's friends put his case before the people in an address published in the summer of 1812. The address attacked the congressional nominating system and the Virginia Dynasty and charged the administration with mismanaging the war. Virginia's domination of the presidency, the address said, had given rise to charges of "*Virginia influence,*" pitting the agricultural states against the commercial ones. To put an end to this divisiveness, the address recommended Clinton as a man who would provide "vigor in war, and a determined character in the relations of peace."

Clinton's nomination posed a dilemma for Federalists. Should they maintain their purity by supporting a Federal candidate—a course sure to lead to defeat—or should they vote for Clinton, a man long associated with the Republican party but considered friendly to commerce and anxious for peace? In New York and Virginia, the prevailing sentiment was for a Federal candidate, the favorites being Rufus King, John Marshall, and Charles Cotesworth Pinckney. Elsewhere there was considerable support for Clinton because, as one Federalist put it, he "wd. engage, if chosen President, to make immediate Peace with England." The sentiment for Clinton was particularly strong among Federalists in Pennsylvania and Massachusetts. In mid-summer a Philadelphia committee of correspondence sent out a circular recommending Clinton because of "his residence and attachments, his asserted freedom from foreign influence, his avowed hostility to the anti-commercial system, . . . combined with the positive declarations which have been made that he is desirous of the restoration of peace."

To fix their election strategy, Federalists held a convention in New York City in September of 1812. Seventy delegates from eleven states attended, though most were from New York, Pennsylvania, and New Jersey. Rufus King spearheaded the opposition to Clinton, believing that he was nothing more than the "Leader of a Faction." King thought "it was of less importance that the Federalists should acquire a temporary ascendency by the aid of a portion of the Repubs. than that their reputation and integrity shd. be preserved unblemished." Many of the delegates disagreed, not because they had any great confidence in Clinton but because they saw him as the lesser of two evils. As Timothy Pickering of Massachusetts put it, "I am far enough from desiring Clinton for President . . . but I would vote for any man in preference to Madison."

Harrison Gray Otis delivered an impassioned appeal on behalf of Clinton. According to one observer, "Mr. Otis arose, apparently much embarrassed, holding his hat in his hand, and seeming as if he were almost sorry he had arisen. Soon he warmed with his subject, his hat fell from his hand, and he poured forth a strain of eloquence that chained all present to their seats." Otis's appeal carried the day, but the convention stopped short of formally endorsing Clinton, fearing that this would undermine his Republican support. Instead, the delegates simply urged Federalists to support presidential electors "most likely by their votes to effect a change in the present course of measures." The convention made no provision for the vice presidency, but Jared Ingersoll became the accepted candidate when he was nominated by Federalists in Lancaster County, Pennsylvania.

None of the candidates openly campaigned for office, but the followers of each were busy, particularly in the middle states. "Never did I witness a more spirited preparation for an election," said a New Yorker. The answer was the principal issue in the campaign. Madison's supporters insisted that the contest was necessary to vindicate the nation's rights and to uphold its independence. "It is a war of right against lawless aggression," said a South Carolina campaign document, "of Justice against perfidy and violence." Republicans also argued that the president could not be blamed for setbacks in the field, that it was unfair "to impute to Mr. Madison the failure of every military expedition, or the defection of every military chief." In response to this, the Clintonians accused Madison's followers of embracing "the British maxim—*the king can do no wrong,*" and of applying it "to the President in its full force."

The Clintonians sought to win northern support by portraying their candidate as a bold and energetic leader who was friendly to commerce and the navy and in no way tied to France. In pro-war states, Clinton's followers emphasized that he would shorten the war by prosecuting it more vigorously, while in anti-war states he was portrayed as a man who would achieve this end by negotiating with the British. Friends of the administration were quick to exploit this inconsistency. "In the west," said one critic, "Mr. Clinton is recommended as a friend of war . . . in the East he is presented as a friend of peace." A character in a contemporary play echoed this sentiment: "He cannot have *war* and *peace at the same time.*"

The Clintonians claimed that there had been a breakdown in presidential leadership, a charge that some of Madison's followers privately conceded.

According to a New Hampshire War Hawk, "many of the friends of the Administration believe, that the Executive are not disposed to prosecute the war with vigor, provided they can find any *hole* through which they can creep out, and avoid the contest." Even in Madison's home state a "horrible spirit of disaffection or distrust" was said to be afoot. "[A]ll the misfortunes of our arms," reported a Virginia Republican, "are here Publicly ascribed to the mismanagement of the Genl Government." Many people wondered whether "Little Jemmy" (who was only five feet four inches tall) was big enough for the job. "Mr. Madison is wholly unfit for the storms of War," Henry Clay confided to a friend. "Nature has cast him in too benevolent a mould."

The Republicans sought to counter charges of Madison's weakness by attacking Clinton's character. One called him "the modern *Cromwell,*" a second described him as a "sprig of upstart nobility," while a third compared him to "*Judas Iscariot.*" The Republicans also tried to discredit Clinton by focusing on his alliance with the Federalists. According to a Philadelphia campaign document, this alliance was "unanswerable evidence, that Mr. Clinton has sacrificed his democratic principles on the altar of his ambition." "[C]ourting the interest and votes of the *Essex Junto,*" said another Republican, "ought forever [to] damn him with Democrats."

The means of selecting presidential electors varied from state to state. Half of the states chose their electors by popular vote, while the rest left the decision to the legislature. Each state followed its own timetable, and the results drifted in over a two-month period in the fall of 1812. The outcome was by no means certain. According to congressman Samuel Latham Mitchill, November was "a dark and dismal month" in the White House because news of election defeats coupled with military reverses rolled in "[day] after day, like the tidings of Job's disasters."

The voting followed the same sectional pattern as the vote on the declaration of war. Clinton fared best in the North, Madison in the South and West. The outcome hinged on the results in New York and Pennsylvania, the two populous middle Atlantic states. Clinton needed both to win. He had no trouble in New York, winning all of that state's twenty-nine electoral votes. This result was due mainly to shrewd maneuvering in the legislature by twenty-nine-year-old Martin Van Buren, who henceforth would be known as the "Little Magician." Madison, however, prevailed in Pennsylvania, winning all twenty-five electoral votes and proving again that this state was the "Keystone in the Democratic Arch." The election was "pretty close work," concluded Richard Rush, "and Pennsylvania, as usual, carries the union on her back." Madison was aided in no small degree by Pennsylvania's booming prosperity, which was based on military spending and an extensive overseas trade. "Never did the abundant harvests of Pennsylvania find a quicker or a better market," crowed a Republican campaign document. In all, Madison won 128 electoral votes to Clinton's 89. (By contrast, Madison had defeated Charles Cotesworth Pinckney in 1808 by a margin of 122 to 47.)

The Republicans also lost ground in the congressional elections. The proportion of seats they held fell from 75 to 63 percent in the House and from 82 to 78 percent in the Senate. Their losses were particularly heavy in

New York, Massachusetts, and New Hampshire. The Republicans lost control of several states, too. In 1811 they had won every state except Connecticut, Rhode Island, and Delaware. In 1812 they lost these states as well as Massachusetts, New Jersey, and Maryland. They also lost their majority in the New York assembly and suffered small or moderate losses in almost every other state east of the Appalachian Mountains. Although the Republicans remained in charge of the nation's destinies, their popularity appeared to be waning. The Federalists, on the other hand, had every reason to be pleased. By capitalizing on the mismanagement and unpopularity of the war and by exploiting the gruesome violence at Baltimore, they had achieved their most impressive electoral gains since the 1790s.

With the elections safely behind them, Republican leaders urged President Madison to strengthen his cabinet. Ever since the previous spring, Secretary of War William Eustis and Secretary of the Navy Paul Hamilton had been under heavy fire. By the end of the year this criticism had reached such a torrent that it threatened to engulf the president himself. "Our executive officers are most incompetent men," said John C. Calhoun. "We are literally boren down under the effects of errors and mismanagement." "The clamor against the gentlemen who are at the head of the War and Navy Departments," said another congressman, "is loud & very general." If these men are not removed, added a Georgia senator, the president "must be content, with defeat, and disgrace in all his efforts, during the war." Although Madison was reluctant to act, he finally accepted the resignations of both men in December.

To replace Hamilton, Madison chose William Jones, a Philadelphia merchant and former congressman who had fought at Trenton and Princeton and served on a privateer during the Revolution. Though later discredited for mismanaging the national bank, Jones had considerable ability. With some justice, Madison later claimed that he was "the fittest minister who had ever been charged with the Navy Department." Far more knowledgeable about naval affairs than his predecessor, he was a good administrator who brought energy and efficiency to the department and won the admiration of his contemporaries. "I know of Some," said Nathaniel Macon in 1814, "who once thought little of his talents, [but] now consider him, the most useful member of the administration."

It was much harder to find a new secretary of war because this office was such an administrative nightmare. "[W]ith all its horrors & perils," said Gallatin, the office "frightens those who know best its difficulties." Finding a candidate who is "qualified, popular, and willing to accept is extremely difficult." Secretary of State James Monroe agreed to serve temporarily but refused to take the office permanently because he was hoping for a command in the field. Senator William H. Crawford and General Henry Dearborn also declined.

The president finally settled on John Armstrong of New York. Although knowledgeable about military affairs, Armstrong was abrasive and indolent and a known enemy of the Virginia Dynasty. In 1783 he had written the Newurgh Letters inciting the Continental Army to mutiny, and many people considered this "an indelible stain" upon his character. He also had a reputation for intrigue, a reputation that was largely justified. Given his liabilities, his confirmation in the Senate was doubtful. "Armstrong will rub hard, if he gets through at all," said one Republican. Though the Senate finally approved him, the vote was 18–15, with both Virginia senators abstaining.

The new appointments improved the efficiency of the administration but not without a price. Armstrong lived up to his reputation for intrigue and alienated his colleagues. Monroe saw him as a rival for the presidential succession and was constantly at odds with him. Monroe finally told Madison that if Armstrong were not removed he would "ruin not you and the admn. only, but the whole republican party and cause." Gallatin also despised him. Armstrong sided with Gallatin's enemies (particularly in Pennsylvania) and distributed his patronage accordingly. The crowning insult came when he awarded an army staff position to William Duane, the editor of the virulently anti-Gallatin Philadelphia *Aurora.* "The appointment of Duane," lamented Gallatin, "has appeared to me so gross an outrage on decency and self respect . . . that I felt no wish to remain associated with an administration which would employ such a miscreant." By the summer of 1813, William Jones had lost confidence in Armstrong, too. "[M]any begin to believe," he said, "that the 'Old Soldier' [Armstrong's nom de plume] is not a legitimate son of Mars." . . .

Throughout the war the Republicans had hoped that favorable election results would shore up their majorities and silence the opposition, but their hopes were never fulfilled. In the elections of 1812, the Federalists had gained control of six of the eighteen states (Massachusetts, Connecticut, Rhode Island, New Jersey, Delaware, and Maryland). The following year they lost New Jersey but won Vermont and New Hampshire, which gave them control over all of New England. In 1814 they retained control of these same seven states.

The Republicans fared no better in congressional elections. Most states held their elections for the Fourteenth Congress in 1814 even though this Congress did not convene until the end of 1815. In the House, Republican strength, which had declined from 75 percent in the Twelfth Congress to 63 percent in the Thirteenth, rose slightly to 65 percent in the Fourteenth Congress. In the Senate, however, Republican strength continued to slide: from 82 percent in the Twelfth Congress to 78 percent in the Thirteenth, to 67 percent in the Fourteenth. Although the leading Senate "Invisibles"—Samuel Smith, William Branch Giles, and Michael Leib—were not returned to the Fourteenth Congress, the regular Republicans were little better off than they had been in the Thirteenth Congress.

Thus in neither Congress nor the country were the Republicans able to win the decisive majorities they sought. Although they counted on the war to enhance their popularity and silence the Federalists, the effect of the conflict was just the opposite. In New England especially, the war served as a catalyst for a Federalist revival. As a result, Federalists achieved a more commanding position in this region than at any time since the 1790s.

It was not only the Federalists who opposed the administration. Many Republicans did, too. The Clintonians and "Invisibles" disliked the administration's management of the war, and the Old Republicans objected to the war itself. The election of 1812 had revealed deep-seated hostility to the Virginia

Dynasty, and by 1814 even regular Republicans had become disillusioned with the party's leadership. "If we have another disastrous campaign in Canada," said George Hay of Virginia, "the republican cause is ruined, and Mr. M[adison] will go out covered with the Scorn of one party, and the reproaches of the other." "Without a change in the management of the war on the Canadian frontier," added Nathaniel Macon, "the republican party must go down[.] The people of every part of the Nation, will be disgusted with an administration, who have declared war, without ability to conduct it, to a favorable issue."

With the disasters of 1814—particularly the burning of Washington—the president and his advisors suffered a further loss in public esteem. "The President is much railed at by many of the Democrats," said a Philadelphia merchant. "The whole administration is blamed for the late disastrous occurrences at Washington," declared a Virginia Republican. "Without money, without soldiers & without courage," said Rufus King, "the President and his Cabinet are the objects of very general execration."

The War of 1812 lasted only two years and eight months—from June18, 1812, to February 17, 1815. Though the war was not long, the United States was beset by problems from the beginning. Many of the nation's military leaders were incompetent, and enlistments in the army and navy lagged behind need. The militia were costly and inefficient and repeatedly refused to cross into Canada or to hold their positions under enemy fire. It was difficult to fill the war loans, and the nation's finances became increasingly chaotic. There was also extensive trade with the enemy—trade that Federalists and republicans alike freely took part in. A combination of Federalist opposition, Republican factionalism, and general public apathy undermined the entire war effort.

Congress was partly responsible for this state of affairs. Endless debate and deep divisions delayed or prevented the adoption of much-needed legislation. Congress was particularly negligent on financial matters. Hoping for a quick war and fearing the political consequences of unpopular measures, Republicans postponed internal taxes and delayed a national bank. As a result, public credit collapsed in 1814, and a general suspension of specie payments ensued. By the end of the war, the administration had to rely on depreciated bank paper and treasury notes. If the contest had continued much longer, the Revolutionary War phrase "not worth a continental" might have been replaced by "not worth a treasury note."

A strong president might have overcome some of these problems, but Madison was one of the weakest war leaders in the nation's history. Although his opponents called the contest "Mr. Madison's War," it never bore his stamp. Cautious, shy, and circumspect, Madison was unable to supply the bold and vigorous leadership that was needed. In some respects, to be sure, his caution served the nation well. Unlike other war presidents, he showed remarkable respect for the civil rights of his domestic foes. Despite pleas from other Republicans, he refused to resort to a sedition law. Thus, even though Federalists had to face mob violence (particularly at the beginning of the war), they never had to contend with government repression. Madison's treatment of enemy aliens and prisoners of war was also commendably humane, and his circumspect policy toward New England disaffection was undoubtedly well judged, too.

In other ways, however, Madison's cautious brand of leadership undermined the nation's war effort. He allowed incompetents like Eustis and Hamilton to hold key positions, he tolerated Armstrong's intrigues and Monroe's backbiting in the cabinet, and he retained Gideon Granger as postmaster general long after his hostility to the administration had become notorious. Madison was also slow to get rid of incompetent generals in the field or to promote officers who had proven themselves in battle. Because he lacked a commanding influence in Congress, he was unable to secure vital legislation, and because he lacked a strong following in the country, he was unable to inspire people to open their hearts and purses.

Contemporaries were aware of Madison's shortcomings, and even Republicans criticized his leadership. "Our President," said John C. Calhoun in 1812, "has not . . . those commanding talents, which are necessary to controul those about him." "[H]is spirit and capacity for a crisis of war," declared a Pennsylvania congressman in 1814, "are very generally called in question." "Mr. Madison," added a western congressman in 1815, "is perhaps 'too good' a man for the responsible office he holds. He does not like to offend his fellow men for any cause." Even Virginia Republicans considered Madison "*too tender* of the feelings of other people." "The amiable temper and delicate sensibility of Mr Madison," declared one Virginian, "are the real sources of our embarrassments."

No doubt poor leadership in Washington and in the field drove up the cost of this war. At the beginning of the contest, a Federalist newspaper predicted that the war would cost 30,000 lives and $180,000,000 and lead to a French-style conscription. This prediction was close to the mark. Official sources, which are not entirely reliable, indicate that the total number of American troops engaged in the contest was 528,000: 57,000 regulars, 10,000 volunteers, 3,000 rangers, and 458,000 militia. Another 20,000 served in the navy and marines. The battle casualties were comparatively light. The official figures are 2,260 killed and 4,505 wounded.

There is no record of how many soldiers died from disease, but before the advent of modern medicine, deaths from disease invariably exceeded those from enemy fire. Epidemics were common, and field commanders sometimes reported 30, 40, or even 50 percent of their troops on the sick list. There were numerous reports of multiple deaths from dysentery, typhoid fever, pneumonia, malaria, measles, typhus, and smallpox. In 1812, a soldier at Buffalo said: "Every day three or four are carried off to their Graves." In 1813, Governor Isaac Shelby said: "They are dying more or less every day on our March." And in 1814, General George Izard called the mortality rate from disease and exposure among his troops "prodigious."

After sampling army records, one scholar has concluded that two and a half times as many soldiers died from disease or accident as were killed or wounded in battle. If this sample is representative, the total number of nonbattle military deaths must have been about 17,000. The army executed an additional 205 men, mainly for repeated desertion, and the navy executed a few men, too. Some privateersmen also died in the war, primarily from disease in British prisons. There were a few civilian casualties as well—mostly victims of Indian raids in the West. Adding all the pertinent figures together suggests that the total number of deaths attributable to the war must have been about 20,000.

The cost of the war (excluding property damage and lost economic opportunities) was $158,000,000. This includes $93,000,000 in army and navy expenditures, $16,000,000 for interest on the war loans, and $49,000,000 in veterans' benefits. (The last veteran died in 1905, the last pensioner—the daughter of a veteran—in 1946.) The government also awarded land bounties to some 224,000 people who had served in the war. The national debt, which Republicans had reduced from $83,000,000 in 1801 to $45,000,000 in 1812, rose to $127,000,000 by the end of 1815. The government borrowed $80,000,000 during the war, but because of discounts offered and paper money received, it got only $34,000,000 specie value.

What did the war accomplish? Although militarily the conflict ended in a draw, in a larger sense it represented a failure or Republican policy makers. The nation was unable to conquer Canada or to achieve any of the maritime goals for which it was contended. Indeed, these issues were not even mentioned in the peace treaty, which merely provided for restoring all conquered territory and returning to the *status quo ante bellum*. . . .

The Battle of New Orleans, though fought after Great Britain had signed and ratified the peace treaty, played a particularly important role in forging the myth of American victory. Even before the peace terms were known, Republicans were touting this battle as a decisive turning point in the war. "The terms of the treaty are yet unknown to us," said Congressman Charles J. Ingersoll in early 1815. "But the victory at Orleans has rendered them glorious and honorable, be they what they may. . . . Who is not proud to feel himself an American—our wrongs revenged—our rights recognized!"

Republicans boasted of how they had defeated "the heroes of Wellington," "Wellington's *invincibles,*" and "the conquerors of the conquerors of Europe." "[W]e have unqueened the self-stiled Queen of the Ocean," crowed the Boston *Yankee,* and "we have beaten at every opportunity, *Wellington's Veterans!*" The myth of American victory continued to grow so that by 1816 *Niles' Register* could unabashedly claim that "we did virtually dictate the treaty of Ghent." Several months later a Republican congressman declaimed on the nation's triumph. "The glorious achievements of the late war," said Henry Southard of New Jersey, "have sealed the destinies of this country, perhaps for centuries to come, and the Treaty of Ghent has secured our liberties, and established our national independence, and placed this nation on high and honorable ground."

As the years slipped by, most people forgot the causes of the war. They forgot the defeats on land and sea and lost sight of how close the nation had come to military and financial collapse. According to the emerging myth, the United States had won the war as well as the peace. Thus the War of 1812 passed into history not as a futile and costly struggle in which the United States had barely escaped dismemberment and disunion, but as a glorious triumph in which the nation has single-handedly defeated the conqueror of Napoleon and the Mistress of the Seas.

POSTSCRIPT

Was James Madison an Effective Wartime President?

This issue lends itself to a comparative approach by which James Madison's leadership can be viewed alongside that of other American commanders-in-chief. Hickey argues that Madison compares unfavorably to Abraham Lincoln, Woodrow Wilson, and Franklin Roosevelt, but even those great presidents faced serious criticism. One might expand the comparison by assessing the responses to war by presidents James Polk, William McKinley, John Kennedy, Lyndon Johnson, Richard Nixon, and both George Bushes.

A broad historical context for the War of 1812 can be found in Marshall Smelser, *The Democratic Republic, 1801–1815* (Harper & Row, 1968) and John Mayfield, *The New Nation, 1800–1845* (Hill & Wang, 1982). Early American diplomacy is effectively covered in Lawrence S. Kaplan, *Colonies into Nation: American Diplomacy, 1763–1801* (Macmillan, 1972); Paul A. Varg, *Foreign Policies of the Founding Fathers* (Michigan State University Press, 1963); and Reginald Horsman, *The Diplomacy of the New Republic, 1776–1815* (Harlan Davidson, 1985) but should be complemented by the following monographs: Samuel Flagg Bemis, *Pinckney's Treaty: America's Advantage from Europe's Distress, 1783–1800* (The Johns Hopkins Press, 1926); Harry Ammon, *The Genet Mission* (W. W. Norton, 1973); and Alexander DeConde, *The Quasi-War: The Politics and Diplomacy of the Undeclared War with France, 1797–1801* (Charles Scribner's Sons, 1966).

The critical events leading up to the War of 1812 are covered in Bradford Perkins, *Prologue to War, 1805–1812: England and the United States* (University of California Press, 1961); Louis M. Sears, *Jefferson and the Embargo* (Reprint Services, 1967); and Clifford L. Egan, *Neither Peace nor War: Franco-American Relations, 1803–1812* (Louisiana State University Press, 1983). Clashing interpretations on the causes of the war are presented in Julius W. Pratt, *Expansionists of 1812* (Macmillan, 1925), which focuses on the "War Hawks" and the dream to gain control of Canada; and Roger H. Brown, *The Republic in Peril: 1812* (W. W. Norton, 1964), which describes the American preoccupation with national honor and the protection of republican institutions. Fuller explorations of causation can be found in Reginald Horsman, *The Causes of the War of 1812* (University of Pennsylvania Press, 1962); Harry Lewis Coles, *The War of 1812* (University of Chicago Press, 1965); and Patrick C. T. White, *The Nation on Trial: America and the War of 1812* (John Wiley & Sons, 1965).

James Madison's wartime leadership is discussed in Irving Brant, *James Madison: Commander in Chief, 1812–1836* (Bobbs-Merrill, 1961); Ralph Ketchum, *James Madison* (American Political Biography Press, 2003); J. C. A. Stagg, *Mr. Madison's War: Politics, Diplomacy, and Warfare in the Early Republic,*

1783-1830 (Princeton University Press, 1983); and Jack Rakove, *James Madison and the Creation of the American Republic* (Scott Forsman/Little, Brown, 1990).

The last crucial military victory for the United States receives scholarly treatment in Robert V. Remini, *The Battle of New Orleans: Andrew Jackson and America's First Military Victory* (Viking Adult, 1999). James M. Banner, Jr. discusses the Federalist opposition to the War of 1812 and the consequences of the Hartford Convention in *To the Hartford Convention: The Federalists and the Origins of Party Politics in Massachusetts, 1789-1815* (Random House, 1970).

ISSUE 9

Did the Election of 1828 Represent a Democratic Revolt of the People?

YES: Sean Wilentz, from *The Rise of American Democracy: Jefferson to Lincoln* (Norton, 2005)

NO: Richard P. McCormick, from "New Perspectives on Jacksonian Politics," *The American Historical Review* (January 1960)

ISSUE SUMMARY

YES: Bancroft Prize winner Sean Wilentz argues that in spite of its vulgarities and slanders, the 1828 election campaign "produced a valediction on the faction-ridden jumble of the Era of Bad Feelings and announced the rough arrival of two district national coalitions."

NO: Professor Richard P. McCormick believes that voting statistics demonstrate that a genuine political revolution did not take place until the presidential election of 1840, when fairly well-balanced political parties had been organized in virtually every state.

According to the conventional wisdom, Andrew Jackson's election to the presidency in 1828 began the era of the common man in which the mass of voters, no longer restrained from voting by property requirements, rose up and threw the elite leaders out of our nation's capital. While recent historians are not quite sure what constituted Jacksonian democracy or who supported it, and they question whether there ever existed such an era of egalitarianism, American history textbooks still include the obligatory chapter on the age of Jackson.

There are several reasons the old-fashioned view of this period still prevails. In spite of the new scholarly interest in social history, it is still easier to generalize about political events. Consequently, most texts continue to devote the major portion of their pages to detailed examinations of the successes and failures of various presidential administrations. Whether Jackson was more significant than other presidents is difficult to assess because "Old Hickory's" forceful personality, compounded with his use of strong executive authority, engendered constant controversy in his eight years in office.

Another reason the traditional concept of Jacksonian democracy has not been abandoned is because critics of the progressive interpretation have not been able to come up with an acceptable alternative view. Culminating with Arthur Schlesinger, Jr.'s Pulitzer Prize–winning and beautifully written *The Age of Jackson* (Little, Brown, 1945), the progressive historians viewed Jackson's election in 1828 as the triumph of the common man in politics. Oversimplified as this interpretation may be, there is little doubt that a major change was taking place in our political system during these years. The death of both Thomas Jefferson and John Adams on July 4, 1826, the fiftieth anniversary of our Declaration of Independence from England, signified the end of the revolutionary generation's control over American politics. The first six presidents had been leaders or descendants of leaders in the revolutionary movement. At the Constitutional Convention in 1787, most of the time was spent discussing the powers of the presidency. Because of the recent experience with the British king, the Founding Fathers were fearful of strong executive authority. Therefore, the presidency was entrusted only to those individuals whose loyalty remained unquestioned. Jackson was the first president of the United States who did not come from either Virginia or Massachusetts. Though Jackson was only a teenager at the time of the American Revolution, his career was similar to those of the early Founding Fathers. Like Washington and Jefferson, Jackson became a living legend before he was 50 years old. His exploits as an Indian fighter and the military hero of the Battle of New Orleans in the War of 1812 were more important than his western background in making him presidential material.

During the past two decades, a number of historians have studied the effects of our presidential elections on the development and maintenance of our two-party system. Borrowing concepts and analytical techniques from political scientists and sociologists, the "new political" historians have demonstrated the effectiveness of our parties in selecting candidates, running campaigns, developing legislation, and legitimizing conflicts within our democratic system. By 1815, the first-party system of competition between the Federalists and the Republican-Democrats had broken down, in part because the Federalists had refused to become a legitimate opposition party. A second-party system developed during the Jackson era between Old Hickory's Democratic party and his Whig opponents. It lasted until the 1850s when the slavery issue led to the formation of a new system of party competition between Republicans and Democrats.

The following selections disagree on the significance of the 1828 presidential race as a critical election in the development of the second-party system. Professor Sean Wilentz has won the Pulitzer Prize for his massive tome on *The Rise of American Democracy* (Norton, 2005). He synthesizes the "new political history" with the more favorable earlier interpretation of Andrew Jackson as the champion of the masses. In spite of its vulgarities and slanders, says Wilentz, the 1828 election campaign "pronounced a valediction on the faction-ridden jumble of the Era of Bad Feelings and announced the rough arrival of two distinct national coalitions." But historian Richard P. McCormick revises the traditional interpretation. His analysis of the voting statistics, he argues, demonstrates that a genuine political revolution did not take place until the presidential election of 1840 when fairly well-balanced parties had been organized in virtually every state.

YES 

Sean Wilentz

The Rise of American Democracy: Jefferson to Lincoln

"Under Whip & Spur": Politics, Propaganda, and the 1828 Campaign

Although he looked like a distinguished old warrior, with flashing blue eyes and a shock of whitening steely gray hair, Andrew Jackson was by now a physical wreck. Years of ingesting calomel and watered gin to combat his chronic dysentery had left him almost toothless. (In 1828, he obtained an ill-fitting set of dentures, but he often refused to wear them.) An irritation of his lungs, caused by a bullet he had caught in one of his early duels, had developed into bronchiectasis, a rare condition causing violent coughing spells that would bring up what he called "great quantities of slime." The bullet itself remained lodged in his chest, and another was lodged in his left arm, where it accelerated the onset of osteomyelitis. Rheumatism afflicted his joints, and his head often ached, the effect of a lifetime of chewing and smoking tobacco. He had survived near-total collapse of his health in 1822 and 1825, but for the rest of his life, he enjoyed few days completely free of agony. His outbursts of irascible fury, which sometimes shocked even his old friends and allies, owed partly to his suffering and to his efforts to suppress it. But after the debacle of 1825, they also owed to his determination to vindicate not just his own honor but that of the American people. For Jackson and his admirers, the two had become identical.

Willfulness did not mean rashness. In preparing to wreak his vengeance on Adams (whom he respected) and Clay (whom he despised), Jackson took care not to violate the accepted etiquette of presidential campaigning and appeal directly for the job. He was available to serve his country once more, but to look or sound less elevated than that would have been dishonorable (as well as onerous, given the state of his health). Jackson made only one major public appearance over the months before the election, at a public festivity in New Orleans on January 8, commemorating his great victory thirteen years earlier—an invitation, issued by the Louisiana legislature, that he could not refuse without seeming churlish. Yet while he stuck close to the Hermitage, Jackson threw himself into the fray as no other previous presidential candidate

From *The Rise of the American Democracy: Jefferson to Lincoln* by Sean Wilentz (W. W. Norton, 2005).

before him had, making himself available for visiting delegations of congressmen, giving interviews to interested parties, and writing letters for newspaper publication. When personal attacks on his character began, he became even more active, his sense of honor on the line. Some of his chief supporters, including Van Buren, asked that "we be let alone" and that Jackson "be *still,*" but Jackson would command this campaign just as surely as he had any of his military exploits.

His positions on several key issues were moderate and flexible, replicating much of what he had said in 1824, in generalities that would not upset the national coalition his agents were assembling. On the tariff, the primary political issue in 1828, Jackson remained blandly middle-of-the-road, repeated his support for a "judicious" tariff, and allowed men of different views to imagine that his sympathies lay with them. On internal improvements, Jackson modified his stance somewhat to support a distribution of surplus federal monies to the states for any road and canal projects they wished to undertake, but generally he restated his cautious support for projects that were genuinely national in scope. On the Indian question, he remained persuaded that, for the good of white settlers and natives alike, orderly removal was the only sound solution, but he refrained from saying anything that might be interpreted as an endorsement of the more extreme state-rights removal position.

Instead of a long list of positions and proposals, Jackson's campaign revolved around calls for "reform," a theme broad enough to unite a disparate coalition without merely resorting to platitudes. At one level, "reform" meant undoing what Jackson considered the theft of the presidency in 1825, and ending the political climate that had permitted it. Sometimes, Jackson and his supporters proposed specific changes. Jackson himself said he would exclude from his cabinet any man who sought the presidency—one obvious way to help prevent any future "corrupt bargain." He also called for a constitutional amendment to bar any member of Congress from eligibility for any other federal office (except in the judiciary) for two years beyond his departure from office. Other Jacksonians spoke of the candidate's support for the principle of rotation in office, for limiting presidents to a single term, and for banning the executive from appointing congressmen to civil posts—all means to disrupt insider exclusivity and what Jackson called the "intrigue and management" that had corrupted the government. Otherwise, the Jackson campaign simply reminded the voters of what had happened in 1825—and went further, to charge that "Lucifer" Clay had, during the House negotiations, offered to throw his support to Jackson if Jackson promised he would name him secretary of state.

At another level, "reform" meant returning American government to Jeffersonian first principles and halting the neo-Federalist revival supposedly being sponsored under the cover of the American System. President Adams, Jackson and his men charged, had made the mistake of following his father's footsteps, balancing a "hypocritical veneration for the great principles of republicanism" with artful manipulation of political power. All of "the asperity which marked the struggle of 98 & 1800," Jackson wrote, had returned. Having "gone into power contrary to the voice of the nation," the administration had claimed a mandate it did not possess, and then tried to expand its authority even further. Illegitimate from the start, the new Adams regime raised what

Jackson called the fundamental question at stake in the election: "[S]hall the government or the people rule?"

While Jackson and his closest advisors refined this message and called the shots from Nashville, his supporters built a sophisticated campaign apparatus unlike any previously organized in a presidential election, a combination so effective that it obviated the need for either a congressional caucus nomination or a national convention. At the top, Jackson's most capable Tennessee operatives, including John Overton, William Lewis, and John Eaton, concentrated their efforts in a central committee headquarters established in Nashville, where decisions about strategy and tactics could be taken efficiently, in rapid response to continuing events and with Jackson's approval. (A similar, smaller Jackson committee headquarters was established in Washington, to work closely with the pro- Jackson caucus in Congress that met regularly under Van Buren's aegis.) The central committee in turn dispatched its messages to (and received intelligence from) Jackson campaign committees established in each state. Finally, the Jacksonians responded to the reforms in presidential voting around the country—reforms that, by 1828, had included, in all but two states, giving the power to choose presidential electors directly to the voters—by coordinating activities at the local level. The state pro-Jackson committees linked up with local Jackson committees, sometimes called Hickory Clubs, that stirred up enthusiasm with rallies and parades and made sure that their supporters arrived at the polls.

Even more extraordinary than the campaign committees was the dense network of pro-Jackson newspapers that seemed to arise out of nowhere beginning in the spring of 1827. Early in the campaign, Jackson's congressional supporters had caucused and pledged to establish "a chain of newspaper posts, from the New England States to Louisiana, and branching off through Lexington to the Western States." In North Carolina alone, nine new Jacksonian papers had appeared by the middle of 1827, while in Ohio, eighteen new papers supplemented the five already in existence in 1824. In each state, the Jackson forces arranged for one newspaper to serve as the official organ of their respective state committees, refining the broadcast of an authoritative message while promoting a cadre of prominent loyal editors, including Ritchie at the *Enquirer,* Amos Kendall at the *Argus of Western America,* Edwin Croswell at the *Albany Argus,* Isaac Hill at the New Hampshire *Patriot,* and, above all, in Washington, Calhoun's friend Duff Green at the anti-administration *United States Telegraph.*

Funding (as well as copy) for the campaign sheets came directly from Jackson's congressional supporters and their friends, who pioneered numerous fund-raising gimmicks, including five-dollar-a-plate public banquets and other ticketed festivities. More substantial sums, including money raised from local bankers and businessmen in the New York–Philadelphia region, were collected and disbursed by Martin Van Buren, who served as the campaign's de facto national treasurer. Some of these monies went to the newspaper editors; others were spent on printing campaign books and pamphlets and producing paraphernalia such as campaign badges. Much of this material made its way to supporters at government cost, thanks to Jacksonian congressmen's liberal partisan use of their personal postal franking privileges.

Jackson's friends made special efforts to solidify their connections to various popular democratic movements, urban and rural, while also winning over more established and politically influential men. The alliances ranged from complete mergers to testy but effective ententes. Kentucky was a special prize for the Jacksonians, having cast its congressional vote for Adams in 1825 at Henry Clay's insistence. The 1828 tariff's high protective rates for hemp growers and manufacturers helped Van Buren offset Clay's advantage among the Kentucky elite, recently aligned with the Old Court Party—but the Jacksonians mainly pinned their hopes on Amos Kendall, Francis Blair, and the revitalized New Court Party machine. In protection-mad Pennsylvania, where the tariff proved extremely popular among the state's ironmongers, the Jacksonians appealed to all of the elements of the old Jeffersonian coalition—including manufacturers, western farmers, and rural Germans—with a propaganda effort headed by the papermaking magnate Congressman Samuel Ingham. In Philadelphia, the presence of numerous New School candidates for state and local office on the Jacksonian ticket alienated the new Working Men's Party, but Jackson's friends reached out to the labor insurgents in various ways, including a direct fifteen-hundred-dollar contribution to rescue Stephen Simpson's financially strapped paper, the *Columbian Observer.* Ultimately, the Workies devised their own Jackson ticket, picking and choosing among the official nominees, offering joint nominations to those they deemed reliable, but running their own candidates for the other slots.

New York, which Jackson had lost in 1824, was a different and, as ever, more difficult story. Under the revised state constitution, voters now chose the state's presidential electors. Unlike in most other states, however, New York's electoral votes would be apportioned on a district-by-district basis, meaning that even if Van Buren's agents carried the overall popular vote, Adams was bound to win a portion of the state's Electoral college total. DeWitt Clinton's death resolved much of the early bickering within the New York pro-Jackson camp, leaving Van Buren in control, but it also raised the possibility that some pro-Clinton Jackson men, who had supported the Tennessean chiefly to promote Clinton, might now drift over to Adams. And then there was the perplexing Anti-Masonic uprising in western New York, an outburst of democratic outrage that could never be won over to Grand Master Mason Andrew Jackson. Even with all of the southern states plus Pennsylvania likely to support Jackson, it would not be enough to elect him president. New York's result would be crucial.

The outlook for Jackson improved when political operatives determined that the Anti-Masonic movement remained, for the moment, localized, and that its chief advocates, Thurlow Weed and William Henry Seward, were having difficulty merging it with the Adams campaign. The outlook improved even more when Jackson's operatives confirmed that Henry Clay was not only a Mason but, as one delighted Manhattan pol put it, "a Mason of rank." Van Buren, meanwhile, decided to make the most of his New York strongholds, above all New York City, where the old Tammany Society, after a history of recurrent factionalism, turned into one of the most united and reliable pro-Jackson organizations in the state. As early as January, Tammany began hosting giant public events touting Jackson, and after the death of DeWitt Clinton—who was hated by the Tammany braves—the way was cleared for an all-out effort to spike the city's vote. Hickory Clubs appeared in every ward, sponsoring hickory tree–planting ceremonies and barroom gatherings to toast the general's success. A clutch of partisan editors in the already well-established New York press churned out reams of pro-Jackson material. "The more he is known," one pro-Jackson paper boasted of its man, "the less and less the charges against him seem to be true."

Against this juggernaut, Adams's supporters—their candidate an awkward public figure who spurned involvement in campaign organization—were badly overmatched. But they tried their best and performed credibly as organizers. Henry Clay, ignoring advice that he resign and let Adams bear the full brunt of defeat, took charge of creating a national campaign and of stumping at dinners and celebrations around the country to make the administration's case. Daniel Webster pitched in as well, overseeing the canvassing of potential financial backers (fully exploiting his ample personal connections to New England capitalists), collecting substantial sums, and keeping track of accounts. Although they could not equal the Jacksonians, the Adamsites created a substantial pro-administration press, headed in Washington by Joseph Gales and William Seaton's *National Intelligencer* and Peter Force's *National Journal.* The Adamsites printed forests' worth of pamphlets, leaflets, and handbills, organized their own state central committees, and sponsored countless dinners and commemorations. In at least one state, New Jersey, the Adamsites probably outorganized their opponents. And everywhere outside of Georgia, where Jackson ran unopposed, there was a genuine contest under way, with both parties, as one Marylander wrote, "fairly in the field, under *whip & spur.*"

Adamsite strategic and tactical errors at the state and local level repeatedly undermined whatever enthusiasm the administration's loyalists generated. High-minded stubbornness, linked to an aversion to what looked to some National Republicans like Van Buren–style wheeling and dealing, killed Adams's chances of carrying the middle Atlantic states. In upstate New York, the National Republicans insulted the Anti-Masons by rejecting their nominee for governor, a close friend of Thurlow Weed's, and then bidding the insurgents to show their good faith by adopting the pro-administration slate, ruining any chance of an alliance. In New York City, a protectionist movement, geared to halting the dumping of foreign manufactures on the New York market, arose in the spring; and, by autumn, it had gained a sizable following that cut across class and party lines. But the Adamsites, seemingly unable to believe that their protectionism might appeal to urban workers, held back from the movement. The protectionists ran their own ticket, and the opportunity was wasted. Similar shortsightedness prevailed in Philadelphia, where the Adamsites refused to make common cause with the surviving Federalist establishment, encouraging Jacksonian hopes of taking the city.

The Adamsites did excel in one area, the dark art of political slander. In 1827, a Cincinnati editor and friend of Clay's named Charles Hammond took a fact-finding tour into Kentucky and Tennessee, and unearthed some old stories about alleged legal irregularities in Jackson's marriage (supposedly he was a bigamist), along with charges that Jackson's wife, Rachel, was an adulteress and his mother a common prostitute. The charges were not simply mean-spirited: they evoked broader cultural presumptions that stigmatized Jackson as a boorish, lawless, frontier lowlife, challenging the Christian gentleman, John Quincy Adams. Clay immediately recommended his mudslinger friend to Webster, calling Hammond's paper "upon the whole, the most efficient and discreet gazette that espouses our cause," and suggested that the editor get direct financial support. Hammond, meanwhile, became a fountain of wild and inflammatory charges—that Jackson's mother had been brought to America by British soldiers, that she married a mulatto who was Jackson's father—all of which found their way into what may have been the lowest production of the 1828 campaign, a new journal entitled *Truth's Advocate and Monthly Anti-Jackson Expositor.* Jackson, enraged to the point of tears, held Clay responsible and sent John Eaton to confront the Kentuckian. Clay vehemently denied the charges, though his private correspondence with Hammond contains hints he was lying. Jackson continued to blame everything on Clay.

Character assassination in presidential politics was hardly invented in 1828—recall, for example, the lurid attacks on Thomas Jefferson and "Dusky Sally" Hemings—and Clay could easily and rightly complain of the Jackson campaign's unceasing attacks about the corrupt bargain as the basest sort of slander. But the Hammond affair, beginning more than a year before the 1828 electioneering commenced in earnest, marked the arrival of a new kind of calculated, mass cultural politics, pitting a fervent sexual moralism against a more forgiving, secularist, laissez-faire ethic. Hammond's attacks also ensured that a great deal of the campaign would be fought out in the sewer. The Jacksonians spread sensational falsehoods that President Adams was a secret aristocratic voluptuary who, while minister to Russia, had procured an innocent American woman for the tsar. Clay came in for merciless attacks as an embezzler, gambler, and brothel habitué. The Adamsites responded with a vicious handbill, covered with coffins, charging Jackson with the murder of six innocent American militamen during the Creek War, and labeling him "a wild man under whose charge the Government would collapse." The competition turned largely into a propaganda battle of personalities and politically charged cultural styles instead of political issues. A campaign slogan from four years earlier, coined in support of a possible Adams-Jackson ticket, assumed completely new meaning and summed up the differences, contrasting the nominees as "Adams who can write/Jackson who can fight."

And yet, for all of the vulgarities and slander, the campaign of 1828 was not an unprincipled and demagogic theatrical. Neither was it a covert sectional battle between a pro-slavery southerner and an antislavery New Englander; nor was it a head-on clash between pro-development Adamsite capitalists and antidevelopment Jacksonian farmers and workers, although strong views about slavery and economic development certainly came into play. The campaign pronounced a valediction on the faction-ridden jumble of the Era of Bad Feelings and announced the rough arrival of two distinct national coalitions, divided chiefly over the so-called corrupt bargain and the larger political implications of the American System. It was, above all, a contest over contrasting conceptions of politics, both with ties to the ideals of Thomas Jefferson.

For all of his setbacks and suffering, John Quincy Adams had never abandoned his moral vision of energetic government and national uplift. Protective tariffs, federal road and canal projects, and the other mundane features of the American System were always, to him, a means to that larger end. A fugitive from Federalism, Adams embodied one part of the Jeffersonian legacy, devoted to intellectual excellence, rationality, and government by the most talented and virtuous—those whom Jefferson himself, in a letter to Adams's father, had praised as "the natural aristoi." The younger Adams took the legacy a large step further, seeing the federal government as the best instrument for expanding the national store of intelligence, prosperity, beauty, and light.

Objections to the political ramifications of that vision united the opposition—objections rooted in another part of the Jeffersonian legacy, a fear of centralized government linked to a trust in the virtue and political wisdom of ordinary American voters. Jackson and his polyglot coalition contended that human betterment meant nothing without the backing of the people themselves. Lacking that fundamental legitimacy, Adams, Clay, and their entire administration had, the Jacksonians contended, been engaged from the start in a gigantic act of fraud—one that, to succeed, required shifting as much power as possible to Washington, where the corrupt few might more easily oppress the virtuous many, through unjust tariffs, costly federal commercial projects, and other legislative maneuvers. Were the Adamsites not removed as quickly as possible, there was no telling how far they might go in robbing the people's liberties, under the guise of national improvement, the American System, or some other shibboleth. Hence, the opposition's slogan: "Jackson and Reform."

Jackson himself laid out the stakes in a letter to an old friend, on the omens in what he called the Adamsites' exercise of "patronage" (by which he simply meant "power"):

> The present is a contest between the virtue of the people, & the influence of patronage[. S]hould patronage prevail, over virtue, then indeed "the safe precedent," will be established, that the President, appoints his successor in the person of the sec. of state—Then the people may prepare themselves to become "hewers of wood & drawers of water," to those in power, who with the Treasury at command, will wield by its corrupting influence a majority to support it—The present is an important struggle, for the perpetuity of our republican government, & I hope the virtue of the people may prevail, & all may be well.

Or as one of his New York supporters put it (presuming to speak on behalf of "the sound planters, farmers & mechanics of the country"), the Jacksonians beheld the coming election as "a great contest between the aristocracy and democracy of America."

The balloting began in September and, because of widely varying state polling laws, continued until November. Early returns from New England unsurprisingly gave Adams the lead, although not quite the clean sweep he had expected. (In Maine, a hardy band of ex-Crawford Radicals in and around Portland managed to win one of the state's electoral votes for Jackson.) The trend shifted heavily in mid-October, when Pennsylvania (overwhelmingly, including a strong plurality in Philadelphia) and Ohio (narrowly) broke for Jackson. It remains a matter of speculation how much this news affected the vote in other states, where the polls had not yet opened, but the Jacksonians took no chances, especially in New York, where the three days of voting did not commence until November 3. Holding back until the moment was ripe, the New York Jackson committee suddenly spread the word in late October that Jackson's election was virtually assured, in order to demoralize the opposition. In the end, Jackson carried the state's popular vote, although only by about 5,000 ballots out of 275,000 cast.

The state-by-state reporting of the vote, with news of one Jackson victory after another rolling in, heightened the impression that a virtual revolution was underway. The final tallies showed a more complicated reality. As expected, Adams captured New England, and Jackson swept the South below Maryland. But apart from Jackson's lopsided victory in Pennsylvania, the returns from the key battleground states were remarkably even.[1] If a mere 9,000 votes in New York, Ohio, and Kentucky had shifted from one column to the other, and if New York, with an Adams majority, had followed the winner-takes-all rule of most other states, Adams would have won a convincing 149 to 111 victory in the Electoral College. In other races for federal office the Adamsites actually improved their position. Above all, in the U.S. Senate, what had been a strong six-vote opposition majority in the Twentieth Congress would be reduced to a Jacksonian majority of two when the new Congress assembled in December 1829. Despite all their blunders, and despite Adams's unpopularity, the friends of the administration had not lost future political viability.

These wrinkles in the returns were lost amid Jackson's overwhelming victory nationwide. Jackson won 68 percent of the electoral vote and a stunning 56 percent of the popular vote—the latter figure representing a margin of victory that would not be surpassed for the rest of the nineteenth century. The totals came from a vastly larger number of voters than ever before in a presidential election, thanks to the adoption of popular voting for electors in four states and the bitterness of the one-on-one contest in the middle Atlantic states. More than a million white men voted for president in 1828, roughly four times the total of 1824. Jackson alone won three times as many votes as the total cast for all candidates four years earlier. The magnitude of it all left Adamsites, including the normally sanguine Henry Clay, miserable, and Jacksonians jubilant.

Perhaps the only Jacksonian not thoroughly overjoyed was Jackson himself. Well before the voting was over, he had understood what the outcome would be, and the news confirming his election caused no particular stir at the Hermitage. After all the months of campaigning behind the scenes, and now faced with actually assuming the presidency, the victor reported that "my mind is depressed." Sadness turned to panic and then grief in mid-December, when Rachel Jackson, preparing for the move to Washington, suddenly collapsed and, after five days of violent heart seizures, died. Her husband, who sat up with her throughout her ordeal, would never really recover from the shock. His great biographer James Parton wrote that it henceforth "subdued his spirit and corrected his speech," except on rare occasions when, in a calculated effort to intimidate his foes or inspire his allies, he would break into his customary fits of table pounding and swearing. Yet Rachel's death also steeled Jackson for the political battles to come. Her health had been precarious for several years before she died. Jackson was absolutely certain that the slanders of the 1828 campaign had finally broken her. And for that cruel and unforgivable blow, he would forever blame, above all others, his nemesis, Henry Clay.

Note

1. The final results from the key states were as follows:

	Popular Vote		Electoral Vote	
States	**Jackson**	**Adams**	**Jackson**	**Adams**
New York	140,763	135,413	20	16
Ohio	67,597	63,396	16	—
Kentucky	39,397	31,460	14	—

Figures from S&I, 2: 492.

Richard P. McCormick

NO

New Perspectives on Jacksonian Politics

The historical phenomenon that we have come to call Jacksonian democracy has long engaged the attention of American political historians, and never more insistently than in the past decade. From the time of Parton and Bancroft to the present day scholars have recognized that a profoundly significant change took place in the climate of politics simultaneously with the appearance of Andrew Jackson on the presidential scene. They have sensed that a full understanding of the nature of that change might enable them to dissolve some of the mysteries that envelop the operation of the American democratic process. With such a challenging goal before them, they have pursued their investigations with uncommon intensity and with a keen awareness of the contemporary relevance of their findings.

A cursory view of the vast body of historical writing on this subject suggests that scholars in the field have been largely preoccupied with attempts to define the content of Jacksonian democracy and identify the influences that shaped it. What did Jacksonian democracy represent, and what groups, classes, or sections gave it its distinctive character? The answers that have been given to these central questions have been—to put it succinctly—bewildering in their variety. The discriminating student, seeking the essential core of Jacksonianism, may make a choice among urban workingmen, southern planters, venturous conservatives, farm-bred *nouveaux riches,* western frontiersmen, frustrated entrepreneurs, or yeoman farmers. Various as are these interpretations of the motivating elements that constituted the true Jacksonians, the characterizations of the programmatic features of Jacksonian democracy are correspondingly diverse. Probably the reasonable observer will content himself with the conclusion that many influences were at work and that latitudinarianism prevailed among the Jacksonian faithful.

In contrast with the controversy that persists over these aspects of Jacksonian democracy, there has been little dissent from the judgment that "the 1830's saw the triumph in American politics of that democracy which has remained pre-eminently the distinguishing feature of our society." The consensus would seem to be that with the emergence of Jackson, the political pulse of the nation quickened. The electorate, long dormant or excluded from the polls by suffrage barriers, now became fired with unprecedented political excitement. The result was a bursting forth of democratic energies, evidenced by a marked upward surge in voting. Beard in his colorful fashion gave expression to the common viewpoint when he asserted that "the roaring flood of the new democracy was . . . [by 1824] foaming perilously near the crest. . . ." Schlesinger, with his allusion to the "immense popular vote" received by Jackson in 1824, creates a similar image. The Old Hero's victory in 1828 has been hailed as the consequence of a "mighty democratic uprising."

That a "new democracy, ignorant, impulsive, irrational" entered the arena of politics in the Jackson era has become one of the few unchallenged "facts" in an otherwise controversial field. Differences of opinion occur only when attempts are made to account for the remarkable increase in the size of the active electorate. The commonest explanations have emphasized the assertion by the common man of his newly won political privileges, the democratic influences that arose out of the western frontier, or the magnetic attractiveness of Jackson as a candidate capable of appealing with singular effectiveness to the backwoods hunter, the plain farmer, the urban workingman, and the southern planter.

Probably because the image of a "mighty democratic uprising" has been so universally agreed upon, there has been virtually no effort made to describe precisely the dimensions of the "uprising." Inquiry into this aspect of Jacksonian democracy has been discouraged by a common misconception regarding voter behavior before 1824. As the authors of one of our most recent and best textbooks put it: "In the years from the beginning of the government to 1824, a period for which we have no reliable election statistics, only small numbers of citizens seemed to have bothered to go to the polls." Actually, abundant data on pre-1824 elections is available, and it indicates a far higher rate of voting than has been realized. Only by taking this data into consideration can voting behavior after 1824 be placed in proper perspective.

The question of whether there was indeed a "mighty democratic uprising" during the Jackson era is certainly crucial in any analysis of the political character of Jacksonian democracy. More broadly, however, we need to know the degree to which potential voters participated in elections before, during, and after the period of Jackson's presidency as well as the conditions that apparently influenced the rate of voting. Only when such factors have been analyzed can we arrive at firm conclusions with respect to the dimensions of the political changes that we associate with Jacksonian democracy. Obviously in studying voter participation we are dealing with but one aspect of a large problem, and the limitations imposed by such a restrictive focus should be apparent.

In measuring the magnitude of the vote in the Jackson elections it is hardly significant to use the total popular vote cast throughout the nation. A comparison of the total vote cast in 1812, for example, when in eight of the seventeen states electors were chosen by the legislature, with the vote in 1832, when every state except South Carolina chose its electors by popular vote, has limited meaning. Neither is it revealing to compare the total vote in 1824 with that in 1832 without taking into consideration the population increase during the interval. The shift from the legislative choice of electors to their election by popular vote, together with the steady population growth, obviously swelled the presidential vote. But the problem to be investigated is whether the Jackson elections brought voters to the polls in such enlarged or unprecedented proportions as to indicate that a "new democracy" had burst upon the political scene.

The most practicable method for measuring the degree to which voters participated in elections over a period of time is to relate the number of votes cast to the number of potential voters. Although there is no way of calculating precisely how many eligible voters there were in any state at a given time, the evidence at hand demonstrates that with the exception of Rhode Island, Virginia, and Louisiana the potential electorate after r824 was roughly equivalent to the adult white male population. A meaningful way of expressing the rate of voter participation, then, is to state it in terms of the percentage of the adult white males actually voting. This index can be employed to measure the variations that occurred in voter participation over a period of time and in both national and state elections. Consequently a basis is provided for comparing the rate of voting in the Jackson elections with other presidential elections before and after his regime as well as with state elections.

Using this approach it is possible, first of all, to ascertain whether or not voter participation rose markedly in the three presidential elections in which Jackson was a candidate. Did voter participation in these elections so far exceed the peak participation in the pre-1824 elections as to suggest that a mighty democratic uprising was taking place? The accompanying data (Table 1) provides an answer to this basic question.

In the 1824 election not a single one of the eighteen states in which the electors were chosen by popular vote attained the percentage of voter participation that had been reached before 1824. Prior to that critical election, fifteen of those eighteen states had recorded votes in excess of 50 percent of their adult white male population, but in 1824 only two states—Maryland and Alabama—exceeded this modest mark. The average rate of voter participation in the election was 26.5 per cent. This hardly fits the image of the "roaring flood of the new democracy . . . foaming perilously near the crest. . . ."

There would seem to be persuasive evidence that in 1828 the common man flocked to the polls in unprecedented numbers, for the proportion of adult white males voting soared to 56.3 per cent, more than double the 1824 figure. But this outpouring shrinks in magnitude when we observe that in only six of the twenty-two states involved were new highs in voter participation established. In three of these—Maryland, Virginia, and Louisiana—the recorded gain was inconsiderable, and in a fourth—New York—the bulk of the increase might be attributed to changes that had been made in suffrage qualifications as recently as 1821 and 1826. Six states went over the 70 per cent mark, whereas ten had bettered that performance before 1824. Instead of a "mighty democratic uprising" there was in 1828 a voter turnout that approached—but in only a few instances matched or exceeded—the maximum levels that had been attained before the Jackson era.

The advance that was registered in 1828 did not carry forward to 1832. Despite the fact that Jackson was probably at the peak of his personal popularity, that he was engaged in a campaign that was presumably to decide issues of

Table 1

Percentages of Adult White Males Voting in Elections

State	Highest Known % AWM Voting before 1824		Presidential Elections					
	Year	% AWM	1824	1828	1832	1836	1840	1844
Maine	1812[g]	62.0	18.9	42.7	66.2*	37.4	82.2	67.5
New Hampshire	1814[g]	80.8	16.8	76.5	74.2	38.2	86.4*	65.6
Vermont	1812[g]	79.9	–	55.8	50.0	52.5	74.0	65.7
Massachusetts	1812[g]	67.4	29.1	25.7	39.3	45.1	66.4	59.3
Rhode Island	1812[g]	49.4	12.4	18.0	22.4	24.1	33.2	39.8
Connecticut	1819[1]	54.4	14.9	27.1	45.9	52.3	75.7*	76.1
New York	1810[g]	41.5	–	70.4*	72.1	60.2	77.7	73.6
New Jersey	1808[p]	71.8	31.1	70.9	69.0	69.3	80.4*	81.6
Pennsylvania	1808[g]	71.5	19.6	56.6	52.7	53.1	77.4*	75.5
Delaware	1804[g]	81.9	–	–	67.0	69.4	82.8*	85.0
Maryland	1820[1]	69.0	53.7	76.2*	55.6	67.5	84.6	80.3
Virginia	1800[p]	25.9	11.5	27.6*	30.8	35.1	54.6	54.5
North Carolina	1823[c]	70.0#	42.2	56.8	31.7	52.9	83.1*	79.1
Georgia	1812[c]	62.3	–	35.9	33.0	64.9*	88.9	94.0
Kentucky	1820[g]	74.4	25.3	70.7	73.9	61.1	74.3	80.3*
Tennessee	1817[g]	80.0	26.8	49.8	28.8	55.2	89.6*	89.6
Louisiana	1812[g]	34.2	–	36.3*	24.4	19.2	39.4	44.7
Alabama	1819[g]	96.7	52.1	53.6	33.3	65.0	89.8	82.7
Mississippi	1823[g]	79.8	41.6	56.6	32.8	62.8	88.2*	89.7
Ohio	1822[g]	46.5	34.8	75.8*	73.8	75.5	84.5	83.6
Indiana	1822[g]	52.4	37.5	68.3*	61.8	70.1	86.0	84.9
Illinois	1822[g]	55.8	24.2	51.9	45.6	43.7	85.9*	76.3
Missouri	1820[g]	71.9	20.1	54.3	40.8	35.6	74.0*	74.7
Arkansas		–	–	–	–	35.0	86.4	68.8
Michigan		–	–	–	–	35.7	84.9	79.3
National Average			26.5	56.3	54.9	55.2	78.0	74.9

* Exceeded pre-1824 high
g Gubernatorial election
p Presidential election
Estimate based on incomplete returns
c Congressional election
1 Election of legislature

great magnitude, and that in the opinion of some authorities a "well-developed two party system on a national scale" had been established, there was a slight decline in voter participation. The average for the twenty-three states participating in the presidential contest was 54.9 per cent. In fifteen states a smaller percentage of the adult white males went to the polls in 1832 than in 1828. Only five states bettered their pre-1824 highs. Again the conclusion would be that it was essentially the pre-1824 electorate—diminished in most states and augmented in a few—that voted in 1832. Thus, after three Jackson elections, sixteen states had not achieved the proportions of voter participation that they had reached before 1824. The "new democracy" had not yet made its appearance.

A comparison of the Jackson elections with earlier presidential contests is of some interest. Such comparisons have little validity before 1808 because few states chose electors by popular vote, and for certain of those states the complete returns are not available. In 1816 and 1820 there was so little opposition to Monroe that the voter interest was negligible. The most relevant elections, therefore, are those of 1808 and 1812. The accompanying table (Table 2) gives the percentages of adult white males voting in 1808 and 1812 in those states for which full returns could be found, together with the comparable percentages for the elections of 1824 and 1828. In 1824 only one state—Ohio—surpassed the highs established in either 1808 or 1812. Four more joined this list in 1828—Virginia, Maryland, Pennsylvania, and New Hampshire—although the margin in the last case was so small as to be inconsequential. The most significant conclusion to be drawn from this admittedly limited and unrepresentative data is that in those states where there was a vigorous two-party contest in 1808 and 1812 the vote was relatively high. Conversely, where there was little or no contest in 1824 or 1828, the vote was low.

Table 2

Percentages of Adult White Males Voting in Presidential Elections

State	1808	1812	1824	1828
Maine	Legis.	50.0	18.9	42.7
New Hampshire	62.1	75.4	16.8	76.5
Massachusetts	Legis.	51.4	29.1	25.7
Rhode Island	37.4	37.7	12.4	18.0
New Jersey	71.8	Legis.	31.1	70.9
Pennsylvania	34.7	45.5	19.6	56.6
Maryland	48.4	56.5	53.7	76.2
Virginia	17.7	17.8	11.5	27.6
Ohio	12.8	20.0	34.8	75.8

Note: No complete returns of the popular vote cast for electors in Kentucky or Tennessee in 1808 and 1812 and in North Carolina in 1808 could be located.

When an examination is made of voting in other than presidential elections prior to 1824, the inaccuracy of the impression that "only small numbers of citizens" went to the polls becomes apparent. Because of the almost automatic succession of the members of the "Virginia dynasty" and the early deterioration of the national two-party system that had seemed to be developing around 1800, presidential elections did not arouse voter interest as much as did those for governor, state legislators, or even members of Congress. In such elections at the state level the "common man" was stimulated by local factors to cast his vote, and he frequently responded in higher proportions than he did to the later stimulus provided by Jackson.

The average voter participation for all the states in 1828 was 56.3 per cent. Before 1824 fifteen of the twenty-two states had surpassed that percentage. Among other things, this means that the 1828 election failed to bring to the polls the proportion of the electorate that had voted on occasion in previous elections. There was, in other words, a high potential vote that was frequently realized in state elections but which did not materialize in presidential elections. The unsupported assumption that the common man was either apathetic or debarred from voting by suffrage barriers before 1824 is untenable in the light of this evidence.

In state after state (see Table 1) gubernatorial elections attracted 70 per cent or more of the adult white males to the polls. Among the notable highs recorded were Delaware with 81.9 per cent in 1804, New Hampshire with 80.8 per cent in 1814, Tennessee with 80.0 per cent in 1817, Vermont with 79.9 per cent in 1812, Mississippi with 79.8 per cent in 1823, and Alabama with a highly improbable 96.7 per cent in its first gubernatorial contest in 1819. There is reason to believe that in some states, at least, the voter participation in the election of state legislators was even higher than in gubernatorial elections. Because of the virtual impossibility of securing county-by-county or district-by-district returns for such elections, this hypothesis is difficult to verify.

Down to this point the voter turnout in the Jackson elections has been compared with that in elections held prior to 1824. Now it becomes appropriate to inquire whether during the period 1824 through 1832 voters turned out in greater proportions for the three presidential contests than they did for the contemporary state elections. If, indeed, this "new democracy" bore some special relationship to Andrew Jackson or to his policies, it might be anticipated that interest in the elections in which he was the central figure would stimulate greater voter participation than gubernatorial contests, in which he was at most a remote factor.

Actually, the election returns show fairly conclusively that throughout the eight-year period the electorate continued to participate more extensively in state elections than in those involving the presidency. Between 1824 and 1832 there were fifty regular gubernatorial elections in the states that chose their electors by popular vote. In only sixteen of these fifty instances did the vote for President surpass the corresponding vote for governor. In Rhode Island, Delaware, Tennessee, Kentucky, Illinois, Mississippi, Missouri, and Georgia the vote for governor consistently exceeded that for President. Only in Connecticut was the reverse true. Viewed from this perspective, too, the remarkable feature of the vote in the Jackson elections is not its immensity but rather its smallness.

Finally, the Jackson elections may be compared with subsequent presidential elections. Once Jackson had retired to the Hermitage, and figures of less dramatic proportions took up the contest for the presidency, did voter participation rise or fall? This question can be answered by observing the percentage of adult white males who voted in each state in the presidential elections of 1836 through 1844 (Table 1). Voter participation in the 1836 election remained near the level that had been established in 1828 and 1832, with 55.2 per cent of the adult white males voting. Only five states registered percentages in excess of their pre-1824 highs. But in 1840 the "new democracy" made its appearance with explosive suddenness.

In a surge to the polls that has rarely, if ever, been exceeded in any presidential election, four out of five (78.0 per cent) of the adult white males cast their votes for Harrison or Van Buren. This new electorate was greater than that of the Jackson period by more than 40 per cent. In all but five states—Vermont, Massachusetts, Rhode Island, Kentucky, and Alabama—the peaks of voter participation reached before 1824 were passed. Fourteen of the twenty-five states involved set record highs for voting that were not to be broken throughout the remainder of the ante bellum period. Now, at last, the common man—or at least the man who previously had not been sufficiently aroused to vote in presidential elections—cast his weight into the political balance. This "Tippecanoe democracy," if such a label is permissible, was of a different order of magnitude from the Jacksonian democracy. The elections in which Jackson figured brought to the polls only those men who were accustomed to voting in state or national elections, except in a very few states. The Tippecanoe canvass witnessed an extraordinary expansion of the size of the presidential electorate far beyond previous dimensions. It was in 1840, then, that the "roaring flood of the new democracy" reached its crest. And it engulfed the Jacksonians.

The flood receded only slightly in 1844, when 74.9 per cent of the estimated , potential dectorate went to the polls. Indeed, nine states attained their record highs for the period. In 1848 and 1852 there was a general downward trend in voter participation, followed by a modest upswing in 1856 and 1860. But the level of voter activity remained well above that of the Jackson elections. The conclusion to be drawn is that the "mighty democratic uprising" came after the period of Jackson's presidency.

Now that the quantitative dimensions of Jacksonian democracy as a political phenomenon have been delineated and brought into some appropriate perspective, certain questions still remain to be answered. Granted that the Jacksonian electorate—as revealed by the comparisons that have been set forth—was not really very large, how account for the fact that voter participation doubled between the elections of 1824 and 1828? It is true that the total vote soared from around 359,000 to 1,155,400 and that the percentage of voter participation more than doubled. Traditionally, students of the Jackson period have been impressed by this steep increase in voting and by way of explanation have identified the causal factors as the reduction of suffrage qualifications, the democratic influence of the West, or the personal magnetism of Jackson. The validity of each of these hypotheses needs to be reexamined.

In no one of the states in which electors were chosen by popular vote was any significant change made in suffrage qualifications between 1824 and 1828. Subsequently, severe restrictions were maintained in Rhode Island until 1842, when some liberalization was effected, and in Virginia down to 1850. In Louisiana, where the payment of a tax was a requirement, the character of the state tax system apparently operated to restrict the suffrage at least as late as 1845. Thus with the three exceptions noted, the elimination of suffrage barriers was hardly a factor in producing an enlarged electorate during the Jackson and post-Jackson periods. Furthermore, all but a few states had extended the privilege of voting either to all male taxpayers or to all adult male citizens by 1810. After Connecticut eliminated its property qualification in 1818, Massachusetts in 1821, and New York in 1821 and 1826, only Rhode Island, Virginia, and Louisiana were left on the list of "restrictionist" states. Neither Jackson's victory nor the increased vote in 1828 can be attributed to the presence at the polls of a newly enfranchised mass of voters.

Similarly, it does not appear that the western states led the way in voter participation. Prior to 1824, for example, Ohio, Indiana, and Illinois had never brought to the polls as much as 60 percent of their adult white males. Most of the eastern states had surpassed that level by considerable margins. In the election of 1828 six states registered votes in excess of 70 per cent of their adult white male populations. They were in order of rank: New Hampshire, Maryland, Ohio, New Jersey, Kentucky, and New York. The six leaders in 1832 were: New Hampshire, Kentucky, Ohio, New York, New Jersey, and Delaware. It will be obvious that the West, however that region may be defined, was not leading the "mighty democratic uprising." Western influences, then, do not explain the increased vote in 1828.

There remains to be considered the factor of Jackson's personal popularity. Did Jackson, the popular hero, attract voters to the polls in unprecedented proportions? The comparisons that have already been made between the Jackson elections and other elections—state and national—before, during, and after his presidency would suggest a negative answer to the question. Granted that a majority of the voters in 1828 favored Jackson, it is not evident that his partisans stormed the polls any more enthusiastically than did the Adams men. Of the six highest states in voter participation in 1828, three favored Adams and three were for Jackson, which could be interpreted to mean that the convinced Adams supporters turned out no less zealously for their man than did the ardent Jacksonians. When Van Buren replaced Jackson in 1836, the voting average increased slightly over 1832. And, as has been demonstrated, the real manifestation of the "new democracy" came not in 1828 but in 1840.

The most satisfactory explanation for the increase in voter participation between 1824 and 1828 is a simple and obvious one. During the long reign of the Virginia dynasty, interest in presidential elections dwindled. In 1816 and 1820 there had been no contest. The somewhat fortuitous termination of the Virginia succession in 1824 and the failure of the congressional caucus to solve the problem of leadership succession threw the choice of a President upon the electorate. But popular interest was dampened by the confusion of choice presented by the multiplicity of candidates, by the disintegration of the old national parties, by the fact that in most states one or another of the candidates was so overwhelmingly popular as to forestall any semblance of a contest, and possibly by the realization that the election would ultimately be decided by the House of Representatives. By 1828 the situation had altered. There were but two candidates in the field, each of whom had substantial sectional backing. A clear-cut contest impended, and the voters became sufficiently aroused to go to the polls in moderate numbers.

One final question remains. Why was the vote in the Jackson elections relatively low when compared with previous and contemporary state elections and with presidential votes after 1840? The answer, in brief, is that in most states either Jackson or his opponent had such a one-sided advantage that the result was a foregone conclusion. Consequently there was little incentive for the voters to go to the polls.

This factor can be evaluated in fairly specific quantitative terms. If the percentage of the total vote secured by each candidate in each state in the election of 1828 is calculated, the difference between the percentages can be used as an index of the closeness, or one-sidedness, of the contest. In Illinois, for example, Jackson received 67 percent of the total vote and Adams, 33; the difference—thirty-four points—represents the margin between the candidates. The average difference between the candidates, taking all the states together, was thirty-six points. Expressed another way this would mean that in the average state the winning candidate received more than twice the vote of the loser. Actually, this was the case in thirteen of the twenty-two states (see Table 3). Such a wide margin virtually placed these states in f the "no contest" category.

A remarkably close correlation existed between the size of the voter turnout and the relative closeness of the contest. The six states previously listed as having the greatest voter participation in 1828 were among the seven states with the smallest margin of difference between the candidates. The exception was Louisiana, where restrictions on the suffrage curtailed the vote. Even in this instance, however, it is significant that voter participation in Louisiana reached a record high. In those states, then, where there was a close balance of political forces the vote was large, and conversely, where the contest was very one sided, the vote was low.

Most of the states in 1828 were so strongly partial to one or another of the candidates that they can best be characterized as one-party states. Adams encountered little opposition in New England, except in New Hampshire, and Jackson met with hardly any resistance in the South. It was chiefly in the middle states and the older West that the real battle was waged. With the removal of Adams from the scene after 1828, New England became less of a one-party section, but the South remained extremely one sided. Consequently it is not surprising that voter participation in 1832 failed even to match that of 1828.

Here, certainly, is a factor of crucial importance in explaining the dimensions of the voter turnout in the Jackson elections. National parties were still in a rudimentary condition and were highly unbalanced from state to state. Indeed, a two-party system scarcely could be said to exist in more than half of

Table 3

Differential between Percentages of Total Vote Obtained by Major Presidential Candidates, 1828–1844

State	1828	1832	1836	1840	1844
Maine	20	10	20	1	13
New Hampshire	7	13	50	11	19
Vermont	50	10	20	29	18
Massachusetts	66	30	9	16	12
Rhode Island	50	14	6	23	20
Connecticut	50	20	1	11	5
New York	2	4	9	4	1
New Jersey	4	1	1	4	1
Pennsylvania	33	16	4	1	2
Delaware	—	2	6	10	3
Maryland	2	1	7	8	5
Virginia	38	50	13	1	6
North Carolina	47	70	6	15	5
Georgia	94	100	4	12	4
Kentucky	1	9	6	29	8
Tennessee	90	90	16	11	1
Louisiana	6	38	3	19	3
Alabama	80	100	11	9	18
Mississippi	60	77	2	7	13
Ohio	3	3	4	9	2
Indiana	13	34	12	12	2
Illinois	34	37	10	2	12
Missouri	41	32	21	14	17
Arkansas	—	—	28	13	26
Michigan	—	—	9	4	6
Average Differential	36	36	11	11	9

the states until after 1832. Where opposing parties had been formed to contest the election, the vote was large, but where no parties, or only one, took the field, the vote was low. By 1840, fairly well-balanced parties had been organized in virtually every state. In only three states did the margin between Harrison and Van Buren exceed twenty points, and the average for all the states was only eleven points. The result was generally high voter participation.[1]

When Jacksonian democracy is viewed from the perspectives employed in this analysis, its political dimensions in so far as they relate to the behavior of the electorate can be described with some precision. None of the Jackson elections involved a "mighty democratic uprising" in the sense that voters were drawn to the polls in unprecedented proportions. When compared with the peak participation recorded for each state before 1824, or with contemporaneous gubernatorial elections, or most particularly with the vast outpouring of the electorate in 1840, voter participation in the Jackson elections was unimpressive. They key to the relatively low presidential vote would seem to be the extreme political imbalance that existed in most states as between the Jacksonians and their opponents. Associated with this imbalance was the immature development of national political parties. Indeed, it can be highly misleading to think in terms of national parties in connection with the Jackson elections. As balanced, organized parties subsequently made their appearance from state to state, and voters were stimulated by the prospect of a genuine contest, a marked rise in voter participation occurred. Such conditions did not prevail generally across the nation until 1840, and then at last the "mighty democratic uprising" took place.

Note

1. Careful analysis of the data in Table 3 will suggest that there were three fairly distinct stages in the emergence of a nationally balanced two-party system. Balanced parties appeared first in the middle states between 1824 and 1828. New England remained essentially a one-party section until after Adams had passed from the scene; then competing parties appeared. In the South and the newer West, a one-party dominance continued until divisions arose over who should succeed Jackson. Sectional loyalties to favorite sons obviously exerted a determining influence on presidential politics, and consequently on party formation, in the Jackson years.

POSTSCRIPT

Did the Election of 1828 Represent a Democratic Revolt of the People?

The two essays in this issue discuss the presidential election of 1828 from different approaches. Professor Richard McCormick, a veteran analyzer of nineteenth-century politics, views the 1828 election through the lens of quantitative history. He uses statistics to break down a number of generalizations about the significance of Jackson's election. The Rutgers University professor discounts the removal of property qualifications for voting, the influence of the western states, and the charisma of Jackson as the major reasons why twice as many voters turned out in the 1828 presidential race than they did four years earlier. He argues that in spite of such statistics, a higher percentage of voters had turned out for earlier gubernatorial and legislative elections in most states than for the 1828 presidential election. In McCormick's view, the key election was 1840, not 1828. Why? Because by this time, the two parties—Whigs and Democrats—were equally balanced in all sections of the country, and voters turn out in larger numbers when they perceive a closely contested presidential race.

McCormick's article raises a number of questions. Is he comparing apples and oranges in contrasting local and national elections? Using McCormick's data, is it possible for other historians to reach different conclusions? How does one explain a 50 percent increase in voter turnout between 1824 and 1828?

In the second selection from his Pulitzer Prize–winning book on *The Rise of American Democracy* (W.W. Norton & Co., 2005), Professor Sean Wilentz restores Jackson to the center of the era. He disagrees with McCormick and other historians such as Lee Benson whose *Concept of Jacksonian Democracy: New York as a Test Case* (Princeton Paperback, 1970) stressed ethno-cultural factors in determining voting patterns and removed Jackson from the center of the era. Wilentz disagrees with McCormick and argues that the second-party system started with the presidential election of 1828 when Jackson's personality enabled state coalitions in New York, Ohio, and Kentucky, among others, to organize a national presidential campaign in support of Jackson. McCormick is correct in arguing that some state and local elections prior to 1828 had a larger proportional turnout of voters. But local elections and issues were far more important to a nation barely unified in its transportation and economic systems. Jackson's election and presidency shifted the locus of power to Washington, D.C.

Wilentz's 1,000-page book, which weighs more than *Webster's dictionary,* is especially strong on the development and mobilization of political organizations in the years from Jefferson through Lincoln. His description of the campaign with its sloganeering, mobilization of voters, and mudslinging (Jackson's wife was called a "harlot" and Adams a "pimp), set the tone for the way presidential elections would be run in the future. Contemporaries realized the shift when on inauguration day, March 4, 1829, twenty thousand people from all parts of the country converged on Washington, broke into the White House reception, and cheered wildly for Jackson. Wrote one sour contemporary: "It was like the inundation of the northern barbarians into Rome, save that the tumultuous tide came in from all parts of the compass."

Finally, Wilentz points out that the democratic triumphs led to the rise of "interest group" politics. Men and women, who were outside the normal political process, could use the "new tools" of "a mass press, popular conventions, petition campaigns, and other means to rouse support for . . . such outlandish things as granting women the vote, banning liquor, restricting immigration, and abolishing slavery."

Richard P. McCormick has a full-length study of *The Second American Party System: Party Formation in the Jacksonian Era* (University of North Carolina Press, 1966). A shorter version, "Political Development and the Second Party System" along with other important essays by historians and political scientists, is in William Nisbet Chambers and Water Dean Burnham, eds., *The American Party Systems: Stages of Political Development* (New York, 1967). The fullest account of *The Presidential Election of 1828* (J.P. Lippincott, 1963) is by Jackson's best-known biographer Robert V. Remini. See his shorter version of the "Election of 1828" in Arthur M. Schlesinger, Jr., ed., *The Coming to Power: Critical Presidential Elections in American History* (Chelsea House Publishers, 1971, 1972).

On the political culture of the 1820s and 1830s, see the classic *Andrew Jackson: Symbol for an Age* (Oxford University Press, 1955, 1983) by the late John William Ward. Influencing Wilentz's work were two books on Michigan and Massachusetts politics by Ronald P. Formisano. The first chapter of *The Transformation of Political Culture: Massachusetts Parties, 1790–1840* (Oxford University Press, 1983) talks about how divisions between the "Core and Periphery" destroyed the older form of deferential politics. Daniel Howe's *The Political Culture of American Wings* (University of Chicago Press, 1979) examines the party's pro-business and moralistic outlook.

Useful review essays on the politics of the Jacksonian era are Ronald Formisano, "Toward a Reconstruction of Jacksonian Politics: A Review of the Literature, 1959–1975," *Journal of American History* 63 (1976); Sean Wilentz, "On Class and Politics in Jacksonian America," *Reviews in American History* 10 (1982); Daniel Feller, "Politics and Society: Toward a Jacksonian Synthesis," *Journal of the Early American Republic* 10 (1990); the most recent are the essays by Jonathan Atkins," The Jacksonian Era, 1825–1844" and Jon Ashworth, "The Sectionalization of American Politics, 1845–1860" in *A Companion to 19th-Century America* (Blackwell Publishers, 2001).

ISSUE 10

Did the Industrial Revolution Provide More Economic Opportunities for Women in the 1830s?

YES: Thomas Dublin, from "Women, Work, and Protest in the Early Lowell Mills: 'The Oppressing Hand of Avarice Would Enslave Us'," *Labor History* (Winter 1975)

NO: Gerda Lerner, from "The Lady and the Mill Girl: Changes in the Status of Women in the Age of Jackson," *American Studies* (Spring 1969)

ISSUE SUMMARY

YES: Professor Thomas Dublin argues that the women who worked in the Lowell mills in the 1830s were a close-knit community who developed bonds of mutual dependence in both their boarding houses and the factory.

NO: According to Professor Gerda Lerner, while Jacksonian democracy provided political and economic opportunities for men, both the "lady" and the "mill girl" were equally disenfranchised and isolated from vital centers of economic opportunity.

In 1961 President John F. Kennedy established the Commission on the Status of Women to examine "the prejudice and outmoded customs that act as barriers to the full realization of women's basic rights." The roots of Friedan's "feminine mystique" go back much earlier than the post–World War II "baby boom" generation of suburban America. Women historians have traced the origins of the modern family to the early nineteenth century. As the nation became more stable politically, the roles of men, women, and children became segmented in ways that still exist today.

In nineteenth-century America, most middle-class white women stayed home. Those who entered the workforce as teachers or became reformers were usually extending the values of the Cult of True Womanhood to the outside world. This was true of the women reformers in the Second Great Awakening and the peace, temperance, and abolitionist movements before the

Civil War. The first real challenge to the traditional values system occurred when a handful of women showed up at Seneca Falls, New York, in 1848 to sign the Women's Declaration of Rights.

It soon became clear that if they were going to pass reform laws, women would have to obtain the right to vote. After an intense struggle the Nineteenth Amendment was ratified on August 26, 1920. Once the women's movement obtained the vote, there was no agreement on future goals. The problems of the Great Depression and World War II overrode women's issues.

World War II brought about major changes for working women. Six million women entered the labor force for the first time, many of whom were married. "The proportion of women in the labor force," writes Lois Banner, "increased from 25 percent in 1940 to 36 percent in 1945." Many women moved into high-paying, traditionally men's jobs as policewomen, firefighters, and precision toolmakers. The federal government also erected federal child-care facilities, but when the war ended in 1945 many working women lost their nontraditional jobs. The federal day-care program was eliminated, and the government told women to go home even though a 1944 study by the Women's Bureau concluded that 80 percent of working women wanted to continue in their jobs after the war. Most history texts emphasized that women did return home, moved to the suburbs, and created a baby boom generation, which reversed the downward size of families between 1946 and 1964. What is lost in this description is the fact that after 1947 the number of working women again began to rise. By 1951 the proportion had reached 31 percent. Twenty-two years later, at the height of the women's liberation movement, it reached 42 percent.

Ironically modern feminists were unaware of their past. But the situation changed rapidly. The women's movement brought a new wave of female scholars into the profession who were interested in researching and writing about their past.

Issue 10 brings us back to the 1830s when the textile mills along the river systems of Rhode Island, Connecticut, and Massachusetts created the first factory system. Did this "market revolution," a term now favored by current historians, help or hinder the economic opportunities for women?

In the first selection, Professor Thomas Dublin sees positive changes taking place in the lives of the mill girls. He maintains that the girls who worked in the Lowell, Massachusetts factories in the 1830s were a close-knit community of young women who developed bonds of mutual dependence in both their boarding houses and the factory. But Professor Gerda Lerner disagrees. The Jacksonian era may have provided political and economic opportunities for men, but it was different for women. By the 1850s, immigrant women from Ireland had replaced the native-born Lowell females in the low-wage factories while middle-class women were excluded from the medical, legal, and business professions.

Thomas Dublin

Women, Work, and Protest in the Early Lowell Mills: "The Oppressing Hand of Avarice Would Enslave Us"

In the years before 1850 the textile mills of Lowell, Massachusetts were a celebrated economic and cultural attraction. Foreign visitors invariably included them on their American tours. Interest was prompted by the massive scale of these mills, the astonishing productivity of the power-driven machinery, and the fact that women comprised most of the workforce. Visitors were struck by the newness of both mills and city as well as by the culture of the female operatives. The scene stood in sharp contrast to the gloomy mill towns of the English industrial revolution.

Lowell, was, in fact, an impressive accomplishment. In 1820, there had been no city at all—only a dozen family farms along the Merrimack River in East Chelmsford. In 1821, however, a group of Boston capitalists purchased land and water rights along the river and a nearby canal, and began to build a major textile manufacturing center. Opening two years later, the first factory employed Yankee women recruited from the nearby countryside. Additional mills were constructed until, by 1840, ten textile corporations with thirty-two mills valued at more than ten million dollars lined the banks of the river and nearby canals. Adjacent to the mills were rows of company boarding houses and tenements which accommodated most of the eight thousand factory operatives.

As Lowell expanded, and became the nation's largest textile manufacturing center, the experiences of women operatives changed as well. The increasing number of firms in Lowell and in the other mill towns brought the pressure of competition. Overproduction became a problem and the prices of finished cloth decreased. The high profits of the early years declined and so, too, did conditions for the mill operatives. Wages were reduced and the pace of work within the mills was stepped up. Women operatives did not accept these changes without protest. In 1834 and 1836 they went on strike to protest wage cuts, and between 1843 and 1848 they mounted petition campaigns aimed at reducing the hours of labor in the mills.

These labor protests in early Lowell contribute to our understanding of the response of workers to the growth of industrial capitalism in the first half of the nineteenth century. They indicate the importance of values and attitudes dating back to an earlier period and also the transformation of these values in a new setting.

The major factor in the rise of a new consciousness among operatives in Lowell was the development of a close-knit community among women working in the mills. The structure of work and the nature of housing contributed to the growth of this community. The existence of community among woman, in turn, was an important element in the repeated labor protests of the period.

The organization of this paper derives from the logic of the above argument. It will examine the basis of community in the experiences of women operatives and then the contribution that the community of women made to the labor protests in these years as well as the nature of the new consciousness expressed by these protests.

The pre-conditions for the labor unrest in Lowell before 1850 may be found in the study of the daily worklife of its operatives. In their everyday, relatively conflict-free lives, mill women created the mutual bonds which made possible united action in times of crisis. The existence of a tight-knit community among them was the most important element in determining the collective, as opposed to individual, nature of this response.

Before examining the basis of community among women operatives in early Lowell, it may be helpful to indicate in what sense "community" is being used. The women are considered a "community" because of the development of bonds of mutual dependence among them. In this period they came to depend upon one another and upon the larger group of operatives in very important ways. Their experiences were not simply similar or parallel to one another, but were inextricably intertwined. Furthermore, they were conscious of the existence of community, expressing it very clearly in their writings and in labor protests. "Community" for them had objective and subjective dimensions and both were important in their experience of women in the mills.

The mutual dependence among women in early Lowell was rooted in the structure of mill work itself. Newcomers to the mills were particularly dependent on their fellow operatives, but even experienced hands relied on one another for considerable support.

New operatives generally found their first experiences difficult, even harrowing, though they may have already done considerable hand-spinning and weaving in their own homes. The initiation of one of them is described in fiction in the *Lowell Offering:*

> The next morning she went into the Mill; and at first the sight of so many bands, and wheels, and springs in constant motion, was very frightful. She felt afraid to touch the loom, and she was almost sure she could never learn to weave . . . the shuttle flew out, and made a new bump on her head; and the first time she tried to spring the lathe, she broke out a quarter of the treads.

While other accounts present a somewhat less difficult picture, most indicate that women only became proficient and felt satisfaction in their work after several months in the mills.

The textile corporations made provisions to ease the adjustment of new operatives. Newcomers were not immediately expected to fit into the mill's regular work routine. They were at first assigned work as sparehands and were paid a daily wage independent of the quantity of work they turned out. As a sparehand, the newcomer worked with an experienced hand who instructed her in the intricacies of the job. The sparehand spelled her partner for short stretches of time, and occasionally took the place of an absentee. One woman described the learning process in a letter reprinted in the *Offering*:

> Well, I went into the mill, and was put to learn with a very patient girl. . . . You cannot think how odd everything seems. . . . They set me to threading shuttles, and tying weaver's knots, and such things, and now I have improved so that I can take care of one loom. I could take care of two if only I had eyes in the back part of my head. . . .

After the passage of some weeks or months, when she could handle the normal complement of machinery—two looms for weavers during the 1830s—and when a regular operative departed, leaving an opening, the sparehand moved into a regular job.

Through this system of job training, the textile corporations contributed to the development of community among female operatives. During the most difficult period in an operative's career, the first months in the mill, she relied upon other women workers for training and support. And for every sparehand whose adjustment to mill work was aided in this process, there was an experienced operative whose work was also affected. Women were relating to one another during the work process and not simply tending their machinery. Given the high rate of turnover in the mill workforce, a large proportion of women operatives worked in pairs. At the Hamilton Company in July 1836, for example, more than a fifth of all females on the Company payroll were sparehands. Consequently, over forty per cent of the females employed there in this month worked with one another. Nor was this interaction surreptitious, carried out only when the overseer looked elsewhere; rather it was formally organized and sanctioned by the textile corporations themselves.

In addition to the integration of sparehands, informal sharing of work often went on among regular operatives. A woman would occasionally take off a half or full day from work either to enjoy a brief vacation or to recover from illness, and fellow operatives would each take an extra loom or side of spindles so that she might continue to earn wages during her absence. Women were generally paid on a piece rate basis, their wages being determined by the total output of the machinery they tended during the payroll period. With friends helping out during her absence, making sure that her looms kept running, an operative could earn almost a full wage even though she was not physically present. Such informal work-sharing was another way in which mutual dependence developed among women operatives during their working hours.

Living conditions also contributed to the development of community among female operatives. Most women working in the Lowell mills of these years were housed in company boarding houses. In July 1836, for example, more than 73 percent of females employed by the Hamilton Company resided in company housing adjacent to the mills. Almost three-fourths of them, therefore, lived and worked with each other. Furthermore, the work schedule was such that women had little opportunity to interact with those not living in company dwellings. They worked, in these years, an average of 73 hours a week. Their work day ended at 7:00 or 7:30 P.M., and in the hours between supper and the 10:00 curfew imposed by management on residents of company boarding houses there was little time to spend with friends living "off the corporation."

Women in the boarding houses lived in close quarters, a factor that also played a role in the growth of community. A typical boarding house accommodated twenty-five young women, generally crowded four to eight in a bedroom. There was little possibility of privacy within the dwelling, and pressure to conform to group standards was very strong (as will be discussed below). The community of operatives which developed in the mills it follows, carried over into life at home as well.

The boarding house became a central institution in the lives of Lowell's female operatives in these years, but it was particularly important in the initial integration of newcomers into urban industrial life. Upon first leaving her rural home for work in Lowell, a woman entered a setting very different from anything she had previously known. One operative, writing in the *Offering*, described the feelings of a fictional character: ". . . the first entrance into a factory boarding house seemed something dreadful. The room looked strange and comfortless, and the women cold and heartless; and when she sat down to the supper table, where among more than twenty girls, all but one were strangers, she could not eat a mouthfull."

In the boarding house, the newcomer took the first steps in the process which transformed her from an "outsider" into an accepted member of the community of women operatives.

Recruitment of newcomers into the mills and their initial hiring was mediated through the boarding house system. Women generally did not travel to Lowell for the first time entirely on their own. They usually came because they knew someone—an older sister, cousin, or friend—who had already worked in Lowell. The scene described above was a lonely one—but the newcomer did know at least one boarder among the twenty seated around the supper table. The Hamilton Company Register Books indicated that numerous pairs of operatives, having the same surname and coming from the same town in northern New England, lived in the same boarding houses. If the newcomer was not accompanied by a friend or relative, she was usually directed to "Number 20, Hamilton Company," or to a similar address of one of the other corporations where her acquaintance lived. Her first contact with fellow operatives generally came in the boarding houses and not in the mills. Given the personal nature of recruitment in this period, therefore, newcomers usually had the company and support of a friend or relative in their first adjustment to Lowell.

Like recruitment, the initial hiring was a personal process. Once settled in the boarding house a newcomer had to find a job. She would generally go to the mills with her friend or with the boarding house keeper who would introduce her to an overseer in one of the rooms. If he had an opening, she might start work immediately. More likely, the overseer would know of an opening elsewhere in the mill, or would suggest that something would probably develop within a few days. In one story in the *Offering*, a newcomer worked on some quilts for her house keeper, thereby earning her board while she waited for a job opening.

Upon entering the boarding house, the newcomer came under pressure to conform with the standards of the community of operatives. Stories in the *Offering* indicate that newcomers at first stood out from the group in terms of their speech and dress. Over time, they dropped the peculiar "twang" in their speech which so amused experienced hands. Similarly, they purchased clothing more in keeping with urban than rural styles. It was an unusual and strong-willed individual who could work and live among her fellow operatives and not conform, at least outwardly, to the customs and values of this larger community.

The boarding houses were the centers of social life for women operatives after their long days in the mills. There they ate their meals, rested, talked, sewed, wrote letters, read books and magazines. From among fellow workers and boarders they found friends who accompanied them to shops, to Lyceum lectures, to church and church-sponsored events. On Sundays or holidays, they often took walks along the canals or out into the nearby countryside. The community of women operatives, in sum, developed in a setting where women worked and lived together, twenty-four hours a day.

Given the all-pervasiveness of this community, one would expect it to exert strong pressures on those who did not conform to group standards. Such appears to have been the case. The community influenced newcomers to adopt its patterns of speech and dress as described above. In addition, it enforced an unwritten code of moral conduct. Henry Miles, a minister in Lowell, described the way in which the community pressured those who deviated from accepted moral conduct:

> A girl, suspected of immoralities, or serious improprieties, at once loses caste. Her fellow boarders will at once leave the house, if the keeper does not dismiss the offender. In self-protection, therefore, the patron is obliged to put the offender away. Nor will her former companions walk with her, or work with her; till at length, finding herself everywhere talked about, and pointed at, and shunned, she is obliged to relieve her fellow-operatives of a presence which they feel brings disgrace.

The power of the peer group described by Miles may seem extreme, but there is evidence in the writing of women operatives to corroborate his account. Such group pressure is illustrated by a story (in the *Offering*)—in which, operatives in a company boarding house begin to harbor suspicions about a fellow boarder, Hannah, who received repeated evening visits from a man whom she does not introduce to the other residents. Two boarders declare that they will leave if she is allowed to remain in the household. The house keeper finally informed Hannah that she must either depart or not see the man again. She does not accept the ultimatum, but is promptly discharged after the overseer is informed, by one of the boarders, about her conduct. And, only one of Hannah's former friends continues to remain on cordial terms.

One should not conclude, however, that women always enforced a moral code agreeable to Lowell's clergy, or to the mill agents and overseers for that matter. After all, the kind of peer pressure imposed on Hannah could be brought to bear on women in 1834 and 1836 who on their own would not have protested wage cuts. It was much harder to go to work when one's roommates were marching about town, attending rallies, circulating strike petitions. Similarly, the ten-hour petitions of the 1840s were certainly aided by the fact of a tight-knit community of operatives living in a dense neighborhood of boarding houses. To the extent that women could not have completely private lives in the boarding houses, they probably had to conform to group norms, whether these involved speech, clothing, relations with men, or attitudes toward the ten-hour day. Group pressure to conform, so important to the community of women in early Lowell, played a significant role in the collective response of women to changing conditions in the mills.

In addition to the structure of work and housing in Lowell, a third factor, the homogeneity of the mill workforce, contributed to the development of community among female operatives. In this period the mill workforce was homogeneous in terms of sex, nativity, and age. Payroll and other records of the Hamilton Company reveal that more than 85 per cent of those employed in July, 1836, were women and that over 96 per cent were native-born. Furthermore, over 80 per cent of the female workforce was between the ages of 15 and 30 years old; and only ten per cent was under 15 or over 40.

Workforce homogeneity takes on particular significance in the context of work structure and the nature of worker housing. These three factors combined meant that women operatives had little interaction with men during their daily lives. Men and women did not perform the same work in the mills, and generally did not even labor in the same rooms. Men worked in the picking and initial carding processes, in the repair shop and on the watchforce, and filled all supervisory positions in the mills. Women held all sparehand and regular operative jobs in drawing, speeding, spinning, weaving and dressing. A typical room in the mill employed eighty women tending machinery, with two men overseeing the work and two boys assisting them. Women had little contact with men other than their supervisors in the course of the working day. After work, women returned to their boarding houses, where once again there were few men. Women, then, worked and lived in a predominantly female setting.

Ethnically the workforce was also homogeneous. Immigrants formed only 3.4 per cent of those employed at Hamilton in July, 1836. In addition, they comprised only 3 per cent of residents in Hamilton company housing. The community of women operatives was composed of women of New England stock drawn from the hill-country farms surrounding Lowell. Consequently, when experienced hands made fun of the speech and dress of newcomers, it was understood that they, too, had been "rusty" or "rustic" upon first coming to Lowell. This common background was another element shared by women workers in early Lowell.

The work structure, the workers' housing, and workforce homogeneity were the major elements which contributed to the growth of community among Lowell's women operatives. To best understand the larger implications of community it is necessary to examine the labor protests of this period. For in these struggles, the new values and attitudes which developed in the community of women operatives are most visible.

II

In February, 1834, 800 of Lowell's women operatives "turned-out"—went on strike—to protest a proposed reduction in their wages. They marched to numerous mills in an effort to induce others to join them; and, at an outdoor rally, they petitioned others to discontinue their labors until terms of reconciliation are made. Their petition concluded:

> Resolved, That we will not go back into the mills to work unless our wages are continued . . . as they have been.
>
> Resolved, That none of us will go back, unless they receive us all as one.
>
> Resolved, That if any have not money enough to carry them home, they shall be supplied.

The strike proved to be brief and failed to reverse the proposed wage reductions. Turning-out on a Friday, the striking women were paid their back wages on Saturday, and by the middle of the next week had returned to work or left town. Within a week of the turn-out, the mills were running near capacity.

This first strike in Lowell, is important not because it failed or succeeded, but simply because it took place. In an era in which women had to overcome opposition simply to work in the mills, it is remarkable that they would further overstep the accepted middle-class bounds of female propriety by participating in a public protest. The agents of the textile mills certainly considered the turn-out unfeminine. William Austin, agent of the Lawrence Company, described the operatives' procession as an "amizonian [sic] display." He wrote further, in a letter to his company treasurer in Boston: "This afternoon we have paid off several of these Amazons & presume that they will leave town on Monday." The turn-out was particularly offensive to the agents because of the relationship they thought they had with their operatives. William Austin probably expressed the feelings of other agents when he wrote: ". . . notwithstanding the friendly and disinterested advice which has been on all proper occassions [sic] communicated to the girls of the Lawrence mills a spirit of evil omen . . . has prevailed, and overcome the judgement and discretion of too many, and this morning a general turn-out from most of the rooms has been the consequence."

Mill agents assumed an attitude of benevolent paternalism toward their female operatives, and found it particularly disturbing that the women paid such little heed to their advice. The strikers were not merely unfeminine, they were ungrateful as well.

Such attitudes not withstanding, women chose to turn-out. They did so for two principal reasons. First, the wage cuts undermined the sense of dignity and social equality which was an important element in their Yankee heritage. Second, these wage cuts were seen as an attack on their economic independence.

Certainly a prime motive for the strike was outrage at the social implications of the wage cuts. In a statement of principles accompanying the petition which was circulated among operatives, women expressed well the sense of themselves which prompted their protest of these wage cuts:

Union Is Power

> Our present object is to have union and exertion, and we remain in possession of our unquestionable rights. We circulate this paper wishing to obtain the names of all who imbibe the spirit of our Patriotic Ancestors, who preferred privation to bondage, and parted with all that renders life desirable—and even life itself—to procure independence for their children. The oppressing hand of avarice would enslave us, and to gain their object, they gravely tell us of the pressure of the time, this we are already sensible of, and deplore it. If any are in want of assistance, the Ladies will be compassionate and assist them; but we prefer to have the disposing of our charities in our own hands; and as we are free, we would remain in possession of what kind Providence has bestowed upon us; and remain daughters of freemen still.

At several points in the proclamation the women drew on their Yankee heritage. Connecting their turn-out with the efforts of their "Patriotic Ancestors" to secure independence from England, they interpreted the wage cuts as an effort to "enslave" them—to deprive them of their independent status as "daughters of freemen."

Though very general and rhetorical, the statement of these women does suggest their sense of self, of their own worth and dignity. Elsewhere, they expressed the conviction that they were the social equals of the overseers, indeed of the millowners themselves. The wage cuts, however struck at this assertion of social equality. These reductions made it clear that the operatives were subordinate to their employers, rather than equal partners in a contract binding on both parties. By turning-out the women emphatically denied that they were subordinates; but by returning to work the next week, they demonstrated that in economic terms they were no match for their corporate superiors.

In point of fact, these Yankee operatives were subordinate in early Lowell's social and economic order, but they never consciously accepted this status. Their refusal to do so became evident whenever the mill owners attempted to exercise the power they possessed. This fundamental contradiction between the objective status of operatives and their consciousness of it was at the root of the 1834 turn-out and of subsequent labor protests in Lowell before 1850. The corporations could build mills, create thousands of jobs, and recruit women to fill them. Nevertheless, they bought only the workers' labor power, and then only for as long as these workers chose to stay. Women could always return to their rural homes, and they had a sense of their own worth and dignity, factors limiting the actions of management.

Women operatives viewed the wage cuts as a threat to their economic independence. This independence had two related dimensions. First, the women were self-supporting while they worked in the mills and, consequently, were independent of their families back home. Second, they were able to save out of their monthly earnings and could then leave the mills for the old homestead whenever they so desired. In effect, they were not totally dependent upon mill work. Their independence was based largely on the high level of wages in the mills. They could support themselves and still save enough to return home periodically. The wage cuts threatened to deny them this outlet, substituting instead the prospect of total dependence on mill work. Small wonder, then, there was alarm that "the oppressing hand of avarice would enslave us." To be forced, out of economic necessity, to lifelong labor in the mills would have indeed seemed like slavery. The Yankee operatives spoke directly to the fear of a dependency based on impoverishment when offering to assist any women workers who "have not money enough to carry them home." Wage reductions, however, offered only the *prospect* of a future dependence on mill employment. By striking, the women asserted their actual economic independence of the mills and their determination to remain "daughters of freemen still."

While the women's traditional conception of themselves as independent daughters of freemen played a major role in the turn-out, this factor acting alone would not necessarily have triggered the 1834 strike. It would have led women as individuals to quit work and return to their rural homes. But the turn-out was a collective protest. When it was announced that wage reductions were being considered, women began to hold meetings in the mills during meal breaks in order to assess tactical possibilities. Their turn-out began at one mill when the agent discharged a woman who had presided at such a meeting. Their procession through the streets passed by other mills, expressing a conscious effort to enlist as much support as possible for their cause. At a mass meeting, the women drew up a resolution which insisted that none be discharged for their participation in the turn-out. This strike, then, was a collective response to the proposed wage cuts—made possible because women had come to form a "community" of operatives in the mill, rather than simply a group of individual workers. The existence of such a tight-knit community turned individual opposition of the wage cuts into a collective protest.

In October, 1836, women again went on strike. This second turn-out was similar to the first in several respects. Its immediate cause was also a wage reduction; marches and a large outdoor rally were organized; again, like the earlier protest, the basic goal was not achieved; the corporations refused to restore wages; and operatives either left Lowell or returned to work at the new rates.

Despite these surface similarities between the turn-outs, there were some real differences. One involved scale: over 1500 operatives turned out in 1836, compared to only 800 earlier. Moreover, the second strike lasted much longer than the first. In 1834 operatives stayed out for only a few days; in 1836, the mills ran far below capacity for several months. Two weeks after the second turn-out began, a mill agent reported that only a fifth of the strikers had returned to work: "The rest manifest *good 'spunk'* as they call it." Several days later he described the impact of the continuing strike on operations in his mills: "we must be feeble for months to come as probably not less than

250 of our former scanty supply of help have left town." These lines read in sharp contrast to the optimistic reports of agents following the turnout in February, 1834.

Differences between the two turn-outs were not limited to the increased scale and duration of the later one. Women displayed a much higher degree of organization in 1836 than earlier. To co-ordinate strike activities, they formed a Factory Girls' Association. According to one historian, membership in the short-lived association reached 2500 at its height. The larger organization among women was reflected in the tactics employed. Strikers, according to one mill agent, were able to halt production to a greater extent than numbers alone could explain; and, he complained, although some operatives were willing to work, "it has been impossible to give employment to many who remained." He attributed this difficulty to the strikers' tactics: "This was in many instances no doubt the result of calculation and contrivance. After the original turn-out they, [the operatives] would assail a particular room—as for instance, all the warpers, or all the warp spinners, or all the speeder and stretcher girls, and this would close the mill as effectually as if all the girls in the mill had left."

Now giving more thought than they had in 1834 to the specific tactics of the turn-out, the women made a deliberate effort to shut down the mills in order to win their demands. They attempted to persuade less committed operatives, concentrating on those in crucial departments within the mill. Such tactics anticipated those of skilled mulespinners and loomfixers who went out on strike in the 1880s and 1890s.

In their organization of a Factory Girl's Association and in their efforts to shut down the mills, the female operatives revealed that they had been changed by their industrial experience. Increasingly, they acted not simply as "daughters of freemen" offended by the impositions of the textile corporations, but also as industrial workers intent on improving their position within the mills.

There was a decline in protest among women in the Lowell mills following these early strike defeats. During the 1837–1843 depression, textile corporations twice reduced wages without evoking a collective response from operatives. Because of the frequency of production cutbacks and lay-offs in these years, workers probably accepted the mill agents' contention that they had to reduce wages or close entirely. But with the return of prosperity and the expansion of production in the mid-1840's, there were renewal labor protests among women. Their actions paralleled those of working men and reflected fluctuations in the business cycle. Prosperity itself did not prompt turn-outs, but it evidently facilitated collective actions by women operatives.

In contrast to the protests of the previous decade, the struggles now were primarily political. Women did not turn-out in the 1840s; rather, they mounted annual petition campaigns calling on the State legislature to limit the hours of labor within the mills. These campaigns reached their height in 1845 and 1846, when 2,000 and 5,000 operatives respectively signed petitions. Unable to curb the wage cuts, or the speed-up and stretch-out imposed by mill owners, operatives sought to mitigate the consequences of these changes by reducing the length of the working day. Having been defeated earlier in economic struggles, they now sought to achieve their new goal through political action. The

Ten Hour Movement, seen in these terms, was a logical outgrowth of the unsuccessful turn-outs of the previous decade. Like the earlier struggles, the Ten Hour Movement was an assertion of the dignity of operatives and an attempt to maintain that dignity under the changing conditions of industrial capitalism.

The growth of relatively permanent labor organizations and institutions among women was a distinguishing feature of the Ten Hour Movement of the 1840s. The Lowell Female Labor Reform Association was organized in 1845 by women operatives. It became Lowell's leading organization over the next three years, organizing the city's female operatives and helping to set up branches in other mill towns. The Association was affiliated with the New England Workingmen's Association and sent delegates to its meetings. It acted in concert with similar male groups, and yet maintained its own autonomy. Women elected their own officers, held their own meetings, testified before a state legislative committee, and published a series of "Factory Tracts" which exposed conditions within the mills and argued for the ten-hour day.

An important educational and organizing tool of the Lowell Female Labor Reform Association was the *Voice of Industry*, a labor weekly published in Lowell between 1845 and 1848 by the New England Workingmen's Association. Female operatives were involved in every aspect of its publication and used the *Voice* to further the Ten Hour Movement among women. Their Association owned the press on which the *Voice* was printed. Sarah Bagley, the Association president, was a member of the three-person publishing committee of the *Voice* and for a time served as editor. Other women were employed by the paper as travelling editors. They wrote articles about the Ten Hour Movement in other mill towns, in an effort to give ten-hour supporters a sense of the larger cause of which they were a part. Furthermore, they raised money for the *Voice* and increased its circulation by selling subscriptions to the paper in their travels about New England. Finally, women used the *Voice* to appeal directly to their fellow operatives. They edited a separate "Female Department," which published letters and articles by and about women in the mills.

Another aspect of the Ten Hour Movement which distinguished it from the earlier labor struggles in Lowell was that it involved both men and women. At the same time that women in Lowell formed the Female Labor Reform Association, a male mechanics' and laborers' association was also organized. Both groups worked to secure the passage of legislation setting ten hours as the length of the working day. Both groups circulated petitions to this end and when the legislative committee came to Lowell to hear testimony, both men and women testified in favor of the ten-hour day.

The two groups, then, worked together, and each made an important contribution to the movement in Lowell. Women had the numbers, comprising as they did over eighty per cent of the mill workforce. Men, on the other hand, had the votes, and since the Ten Hour Movement was a political struggle, they played a crucial part. After the State committee reported unfavorably on the ten-hour petitions, the Female Labor Reform Association denounced the committee chairman, a State representative from Lowell, as a corporation "tool." Working for his defeat at the polls, they did so successfully and then passed the following post-election resolution: "*Resolved,* That the members of this Association tender their grateful acknowledgments to the voters of Lowell, for consigning William Schouler to the obscurity he so justly deserves. . . ." Women took a more prominent part in the Ten Hour Movement in Lowell than did men, but they obviously remained dependent on male voters and legislators for the ultimate success of their movement.

Although co-ordinating their efforts with those of working men, women operatives organized independently within the Ten Hour Movement. For instance, in 1845 two important petitions were sent from Lowell to the State legislature. Almost ninety per cent of the signers of one petition were females, and more than two-thirds of the signers of the second were males. Clearly the separation of men and women in their daily lives was reflected in the Ten Hour petitions of these years.

The way in which the Ten Hour Movement was carried from Lowell to other mill towns also illustrated the independent organizing of women within the larger movement. For example, at a spirited meeting in Manchester, New Hampshire in December, 1845—one presided over by Lowell operatives—more than a thousand workers, two-thirds of them women, passed resolutions calling for the ten-hour day. Later, those in attendance divided along male-female lines each meeting separately to set up parallel organizations. Sixty women joined the Manchester Female Labor Reform Association that evening, and by the following summer it claimed over three hundred members. Female operatives met in company boarding houses to involve new women in the movement. In their first year of organizing, Manchester workers obtained more than 4,000 signatures on ten-hour petitions. While men and women were both active in the movement, they worked through separate institutional structures from the outset.

The division of men and women within the Ten Hour Movement also reflected their separate daily lives in Lowell and in other mill towns. To repeat, they held different jobs in the mills and had little contact apart from the formal, structured overseer-operative relation. Outside the mill, we have noted, women tended to live in female boarding houses provided by the corporations and were isolated from men. Consequently, the experiences of women in these early mill towns were different from those of men, and in the course of their daily lives they came to form a close-knit community. It was logical that women's participation in the Ten Hour Movement mirrored this basic fact.

The women's Ten Hour Movement, like the earlier turnouts, was based in part on the participants' sense of their own worth and dignity as daughters of freemen. At the same time, however, it also indicated the growth of a new consciousness. It reflected a mounting feeling of community among women operatives and a realization that their interests and those of their employers were not identical, that they had to rely on themselves and not on corporate benevolence to achieve a reduction in the hours of labor. One woman, in an open letter to a State legislator, expressed this rejection of middle-class paternalism: "Bad as is the condition of so many women, it would be much worse if they had nothing but your boasted protection to rely upon; but they have at last learnt the lesson which a bitter experience teaches, that not to those who style themselves their "natural protectors" are they to look for the needful help, but to the strong and resolute of their own sex. Such an attitude, underlying the self-organizing of women in the ten-hour petition campaigns, was clearly the product of the industrial experience in Lowell.

Both the early turn-outs and the Ten Hour Movement were, as noted above, in large measure dependent upon the existence of a close-knit community of women operatives. Such a community was based on the work structure, the nature of worker housing, and workforce homogeneity. Women were drawn together by the initial job training of newcomers; by the informal work sharing among experienced hands, by living in company boarding houses, by sharing religious, educational, and social activities in their leisure hours. Working and living in a new and alien setting, they came to rely upon one another for friendship and support. Understandably, a community feeling developed among them.

This evolving community as well as the common cultural traditions which Yankee women carried into Lowell were major elements that governed their response to changing mill conditions. The pre-industrial tradition of independence and self-respect made them particularly sensitive to management labor policies. The sense of community enabled them to transform their individual opposition to wage cuts and to the increasing pace of work into public protest. In these labor struggles women operatives expressed a new consciousness of their rights both as workers and as women. Such a consciousness, like the community of women itself, was one product of Lowell's industrial revolution.

The experiences of Lowell women before 1850 present a fascinating picture of the contradictory impact of industrial capitalism. Repeated labor protests reveal that female operatives felt the demands of mill employment to be oppressive. At the same time, however, the mills, provided women with work outside of the home and family, thereby offering them an unprecedented opportunity. That they came to challenge employer paternalism was a direct consequence of the increasing opportunities offered them in these years. The Lowell mills both exploited and liberated women in ways unknown to the preindustrial political economy.

Gerda Lerner

NO

The Lady and the Mill Girl: Changes in the Status of Women in the Age of Jackson

The period 1800–1840 is one in which decisive changes occurred in the status of American women. It has remained surprisingly unexplored. With the exception of a recent, unpublished dissertation by Keith Melder and the distinctive work of Elisabeth Dexter, there is a dearth of descriptive material and an almost total absence of interpretation. Yet the period offers essential clues to an understanding of later institutional developments, particularly the shape and nature of the woman's rights movement. This analysis will consider the economic, political, and social status of women and examine the changes in each area. It will also attempt an interpretation of the ideological shifts which occurred in American society concerning the "proper" role for women.

Periodization always offers difficulties. It seemed useful here, for purposes of comparison, to group women's status before 1800 roughly under the "colonial" heading and ignore the transitional and possibly atypical shifts which occurred during the American Revolution and the early period of nationhood. Also, regional differences were largely ignored. The South was left out of consideration entirely because its industrial development occurred later.

The status of colonial women has been well studied and described and can briefly be summarized for comparison with the later period. Throughout the colonial period there was a marked shortage of women, which varied with the regions and always was greatest in the frontier areas. This (from the point of view of women) favorable sex ratio enhanced their status and position. The Puritan world view regarded idleness as sin; life in an underdeveloped country made it absolutely necessary that each member of the community perform an economic function. Thus work for women, married or single, was not only approved, it was regarded as a civic duty. Puritan town councils expected single girls, widows, and unattached women to be self-supporting and for a long time provided needy spinsters with parcels of land. There was no social sanction against married women working; on the contrary, wives were expected to help their husbands in their trade and won social approval for doing extra work in or out of the home. Needy children, girls as well as boys, were indentured or apprenticed and were expected to work for their keep.

The vast majority of women worked within their homes, where their labor produced most articles needed for the family. The entire colonial production of cloth and clothing and in part that of shoes was in the hands of women. In addition to these occupations, women were found in many different kinds of employment. They were butchers, silversmiths, gunsmiths, upholsterers. They ran mills, plantations, tan yards, shipyards, and every kind of shop, tavern and boarding house. They were gate keepers, jail keepers, sextons, journalists, printers, "doctoresses," apothecaries, midwives, nurses, and teachers. Women acquired their skills the same way as did the men, through apprenticeship training, frequently within their own families.

Absence of a dowry, ease of marriage and remarriage, and a more lenient attitude of the law with regard to women's property rights were manifestations of the improved position of wives in the colonies. Under British common law, marriage destroyed a woman's contractual capacity; she could not sign a contract even with the consent of her husband. But colonial authorities were more lenient toward the wife's property rights by protecting her dower rights in her husband's property, granting her personal clothing, and upholding prenuptial contracts between husband and wife. In the absence of the husband, colonial courts granted women "femme sole" rights, which enabled them to conduct their husband's business, sign contracts, and sue. The relative social freedom of women and the esteem in which they were held was commented upon by most early foreign travelers in America.

But economic, legal, and social status tells only part of the story. Colonial society as a whole was hierarchical, and rank and standing in society depended on the position of the men. Women did not play a determining role in the ranking pattern; they took their position in society through the men of their own family or the men they married. In other words, they participated in the hierarchy only as daughters and wives, not as individuals. Similarly, their occupations were, by and large, merely auxiliary, designed to contribute to family income, enhance their husbands' business or continue it in case of widowhood. The self-supporting spinsters were certainly the exception. The underlying assumption of colonial society was that women ought to occupy an inferior and subordinate position. The settlers had brought this assumption with them from Europe; it was reflected in their legal concepts, their willingness to exclude women from political life, their discriminatory educational practices. What is remarkable is the extent to which this felt inferiority of women was constantly challenged and modified under the impact of environment, frontier conditions, and a favorable sex ratio.

By 1840 all of American society had changed. The Revolution had substituted an egalitarian ideology for the hierarchical concepts of colonial life. Privilege based on ability rather than inherited status, upward mobility for all groups of society, and unlimited opportunities for individual self-fulfillment had become ideological goals, if not always realities. For men, that is; women were, by tacit concensus, excluded from the new democracy. Indeed their actual situation had in many respects deteriorated. While, as wives, they had benefitted from increasing wealth, urbanization, and industrialization, their role as economic producers and as political members of society differed sharply from that of men. Women's work outside of the home no longer met with social approval; on the contrary, with two notable exceptions, it was condemned. Many business and professional occupations formerly open to women were now closed, many others restricted as to training and advancement. The entry of large numbers of women into low status, low pay, and low skill industrial work had fixed such work by definition as "woman's work." Women's political status, while legally unchanged, had deteriorated relative to the advances made by men. At the same time the genteel lady of fashion had become a model of American femininity, and the definition of "woman's proper sphere" seemed narrower and more confined than ever.

Within the scope of this essay only a few of these changes can be more fully explained. The professionalization of medicine and its impact on women may serve as a typical example of what occurred in all the professions.

In colonial America there were no medical schools, no medical journals, few hospitals, and few laws pertaining to the practice of the healing arts. Clergymen and governors, barbers, quacks, apprentices, and women practiced medicine. Most practitioners acquired their credentials by reading Paracelsus and Galen and serving an apprenticeship with an established practitioner. Among the semi-trained "physics," surgeons, and healers the occasional "doctoress" was fully accepted and frequently well rewarded. County records of all the colonies contain references to the work of the female physicians. There was even a female Army surgeon, a Mrs Allyn, who served during King Philip's war. Plantation records mention by name several slave women who were granted special privileges because of their useful service as midwives and "doctoresses."

The period of the professionalization of American medicine dates from 1765, when Dr. William Shippen began his lectures on midwifery in Philadelphia. The founding of medical faculties in several colleges, the standardization of training requirements, and the proliferation of medical societies intensified during the last quarter of the 18th century. The American Revolution dramatized the need for trained medical personnel, afforded first-hand battlefield experience to a number of surgeons and brought increasing numbers of semi-trained practitioners in contact with the handful of European-trained surgeons working in the military hospitals. This was an experience from which women were excluded. The resulting interest in improved medical training, the gradual appearance of graduates of medical colleges, and the efforts of medical societies led to licensing legislation. In 1801 Maryland required all medical practitioners to be licensed; in 1806 New York enacted a similar law, followed by all but three states. This trend was reversed in the 1830s and 40s when most states repealed their licensure requirements. This was due to pressure from eclectic, homeopathic practitioners, the public's dissatisfaction with the "heroic medicine" then practiced by licensed physicians, and to the distrust of state regulation, which was widespread during the Age of Jackson. Licensure as prime proof of qualification for the practice of medicine was reinstituted in the 1870s.

In the middle of the 19th century it was not so much a license or an M.D. which marked the professional physician as it was graduation from an approved medical college, admission to hospital practice and to a network of referrals through other physicians. In 1800 there were four medical schools, in 1850, forty-two. Almost all of them excluded women from admission. Not surprisingly, women turned to eclectic schools for training. Harriot Hunt, a Boston physician, was trained by apprenticeship with a husband and wife team of homeopathic physicians. After more than twenty years of practice she attempted to enter Harvard Medical school and was repeatedly rebuffed. Elizabeth Blackwell received her M.D. from Geneva (New York) Medical College, an eclectic school. Sarah Adamson found all regular medical schools closed against her and earned an M.D. in 1851 from Central College at Syracuse, an eclectic institution. Clemence Lozier graduated from the same school two years later and went on to found the New York Medical College and Hospital for women in 1863, a homeopathic institution which was later absorbed into the Flower-Fifth Avenue Hospital.

Another way in which professionalization worked to the detriment of women can be seen in the cases of Drs. Elizabeth and Emily Blackwell, Marie Zakrzewska, and Ann Preston, who despite their M.D.s and excellent training were denied access to hospitals, were refused recognition by county medical societies, and were denied customary referrals by male colleagues. Their experiences were similar to those of most of the pioneer women physicians. Such discrimination caused the formation of alternate institutions for the training of women physicians and for hospitals in which they might treat their patients. The point here is not so much that any one aspect of the process of professionalization excluded women but that the process, which took place over the span of almost a century, proceeded in such a way as to institutionalize an exclusion of women, which had earlier been accomplished irregularly, inconsistently, and mostly by means of social pressure. The end result was an *absolute* lowering of status for all women in the medical profession and a *relative* loss. As the professional status of all physicians advanced, the status differential between male and female practitioners was more obviously disadvantageous and underscored women's marginality. Their virtual exclusion from the most prestigious and lucrative branches of the profession and their concentration in specializations relating to women and children made such disadvantaging more obvious by the end of the 19th century.

This process of pre-emption of knowledge, of institutionalization of the profession, and of legitimation of its claims by law and public acceptance is standard for the professionalization of the sciences, as George Daniels has pointed out. It inevitably results in the elimination of fringe elements from the profession. It is interesting to note that women had been pushed out of the medical profession in 16th-century Europe by a similar process. Once the public had come to accept licensing and college training as guarantees of up-to-date practice, the outsider, no matter how well qualified by years of experience, stood no chance in the competition. Women were the casualties of medical professionalization.

In the field of midwifery the results were similar, but the process was more complicated. Women had held a virtual monopoly in the profession in colonial America. In 1646 a man was prosecuted in Maine for practicing as a midwife. There are many records of well-trained midwives with diplomas from European institutions working in the colonies. In most of the colonies midwives were licensed, registered, and required to pass an examination before a board. When Dr. Shippen announced his pioneering lectures on midwifery, he did it to "combat the widespread popular prejudice against the man-midwife" and because he considered most midwives ignorant and improperly trained.

Yet he invited "those women who love virtue enough, to own their Ignorance, and apply for instruction" to attend his lectures, offering as an inducement the assurance that female pupils would be taught privately. It is not known if any midwives availed themselves of the opportunity.

Technological advances, as well as scientific, worked against the interests of female midwives. In 16th-century Europe the invention and use of obstetrical forceps had for three generations been the well-kept secret of the Chamberlen family and had greatly enhanced their medical practice. Hugh Chamberlen was forced by circumstances to sell the secret to the Medical College in Amsterdam, which in turn transmitted the precious knowledge to licensed physicians only. By the time the use of the instrument became widespread it had become associated with male physicians and male midwives. Similarly in America, introduction of the obstetrical forceps was associated with the practice of male midwives and served to their advantage. By the end of the 18th century a number of male physicians advertised their practice of midwifery. Shortly thereafter female midwives also resorted to advertising, probably in an effort to meet the competition. By the early 19th century male physicians had virtually monopolized the practice of midwifery on the Eastern seaboard. True to the generally delayed economic development in the Western frontier regions, female midwives continued to work on the frontier until a much later period. It is interesting to note that the concepts of "propriety" shifted with the prevalent practice. In 17th-century Maine the attempt of a man to act as a midwife was considered outrageous and illegal; in mid-19th-century America the suggestion that women should train as midwives and physicians was considered equally outrageous and improper.

Professionalization, similar to that in medicine with the elimination of women from the upgraded profession, occurred in the field of law. Before 1750, when law suits were commonly brought to the courts by the plaintiffs themselves or by deputies without specialized legal training, women as well as men could and did act as "attorneys-in-fact." When the law became a paid profession and trained lawyers took over litigation, women disappeared from the court scene for over a century.

A similar process of shrinking opportunities for women developed in business and in the retail trades. There were fewer female storekeepers and business women in the 1830s than there had been in colonial days. There was also a noticeable shift in the kind of merchandise handled by them. Where previously women could be found running almost every kind of retail shop, after 1830 they were mostly found in businesses which served women only.

The only fields in which professionalization did not result in the elimination of women from the upgraded profession were nursing and teaching. Both were characterized by a severe shortage of labor. Nursing lies outside the field of this inquiry since it did not become an organized profession until after the Civil War. Before then it was regarded peculiarly as a woman's occupation, although some of the hospitals and the Army during wars employed male nurses. These bore the stigma of low skill, low status, and low pay. Generally, nursing was regarded as simply an extension of the unpaid services performed by the housewife—a characteristic attitude that haunts the profession to this day.

Education seems, at first glance, to offer an entirely opposite pattern from that of the other professions. In colonial days women had taught "Dame schools" and grade schools during summer sessions. Gradually, as educational opportunities for girls expanded, they advanced just a step ahead of their students. Professionalization of teaching occurred between 1820 and 1860, a period marked by a sharp increase in the number of women teachers. The spread of female seminaries, academies, and normal schools provided new opportunities for the training and employment of female teachers.

This trend, which runs counter to that found in the other professions, can be accounted for by the fact that women filled a desperate need created by the challenge of the common schools, the ever-increasing size of the student body, and the westward growth of the nation. America was committed to educating its children in public schools, but it was insistent on doing so as cheaply as possible. Women were available in great numbers, and they were willing to work cheaply. The result was another ideological adaptation: in the very period when the gospel of the home as woman's only proper sphere was preached most loudly, it was discovered that women were the natural teachers of youth, could do the job better than men, and were to be preferred for such employment. This was always provided, of course, that they would work at the proper wage differential—30 to 50 per cent of the wages paid male teachers was considered appropriate. The result was that in 1888 in the country as a whole 63 per cent of all teachers were women, while the figure for the cities only was 90.04 per cent.

It appeared in the teaching field, as it would in industry, that role expectations were adaptable provided the inferior status group filled a social need. The inconsistent and peculiar patterns of employment of black labor in the present-day market bear out the validity of this generalization.

There was another field in which the labor of women was appreciated and which they were urged to enter—industry. From Alexander Hamilton to Matthew Carey and Tench Coxe, advocates of industrialization sang the praises of the working girl and advanced arguments in favor of her employment. The social benefits of female labor particularly stressed were those bestowed upon her family, who now no longer had to support her. Working girls were "thus happily preserved from idleness and its attendant vices and crimes," and the whole community benefitted from their increased purchasing power.

American industrialization, which occurred in an underdeveloped economy with a shortage of labor, depended on the labor of women and children. Men were occupied with agricultural work and were not available or were unwilling to enter the factories. This accounts for the special features of the early development of the New England textile industry: the relatively high wages, the respectability of the job and relatively high status of the mill girls, the patriarchal character of the model factory towns, and the temporary mobility of women workers from farm to factory and back again to farm. All this was characteristic only of a limited area and of a period of about two decades. By the late 1830s the romance had worn off: immigration had supplied a strongly competitive, permanent work force willing to work for subsistence wages; early efforts at trade union organization had been shattered, and mechanization had turned semi-skilled factory labor into unskilled labor. The process led to the replacement of the New England-born farm girls by immigrants in the mills and was accompanied by a loss of status and respectability for female workers.

The lack of organized social services during periods of depression drove ever greater numbers of women into the labor market. At first, inside the factories distinctions between men's and women's jobs were blurred. Men and women were assigned to machinery on the basis of local need. But as more women entered industry the limited number of occupations open to them tended to increase competition among them, thus lowering pay standards. Generally, women regarded their work as temporary and hesitated to invest in apprenticeship training, because they expected to marry and raise families. Thus they remained untrained, casual labor and were soon, by custom, relegated to the lowest paid, least skilled jobs. Long hours, overwork, and poor working conditions would characterize women's work in industry for almost a century.

Another result of industrialization was in increasing differences in life styles between women of different classes. When female occupations, such as carding, spinning, and weaving, were transferred from home to factory, the poorer women followed their traditional work and became industrial workers. The women of the middle and upper classes could use their newly gained time for leisure pursuits: they became ladies. And a small but significant group among them chose to prepare themselves for professional careers by advanced education. This group would prove to be the most vocal and troublesome in the near future.

As class distinctions sharpened, social attitudes toward women became polarized. The image of "the lady" was elevated to the accepted ideal of femininity toward which all women would strive. In this formulation of values lower-class women were simply ignored. The actual lady was, of course, nothing new on the American scene; she had been present ever since colonial days. What was new in the 1830s was the cult of the lady, her elevation to a status symbol. The advancing prosperity of the early 19th century made it possible for middle-class women to aspire to the status formerly reserved for upper-class women. The "cult of true womanhood" of the 1830s became a vehicle for such aspirations. Mass circulation newspapers and magazines made it possible to teach every woman how to elevate the status of her family by setting "proper" standards of behavior, dress, and literary tastes. *Godey's Lady's Book* and innumerable gift books and tracts of the period all preach the same gospel of "true womanhood"—piety, purity, domesticity. Those unable to reach the goal of becoming ladies were to be satisfied with the lesser goal—acceptance of their "proper place" in the home.

It is no accident that the slogan "woman's place is in the home" took on a certain aggressiveness and shrillness precisely at the time when increasing numbers of poorer women *left* their homes to become factory workers. Working women were not a fit subject for the concern of publishers and mass media writers. Idleness, once a disgrace in the eyes of society, had become a status symbol. Thorstein Veblen, one of the earliest and sharpest commentators on the subject, observed that it had become almost the sole social function of the lady "to put in evidence her economic unit's ability to pay." She was "a means of conspicuously unproductive expenditure," devoted to displaying her husband's wealth. Just as the cult of white womanhood in the South served to preserve a labor and social system based on race distinctions, so did the cult of the lady in an egalitarian society serve as a means of preserving class distinctions. Where class distinctions were not so great, as on the frontier, the position of women was closer to what it had been in colonial days; their economic contribution was more highly valued, their opportunities were less restricted, and their positive participation in community life was taken for granted.

In the urbanized and industrialized Northeast the life experience of middle-class women was different in almost every respect from that of the lower-class women. But there was one thing the society lady and the mill girl had in common—they were equally disfranchised and isolated from the vital centers of power. Yet the political status of women had not actually deterioriated. With very few exceptions women had neither voted nor stood for office during the colonial period. Yet the spread of the franchise to ever wider groups of white males during the Jacksonian age, the removal of property restrictions, the increasing numbers of immigrants who acquired access to the franchise, made the gap between these new enfranchised voters and the disfranchised women more obvious. Quite naturally, educated and propertied women felt this deprivation more keenly. Their own career expectations had been encouraged by widening educational opportunities; their consciousness off their own abilities and of their potential for power had been enhanced by their activities in the reform movements of the 1830s; the general spirit of upward mobility and venturesome entrepreneurship that pervaded the Jacksonian era was infectious. But in the late 1840s a sense of acute frustration enveloped these educated and highly spirited women. Their rising expectations had met with frustration, their hopes had been shattered; they were bitterly conscious of a relative lowering of status and a loss of position. This sense of frustration led them to action; it was one of the main factors in the rise of the woman's rights movement.

The women, who at the first woman's rights convention at Seneca Falls, New York, in 1848 declared boldly and with considerable exaggeration that "the history of mankind is a history of repeated injuries and usurpations on the part of man toward woman, having in direct object the establishment of an absolute tyranny over her," did not speak for the truly exploited and abused working woman. As a matter of fact, they were largely ignorant of her condition and, with the notable exception of Susan B. Anthony, indifferent to her fate. But they judged from the realities of their own life experience. Like most revolutionaries, they were not the most downtrodden but rather the most status-deprived group. Their frustrations and traditional isolation from political power funneled their discontent into fairly utopian declarations and immature organizational means. They would learn better in the long, hard decades of practical struggle. Yet it is their initial emphasis on the legal and political "disabilities" of women which has provided the framework for most of the historical work on women.[1] For almost a hundred years sympathetic historians have told the story of women in America by deriving from the position of middle-class women a generalization concerning all American women. To avoid distortion, any valid generalization concerning American women after the 1830s should reflect a recognition of class stratification.

For lower-class women the changes brought by industrialization were actually advantageous, offering income and advancement opportunities, however limited, and a chance for participation in the ranks of organized labor.[2] They, by and large, tended to join men in their struggle for economic advancement and became increasingly concerned with economic gains and protective labor legislation. Middle- and upper-class women, on the other hand, reacted to actual and fancied status deprivation by increasing militancy and the formation of organizations for woman's rights, by which they meant especially legal and property rights.

The four decades preceding the Seneca Falls Convention were decisive in the history of American women. They brought an actual deterioration in the economic opportunities open to women, a relative deterioration in their political status, and a rising level of expectation and subsequent frustration in a privileged elite group of educated women. It was in these decades that the values and beliefs that clustered around the assertion "Woman's place is in the home" changed from being descriptive of an existing reality to becoming an ideology. "The cult of true womanhood" extolled woman's predominance in the domestic sphere, while it tried to justify women's exclusion from the public domain, from equal education and from participation in the political process by claims to tradition, universality, and a history dating back to antiquity, or at least to the *Mayflower.* In a century of modernization and industrialization women alone were to remain unchanging, embodying in their behavior and attitudes the longing of men and women caught in rapid social change for a mythical archaic past of agrarian family self-sufficiency. In pre-industrial America the home was indeed the workplace for both men and women, although the self-sufficiency of the American yeoman, whose economic well-being depended on a network of international trade and mercantilism, was even then more apparent than real. In the 19th and 20th centuries the home was turned into the realm of woman, while the workplace became the public domain of men. The ideology of "woman's sphere" sought to upgrade women's domestic function by elaborating the role of mother, turning the domestic drudge into a "homemaker" and charging her with elevating her family's status by her exercise of consumer functions and by her display of her own and her family's social graces. These prescribed roles never *were* a reality. In the 1950s Betty Friedan would describe this ideology and rename it "the feminine mystique," but it was no other than the myth of "woman's proper sphere" created in the 1840s and updated by consumerism and the misunderstood dicta of Freudian psychology.

The decades 1800–1840 also provide the clues to an understanding of the institutional shape of the later women's organizations. These would be led by middle-class women whose self-image, life experience, and ideology had largely been fashioned and influenced by these early, transitional years. The concerns of middle-class women—property rights, the franchise, and moral uplift—would dominate the woman's rights movement. But side by side with it, and at times cooperating with it, would grow a number of organizations serving the needs of working women.

American women were the largest disfranchised group in the nation's history, and they retained this position longer than any other group. Although they found ways of making their influence felt continuously, not only as individuals but as organized groups, power eluded them. The mill girl and the lady, both born in the age of Jackson, would not gain access to power until they learned to cooperate, each for her own separate interests. It would take almost six decades before they would find common ground. The issue around which they finally would unite and push their movement to victory was the "impractical and utopian" demand raised at Seneca Falls—the means to power in American society—female suffrage.

Notes

1. To the date of the first printing of this article (1969).
2. In 1979, I would not agree with this optimistic generalization.

POSTSCRIPT

Did the Industrial Revolution Provide More Economic Opportunities for Women in the 1830s?

Professor Gerda Lerner was a pioneer in women's history. A European refugee and playwright, she entered the New School of Social Research at the age of 40 where she also taught the earliest course on women's history in 1962. At the same time, she developed an interest in African American history when she wrote the screen play for the film directed by her husband, *Black Like Me,* based on a best-selling memoir about a white man who dyed his skin black in order to experience what it was like to be non-white.

As a forty-three-year-old graduate student at Columbia University, she convinced her mentors that a dissertation about the Grimke sisters, who were southern abolitionists, was a viable subject. She published *The Grimke Sisters from South Carolina, Rebels Against Slavery* (Houghton Mifflin, 1967), though a number of major publishers rejected the manuscript because it lacked information about the psychological failings of the sisters.

Recognizing that women "are and always have been at least half of humankind and most of the time have been a majority," Lerner argued that women have their own history, which should not be marginalized by men nor forced to be subject to the traditional male framework of political/military/diplomatic/economic history. Along with other pioneers, she led the search for nontraditional sources that provided information about women: demographic records; census figures; parish and birth records; property taxes; organizational files of churches, schools, police, and hospital records; finally, diaries, family letters, and autobiographies that are more attuned to a women's point of view.

Lerner suggested that the writing of women's history could be divided into four parts: (1) "compensatory history" where historians search for women whose experiences deserve to be well known; (2) "contribution history" of women worthy to topics and issues deemed important to the American mainstream; (3) test familiar narratives and rewrite generalizations when they appear to be wrong; and (4) understand gender as a social construct, and rewrite and develop new frameworks and concepts to understand women's history.

The Lady and the Mill Girl is a classic article that uses the conceptual framework of the "cult of motherhood" to demonstrate how the experiences of middle-class and working-class women in the Jacksonian period was different from men because they were unable to vote and were driven out of the medical, legal, and business professions, which provided occupations of upward mobility for men. Written a decade before historians began to use the term "market revolution," Lerner's article argues that industrialization retarded women's attempts at economic advancements outside the home. The two professions dominated by women—teaching and nursing—were both poorly paid and were an extension of the family values carried outside the home.

Professor Dublin's article and subsequent books are based upon the two new approaches to women's history and labor history. Both fields are part of the new social history developed in the late 1960s, which looks at history from the bottom up rather than from the top down. Dublin's Lowell factory workers developed a collective consciousness because they spent all the leisure hours in boarding houses and their 72-hour workweek tending the looms. Their contact with the male owners was nonexistent. The modern corporation that separated owners and management was true at Lowell where the Boston capitalists who started the company rarely appeared. Usually the women tending the mills would have their only contact with their immediate male supervisors. Consequently, the women could enforce their moral standards in the boarding house and get rid of women whom they deemed promiscuous. Their collective consciousness also made it easier for the women to organize strikes when their owners cut the wages as they did in 1834 and 1836.

Dublin points out that the strikes did not succeed. He is unclear about the reasons for their failures. The major one could be that women viewed the work at Lowell as temporary, a chance to build up a dowry that they could use to get married. The cult of motherhood was strong even for female factory workers. Marriage was still their primary goal.

The Lowell experiment was short-lived. Though the female workers supported the Ten Hour Movement with men working in separate organizations, the early labor movement, like the protesters in the 1880s and 1890s, failed to achieve their objectives. By the 1850s, the "Daughters of Free Men" were replaced by Irish immigrants.

The bibliography on women's history since the 1960s is enormous. The starting points for reinterpreting the field are the oft reprinted articles by Barbara Welter, "The Cult of True Womanhood: 1820–1860," *American Quarterly* 18 (Summer 1966); Carol Smith-Rosenberg, "The Female World of Love and Ritual: Relations Between Women in Nineteenth-Century America," *Signs* 1 (1975); and the collection of essays including a brief autobiography by Gerder Lerner in *The Majority Finds Its Past: Placing Women in History* (Oxford, 1979). Also important for its primary research is Nancy F. Cott, *The Bounds of Womanhood: "Women's Sphere" in New England, 1780–1835* (Yale University Press, 1977).

Thomas Dublin's essay was drawn from his doctoral dissertation at Columbia University, which the press published in 1979 as *Women at Work: The Transformation of Work and Community in Lowell, Massachusetts, 1826–1860.* Dublin also published a primary source collection *From Farm to Factory: Women's Letters 1830–1860* (Columbia University Press, 1981 and 2nd ed., 1993). Other important works about women in the workforce include Alice Kessler-Harris, *Out to Work: A History of Wage-Earning Women in the United States* (Oxford University Press, 1982); Jeanne Boydston, *Home and Work: Housework, Wages and the Ideology of Labor in the Early Republic* (Oxford

University Press, 1990); and Ava Baron, ed., *Work Engendered: Toward a New History of American Labor* (Cornell University Press, 1992).

Issue 10 deals primarily with white working-class and middle-class women and does not treat the different experiences of western women, Native Americans, African Americans, Mexican Americans, or the white immigrants. For an example of the immigrants who succeeded the "Daughters of Freemen" at Lowell, see Hasia Diner, *Erin's Daughters in America: Irish Immigrant Women in the Nineteenth Century* (Johns Hopkins University Press, 1983).

Internet References . . .

Birth of a Nation & Antebellum America

This site, maintained by Mike Madin, provides links to a wide assortment of topics from the early national and antebellum eras.

http://www.academicinfo.net/usindnew.html

The Atlantic Slave Trade and Slave Life in the Americas: A Visual Record

This site, maintained by Jerome S. Handler and Michael L. Tuite, Jr., is a project of the Virginia Foundation for the Humanities and the Digital Media Lab at the University of Virginia Library. The site includes information and images on various aspects of slave life, including family organization.

http://hitchcock.itc.virginia.edu/Slavery/

The Descendents of Mexican War Veterans

An excellent source for the history of the Mexican-American War (1846–1848), which includes images, primary documents, and maps.

http://www.dmwv.org/mexwar/mexwar1.htm

John Brown's Holy War

This site was developed to complement the Public Broadcasting System's program on John Brown. It includes interactive maps, information on many of Brown's abolitionist acquaintances, links to virtual tours of the farmhouse where Brown and his followers gathered prior to the Harpers Ferry raid, as well as the transcript of the video itself.

http://www.pbs.org/wgbh/amex/brown

UNIT 3

Antebellum America

Pressures and trends that began building in the early years of the American nation continued to gather momentum until conflict was almost inevitable. Population growth and territorial expansion brought the country into conflict with other nations. The United States had to respond to challenges from Americans who felt alienated from or forgotten by the new nation because the ideals of human rights and democratic participation that guided the founding of the nation had been applied only to selected segments of the population.

- Did Slavery Destroy the Black Family?
- Was the Mexican War an Exercise in American Imperialism?
- Was John Brown an Irrational Terrorist?

ISSUE 11

Did Slavery Destroy the Black Family?

YES: Wilma A. Dunaway, from *The African-American Family in Slavery and Emancipation* (Cambridge University Press, 2003)

NO: Eugene D. Genovese, from *Roll, Jordan, Roll: The World the Slaves Made* (Random House, 1974)

ISSUE SUMMARY

YES: Professor Wilma A. Dunaway believes that modern historians have exaggerated the amount of control slaves exercised over their lives and underplayed the cruelty of the slave experience—family separations, nutritional deficiencies, sexual exploitation and physical abuse that occurred on the majority of small plantations.

NO: Professor Genovese argues that slaves developed their own system of family and cultural values within the Southern paternalistic and pre-capitalistic slave society.

All the North American colonies had some slaves in the seventeenth century. But by the 1670s, slaves became the most important workforce in the southern colonies because of the intensive labor needed to cultivate the tobacco fields and rice paddies. The enlightment philosophy that permeated the American Revolutionaries belief that "all men were created equal" might have caused slavery's eventual demise. But the invention of the cotton gin and the development of a "market revolution" of textile factories in Old and New England gave slavery a rebirth as millions of slaves were sold from the traditional tobacco-growing areas of the upper South to cotton-producing regions in Alabama and Mississippi and the sugar fields of Louisiana.

Until recently, historians debated the slavery issue with the same arguments used over a century ago by the abolitionists and plantation owners. Slavery had been viewed as a paternalistic institution that civilized and Christianized the heathen African who, though bought and sold by his masters, was better off than many free northern workers; he was, at least, cared for in his non-working hours and old age by his masters. The prodigious research of Georgia-born professor Ulrich B. Phillips and his followers, who mined the records of the large plantation owners, gave a picture of slavery that reflected the views of those slave masters. Because Phillips considered blacks intellectually inferior to whites, his books seem woefully outdated to the American student. But Phillips' book such as *American Negro Slavery* (New York, 1918; reprint, Louisiana State University Press, 1966) and those of his students dominated the field for over thirty years.

The climate of opinion changed after World War II. Hitler made the concept of "race" a dirty word that no respected biologist or social scientist would use. Assuming that "the slaves were merely ordinary human beings and that innately Negroes were, after all, only white men with black skins," Professor Kenneth Stampp wrote a history of slavery from a northern white liberal, or abolitionist, point of view. *The Peculiar Institution* (Vintage, 1956) utilized many of the same sources as Phillips's books but came to radically different conclusions; slavery was now considered an inhuman institution.

In 1959 Stanley Elkins synthesized these seemingly contradictory interpretations in his controversial but path-breaking study *Slavery: A Problem in American Institutional and Intellectual Life,* 3rd edition (University of Chicago Press, 1976). Elkins clearly accepted Stampp's emphasis on the harshness of the slave system by hypothesizing that slavery was a "closed" system in which masters dominated their slaves in the same way that Nazi concentration camp guards in World War II had controlled the lives of their prisoners. Such an environment, he insisted, generated severe psychological dysfunctions that produced the personality traits of Phillips's "Sambo" character type. Elkins book provoked an intense debate in the 1960s and 1970s. Although his image of the slave as "Sambo" was rejected by scholars, *Slavery* was an important work because it forced historians to reconceptualize and tell slavery from the point of view of the slaves themselves.

In the second selection, Professor Eugene Genovese agreed with Elkins that it was important to view slavery through the eyes of the slave owners. But like many writers in the 1970s, Genovese disagreed with Elkins about the use of traditional sources to uncover slave culture. In his many books and articles, Genovese combined a search through the plantation records with a careful reading of slave autobiographies and the controversial records of the former slave interviews recorded in the 1930s by writers working for the federal Works Progress Administration (WPA). As a Marxist who defended Ulrich Phillips's conception of the plantation as a pre-capitalist feudal institution, Genovese's later writings reflected less concern for the economic aspects and more for the cultural interactions of blacks and whites in the antebellum South. He argues that southern slavery existed in a pre-capitalistic society dominated by a paternalistic ruling class of white slaveholders who ruled over their white and slave families. Under this system of paternalism, cultural bonds were forged between master and slave which recognized the slaves' humanity and enabled them to develop their own system of family and cultural values.

Have modern historians romanticized the ability of the slaves to maintain strong family ties? In the first selection, professor Wilma A. Dunaway argues that modern historians have exaggerated the amount of control slaves exercised over their lives and underplayed the cruelty of the slave experience—family separations, nutritional deficiencies, sexual exploitation, and physical abuse, which occurred on the majority of small plantations.

Wilma A. Dunaway

Introduction

. . . The conventional wisdom is that owners rarely broke up slave families; that slaves were adequately fed, clothed, and sheltered; and that slave health or death risks were no greater than those experienced by white adults. Why have so many investigations come to these optimistic conclusions? U.S. slavery studies have been handicapped by four fundamental weaknesses:

- a flawed view of the slave family,
- scholarly neglect of small plantations,
- limited analysis of Upper South enslavement,
- academic exaggeration of slave agency.

The Flawed View of the Slave Family

U.S. slavery studies have been dominated by the view that it was not economically rational for masters to break up black families. According to Fogel and Engerman, households were the units through which work was organized and through which the rations of basic survival needs were distributed. By discouraging runaways, families also rooted slaves to owners. Gutman's work established the view that slave families were organized as stable, nuclear, single-residence households grounded in long-term marriages. After thirty years of research, Fogel is still convinced that two-thirds of all U.S. slaves lived in two-parent households. Recent studies, like those of Berlin and Rowland, are grounded in and celebrate these optimistic generalizations about the African-American slave family.

None of these writers believes that U.S. slave owners interfered in the construction or continuation of black families. Fogel argues that such intervention would have worked against the economic interests of the owners, while Gutman focuses on the abilities of slaves to engage in day-to-day resistance to keep their households intact. Fogel and most scholars argue that sexual exploitation of slave women did not happen very often. Moreover, the conventional wisdom has been that slaveholders discouraged high fertility because female laborers were used in the fields to a greater extent than male workers. Consequently, the predominant view is that most slave women did not have their first child until about age twenty-one and that teenage pregnancies were rare. To permit women to return to work as quickly as possible, owners protected children by providing collectivized child care.

Scholarly Neglect of Small Plantations

Those who have supported the dominant paradigm neglected small slaveholdings, the second methodological blunder of U.S. slave studies. Gutman acknowledged this inadequacy of his own work when he commented in passing that "little is yet known about the domestic arrangements and kin networks as well as the communities that developed among slaves living on farms and in towns and cities." Fogel stressed that "failure to take adequate account of the differences between slave experiences and culture on large and small plantations" has been a fundamental blunder by slavery specialists. Because findings have been derived from analysis of plantations that owned more than fifty slaves, generalizations about family stability have been derived from institutional arrangements that represented the life experiences of a small minority of the enslaved population. In reality, more than 88 percent of U.S. slaves resided at locations where there were fewer than fifty slaves.

Revisionist researchers provide ample evidence that slave family stability varied with size of the slaveholding. Analyzing sixty-six slave societies around the world in several historical eras, Patterson found that slavery was most brutal and most exploitative in those societies characterized by smallholdings. Contrary to the dominant paradigm, Patterson found that family separations, slave trading, sexual exploitation, and physical abuse occurred much more often in societies where the masters owned small numbers of slaves. There were several factors that were more likely to destabilize family life on small plantations than on large ones. According to Patterson, small slaveholdings allowed "far more contact with (and manipulation of) the owner" and "greater exposure to sexual exploitation." Compared to large plantations, slave families on small plantations were more often disrupted by masters, and black households on small plantations were much more frequently headed by one parent. Stephen Crawford showed that slave women on small plantations had their first child at an earlier age and were pregnant more frequently than black females on large plantations. Steckel argued that hunger and malnutrition were worse on small plantations, causing higher mortality among the infants, children, and pregnant women held there.

Scholarly Neglect of the Upper South

In addition to their neglect of small plantations, scholars who support the dominant paradigm have directed inadequate attention to enslavement in the Upper South. Instead, much of what is accepted as conventional wisdom is grounded in the political economy and the culture of the Lower South. Why is it so important to study the Upper South? In the United States, world demand for cotton triggered the largest domestic slave trade in the history of the world. Between 1790 and 1860, the Lower South slave population nearly quadrupled because the Upper South exported nearly one million black laborers. In a fifty-year period, two-fifths of the African-Americans who were enslaved in the Upper South were forced to migrate to the cotton economy; the vast majority were sold through interstate transactions, and about 15 percent were removed in relocations with owners.

Because of that vast interregional forced migration, Upper South slaves experienced family histories that contradict the accepted wisdom in U.S. slave studies. Though their arguments still have not altered the dominant paradigm, revisionist researchers offer evidence that slave family stability varied with southern subregion. Tadman contends that, after the international slave trade closed in 1808, the Upper South operated like a "stock-raising system" where "a proportion of the natural increase of its slaves was regularly sold off." As a result, the chances of an Upper South slave falling into the hands of interstate traders were quite high. Between 1820 and 1860, one-tenth of all Upper South slaves were relocated to the Lower South each decade. Nearly one of every three slave children living in the Upper South in 1820 was gone by 1860. Among Mississippi slaves who had been removed from the Upper South, nearly half the males and two-fifths of the females had been separated from spouses with whom they had lived at least five years. Stevenson contends that Virginia slave families were disproportionately matrifocal because of the slave trading and labor strategies of Upper South masters. Clearly, the fifty-year forced labor migration of slaves must be taken into account in scholarly assessments of family stability and of household living conditions.

Scholarly Preoccupation with Slave Agency

The fourth weakness in U.S. slavery studies has been a preoccupation with slave agency. As Kolchin has observed, most scholars "have abandoned the victimization model in favor of an emphasis on the slaves' resiliency and autonomy." Like a number of other scholars, I have grown increasingly concerned that too many recent studies have the effect of whitewashing from slavery the worst structural constraints. Because so much priority has been placed on these research directions, there has been inadequate attention directed toward threats to slave family maintenance. Notions like "windows of autonomy within slavery" or an "independent slave economy" seriously overstate the degree to which slaves had control over their own lives, and they trivialize the brutalities and the inequities of enslavement. Patterson is scathing in his criticism of the excesses of studies that assign too much autonomy to slaves.

> During the 1970s, a revisionist literature emerged in reaction to the earlier scholarship on slavery that had emphasized the destructive impact of the institution on Afro-American life. In their laudable attempts to demonstrate that slaves, in spite of their condition, did exercise some agency and did develop their own unique patterns of culture and social organization, the revisionists went to the opposite extreme, creating what Peter Parish calls a "historiographical hornet's nest," which came "dangerously close to writing the slaveholder out of the story completely."

In their haste to celebrate the resilience and the dignity of slaves, scholars have underestimated the degree to which slaveholders placed families at risk. Taken to its extreme, the search for individual agency shifts to the oppressed the blame for the horrors and inequalities of the institutions that enslaved them. If, for example, we push to its rhetorical endpoint the claim of Berlin and Rowland that slaves "manipulated to their own benefit the slaveowners' belief that regular family relations made for good business," then we would arrive at the inaccurate conclusion (as some have) that the half of the U.S. slave population who resided in single-parent households did so as an expression of their African-derived cultural preferences, not because of any structural interference by owners. If we push to its rhetorical endpoint the claim that there was an independent slave economy, then we must ultimately believe that a hungry household was just not exerting enough personal agency at "independent" food cultivation opportunities. Such views are simply not supported by the narratives of those who experienced enslavement. Nowhere in the 600 slave narratives that I have analyzed (within and outside the Mountain South) have I found a single slave who celebrated moments of independence or autonomy in the manner that many academics do. Some slaves did resist, but ex-slaves voiced comprehension that their dangerous, often costly acts of civil disobedience resulted in no long-term systemic change.

The Target Area for This Study

In sharp contrast to previous studies, I will test the dominant paradigm of the slave family against findings about a slaveholding region that was *typical* of the circumstances in which a majority of U.S. slaves were held. That is, I will examine enslavement in a region that was *not* characterized by large plantations and that did *not* specialize in cotton production. Even though more than half of all U.S. slaves lived where there were fewer than four slave families, there is very little research about family life in areas with low black population densities. Despite Crawford's groundbreaking finding that plantation size was the most significant determinant of quality of slave life, this is the first study of a multistate region of the United States that was characterized by small plantations.

This study breaks new ground by investigating the slave family in a slaveholding region that has been ignored by scholars. I will explore the complexities of the Mountain South where slavery flourished amidst a nonslaveholding majority and a large surplus of poor white landless laborers. In geographic and geological terms, the Mountain South (also known as Southern Appalachia) makes up that part of the U.S. Southeast that rose from the floor of the ocean to form the Appalachian Mountain chain 10,000 years ago. In a previous book, I documented the historical integration of this region into the capitalist world system. The incorporation of Southern Appalachia entailed nearly one hundred fifty years of ecological, politico-economic, and cultural changes. . . . Fundamentally, the Mountain South was a *provisioning zone,* which supplied raw materials to other agricultural or industrial regions of the world economy.

On the one hand, this inland region exported foodstuffs to other peripheries and semiperipheries of the western hemisphere, those areas that specialized in cash crops for export. The demand for flour, meal, and grain liquors was high in plantation economies (like the North American South and most of Latin America), where labor was budgeted toward the production of staple crops. So it was not accidental that the region's surplus producers concentrated their land and labor resources into the generation of wheat and corn, often in terrain where such production was ecologically unsound. Nor was it a chance occurrence that the Southern Appalachians specialized in the production of livestock, as did inland mountainous sections of other zones of the New World. There was high demand for work animals, meat, animal by-products, and leather in those peripheries and semiperipheries that did not allocate land to less-profitable livestock production.

On the other hand, the Mountain South supplied raw materials to emergent industrial centers in the American Northeast and western Europe. The appetite for Appalachian minerals, timber, cotton, and wool was great in those industrial arenas. In addition, regional exports of manufactured tobacco, grain liquors, and foodstuffs provisioned those sectors of the world economy where industry and towns had displaced farms. By the 1840s, the northeastern United States was specializing in manufacturing and international shipping, and that region's growing trade/production centers were experiencing food deficits. Consequently, much of the Appalachian surplus received in Southern ports was reexported to the urban-industrial centers of the American Northeast and to foreign plantation zones of the world economy. In return for raw ores and agricultural products, Southern markets—including the mountain counties—consumed nearly one-quarter of the transportable manufacturing output of the North and received a sizeable segment of the redistributed international imports (e.g., coffee, tea) handled by Northeastern capitalists.

Beginning in the 1820s, Great Britain lowered tariffs and eliminated trade barriers to foreign grains. Subsequently, European and colonial markets were opened to North American commodities. Little wonder, then, that flour and processed meats were the country's major nineteenth-century exports, or that more than two-thirds of those exports went to England and France. Outside the country, then, Appalachian commodities flowed to the manufacturing centers of Europe, to the West Indies, to the Caribbean, and to South America. Through far-reaching commodity flows, Appalachian raw materials—in the form of agricultural, livestock, or extractive resources—were exchanged for core manufactures and tropical imports.

Slavery in the American Mountain South

Peripheral capitalism unfolded in Southern Appalachia as a mode of production that combined several forms of land tenure and labor. Because control over land—the primary factor of production—was denied to them, the unpropertied majority of the free population was transformed into an impoverished *semi-proletariat.* However, articulation with the world economy did not trigger only the appearance of free wage labor or white tenancy. Capitalist dynamics in the Mountain South also generated a variety of unfree labor mechanisms. To use the words of Phillips, "the process of incorporation . . . involved the subordination of the labor force to the dictates of export-oriented commodity production, and thus occasioned increased coercion of the labor force as commodity production became generalized." As a result, the region's landholders combined *free* laborers from the ranks of the landless tenants, croppers, waged workers, and poor women with *unfree* laborers from four sources. Legally restricted from free movement in the marketplace, the region's free blacks, Cherokee households, and indentured paupers contributed coerced labor to the region's farms. However, Southern Appalachia's largest group of unfree laborers were nearly three hundred thousand slaves who made up about 15 percent of the region's 1860 population. About three of every ten adults in the region's labor force were enslaved. In the Appalachian zones of Alabama, Georgia, South Carolina, and Virginia, enslaved and free blacks made up one-fifth to one-quarter of the population. In the Appalachian zones of Maryland, North Carolina, and Tennessee, blacks accounted for only slightly more than one-tenth of the population. West Virginia and eastern Kentucky had the smallest percentage of blacks in their communities. The lowest incidence of slavery occurred in the *mountainous* Appalachian counties where 1 of every 6.4 laborers was enslaved. At the other end of the spectrum, the *ridge-valley* counties utilized unfree laborers more than twice as often as they were used in the zones with the most rugged terrain.

Consisting of 215 mountainous and hilly counties in nine states, this large land area was characterized in the antebellum period by nonslaveholding farms and enterprises, a large landless white labor force, small plantations, mixed farming, and extractive industry. Berlin's conceptualization of a *slave society* caused us to predict that slavery did not dominate the Mountain South because there were not large numbers of plantations or slaves. I contested that assumption in a previous book. A region was not buffered from the political, economic, and social impacts of enslavement simply because it was characterized by low black population density and small slaveholdings. On the one hand, a Lower South farm owner was twelve times more likely to run a large plantation than his Appalachian counterpart. On the other hand, Mountain slaveholders monopolized a much higher proportion of their communities' land and wealth than did Lower South planters. This region was linked by rivers and roads to the coastal trade centers of the Tidewater and the Lower South, and it lay at the geographical heart of antebellum trade routes that connected the South to the North and the Upper South to the Lower South. Consequently, two major slave-trading networks cut directly through the region and became major conduits for overland and river transport of slave coffles. No wonder, then that the political economies of all Mountain South counties were in the grip of slavery. Even in counties with the smallest slave populations (including those in Kentucky and West Virginia), slaveholders owned a disproportionate share of wealth and land, held a majority of important state and county offices, and championed proslavery agendas rather than the social and economic interests of the nonslaveholders in their own communities. Moreover, public policies were enacted by state legislatures controlled and manipulated by slaveholders. In addition, every Appalachian county and every white citizen benefited in certain ways and/or was damaged by enslavement, even when there were few black laborers in the county and even when the individual citizen owned no slaves. For example, slaves were disproportionately represented among hired laborers in the public services and transportation systems that benefited whites of all Appalachian counties, including those with small slave populations. Furthermore, the lives of poor white Appalachians were made more miserable because slaveholders restricted economic diversification, fostered ideological demeaning of the poor, expanded tenancy and sharecropping, and prevented emergence of free public education. Moreover, this region was more politically divided over slavery than any other section of the South. Black and poor white Appalachians were disproportionately represented among the soldiers and military laborers for the Union Army. The Civil War tore apart Appalachian communities, so that the Mountain South was probably more damaged by army and guerilla activity than any other part of the country.

In an earlier work, I identified six indicators that distinguish the Mountain South from the Lower South.

- One of every 7.5 enslaved Appalachians was either a Native American or descended from a Native American. Thus, black Appalachians were 4.5 times more likely than other U.S. slaves to be Native American or to have Indian heritage, reflecting the presence of eight indigenous peoples in this land area.
- Mountain slaves were employed outside agriculture much more frequently than Lower South slaves. At least one-quarter of all mountain slaves were employed full time in nonagricultural occupations. Thus, slaves were disproportionately represented in the region's town commerce, travel capitalism, transportation networks, manufactories, and extractive industries.
- In comparison to areas of high black population density, mountain plantations were much more likely to employ ethnically mixed labor forces and to combine tenancy with slavery.
- Compared to the Lower South, mountain plantations relied much more heavily on women and children for field labor.
- Fogel argued that "the task system was never used as extensively in the South as the gang system." Except for the few large slaveholders, Mountain South plantations primarily managed laborers by assigning daily or weekly tasks and by rotating workers to a variety of occupations. Moreover, small plantations relied on community pooling strategies, like corn huskings, when they needed a larger labor force. Since a majority of U.S. slaves resided on holdings smaller than fifty, like those of the Mountain South, it is likely that gang labor did not characterize Southern plantations to the extent that Fogel claimed.
- Mountain slaves almost always combined field work with nonfield skills, and they were much more likely to be artisans than other U.S. slaves.

Several findings about the Mountain South cry out for scholarly rethinking of assumptions about areas with low black population densities and small plantations.

- On small plantations, slave women worked in the fields, engaged in resistance, and were whipped just about as often as men.
- Mountain masters meted out the most severe forms of punishment to slaves much more frequently than their counterparts in other Southern regions. Appalachian ex-slaves reported frequent or obsessive physical

punishment nearly twice as often as other WPA interviewees. There was greater brutality and repression on small plantations than on large plantations. Moreover, areas with low black population densities were disproportionately represented in court convictions of slaves for capital crimes against whites. As on large plantations, small plantations punished slaves primarily for social infractions, not to motivate higher work productivity.

- As Berlin observed, "the Africanization of plantation society was not a matter of numbers." Thus, slaves on small plantations engaged in much more day-to-day resistance and counter-hegemonic cultural formation than had been previously thought. . . .

Methods, Sources, and Definitions

To research this complex topic, I have triangulated quantitative, archival, primary, and secondary documents. I derived my statistical analysis from a database of nearly twenty-six thousand households drawn from nineteenth-century county tax lists and census manuscripts. In addition to those samples, I relied on archived records from farms, plantations, commercial sites, and industries. A majority of the slaveholder collections utilized for this research derived from *small* and *middling* plantations. However, I did not ignore rich Appalachian planters, like Thomas Jefferson or John Calhoun. Never to quote or cite an Appalachian planter is to deny that they existed and to ignore that they were the richest, most politically powerful families in Appalachian counties. Indeed, I present information about them to demonstrate that they are similar to their Lower South counterparts and, therefore, very different from the typical farmers in their communities. It is also necessary to draw upon planter documents to show that larger plantations implemented different crop choices, surveillance strategies, and labor management practices than did smallholdings. Still, those rich planters account for less than 1 percent of all the citations and details provided in this study.

. . . I have used the term *plantation* consistently to refer to a slaveholding enterprise. I have purposefully done this to distinguish such economic operations from the nonslaveholding farms that characterized the Mountain South. Far too many scholars confront me at meetings with the mythological construct that the typical Appalachian slaveholder was a benign small farmer who only kept a couple of slaves to help his wife out in the kitchen. By using *plantation* to distinguish all slaveholding farms, I seek to erode the stereotype that small plantations might be the social, political, and economic equivalent of small nonslaveholding farms in their communities. On the one hand, small plantations could not have owned black laborers if those families had not accumulated surplus wealth far in excess of the household assets averaged by the majority of nonslaveholding Appalachians. On the other hand, planters and smallholders alike controlled far more than their equitable share of the political power and economic resources in their communities. Because small slaveholders aspired to be planters, they did not often align themselves with the political and economic interests of nonslaveholders. According to Berlin, "what distinguished the slave plantation from other forms of production was neither the particularities of the crop that was cultivated nor the scale of its cultivation. . . . The plantation's distinguishing mark was its peculiar social order, which conceded nearly everything to the slaveowner and nothing to the slave." That social order was grounded in a racial ideology in which chattel bondage and white supremacy became entwined. For that reason, it is crucial to distinguish a nonslaveholding farm from a slaveholding farm. In the Mountain South, a slaveholder did not have to reach planter status to be set apart from neighbors whose antagonism to enslavement would cause them to align themselves with the Union in greater numbers than in any other region of the American South. To distinguish plantations by size, I utilize the definitions that are typically applied by U.S. slavery specialists. A *planter* or *large plantation* held fifty or more slaves, while a *middling plantation* or slaveholder owned twenty to forty-nine slaves. Thus, a *small plantation* was one on which there were nineteen or fewer slaves. . . .

Slave Narratives from the Mountain South

I grounded this study in analysis of narratives of nearly three hundred slaves and more than four hundred white Civil War veterans. I spent many months locating Appalachian slave narratives within the Federal Writers Project, at regional archives, and among published personal histories. Beginning with Rawick's forty-one published volumes of the WPA slave narratives, I scrutinized every page for county of origin, for interregional sales or relocations that shifted slaves into or out of the Mountain South, and for occurrences during the Civil War that displaced slaves. After that process, I identified other archival and published accounts, finding several narratives in unusual locations, including archives at Fisk University and the University of Kentucky. In this way, I did not ignore the life histories of slaves who were born outside the Mountain South and migrated there or those who were removed to other regions. Ultimately, I aggregated the first comprehensive list of Mountain South slave narratives.

How representative of the region are these narratives? In comparison to the entire WPA collection, Appalachian slave narratives are exceptional in the degree to which they depict small plantations. By checking the slave narratives against census manuscripts and slave schedules, I established that the vast majority of the Appalachian narratives were collected from individuals who had been enslaved on plantations that held fewer than twenty slaves. Consequently, Blue Ridge Virginia is underrepresented while the Appalachian counties of Kentucky, North Carolina, and West Virginia are overrepresented. Thus, those areas that held the fewest slaves in this region are more than adequately covered. Appalachian slave narratives are not handicapped by the kinds of shortcomings that plague the national WPA collection. Large plantations, males, and house servants are overrepresented among the entire universe of respondents. In addition, two-fifths of the ex-slaves had experienced fewer than ten years of enslavement. The most serious distortions derived from the class and racial biases of whites who conducted the vast majority of the interviews. Most of the mountain respondents had been field hands, and very few were employed full time as artisans or domestic servants. In terms of gender differentiation, the Appalachian sample is almost evenly divided. In contrast to the entire WPA collection, three-quarters of the mountain ex-slaves were older than ten when freed. Indeed, when emancipated, one-third of the respondents were sixteen or older, and 12 percent were twenty-five or older. Thus, nearly half the Appalachian ex-slaves had endured fifteen years or more of enslavement, and they were old enough to form and to retain oral histories. Perhaps the greatest strength of this regional collection has to do with the ethnicity of interviewers. More than two-fifths of the narratives were written by the ex-slaves themselves or collected by black field workers, including many Tennessee and Georgia interviews that were conducted under the auspices of Fisk University and the Atlanta Urban League. Because the mountain narratives were collected over a vast land area in nine states, this collection offers another advantage. The geographical distances between respondents offer opportunities for testing the widespread transmission of African-Amemrican culture.

I have come away from this effort with a deep respect for the quality and the reliability of these indigenous narratives. When I tested ex-slave claims against public records, I found them to be more accurate than most of the slaveholder manuscripts that I scrutinized, and quite often much less ideologically blinded than many of the scholarly works I have consulted. Therefore, I made the conscious intellectual decision to engage in "the making of *history* in the final instance" by respecting the indigenous knowledge of the ex-slaves whose transcripts I analyzed. That means that I did not dismiss and refuse to explore every slave voice that challenged conventional academic rhetoric. In most instances, I triangulated the indigenous view against public records and found the slave's knowledge to be more reliable than some recent scholarly representations. In other instances, I perceived that Appalachian slaves are a *people without written history* and that it is important to document the oral myths in which they grounded their community building. Because mountain slave narratives present a view of enslavement that attacks the conventional wisdom, I recognized that they and I were engaging in a process that Trouillot calls "the production of alternative narratives." When contacted by a Fisk University researcher in 1937, one Chattanooga ex-slave comprehended that he possessed a knowledge about slavery that was different from the social constructions of the African-American interviewer. "I don't care about telling about it [slavery] sometime," he commented cynically, "because there is always somebody on the outside that knows more about it than I do, and I was right in it." Clearly, this poorly educated man understood that historical facts are not created equal and that knowledge construction is biased by differential control of the means of historical production. On the one hand, I set myself the difficult goal of avoiding the kind of intellectual elitism the ex-slave feared while at the same time trying to avoid the pitfall of informant misrepresentation. On the other hand, I heeded the advice of C. Vann Woodward and did not view the use of slave narratives as any more treacherous or unreliable than other sources or research methods. . . .

Toward a New Paradigm of the U.S. Slave Family

In his 1989 capstone study, Fogel argued that enslavement was morally reprehensible because owners denied to African-Americans freedom from domination, economic opportunity, citizenship, and cultural self-determination. It is disturbing that Fogel excluded from his moral indictment the forcible removal of kin and masters' disruptions of black households. While I strongly endorse his call for an "effort to construct a new paradigm on the slave family," I would hope to see writers assign greater priority to the human pain of family separations than has occurred over the last three decades. Celebration of resistance and cultural persistence to the exclusion of investigations of those forces that broke families will not advance a new school of thought in directions that are any more accurate and reliable than previous generalizations. As we move toward a new paradigm, we need to follow nine lines of new inquiry.

- We need new research that documents slave family life in institutional arrangements that represent the residential and work circumstances of a majority of African-Americans. That requires directing greater attention to plantations smaller than fifty, to the Upper South and slave-selling areas, and to nonagricultural laborers.
- We need to make realistic assessments of all labor migrations. Adherents to the dominant paradigm have been preoccupied with slave selling and have presumed that permanent separations were not caused by hireouts, migrations with owners, slave inheritance within the owner's family, and assignment to distant work sites. However, it is clear in the slave narratives that all these forced migrations severed kinship ties, threatened marriages, generated great numbers of female-headed households, and weakened bonds between children and fathers.
- New research needs to reevaluate the strengths and weaknesses of *abroad marriages* because scholars have tended to presume that such relationships were more stable than they actually were. Such arrangements left women to generate the survival needs of their households and to protect children without the daily support of husbands or other adult males. Moreover, masters withdrew family visits so routinely that households could not count on regular reunions of spouses or of parents and children.
- In future approaches, we need to define family disruption more broadly. Marriage breakups are only one indicator. Loss of children occurred much more frequently, breaking ties between parents and offspring and between siblings. Moreover, few African-Americans maintained long-term connections with extended kin.
- Taking into account variations by size of slaveholding, by subregion, and by type of production, we need to reexamine threats to family persistence caused by inadequate nutrition, shortfalls in basic survival needs, and ecological conditions.
- Scholars need to abandon the myth that family stability is measured in terms of the presence of a *nuclear family.* First, such a family construct did not characterize antebellum white households, and it is

doubtful that this ideal type has ever typified Americans. Second, stability characterizes nonnuclear family constructions in many nonwestern societies. Third, the absence of adult males was not a cultural choice because enslaved women were never in a structural position to control household composition without owners' intervention. Fourth, many enslaved women pooled survival resources by relying on support from other females.

- We need to learn from contemporary demographic trends in many poor countries where high infant mortality rates fuel population growth. On a different conceptual plane than has typified earlier discussions, we need to rethink the connection between high slave child mortality and fertility patterns of enslaved women.
- We need to investigate threats to slave families that occurred during the Civil War and the emancipation process. Families were separated, often permanently, by military labor impressments, enlistment of black soldiers, and the removal of kin to contraband camps. There was an increased incidence of Upper South slave selling and owner migrations throughout the war, magnifying the chances that a slave would be permanently separated from kin. Emancipation came slower in the Upper South, particularly in those counties with large numbers of pro-Union slaveholders or low black population densities. After liberation, most ex-slaves remained with former owners two years or longer, continuing to reside in the same cabins they had occupied during enslavement. Reconstruction labor policies worked against family rebuilding and increased the likelihood of new family disruptions (e.g., indenturement of children to former owners).
- Finally, scholars need to take a fresh look at the historical overlap between African and indigenous enslavement. First, the import of Africans did not trigger so abrsupt an end to Native American enslavement as historians have claimed. Second, researchers have ignored hardships for ethnically mixed slave families caused by forced removals of indigenous peoples from the U.S. Southeast. Third, there was a higher incidence of Native American heritage among southwestern African-Americans who were more often owned by or interacted frequently with Indians.

While Fogel stresses "the critical importance of quantitative consideration," I argue that integrating the perspective of the affected slaves is even more crucial. Even though the existing paradigm is heavily grounded in cliometrics, demography, and sophisticated economic projections, it has still failed to capture the diversity of slave family life on different sized plantations and in different sections of the American South. What we need in the future are approaches that triangulate quantitative analyses with slave accounts to draw comparisons between subregions of the American South, between different parts of the world, and between large and small plantations. The best rationale for a new paradigm can be heard in the painful voices of African-Americans. Elderly ex-slaves mourned the loss of parents, spouses, children, siblings, and grandparents. Even when they had been separated from kin at very early ages, they sensed that a significant element of their souls had been wrenched from them. A mountain slave says it best: "We never met again. . . . That parting I can never forget." In the minds of black Appalachians, poverty, illiteracy, and racial inequality were not the worst legacies of enslavement. Bad as those structural factors were, it was the forced removals of family that broke their hearts and generated a community wound that was not healed by liberation. Moreover, half the Appalachian ex-slaves carried into the twentieth century the structural impacts of past diasporas, exacerbated by new family separations borne of a chaotic war and an inhumane emancipation process.

Eugene D. Genovese

NO

The World of the Slaves

According to the slaveholders, slave men had little sense of responsibility toward their families and abused them so mercilessly that Ole Massa constantly had to intervene to protect the women and children. Skeptics might wonder how these allegedly emasculated men so easily dominated the strong-willed and physically powerful women of the matriarchal legend, but the slaveholders never troubled themselves about such inconsistencies.

"Negroes are by nature tyrannical in their dispositions," Robert Collins of Macon, Ga., announced, "and, if allowed, the stronger will abuse the weaker; husbands will often abuse their wives and mothers their children." Thus, he concluded, masters and overseers must protect the pace of the quarters and punish aggressors.

Life in the quarters, like lower-class life generally, sometimes exploded in violence. Court records, plantation papers and ex-slave accounts reveal evidence of wife-beating but do not remotely sustain the pretension that without white interference the quarters would have rung with the groans of abused womanhood. Too many black men did not believe in beating their wives, and too many black women, made physically strong by hard field work, were not about to be beaten. So, why should slaveholders, who thought nothing of stripping a woman naked and whipping her till she bled, express so much concern? The pontificating of the ideologues might be dismissed as politically serviceable rubbish, but the concern of the slaveholders who wrote in agricultural journals primarily for each other's eyes and who penned private instructions for overseers demands explanation.

The slaveholders needed order and feared that domestic abuse would undermine the morale of the labor force. By asserting himself as the protector of black women and domestic peace, the slaveholder asserted himself as *paterfamilias* and reinforced his claims to being sole father of a "family, black and white." In this light, the efforts of the drivers or plantation preachers or other prestigious slaves to restrain abusive husbands represented an attempt by the quarters to rule themselves.

The slaveholders intuitively grasped something else. A black man whose authority in the house rested on his use of force may have picked the worst way to assert himself, but in a world in which so much conspired to reduce men to "guests in the house" and to emasculate them, even this kind of assertion, however unmanly by external standards, held some positive meaning.

Defending Their Own

The slave women did not often welcome Ole Massa's protection. They preferred to take care of themselves or, when they needed help, to turn to their fathers, brothers or friend. As any policeman in a lower-class neighborhood, white or black, knows, a woman who is getting the worst of a street fight with her man and who is screaming for help usually wants relief from the blows; she does not want her man subjected to an outsider's righteous indignation and may well join him in repelling an attack.

When Ellen Botts' mother—the much respected Mammy of a sugar plantation—showed up with a lump on her head inflicted by her hot-tempered husband, she told her master that she had had an accident. She would deal with her husband herself and certainly did not want to see him whipped. When James Redpath asked a slave woman in South Carolina if slave women expected to leave their husbands when they fell out, he got the contemptuous answer meddlers in other people's love lives ought to expect. "Oh, no, not all us; we sometimes quarrel in de daytime and make all up at night."

The slaveholders, in their tender concern for black women who suffered abuse from their husbands, remained curiously silent about those who fell back on their husbands' protection. Laura Bell's father won her mother's hand by volunteering to take a whipping in her place. Most slaveholders had the sense to prohibit such gallantry, but no few black men braved their wrath by interposing themselves between their wives or daughters and the white man who sought to harm them. Not only husbands but male friends killed, beat or drove off overseers for whipping their women.

Black women fell victims to white lust, but many escaped because the whites knew they had black men who would rather die than stand idly by. In some cases black men protected their women and got off with a whipping or no punishment at all; in other cases they sacrificed their lives.

Even short of death, the pride of assertive manliness could reach fearful proportions. An overseer tried to rape Josiah Henson's mother but was overpowered by his father. Yielding to his wife's pleas and their overseer's promise of no reprisal, the enraged slave desisted from killing him. The overseer broke his promise. Henson's father suffered 100 lashes and had an ear nailed to the whipping post and then severed.

"Previous to this affair my father, from all I can learn, had been a good-humored and light-hearted man, the ringleader in all fun at corn-huskings and Christmas buffoonery. His banjo was the life of the farm, and all night long at a merry-making would he play on it while the other Negroes danced. But from this hour he became utterly changed. Sullen, morose, and dogged, nothing could be done with him."

Threats of being sold south had no effect on him. The thoughts running through his mind as he came to prefer separation from the wife he loved to enduring life there must remain a matter of speculation. His master sold him to Alabama, and he was never heard from again.

Resisting Oppression

The slaveholders deprived black men of the role of provider; refused to dignify their marriages or legitimize their issue; compelled them to submit to physical abuse in the presence of their women and children; made them choose between remaining silent while their wives and daughters were raped or seduced and risking death; and threatened them with separation from their family at any moment.

Many men caved in under the onslaught and became irresponsible husbands and indifferent fathers. The women who had to contend with such men sometimes showed stubborn cheerfulness and sometimes raging bitterness; they raised the children, maintained order at home, and rotated men in and out of bed. Enough men and women fell into this pattern to give rise to the legends of the matriarchy, the emasculated but brutal male, and the fatherless children.

Many men and women resisted the "infantilization," "emasculation" and "dehumanization" inherent in the system's aggression against the slave family. How many? No one will ever know. At issue is the quality of human relationships, which cannot be measured. But there exists as much evidence of resistance and of a struggle for a decent family life as of demoralization. A brutal social system broke the spirit of many and rendered others less responsible than human beings ought to be. But enough men came out of this test of fire whole, if necessarily scarred, to demonstrate that the slaves had powerful inner resources. A terrible system of human oppression took a heavy toll of its victims, but their collective accomplishment in resisting the system constitutes a heroic story. That resistance provided black people with solid norms of family life and role differentiation, even if circumstances caused a dangerously high lapse from those norms. The slaves from their own experience had come to value a two-parent, male-centered household, no matter how much difficulty they had in realizing the ideal.

The role of the male slave as husband and father therefore requires a fresh look. If many men lived up to their assigned irresponsibility, others, probably a majority, overcame all obstacles and provided a positive male image for their wives and children. An ex-slave recalled his boyhood:

"I loved my father. He was such a good man. He was a good carpenter and could do anything. My mother just rejoiced in him. Whenever he sat down to talk she just sat and looked and listened. She would never cross him for anything. If they went to church together she always waited for him to interpret what the preacher had said or what he taught was the will of God. I was small but I noticed all of these things. I sometimes think I learned more in my early childhood about how to live than I have learned since."

Protective fathers appeared in the lullabies slave mothers sang to their children:

> Kink head, wherefore you skeered?
> Old snake crawled off, 'cause he's afeared.
> Pappy will smite him on de back
> With a great big club—Ker whack! Ker whack!

Many ex-slaves recalled their fathers as stern disciplinarians, and the slaveholders' complaints about fathers' abusing their children may be read as supporting evidence. Other slave men left their children a memory of kindness and affection that remained through life. Will Adams' father, a foreman on a Texas plantation, came in exhausted after a long day's work but never failed to take his son out of bed and to play with him for hours. The spirituals and other slave songs reflected the importance of the father in the lives of the children; many of them sang of the reunification of the family in heaven and of the father's return.

Middle-Class Norms

Men knew that they might have to part from their wives and children, but that knowledge did not engender indifference so much as a certain stoical submission to that which had to be endured. Under painful conditions, many did their best even while others succumbed. Mingo White's father, upon being sold, did nothing unusual when he charged a male friend with responsibility for looking after his son. A principle of stewardship had arisen in the quarters. Even in the absence of a father, some male would likely step in to help raise a boy to manhood. When the war ended, men crisscrossed the South to reclaim their families and to assert authority over their children.

Slave children usually did have an image of a strong blackolm man before them. Critical scholars have made the mistake of measuring the slave family by middle-class norms; naturally, they have found it wanting.

Even when a slave boy was growing up without a father in the house, he had as a model a tough, resourceful driver, a skilled mechanic or two, and older field hands with some time for the children of the quarters. Some of those men devoted themselves to playing surrogate father to all the children. They told them stories, taught them to fish and trap animals, and instructed them in the ways of survival in a hostile white world.

The norm in the quarters called for adults to look after children, whether blood relatives or not. Every plantation had some men who played this role. Under the worst of circumstances, one or two would have been enough; usually, however, there were a number. And there were the preachers. To the extent that the slaves heard their preachers, the children saw before them influential black men whose eloquence and moral force commanded the respect of the adults.

The slave children, like the ghetto children of later decades, saw a pattern of behavior that implied clear sexual differentiation and a notion of masculinity with its own strengths and weaknesses.

Don't Mess With Mammy

The daughters of the Confederacy suggested in 1923 that Congress set aside a site in Washington for a suitable memorial to the antebellum plantation Mammy. The good ladies had picked their symbol carefully, for no figure stands out so prominently in the moonlight-and-magnolias legend of the Old South. The hostile reaction of so many blacks confirmed the judgment. As the old regime has come under increasingly critical scrutiny, Mammy has had a steadily worsening press. She remains the most elusive and important black presence in the Big House. To understand her is to move toward understanding the tragedy of plantation paternalism.

First, the white legend, Lewis H. Blair, attacking racial segregation in 1889, wrote:

"Most of us above 30 years of age had our mammy, and generally she was the first to receive us from the doctor's hands, and was the first to proclaim, with heart bursting with pride, the arrival of a fine baby. Up to the age of 10 we saw as much of the mammy as of the mother, perhaps more, and we loved her quite as well. The mammy first taught us to lisp and to walk, played with us and told us wonderful stories, taught us who made us and who redeemed us, dried our tears and soothed our bursting hearts, and saved us many a well-deserved whipping. . . ."

Word Had Force of Law

Mammy comes through the black sources in much the same way, but only so far. Lindey Faucette of North Carolina remembered her grandmother, Mammie Beckie, who "toted de keys," whose word had the force of law with Marse John and Mis' Annie, and who slept in the bed with her mistress when the master's law practice kept him in town all night. Alice Sewell of Alabama especially recalled the plantation Mammy's comforting the relatives of deceased slaves, arranging for the burial, and leading the funeral services. Ellen Botts of Louisiana noted: "All de niggers have to stoop to Aunt Rachel like they curtsy to Missy." And Adeline Johnson, who had served as a Mammy in South Carolina, spoke in her old age in accents that would have warmed the hearts of those Daughters of the Confederacy.

"I hope and prays to git to hebben. Whether I's white or black when I git dere, I'll be satisfied to see my Savior dat my old marster worshipped and my husband preached 'bout. I wants to be in hebben wid all my white folks, just to wait on them and love them and serve them, sorta lak I did in slavery time. Dat will be 'nough hebben for Adeline."

Who were these Mammies? What did they actually do? Primarily, the Mammy raised the white children and ran the Big House either as the mistress' executive officer or her de facto superior. Her power extended over black and white so long as she exercised restraint, and she was not to be crossed.

She carried herself like a surrogate mistress—neatly attired, barking orders, conscious of her dignity, full of self-respect. She played the diplomat and settled the interminable disputes that arose among the house servants; when diplomacy failed, she resorted to her whip and restored order. She served as confidante to the children, the mistress, and even the master. She expected to be consulted on the love affairs and marriages of the white children and might even be consulted on the business affairs of the plantation. She presided over the dignity of the whole plantation and taught the courtesies to the white children as well as to those black children destined to work in the Big House. On the small and medium-sized plantations she had to carry much of the house work herself, and her relationship to the field slaves drew closer.

In general, she gave the whites the perfect slave—a loyal, faithful, contented, efficient, conscientious member of the family who always knew her place; and she gave the slaves a white-approved standard of black behavior. She also had to be a tough, worldly-wise, enormously resourceful woman; that is, she had to develop all the strength of character not usually attributed to an Aunt Jane.

Mammy supposedly paid more attention to the white children than to her own. Even W. E. B. Du Bois, who was rarely taken in by appearances and legends, thought so. He described the Mammy as "one of the most pitiful of the world's Christs. . . . She was an embodied Sorrow, an anomaly crucified on the cross of her own neglected children for the sake of the children of masters who bought and sold her as they bought and sold cattle."

The Mammy typically took her responsibilities to the white family as a matter of high personal honor and in so doing undoubtedly could not give her own children as much love and attention as they deserved. House nannies, white and black, free and slave, have often fallen into this trap. But the idea that the Mammies actually loved the white children more than their own rests on nothing more than wishful white perceptions. That they loved the white children they themselves raised—hardly astonishing for warm, sensitive, generous women—in no way proves that they loved their own children the less. Rather, their position in the Big House, including their close attention to the white children sometimes at the expense of their own, constituted the firmest protection they could have acquired for themselves and their immediate families. Mammies did not often have to worry about being sold or about having their husbands or children sold. The sacrifices they made for the whites earned them genuine affection in return, which provided a guarantee of protection, safety, and privilege for their own children.

Barrier Against Abuse

The relationship between the Mammies and their white folks exhibited that reciprocity so characteristic of paternalism. "Of course," a planter in Virginia told a northern reporter in 1865, "if a servant has the charge of one of my little ones, and I see the child grow fond of her, and that she loves the child, I cannot but feel kindly towards her." Of course, Mom Genia Woodbury, who had been a slave in South Carolina, acknowledged that when white folks treat you kindly, you develop kind feelings toward their children.

The devotion of the white children, who regularly sought her as their protector, confidante, and substitute mother, established a considerable barrier against the abuse of Mammy or her family. "We would not hesitate about coming to see you," Laura S. Tibbets of Louisiana wrote her sister-in-law, "if I could bring my servants, but I could not bring my baby without assistance. She is a great deal fonder of her Mammy than she is of me. She nurses her and it would be a great trial to go without her."

The immunity that Mammy secured for herself did not fully cover husband and children, but it went far enough to shield them from the worst. Mammy distraught, hurt, or angry was not to be borne. More than one overseer learned to his cost to walk gingerly around her and hers. Ma Eppes of Alabama said that an overseer had whipped the plantation Mammy when the mistress was away:

"When Miss Sarah comed back and found it out she was the maddest white lady I ever seed. She sent for the overseer and she say, 'Allen, what you mean by whipping Mammy? You know I don't allow you to touch my house servants . . . I'd rather see them marks on my old shoulders than to see'em on Mammy's. They wouldn't hurt me no worse.' Then she say, 'Allen, take your family and git offen my place. Don't you let sundown catch you here.' So he left. He wasn't nothing but white trash nohow."

Another overseer made the incredible mistake of asking his employer for permission to punish Mammy. The reply: "What! What! Why I would as soon think of punishing my own mother! Why man you'd have four of the biggest men in Mississippi down on you if you even dare suggest such a thing, and she knows it! All you can do is to knuckle down to Mammy."

The plantation Mammy was not, as is so easily assumed, some "white man's nigger," some pathetic appendage to the powerful whites of the Big House. Her strength of character, iron will and impressive self-discipline belie any glib generalizations.

She did not reject her people in order to identify with stronger whites, but she did place herself in a relationship to her own people that reinforced the paternalist social order. Thus, she carried herself with courage, compassion, dignity and self-respect and might have provided a black model for these qualities among people who needed one, had not the constricting circumstances of her own development cut her off, in essential respects, from playing that role. Her tragedy lay not in her abandonment of her own people but in her inability to offer her individual power and beauty to black people on terms they could not accept without themselves sliding further into a system of paternalistic dependency.

Some Chose Freedom

The boldest slaves struck the hardest blow an individual could against the regime: they escaped to freedom. During the 1850s about a thousand slaves a year ran away to the North, Canada, and Mexico. Increased vigilance by the slaveholders and their police apparatus may have reduced the number from 1,011 in 1850 to 803 in 1860 as the census reports insist, but even so, the economic drain and political irritation remained serious.

The slaves in the border states, especially the extreme northern tier, had a much better chance to escape than did those in Mississippi or Alabama. But even in Texas, Arkansas and Louisiana, slaveholders had to exercise vigilance, for many slaves went over the Mexican border or escaped to friendly Indians.

Who ran away? Any slave might slip into the woods for a few days, but those whose departure rated an advertisement and organized chase—those who headed for freedom in the North, the Southern cities, or the swamps—fell into a pattern. At least 80 per cent were men between the ages of 16 and 35. At least one-third of the runaways belonged to the ranks of the skilled and privileged slaves—those with some education and with some knowledge of the outside world—and women occupied these ranks only as house servants.

The whip provided the single biggest provocation to running away. Many slaves ran in anticipation of a whipping or other severe punishment, and others in anger after having suffered it. In some cases—too many—slaves ran not simply from a particular whipping but from the torments regularly inflicted by cruel or sadistic masters or overseers.

A large if underdetermined number of slaves ran away to rejoin loved ones from whom they had been forcibly parted. Newspaper advertisements frequently contained such words as "He is no doubt trying to reach his wife." Slaveholders had great trouble with newly purchased slaves who immediately left to try to find parents or children as well as wives. In some instances the slaves had unexpected success when their masters, touched by the evidence of devotion and courage, reunited the family by resale.

In many more cases family ties prevented slaves from running away or kept them close to home when they did run. Frederick Law Olmsted reported from the lower Mississippi Valley that planters kept a sharp eye on mothers, for few slaves would leave permanently if they had to leave their mothers behind to face the master's wrath.

"The Thousands Obstacles"

Among the deterrents to making the long run to free states none loomed larger than the fear of the unknown. Most knew only the immediate area and often only a narrow strip of that. Even many skilled and relatively sophisticated slaves lacked an elementary knowledge of geography and had no means of transportation.

If most slaves feared to think about flight to the North, many feared even to think of short-term flight to the nearby woods or swamps. The slaves faced particularly difficult conditions in the swampy areas alongside the great plantation districts of Louisiana and the eastern low country. Solomon Northrup, a slave on a Louisiana cotton plantation in the 1840s, wrote:

"No man who has never been placed in such a situation can comprehend the thousand obstacles thrown in the way of the fleeing slave. Every whiteman's hand is raised against him—the patrollers are watching for him—the hounds are ready to follow on his track, and the nature of the country is such as renders it impossible to pass through it with any safety."

And yet, large numbers of slaves did brave the elements, the dogs, and the patrols; did swallow their fears; and did take to the woods. No plantation of any size totally avoided the runaway problem. Everywhere, the slavesholders had to build a certain loss of labor-time and a certain amount of irritation into their yearly calculations.

Slaves from one plantation assisted runaways from other plantations under certain circumstances. The slaves from neighboring plantations often knew each other well. They met for prayer meetings, corn shuckings, Christmas, and other holiday barbecues; often formed close attachments; and sometimes extended their idea of a plantation family to at least some of these friends and acquaintances. Within this wider circle, the slaves would readily help each other if they shunned those they regarded as strangers. But even strangers might find succor if they were fleeing the plantations of slaveholders known to be cruel.

Those who fled to freedom made an inestimable contribution to the people they left behind, which must be weighed against their participation in a safety-valve effect. These were slaves who, short of taking the path of insurrection, most clearly repudiated the regime; who dramatically chose freedom at the highest risk; who never let others forget that there was an alternative to their condition.

POSTSCRIPT

Did Slavery Destroy the Black Family?

Major reinterpretations of slavery occurred in the 1970s. Professor John Blassingame was one of the first African American historians to challenge the Elkins thesis of the slave as "Sambo" and write a history of slavery from the point of view of the slaves themselves.

Blassingame centers his view of *The Slave Community: Plantation Life in the Antebellum South* revised and enlarged edition (Oxford University Press, 1972, 1979) around the slave family. Unlike other slave societies, Blassingame believes the even sex ration between males and females in the antebellum South contributed to the solidarity and generally monogamous relationships between husbands and wives. The author is no romantic, however, because he argues elsewhere that almost one-third of all slave marriages were broken up because of the sale of one partner to another plantation.

Blassingame was the first historian to make use of slave testimonies. A good example of Blassingame's use of sources—speakers, interviews, letters, and autobiographies—are collected in his *Slave Testimony: Two Centuries of Letters, Speeches, Interviews and Autobiographies* (Oxford University Press, 1979).

Several white historians such as Herbert Gutman and Eugene Genovese believed that careful usage of oral interviews greatly enhanced our view of nineteenth-century slavery. In his iconoclastic sprawling view of *The Black Family in Slavery and Freedom, 1750-1925* (Pantheon, 1976), Gutman argues that slaves were more monogamous, were less promiscuous, and did not marry kin as did the white slaveholding families. Furthermore Gutman argues somewhat controversially that the master had no influence on the slave family.

Professor Eugene Genovese has written dozens of journal articles, review essays, and books about the antebellum South. He views the antebellum South as a pre-capitalist agrarian society in which master and slave were bound together in a set of mutual duties and responsibilities similar to the arrangements of lords and serfs under the feudal system of middle ages Europe. Most of Genovese's contentions are rejected by modern historians of slavery. Robert W. Fogel and Stanley L. Engerman, in their controversial study of *Time on the Cross: The Economics of American Slavery*, 2 vols. (Hougton Mifflin, 1974), argued that planters were capitalists, ran plantations that were "35 percent more efficient than the northern system of family farms," and developed a system of rewards for the hardworking slaves who internalized the values of their masters.

In the *Taking Sides* selection from his major synthesis *Roll Jordan Roll* (Pantheon, 1974), Professor Genovese describes the important role men played on the plantation in defending women from advances by the owners at the risk of being beaten, killed, or sold to another plantation. When families were split, children would receive guidance from other males in the quarters. Genovese also explains how important "mammy" was to the "plantation mistress." At the same time, he notes that "mammy" made sure that her own family was treated well and remained intact because of her importance to the owner's family. Finally Genovese sketches the unhappiness that slaves felt about the institution in discussing the thousands of runaways—primarily single males—who attempted to escape under insurmountable odds to free states and Canada.

In the first selection, Professor Wilma Dunaway challenges the dominant paradigm that has celebrated the autonomy of the slave family in the histories of Professors Blassingame, Genovese, Gutman, Rawick, and others. Most of Professor Dunaway's generalizations come from an earlier study on *Slavery in the American Mountain South* (Cambridge University Press, 2003). Her research is rooted in a database of antebellum census returns and tax records from 215 Appalachian countries and almost 400 manuscript collections that range over nine states from Maryland and West Virginia to the deep South states of Georgia and Alabama. She also uses the oral history interviews of former slaves in the 1920s and 1930s by professional historians and New Deal government workers.

Her books demonstrated the strengths and weaknesses of local history. Dunaway argues that the Appalachian region with its medium and small plantations was more typical than the deep South regions with their large cotton-dominated plantations. According to Dunaway, Appalachian slaves were treated harshly by their masters. Whippings were standard practice, slaves sales to the plantations of the deep South were common without regard for family attachments, and fewer than 12 percent of mountain slaves grew market-based gardens because of exhaustion from 14-hour work days. Many slaves were engaged in industrial rather than agricultural jobs. Most grew corn and wheat for the "new global markets" rather than cotton. Slaves worked side by side with "landless tenants, croppers, wage workers, and unfree laborers." Interestingly there were a number of Cherokee Indian slave owners, but also Cherokee Indian slaves who worked with Afro-American slaves and slaves with mixed blood.

But local history has its limitations. Dunaway may also overgeneralize about the Appalachian experience as establishing a new or really pre-1970s paradigm for slavery. Perhaps, as Professor Berlin points out, the slave experience is too varied in terms of time, region, and size to lend itself to easy generalizations.

The two most important historiographical works on slavery are Mark Smith, *Debating Slavery: Economy and Society in the Antebellum American South* (Cambridge University Press, 1998) and Peter J. Parish, *Slavery: History and Historians* (Harper and Row, 1989). The best anthology of primary sources and secondary readings is *Slavery and Emancipation,* edited by Rick Halpern and Enrico Dal Lago (Blackwell Publishing, 2002). Three other useful anthologies of secondary readings are William Dudley, ed., *American Slavery* (Greenhaven

Press, 2000), Lawrence B. Goodhart, et. al., eds., *Slavery in American Society,* 3rd ed. (D.C. Heath and Company, 1993), and the older but still useful Allen Weinstein, et al., eds., *American Negro Slavery,* 3rd ed. (Oxford University Press, 1979).

Finally, in addition to the works of Professor Berlin, *American Slavery 1619-1877* (Hill and Wang, 1993) by Peter Kolchin is an indispensable summary as well as the special issue on the "Genovese Forum" in the *Radical History Review* 88 (Winter 2004), 3-83, an analysis of the work of the "Marxian Conservative" scholar by several of his peers.

ISSUE 12

Was the Mexican War an Exercise in American Imperialism?

YES: Ramón Eduardo Ruiz, from "Manifest Destiny and the Mexican War," in Howard H. Quint, Milton Cantor, and Dean Albertson, eds., *Main Problems in American History,* 5th ed. (Dorsey Press, 1988)

NO: Norman A. Graebner, from "The Mexican War: A Study in Causation," *Pacific Historical Review* (August 1980)

ISSUE SUMMARY

YES: Professor of history Ramón Eduardo Ruiz argues that for the purpose of conquering Mexico's northern territories, the United States waged an aggressive war against Mexico from which Mexico never recovered.

NO: Professor of diplomatic history Norman A. Graebner argues that President James Polk pursued an aggressive policy that he believed would force Mexico to sell New Mexico and California to the United States and to recognize the annexation of Texas without starting a war.

As David M. Plecher points out in his balanced but critical discussion of *The Diplomacy of Annexation: Texas, Oregon and the Mexican War* (University of Missouri Press, 1973), the long-range effects on American foreign policy of the Mexican War were immense. Between 1845 and 1848, the United States acquired more than 1,200 square miles of territory and increased its size by over a third of its present area. This included the annexation of Texas and the subsequent states of the southwest that stretched to the Pacific coast incorporating California and the Oregon territory up to the 49th parallel. European efforts to gain a foothold in North America virtually ceased. By the 1860s, the British gradually abandoned their political aspirations in Central America, "content to compete for economic gains with the potent but unmilitary weapon of their factory system and their merchant marine." Meanwhile, the United States flexed her muscles at the end of the Civil War and used the Monroe Doctrine for the first time to force the French puppet ruler out of Mexico.

The origins of the Mexican War began with the controversy over Texas, a Spanish possession for three centuries. In 1821, Texas became the northernmost province of the newly established country of Mexico. Sparsely populated with a mixture of Hispanics and Indians, the Mexican government encouraged immigration from the United States. By 1835, the Anglo population had swelled to 30,000 plus over 2,000 slaves, while the Mexican population was only 5,000.

Fearful of losing control over Texas, the Mexican government prohibited further immigration from the United States in 1830. But it was too late. The Mexican government was divided and had changed hands several times. The centers of power were thousands of miles from Texas. In 1829, the Mexican government abolished slavery, an edict that was difficult to enforce. Finally General Santa Anna attempted to abolish the federation and impose military rule over the entire country. Whether it was due to Mexican intransigence or the Anglos' assertiveness, the settlers rebelled in September 1835. The war was short-lived. Santa Anna was captured at the battle of San Jacinto in April 1836, and Texas was granted her independence.

For nine years, Texas remained an independent republic. Politicians were afraid that if Texas were annexed it would be carved into four or five states, thereby upsetting the balance of power between the evenly divided free states and slave states that had been created in 1819 by the Missouri Compromise. But the pro-slavery president John Tyler pushed through Congress a resolution annexing Texas in the three days of his presidency in 1845.

The Mexican government was incensed and broke diplomatic relations with the United States. President James K. Polk sent John Slidell as the American emissary to Mexico to negotiate monetary claims of American citizens in Mexico, to purchase California, and to settle the southwestern boundary of Texas at the Rio Grande River and not farther north at the Nueces River, which Mexico recognized as the boundary. Upon Slidell's arrival, news leaked out about his proposals. The Mexican government rejected Slidell's offer. In March 1846, President Polk stationed General Zachary Taylor in the disputed territory along the Rio Grande with an army of 4,000 troops. On May 9, Slidell returned to Washington and informed Polk that he was rebuffed. Polk met with his cabinet to consider war. By chance that same evening, Polk received a dispatch from General Taylor informing him that on April 25 the Mexican army crossed the Rio Grande and killed or wounded 16 of his men. On May 11, Polk submitted his war message claiming "American blood was shed on American soil." Congress voted overwhelmingly for war 174 to 14 in the House and 40 to 2 in the Senate despite the vocal minority of Whig protesters and intellectuals who opposed the war.

In the following selections, Ramón Eduardo Ruiz argues that the United States waged a racist and aggressive war against Mexico for the purpose of conquering what became the American southwest. In his view Manifest Destiny was strictly an ideological rationale to provide noble motives for what were really acts of aggression against a neighboring country. Norman A. Graebner contends that President James Polk pursued the aggressive policy of a stronger nation in order to force Mexico to sell New Mexico and Texas to the United States and to recognize America's annexation of Texas without causing a war.

YES 

Ramón Eduardo Ruiz

Manifest Destiny and the Mexican War

All nations have a sense of destiny. Spaniards braved the perils of unknown seas and the dangers of savage tribes to explore and conquer a New World for Catholicism. Napoleon's armies overran Europe on behalf of equality, liberty, and fraternity. Communism dictates the future of China and the Soviet Union. Arab expansionists speak of Islam. In the United States, Manifest Destiny in the 19th century was the equivalent of these ideologies or beliefs. Next-door neighbor Mexico felt the brunt of its impact first and suffered most from it.

What was Manifest Destiny? The term was coined in December 1845 by John L. O'Sullivan, then editor and cofounder of the *New York Morning News.* Superpatriot, expansionist, war hawk, and propagandist, O'Sullivan lived his doctrine of Manifest Destiny, for that slogan embodied what he believed. O'Sullivan spoke of America's special mission, frequently warned Europe to keep hands off the Weste Hemisphere, later joined a filibustering expedition to Cuba, and had an honored place among the followers of President James K. Polk, Manifest Destiny's spokesman in the Mexican War.

Manifest Destiny voiced the expansionist sentiment that had gripped Americans almost from the day their forefathers had landed on the shores of the New World in the 17th century. Englishmen and their American offspring had looked westward since Jamestown and Plymouth, confident that time and fate would open to them the vast West that stretched out before them. Manifest Destiny, then, was first territorial expansion—American pretensions to lands held by Spain, France, and later Mexico; some even spoke of a United States with boundaries from pole to pole. But Manifest Destiny was greater than mere land hunger; much more was involved. Pervasive was a spirit of nationalism, the belief that what Americans upheld was right and good, that Providence had designated them the chosen people. In a political framework, Manifest Destiny stood for democracy as Americans conceived it; to spread democracy and freedom was the goal. Included also were ideals of regeneration, the conquest of virgin lands for the sake of their development, and concepts of Anglo-Saxon superiority. All these slogans and beliefs played a role in the Mexican question that culminated in hostilities in 1846.

Apostles of these slogans pointed out that Mexicans claimed lands from the Pacific to Texas but tilled only a fraction of them, and then inefficiently.

"No nation has the right to hold soil, virgin and rich, yet unproducing," stressed one U.S. representative. "No race but our own can either cultivate or rule the western hemisphere," acknowledged the *United States Magazine and Democratic Review.* The Indian, almost always a poor farmer in North America, was the initial victim of this concept of soil use; expansionists later included nearly everyone in the New World, and in particular Mexicans. For, Caleb Cushing asked: "Is not the occupation of any portion of the earth by those competent to hold and till it, a providential law of national life?"

Oregon and Texas, and the Democratic Party platform of 1844, kindled the flames of territorial expansion in the roaring forties. Millions of Americans came to believe that God had willed them all of North America. Expansion symbolized the fulfillment of "America's providential mission or destiny"—a mission conceived in terms of the spread of democracy, which its exponents identified with freedom. Historian Albert K. Weinberg has written: "It was because of the association of expansion and freedom in a means-end relationship, that expansion now came to seem most manifestly a destiny."

Americans did not identify freedom with expansion until the forties. Then, fears of European designs on Texas, California, and Oregon, perhaps, prompted an identity of the two. Not only were strategic and economic interests at stake, but also democracy itself. The need to extend the area of freedom, therefore, rose partly from the necessity of keeping absolutistic European monarchs from limiting the area open to American democracy in the New World.

Other factors also impelled Americans to think expansion essential to their national life. Failure to expand imperiled the nation, for, as historian William E. Dodd stated, Westerners especially believed "that the Union gained in stability as the number of states multiplied." Meanwhile, Southerners declared the annexation of Texas essential to their prosperity and to the survival of slavery, and for a congressional balance of power between North and South. Others insisted that expansion helped the individual states to preserve their liberties, for their numerical strength curtailed the authority of the central government, the enemy of local autonomy and especially autonomy of the South. Moreover, for Southerners extension of the area of freedom meant, by implication, expansion of the limits of slavery. Few planters found the two ideas incompatible. Religious doctrines and natural principles, in their opinion, had ruled the Negro ineligible for political equality. That expansion favored the liberties of the individual, both North and South agreed.

In the forties, the pioneer spirit received recognition as a fundamental tenet of American life. Individualism and expansion, the mark of the pioneer, were joined together in the spirit of Manifest Destiny. Expansion guaranteed not just the political liberty of the person, but the opportunity to improve himself economically as well, an article of faith for the democracy of the age. Further, when antiexpansionists declared that the territorial limits of the United States in 1846 assured all Americans ample room for growth in the future, the expansionists-turned-ecologists replied that some 300 million Americans in 1946 would need more land, a prediction that overstated the case of the population-minded experts. And few Americans saw the extension of freedom in terms other than liberty for themselves—white, Anglo-Saxon, and Protestant. All these concepts, principles, and beliefs, then, entered into the expansionist creed of Manifest Destiny.

None of these was a part of the Mexican heritage, the legacy of three centuries of Spanish rule and countless years of pre-Columbian civilization. Mexico and the United States could not have been more dissimilar in 1846. A comparison of colonial backgrounds helps to bring into focus the reasons the two countries were destined to meet on the field of battle. One was weak and the other strong; Mexico had abolished slavery and the United States had not; Americans had their Manifest Destiny, but few Mexicans believed in themselves.

Daughter of a Spain whose colonial policy embraced the Indian, Mexico was a mestizo republic, a half-breed nation. Except for a small group of aristocrats, most Mexicans were descendants of both Spaniards and Indians. For Mexico had a colonial master eager and willing to assimilate pre-Columbian man. Since the days of the conqueror Hernán Cortés, Spaniards had mated with Indians, producing a Mexican both European and American in culture and race. Offspring of the Indian as well as the Spaniard, Mexican leaders, and even the society of the time, had come to accept the Indian, if not always as an equal, at least as a member of the republic. To have rejected him would have been tantamount to the Mexican's self-denial of himself. Doctrines of racial supremacy were, if not impossible, highly unlikely, for few Mexicans could claim racial purity. To be Mexican implied a mongrel status that ruled out European views of race.

Spain bequeathed Mexico not merely a racial attitude but laws, religious beliefs, and practices that banned most forms of segregation and discrimination. For example, reservations for Indians were never a part of the Spanish heritage. Early in the 16th century, the Spaniards had formulated the celebrated Laws of the Indies—legislation that clearly spelled out the place of the Indian in colonial society. Nothing was left to chance, since the Spanish master included every aspect of life—labor, the family, religion, and even the personal relations between Spaniard and Indian. The ultimate aim was full citizenship for the Indian and his descendants. In the meantime, the Church ruled that the Indian possessed a soul; given Christian teachings, he was the equal of his European conqueror. "All of the people of the world are men," the Dominican Bartolomé de las Casas had announced in his justly famous 1550 debate with the scholar Sepúlveda.

Clearly, church and state and the individual Spaniard who arrived in America had more than charity in mind. Dreams of national and personal glory and wealth dominated their outlook. Yet, despite the worldly goals of most secular and clerical conquerors, they built a colonial empire on the principle that men of all colors were equal on earth. Of course, Spain required the labor of the Indian and therefore had to protect him from the avarice of many a conquistador. Spaniards, the English were wont to say, were notorious for their disdain of manual labor of any type. But Spain went beyond merely offering the Indian protection in order to insure his labor. It incorporated him into Hispanic-American society. The modern Mexican is proof that the Indian survived: all Mexicans are Indian to some extent. That the Indian suffered economic exploitation and frequently even social isolation is undoubtedly true, but such was the lot of the poor in the Indies—Indian, half-breed, and even Spaniard.

Spain's empire, as well as the Mexican republic that followed, embraced not just the land but the people who had tilled it for centuries before the European's arrival. From northern California to Central America, the boundaries of colonial New Spain, and later Mexico, the Spaniard had embraced the Indian or allowed him to live out his life. It was this half-breed population that in 1846 confronted and fell victim to the doctrine of Manifest Destiny.

America's historical past could not have been more dissimilar. The English master had no room for the Indian in his scheme of things. Nearly all Englishmen—Puritans, Quakers, or Anglicans—visualized the conquest and settlement of the New World in terms of the exclusive possession of the soil. All new lands conquered were for the immediate benefit of the new arrivals. From the days of the founding of Jamestown and Plymouth, the English had pushed the Indian westward, relentlessly driving him from his homeland. In this activity, the clergy clasped hands with lay authorities; neither offered the red man a haven. Except for a few hardy souls, invariably condemned by their peers, Englishmen of church and state gave little thought to the Indian. Heaven, hell, and the teachings of Christ were the exclusive domain of the conquerors.

Society in the 13 colonies, and in the Union that followed, reflected English and European customs and ways of life. It was a transplanted society. Where the Indian survived, he found himself isolated from the currents of time. Unlike the Spaniards, whose ties with Africa and darker skinned peoples through seven centuries of Moorish domination had left an indelible imprint on them, most Englishmen had experienced only sporadic contact with people of dissimilar races and customs. Having lived a sheltered and essentially isolated existence, the English developed a fear and distrust of those whose ways were foreign to them. The Americans who walked in their footsteps retained this attitude.

Many American historians will reject this interpretation. They will probably allege that American willingness to accept millions of destitute immigrants in the 19th century obviously contradicts the view that the Anglo-Saxon conqueror and settler distrusted what was strange in others. Some truth is present here, but the weight of the evidence lies on the other side. What must be kept firmly in mind is that immigration to the English colonies and later to the United States—in particular, the tidal wave of humanity that engulfed the United States in the post-Civil War era—was European in origin. Whether Italians, Jews, or Greeks from the Mediterranean, Swedes, Scots, or Germans from the North, what they had in common far outweighed conflicting traits and cultural and physical differences. All were European, offspring of one body of traditions and beliefs. Whether Catholics, Protestants, or Jews, they professed adherence to Western religious practices and beliefs. The so-called melting pot was scarcely a melting pot at all; the ingredients were European in origin. All spices that would have given the stew an entirely different flavor were carefully kept out—namely, the Negro and the Indian.

It was logical that Manifest Destiny, that American belief in a Providence of special design, should have racial overtones. Having meticulously kept out the infidel, Americans could rightly claim a racial doctrine of purity and supremacy in the world of 1846. Had not the nation of Polk's era developed free of those races not a part of the European heritage? Had the nation not progressed rapidly? Most assuredly, the answer was yes. When American development was compared to that of the former Spanish-American colonies, the reply was even more emphatically in the affirmative. After all, the Latin republics to the south had little to boast about. All were backward, illiterate, and badly governed states. Americans had just cause for satisfaction with what they had accomplished.

Unfortunately for Latin America, and especially Mexico, American pride had dire implications for the future. Convinced of the innate racial supremacy which the slogan of Manifest Destiny proclaimed throughout the world, many Americans came to believe that the New World was theirs to develop. Only their industry, their ingenuity, and their intelligence could cope fully with the continental challenge. Why should half-breed Mexico—backward, politically a waste-land, and hopelessly split by nature and man's failures—hold Texas, New Mexico, and California? In Mexico's possession, all these lands would lie virgin, offering a home to a few thousand savage Indians, and here and there a Mexican pueblo of people scarcely different from their heathen neighbors. Manifest Destiny simply proclaimed what most Americans had firmly believed—the right of Anglo-Saxons and others of similar racial origin to develop what Providence had promised them. Weak Mexico, prey of its own cupidity and mistakes, was the victim of this belief.

Manifest Destiny, writes Mexican historian Carlos Bosch García, also contradicts an old American view that means are as important as ends. He stresses that the key to the history of the United States, as the doctrine of Manifest Destiny illustrates, lies in the willingness of Americans to accept as good the ultimate result of whatever they have undertaken to do. That the red man was driven from his homeland is accepted as inevitable and thus justifiable. American scholars might condemn the maltreatment of the Indian, but few question the final verdict.

Equally ambivalent, says Bosch García, is the American interpretation of the Mexican War. Though some American scholars of the post–Civil War period severely censured the South for what they called its responsibility for the Mexican War, their views reflected a criticism of the slavocracy rather than a heartfelt conviction that Mexico had been wronged. Obviously, there were exceptions. Hubert H. Bancroft, a California scholar and book collector, emphatically denounced Polk and his cohorts in his voluminous *History of Mexico* (1883–88). Among the politicians of the era, Abraham Lincoln won notoriety—and probably lost his seat in the House of Representatives—for his condemnation of Polk's declaration of war against Mexico. There were others, mostly members of the Whig Party, which officially opposed the war; but the majority, to repeat, was more involved with the problem of the South than with the question of war guilt.

Most Americans, in fact, have discovered ways and means to justify Manifest Destiny's war on Mexico. That country's chronic political instability, its unwillingness to meet international obligations, its false pride in its military establishment—all those, say scholars, led Mexican leaders to plunge their people into a hopeless war. Had Mexico been willing to sell California, one historian declares, no conflict would have occurred. To paraphrase Samuel F. Bemis, distinguished Yale University diplomatic scholar, no American today would undo the results of Polk's war. Put differently, to fall back on Bosch García, American writers have justified the means because of the ends. Manifest Destiny has not only been explained but has been vindicated on the grounds of what has been accomplished in California and New Mexico since 1848. Or, to cite Hermann Eduard von Holst, a late 19th century German scholar whose writings on American history won him a professorship at the University of Chicago, the conflict between Mexico and the United States was bound to arise. A virile and ambitious people whose cause advanced that of world civilization could not avoid battle with a decadent, puerile people. Moral judgments that applied to individuals might find Americans guilty of aggression, but the standards by which nations survive and prosper upheld the cause of the United States. Might makes right? Walt Whitman, then editor of the *Brooklyn Daily Eagle,* put down his answer succinctly:

> We love to indulge in thoughts of the future extent and power of this Republic—because with its increase is the increase in human happiness and liberty. . . . What has miserable Mexico—with her superstition, her burlesque upon freedom, her actual tyranny by the few over the many—what has she to do with the great mission of peopling the New World with a noble race? Be it ours, to achieve that mission! Be it ours to roll down all of the up-start leaven of the old despotism, that comes our way.

The conflict with Mexico was an offensive war without moral pretensions, according to Texas scholar Otis A. Singletary. It was no lofty crusade, no noble battle to right the wrongs of the past or to free a subjugated people, but a war of conquest waged by one neighbor against another. President Polk and his allies had to pay conscience money to justify a "greedy land-grab from a neighbor too weak to defend herself." American indifference to the Mexican War, Professor Singletary concludes, "lies rooted in the guilt that we as a nation have come to feel about it."

American racial attitudes, the product of a unique colonial background in the New World, may also have dictated the scope of territorial conquest in 1848 and, ironically, saved Mexico from total annexation. Until the clash with Mexico, the American experience had been limited to the conquest, occupation, and annexation of empty or sparsely settled territories, or of those already colonized by citizens of the United States, as were Oregon and Texas. American pioneers had been reincorporated into the Union with the annexation of Oregon and Texas, and even with the purchase of Louisiana in 1803, for the alien population proved small and of little importance. White planters, farmers, and pioneers mastered the small Mexican population in Texas and easily disposed of the Indians and half-breeds in the Louisiana territory.

Expansionists and their foes had long considered both Indian and Negro unfit for regeneration; both were looked on as inferior and doomed races. On this point, most Americans were in agreement. While not entirely in keeping with this view, American opinions of Latin Americans, and of Mexicans in particular, were hardly flattering. Purchase and annexation of Louisiana and Florida, and of Texas and Oregon, had been debated and postponed partly but of fear of what many believed would be the detrimental effect on American democracy resulting from the amalgamation of the half-breed and mongrel peoples of these lands. Driven by a sense of national aggrandizement, the expansionists preferred to conquer lands free of alien populations. Manifest Destiny had no place for the assimilation of strange and exotic peoples. Freedom for Americans—this was the cry, regardless of what befell the conquered natives. The location of sparsely held territory had dictated the course of empire.

James K. Polk's hunger for California reflected national opinion on races as well as desire for land. Both that territory and New Mexico, nearly to the same extent, were almost barren of native populations. Of sparsely settled California, in 1845 the *Hartford Times* eloquently declared that Americans could "redeem from unhallowed hands a land, above all others of heaven, and hold it for the use of a people who know how to obey heaven's behests." Thus it was that the tide of conquest—the fruits of the conference table at Guadalupe Hidalgo—stopped on the border of Mexico's inhabited lands, where the villages of a people alien in race and culture confronted the invaders. American concepts of race, the belief in the regeneration of virgin lands—these logically ordered annexation of both California and New Mexico, but left Mexico's settled territory alone.

Many Americans, it is true, gave much thought to the conquest and regeneration of all Mexico, but the peace of 1848 came before a sufficiently large number of them had abandoned traditional thoughts on race and color to embrace the new gospel. Apparently, most Americans were not yet willing to accept dark-skinned people as the burden of the white man.

Manifest Destiny, that mid-19th-century slogan, is now merely a historical question for most Americans. Despite the spectacular plums garnered from the conference table, the war is forgotten by political orators, seldom discussed in classrooms, and only infrequently recalled by historians and scholars.

But Mexicans, whether scholars or not, have not forgotten the war; their country suffered most from Manifest Destiny's claims to California. The war of 1846–48 represents one of the supreme tragedies of their history. Mexicans are intimately involved with it, unlike their late adversaries who have forgotten it. Fundamental reasons explain this paradox. The victorious United States went to a post-Civil War success story unequaled in the annals of Western civilization. Mexico emerged from the peace of Guadalupe Hidalgo bereft of half of its territory, a beaten, discouraged, and divided country. Mexico never completely recovered from the debacle.

Mexicans had known tragedy and defeat before, but their conquest by Generals Zachary Taylor and Winfield Scott represented not only a territorial loss of immense proportions, but also a cataclysmic blow to their morale as a nation and as a people. From the Mexican point of view, their pride in what they believed they had mastered best—the science of warfare—was exposed as a myth. Mexicans could not even fight successfully, and they had little else to recall with pride, for their political development had enshrined bitter civil strife and callous betrayal of principle. Plagued by hordes of scheming politicians, hungry military men, and a backward and reactionary clergy, they had watched their economy stagnate. Guadalupe Hidalgo clearly outlined the scope of their defeat. There was no success story to write about, only tragedy. Mexicans of all classes are still engrossed in what might have been *if* General Antonio López de Santa Anna had repelled the invaders, from the North.

Polk's war message to Congress and Lincoln's famous reply in the House cover some dimensions of the historical problem. Up for discussion are Polk's role in the affair, the responsibility of the United States and Mexico, and the question of war guilt—a question raised by the victorious Americans and their allies at Nuremberg after World War II. For if Polk felt "the blood of this war, like the blood of Abel, is crying to Heaven against him," as Lincoln charged, then not just the war but also Manifest Destiny stand condemned.

Norman A. Graebner

NO

The Mexican War: A Study in Causation

On May 11, 1846, President James K. Polk presented his war message to Congress. After reviewing the skirmish between General Zachary Taylor's dragoons and a body of Mexican soldiers along the Rio Grande, the president asserted that Mexico "has passed the boundary of the United States, has invaded our territory and shed American blood upon the American soil. . . . War exists, and, notwithstanding all our efforts to avoid it, exists by act of Mexico." No country could have had a superior case for war. Democrats in large numbers (for it was largely a partisan matter) responded with the patriotic fervor which Polk expected of them. "Our government has permitted itself to be insulted long enough," wrote one Georgian. "The blood of her citizens has been spilt on her own soil. It appeals to us for vengeance." Still, some members of Congress, recalling more accurately than the president the circumstances of the conflict, soon rendered the Mexican War the most reviled in American history—at least until the Vietnam War of the 1960s. One outraged Whig termed the war "illegal, unrighteous, and damnable," and Whigs questioned both Polk's honesty and his sense of geography. Congressman Joshua R. Giddings of Ohio accused the president of "planting the standard of the United States on foreign soil, and using the military forces of the United States to violate every principle of international law and moral justice." To vote for the war, admitted Senator John C. Calhoun, was "to plunge a dagger into his own heart, and more so." Indeed, some critics in Congress openly wished the Mexicans well.

For over a century such profound differences in perception have pervaded American writings on the Mexican War. Even in the past decade, historians have reached conclusions on the question of war guilt as disparate as those which separated Polk from his wartime conservative and abolitionist critics. . . .

In some measure the diversity of judgment on the Mexican War, as on other wars, is understandable. By basing their analyses on official rationalizations, historians often ignore the more universal causes of war which transcend individual conflicts and which can establish the bases for greater consensus. Neither the officials in Washington nor those in Mexico City ever acknowledged any alternatives to the actions which they took. But governments generally

From *Pacific Historical Review*, vol. 49, no. 3, August 1980, pp. 405–426.

have more choices in any controversy than they are prepared to admit. Circumstances determine their extent. The more powerful a nation, the more remote its dangers, the greater its options between action and inaction. Often for the weak, unfortunately, the alternative is capitulation or war. . . . Polk and his advisers developed their Mexican policies on the dual assumption that Mexico was weak and that the acquisition of certain Mexican territories would satisfy admirably the long-range interests of the United States. Within that context, Polk's policies were direct, timely, and successful. But the president had choices. Mexico, whatever its internal condition, was no direct threat to the United States. Polk, had he so desired, could have avoided war; indeed, he could have ignored Mexico in 1845 with absolute impunity.

In explaining the Mexican War historians have dwelled on the causes of friction in American-Mexican relations. In part these lay in the disparate qualities of the two populations, in part in the vast discrepancies between the two countries in energy, efficiency, power, and national wealth. Through two decades of independence Mexico had experienced a continuous rise and fall of governments; by the 1840s survival had become the primary concern of every regime. Conscious of their weakness, the successive governments in Mexico City resented the superior power and effectiveness of the United States and feared American notions of destiny that anticipated the annexation of Mexico's northern provinces. Having failed to prevent the formation of the Texas Republic, Mexico reacted to Andrew Jackson's recognition of Texan independence in March 1837 with deep indignation. Thereafter the Mexican raids into Texas, such as the one on San Antonio in 1842, aggravated the bitterness of Texans toward Mexico, for such forays had no purpose beyond terrorizing the frontier settlements.

Such mutual animosities, extensive as they were, do not account for the Mexican War. Governments as divided and chaotic as the Mexican regimes of the 1840s usually have difficulty in maintaining positive and profitable relations with their neighbors; their behavior often produces annoyance, but seldom armed conflict. Belligerence toward other countries had flowed through U.S. history like a torrent without, in itself, setting off a war. Nations do not fight over cultural differences or verbal recriminations; they fight over perceived threats to their interests created by the ambitions or demands of others.

What increased the animosity between Mexico City and Washington was a series of specific issues over which the two countries perennially quarreled—claims, boundaries, and the future of Texas. Nations have made claims a pretext for intervention, but never a pretext for war. Every nineteenth-century effort to collect debts through force assumed the absence of effective resistance, for no debt was worth the price of war. To collect its debt from Mexico in 1838, for example, France blockaded Mexico's gulf ports and bombarded Vera Cruz. The U.S. claims against Mexico created special problems which discounted their seriousness as a rationale for war. True, the Mexican government failed to protect the possessions and the safety of Americans in Mexico from robbery, theft, and other illegal actions, but U.S. citizens were under no obligation to do business in Mexico and should have understood the risk of transporting goods and money in that country. Minister Waddy Thompson wrote from Mexico City in 1842 that it would be "with somewhat of bad grace that we should war upon a country because it could not pay its debts when so many of our own states are in the same situation." Even as the United States after 1842 attempted futilely to collect the $2 million awarded its citizens by a claims commission, it was far more deeply in debt to Britain over speculative losses. Minister Wilson Shannon reported in the summer of 1844 that the claims issue defied settlement in Mexico City and recommended that Washington take the needed action to compel Mexico to pay. If Polk would take up the challenge and sacrifice American human and material resources in a war against Mexico, he would do so for reasons other than the enforcement of claims. The president knew well that Mexico could not pay, yet as late as May 9, 1846, he was ready to ask Congress for a declaration of war on the question of unpaid claims alone.

Congress's joint resolution for Texas annexation in February 1845 raised the specter of war among editors and politicians alike. As early as 1843 the Mexican government had warned the American minister in Mexico City that annexation would render war inevitable; Mexican officials in Washington repeated that warning. To Mexico, therefore, the move to annex Texas was an unbearable affront. Within one month after Polk's inauguration on March 4, General Juan Almonte, the Mexican minister in Washington, boarded a packet in New York and sailed for Vera Cruz to sever his country's diplomatic relations with the United States. Even before the Texas Convention could meet on July 4 to vote annexation, rumors of a possible Mexican invasion of Texas prompted Polk to advance Taylor's forces from Fort Jesup in Louisiana down the Texas coast. Polk instructed Taylor to extend his protection to the Rio Grande but to avoid any areas to the north of that river occupied by Mexican troops. Simultaneously the president reinforced the American squadron in the Gulf of Mexico. "The threatened invasion of Texas by a large Mexican army," Polk informed Andrew J. Donelson, the American charge in Texas, on June 15, "is well calculated to excite great interest here and increases our solicitude concerning the final action by the Congress and the Convention of Texas." Polk assured Donelson that he intended to defend Texas to the limit of his constitutional power. Donelson resisted the pressure of those Texans who wanted Taylor to advance to the Rio Grande; instead, he placed the general at Corpus Christi on the Nueces River. Taylor agreed that the line from the mouth of the Nueces to San Antonio covered the Texas settlements and afforded a favorable base from which to defend the frontier.

Those who took the rumors of Mexican aggressiveness seriously lauded the president's action. With Texas virtually a part of the United States, argued the *Washington Union,* "We owe it to ourselves, to the proud and elevated character which America maintains among the nations of the earth, to guard our own territory from the invasion of the ruthless Mexicans." The *New York Morning News* observed that Polk's policy would, on the whole, "command a general concurrence of the public opinion of his country." Some Democratic leaders, fearful of a Mexican attack, urged the president to strengthen Taylor's forces and order them to take the offensive should Mexican soldiers cross the Rio Grande. Others believed the reports from Mexico exaggerated, for there was no apparent relationship between the country's expressions of belligerence and its capacity to act. Secretary of War William L. Marcy admitted that his information was no better than that of other commentators. "I have at no time," he wrote in July, "felt that war with Mexico was probable—and do not now believe it is, yet it is in the range of possible occurrences. I have officially acted on the hypothesis that our peace may be temporarily disturbed without however believing it will be." Still convinced that the administration had no grounds for alarm, Marcy wrote on August 12: "The presence of a considerable force in Texas will do no hurt and possibly may be of great use." In September William S. Parrott, Polk's special agent in Mexico, assured the president that there would be neither a Mexican declaration of war nor an invasion of Texas.

Polk insisted that the administration's show of force in Texas would prevent rather than provoke war. "I do not anticipate that Mexico will be mad enough to declare war," he wrote in July, but "I think she would have done so but for the appearance of a strong naval force in the Gulf and our army moving in the direction of her frontier on land." Polk restated this judgment on July 28 in a letter to General Robert Armstrong, the U.S. consul at Liverpool: "I think there need be but little apprehension of war with Mexico. If however she shall be mad enough to make war we are prepared to meet her." The president assured Senator William H. Haywood of North Carolina that the American forces in Texas would never aggress against Mexico; however, they would prevent any Mexican forces from crossing the Rio Grande. In conversation with Senator William S. Archer of Virginia on September 1, the president added confidently that "the appearance of our land and naval forces on the borders of Mexico & in the Gulf would probably deter and prevent Mexico from either declaring war or invading Texas." Polk's continuing conviction that Mexico would not attack suggests that his deployment of U.S. land and naval forces along Mexico's periphery was designed less to protect Texas than to support an aggressive diplomacy which might extract a satisfactory treaty from Mexico without war. For Anson Jones, the last president of the Texas Republic, Polk's deployments had precisely that purpose:

> Texas never actually needed the protection of the United States after I came into office. . . . There was no necessity for it after the 'preliminary Treaty,' as we were at peace with Mexico, and knew perfectly well that that Government, though she might bluster a little, had not the slightest idea of invading Texas either by land or water; and that nothing would provoke her to (active) hostilities, but the presence of troops in the immediate neighborhood of the Rio Grande, threatening her towns and settlements on the southwest side of that river. . . . But Donelson appeared so intent upon 'encumbering us with help,' that finally, to get rid of his annoyance, he was told he might give us as much protection as he pleased. . . . The protection asked for was only *prospective* and contingent; the *protection* he had in view was *immediate* and *aggressive*.

For Polk the exertion of military and diplomatic pressure on a disorganized Mexico was not a prelude to war. Whig critics of annexation had predicted war; this alone compelled the administration to avoid a conflict over Texas. In his memoirs Jones recalled that in 1845 Commodore Robert F. Stockton, with either the approval or the connivance of Polk, attempted to convince him that he should place Texas "in an attitude of active hostility toward Mexico, so that, when Texas was finally brought into the Union, *she might bring war with her.*" If Stockton engaged in such an intrigue, he apparently did so on his own initiative, for no evidence exists to implicate the administration. Polk not only preferred to achieve his purposes by means other than war but also assumed that his military measures in Texas, limited as they were, would convince the Mexican government that it could not escape the necessity of coming to terms with the United States. Washington's policy toward Mexico during 1845 achieved the broad national purpose of Texas annexation. Beyond that it brought U.S. power to bear on Mexico in a manner calculated to further the processes of negotiation. Whether the burgeoning tension would lead to a negotiated boundary settlement or to war hinged on two factors: the nature of Polk's demands and Mexico's response to them. The president announced his objectives to Mexico's troubled officialdom through his instructions to John Slidell, his special emissary who departed for Mexico in November 1845 with the assurance that the government there was prepared to reestablish formal diplomatic relations with the United States and negotiate a territorial settlement. . . .

Actually, Slidell's presence in Mexico inaugurated a diplomatic crisis not unlike those which precede most wars. Fundamentally the Polk administration, in dispatching Slidell, gave the Mexicans the same two choices that the dominant power in any confrontation gives to the weaker: the acceptance of a body of concrete diplomatic demands or eventual war. Slidell's instructions described U.S. territorial objectives with considerable clarity. If Mexico knew little of Polk's growing acquisitiveness toward California during the autumn of 1845, Slidell proclaimed the president's intentions with his proposals to purchase varying portions of California for as much as $25 million. Other countries such as England and Spain had consigned important areas of the New World through peaceful negotiations, but the United States, except in its Mexican relations, had never asked any country to part with a portion of its own territory. Yet Polk could not understand why Mexico should reveal any special reluctance to part with Texas, the Rio Grande, New Mexico, or California. What made the terms of Slidell's instructions appear fair to him was Mexico's military and financial helplessness. Polk's defenders noted that California was not a sine qua non of any settlement and that the president offered to settle the immediate controversy over the acquisition of the Rio Grande boundary alone in exchange for the cancellation of claims. Unfortunately, amid the passions of December 1845, such distinctions were lost. Furthermore, a settlement of the Texas boundary would not have resolved the California question at all.

Throughout the crisis months of 1845 and 1846, spokesmen of the Polk administration repeatedly warned the Mexican government that its choices were limited. In June 1845, Polk's mouthpiece, the *Washington Union,* had observed characteristically that, if Mexico resisted Washington's demands, "a corps of properly organized volunteers . . . would invade, overrun, and occupy Mexico. They would enable us not only to take California, but to keep it." American officials, in their contempt for Mexico, spoke privately of the need to chastize that country for its annoyances and insults. Parrott wrote to Secretary of State James Buchanan in October that he wished "to see this people well flogged by Uncle Sam's boys, ere we enter upon negotiations. . . . I know [the Mexicans] better, perhaps, than any other American citizen and I am fully persuaded, they can never love or respect us, as we should be loved and respected by them, until we shall have given them a positive proof of our superiority." Mexico's pretensions would continue, wrote Slidell in late December, "until the Mexican people shall be convinced by hostile demonstrations, that our differences must be settled promptly, either by negotiation or the sword." In January 1846 the *Union* publicly threatened Mexico with war if it rejected the just demands of the United States: "The result of such a course on her part may compel us to resort to more decisive measures. . . . to obtain the settlement of our legitimate claims." As Slidell prepared to leave Mexico in March 1846, he again reminded the administration: "Depend upon it, we can never get along well with them, until we have given them a good drubbing." In Washington on May 8, Slidell advised the president "to take the redress of the wrongs and injuries which we had so long borne from Mexico into our own hands, and to act with promptness and energy."

Mexico responded to Polk's challenge with an outward display of belligerence and an inward dread of war. Mexicans feared above all that the United States intended to overrun their country and seize much of their territory. Polk and his advisers assumed that Mexico, to avoid an American invasion, would give up its provinces peacefully. Obviously Mexico faced growing diplomatic and military pressures to negotiate away its territories; it faced no moral obligation to do so. Herrera and Paredes had the sovereign right to protect their regimes by avoiding any formal recognition of Slidell and by rejecting any of the boundary proposals embodied in his instructions, provided that in the process they did not endanger any legitimate interests of the American people. At least to some Mexicans, Slidell's terms demanded nothing less than Mexico's capitulation. By what standard was $2 million a proper payment for the Rio Grande boundary, or $25 million a fair price for California? No government would have accepted such terms. Having rejected negotiation in the face of superior force, Mexico would meet the challenge with a final gesture of defiance. In either case it was destined to lose, but historically nations have preferred to fight than to give away territory under diplomatic pressure alone. Gene M. Brack, in his long study of Mexico's deep-seated fear and resentment of the United States, explained Mexico's ultimate behavior in such terms:

> President Polk knew that Mexico could offer but feeble resistance militarily, and he knew that Mexico needed money. No proper American would

exchange territory and the national honor for cash, but President Polk mistakenly believed that the application of military pressure would convince Mexicans to do so. They did not respond logically, but patriotically. Left with the choice of war or territorial concessions, the former course, however dim the prospects of success, could be the only one.

Mexico, in its resistance, gave Polk the three choices which every nation gives another in an uncompromisable confrontation: to withdraw his demands and permit the issues to drift, unresolved; to reduce his goals in the interest of an immediate settlement; or to escalate the pressures in the hope of securing an eventual settlement on his own terms. Normally when the internal conditions of a country undermine its relations with others, a diplomatic corps simply removes itself from the hostile environment and awaits a better day. Mexico, despite its animosity, did not endanger the security interests of the United States; it had not invaded Texas and did not contemplate doing so. Mexico had refused to pay the claims, but those claims were not equal to the price of a one-week war. Whether Mexico negotiated a boundary for Texas in 1846 mattered little; the United States had lived with unsettled boundaries for decades without considering war. Settlers, in time, would have forced a decision, but in 1846 the region between the Nueces and the Rio Grande was a vast, generally unoccupied wilderness. Thus there was nothing, other than Polk's ambitions, to prevent the United States from withdrawing its diplomats from Mexico City and permitting its relations to drift. But Polk, whatever the language of his instructions, did not send Slidell to Mexico to normalize relations with that government. He expected Slidell to negotiate an immediate boundary settlement favorable to the United States, and nothing less.

Recognizing no need to reduce his demands on Mexico, Polk, without hesitation, took the third course which Mexico offered. Congress bound the president to the annexation of Texas; thereafter the Polk administration was free to formulate its own policies toward Mexico. With the Slidell mission Polk embarked upon a program of gradual coercion to achieve a settlement, preferably without war. That program led logically from his dispatching an army to Texas and his denunciation of Mexico in his annual message of December 1845 to his new instructions of January 1846, which ordered General Taylor to the Rio Grande. Colonel Atocha, spokesman for the deposed Mexican leader, Antonio López de Santa Anna, encouraged Polk to pursue his policy of escalation. The president recorded Atocha's advice:

> He said our army should be marched at once from Corpus Christi to the Del Norte, and a strong naval force assembled at Vera Cruz, that Mr. Slidell, the U.S. Minister, should withdraw from Jalappa, and go on board one of our ships of War at Vera Cruz, and in that position should demand the payment of [the] amount due our citizens; that it was well known the Mexican Government was unable to pay in money, and that when they saw a strong force ready to strike on their coasts and border, they would, he had no doubt, feel their danger and agree to the boundary suggested. He

> said that Paredes, Almonte, & Gen'l Santa Anna were all willing for such an arrangement, but that they dare not make it until it was made apparent to the Archbishop of Mexico & the people generally that it was necessary to save their country from a war with the U. States.

Thereafter Polk never questioned the efficacy of coercion. He asserted at a cabinet meeting on February 17 that "it would be necessary to take strong measures towards Mexico before our difficulties with that Government could be settled." Similarly on April 18 Polk told Calhoun that "our relations with Mexico had reached a point where we could not stand still but must treat all nations whether weak or strong alike, and that I saw no alternative but strong measures towards Mexico." A week later the president again brought the Mexican question before the cabinet. "I expressed my opinion," he noted in his diary, "that we must take redress for the injuries done us into our own hands, that we had attempted to conciliate Mexico in vain, and had forborne until forbearance was no longer either a virtue or patriotic." Convinced that Paredes needed money, Polk suggested to leading senators that Congress appropriate $1 million both to encourage Paredes to negotiate and to sustain him in power until the United States could ratify the treaty. The president failed to secure Calhoun's required support.

Polk's persistence led him and the country to war. Like all escalations in the exertion of force, his decision responded less to unwanted and unanticipated resistance than to the requirements of the clearly perceived and inflexible purposes which guided the administration. What perpetuated the president's escalation to the point of war was his determination to pursue goals to the end whose achievement lay outside the possibilities of successful negotiations. Senator Thomas Hart Benton of Missouri saw this situation when he wrote: "It is impossible to conceive of an administration less warlike, or more intriguing, than that of Mr. Polk. They were *men of peace, with objects to be accomplished by means of war*; so that war was a necessity and an indispensability to their purpose."

Polk understood fully the state of Mexican opinion. In placing General Taylor on the Rio Grande he revealed again his contempt for Mexico. Under no national obligation to expose the country's armed forces, he would not have advanced Taylor in the face of a superior military force. Mexico had been undiplomatic; its denunciations of the United States were insulting and provocative. But if Mexico's behavior antagonized Polk, it did not antagonize the Whigs, the abolitionists, or even much of the Democratic party. Such groups did not regard Mexico as a threat; they warned the administration repeatedly that Taylor's presence on the Rio Grande would provoke war. But in the balance against peace was the pressure of American expansionism. Much of the Democratic and expansionist press, having accepted without restraint both the purposes of the Polk administration and its charges of Mexican perfidy, urged the president on to more vigorous action. . . .

Confronted with the prospect of further decline which they could neither accept nor prevent, [the Mexicans] lashed out with the intention of protecting their self-esteem and compelling the United States, if it was determined to have the Rio Grande, New Mexico, and California, to pay for its prizes with something other than money. On April 23, Paredes issued a proclamation declaring a defensive war against the United States. Predictably, one day later the Mexicans fired on a detachment of U.S. dragoons. Taylor's report of the attack reached Polk on Saturday evening, May 9. On Sunday the president drafted his war message and delivered it to Congress on the following day. Had Polk avoided the crisis, he might have gained the time required to permit the emigrants of 1845 and 1846 to settle the California issue without war.

What clouds the issue of the Mexican War's justification was the acquisition of New Mexico and California, for contemporaries and historians could not logically condemn the war and laud the Polk administration for its territorial achievements. Perhaps it is true that time would have permitted American pioneers to transform California into another Texas. But even then California's acquisition by the United States would have emanated from the use of force, for the elimination of Mexican sovereignty, whether through revolution or war, demanded the successful use of power. If the power employed in revolution would have been less obtrusive than that exerted in war, its role would have been no less essential. There simply was no way that the United States could acquire California peacefully. If the distraught Mexico of 1845 would not sell the distant province, no regime thereafter would have done so. Without forceful destruction of Mexico's sovereign power, California would have entered the twentieth century as an increasingly important region of another country.

Thus the Mexican War poses the dilemma of all international relations. Nations whose geographic and political status fails to coincide with their ambition and power can balance the two sets of factors in only one manner: through the employment of force. They succeed or fail according to circumstances; and for the United States, the conditions for achieving its empire in the Southwest and its desired frontage on the Pacific were so ideal that later generations could refer to the process as the mere fulfillment of destiny. "The Mexican Republic," lamented a Mexican writer in 1848, " . . . had among other misfortunes of less account, the great one of being in the vicinity of a strong and energetic people." What the Mexican War revealed in equal measure is the simple fact that only those countries which have achieved their destiny, whatever that may be, can afford to extol the virtues of peaceful change.

POSTSCRIPT

Was the Mexican War an Exercise in American Imperialism?

According to Graebner, President James Polk assumed that Mexico was weak and that acquiring certain Mexican territories would satisfy "the long-range interests" of the United States. But when Mexico refused Polk's attempts to purchase New Mexico and California, he was left with three options: withdraw his demands, modify and soften his proposals, or aggressively pursue his original goals. According to Graebner, the president chose the third option.

Graebner is one of the most prominent members of the "realist" school of diplomatic historians. His writings were influenced by the cold war realists, political scientists, diplomats, and journalists of the 1950s who believed that American foreign policy oscillated between heedless isolationism and crusading wars without developing coherent policies that suited the national interests of the United States.

Graebner's views on the Mexican War have not gone unchallenged. For example, both David M. Pletcher's *The Diplomacy of Annexation* (University of Missouri Press, 1973), which remains the definitive study of the Polk administration, and Charles Seller's biography *James K. Polk*, 2 vols. (Princeton University Press, 1957–1966) are critical of Polk's actions in pushing the Mexican government to assert its authority in the disputed territory.

Professor Ruiz offers a Mexican perspective on the war in chapter 11 of his book *Triumphs and Tragedy: A History of the Mexican People* (W. W. Norton, 1992), in which he argues that while the United States went on to achieve great economic success after the Civil War, Mexico never recovered from losing half of her territories.

Ruiz also takes issue with Graebner, who considers Manifest Destiny to be mere political rhetoric with very limited goals. In Ruiz's view, Manifest Destiny was a reflection of the racist attitudes shown toward the non-white Native Americans, African Americans, and Mexican Americans who stood in the way of white America's desire for new land.

Both Graebner and Ruiz appear ethnocentric in their analysis of the origins of the war. Graebner neglects the emotionalism and instability of Mexican politics at the time, which may have precluded the rational analysis a realistic historian might have expected in the decision-making process. Ruiz also oversimplifies the motives of the Euroamericans, and he appears to neglect the political divisions between slaveholders and nonslaveholders and between Whig and Democratic politicians over the wisdom of going to war with Mexico.

The best two collections of readings from the major writers on the Mexican War are old but essential: see Archie McDonald, ed., *The Mexican War: Crisis for American Democracy* (D. C. Heath, 1969) and Ramon Eduardo Ruiz, ed., *The Mexican War: Was It Manifest Destiny?* (Holt, Rinehart & Winston, 1963).

There are several nontraditional books that cover the Mexican War, including John H. Schroeder, *Mr. Polk's War: American Opposition and Dissent, 1846–1848* (University of Wisconsin Press, 1973). Robert W. Johannsen summarizes the ways in which contemporaries viewed the war in *To the Halls of the Montezumas: The Mexican War in the American Imagination* (Oxford University Press, 1985).

ISSUE 13

Was John Brown an Irrational Terrorist?

YES: C. Vann Woodward, from *The Burden of Southern History,* 3d ed. (Louisiana State University Press, 1993)

NO: David S. Reynolds, from *John Brown, Abolitionist: The Man Who Killed Slavery, Sparked the Civil War, and Seeded Civil Rights* (Alfred A. Knopf, 2005)

ISSUE SUMMARY

YES: C. Vann Woodward depicts John Brown as a fanatic who committed wholesale murder in Kansas in 1856 and whose ill-fated assault on Harpers Ferry, Virginia, in 1859 was an irrational act of treason against the United States.

NO: David S. Reynolds portrays John Brown as a deeply religious, yet deeply flawed, humanitarian reformer who employed violent means in Kansas and in the raid at Harpers Ferry against proslavery outrages at a time when the United States had failed to live up to its most cherished ideal of human equality.

Opposition to slavery in the area that became the United States dates back to the seventeenth and eighteenth centuries, when Puritan leaders, such as Samuel Sewall, and Quakers, such as John Woolman and Anthony Benezet, published a number of pamphlets condemning the existence of the slave system. This religious link to antislavery sentiment is also evident in the writings of John Wesley as well as in the decision of the Society of Friends in 1688 to prohibit their members from owning bondservants. Slavery was said to be contrary to Christian principles. These attacks, however, did little to diminish the institution. Complaints that the English government had instituted a series of measures that "enslaved" the colonies in British North America raised thorny questions about the presence of *real* slavery in those colonies. How could American colonists demand their freedom from King George III, who was cast in the role of oppressive master, while denying freedom and liberty to African American slaves? Such a contradiction inspired a gradual emancipation movement in the North, which often was accompanied by compensation for the former slave owners.

In addition, antislavery societies sprang up throughout the nation to continue the crusade against bondage. Interestingly, the majority of these organizations were located in the South. Prior to the 1830s, the most prominent antislavery organization was the American Colonization Society, which offered a twofold program: (1) gradual, compensated emancipation of slaves; and (2) exportation of the newly freed to colonies outside the boundaries of the United States, mostly to Africa.

In the 1830s, antislavery activity underwent an important transformation. A new strain of antislavery sentiment expressed itself in the abolitionist movement. Drawing momentum both from the revivalism of the Second Great Awakening and the example set by England (which prohibited slavery in its imperial holdings in 1833), abolitionists called for the immediate end to slavery without compensation to masters for the loss of their property. Abolitionists viewed slavery not so much as a practical problem to be resolved, but rather as a moral offense incapable of resolution through traditional channels of political compromise. In January 1831, William Lloyd Garrison, who for many came to symbolize the abolitionist crusade, published the first issue of *The Liberator,* a newspaper dedicated to the immediate end to slavery. In his first editorial, Garrison expressed the self-righteous indignation of many in the abolitionist movement when he warned slaveholders and their supporters to "urge me not to use moderation in a cause like the present. I am in earnest—I will not equivocate—I will not excuse—I will not retreat a single inch—AND I WILL BE HEARD. . . ."

Unfortunately for Garrison, relatively few Americans were inclined to respond positively to his call. His newspaper generated little interest outside Boston, New York, Philadelphia, and other major urban centers of the North. This situation, however, changed within a matter of months. In August 1831, a slave preacher named Nat Turner led a rebellion of slaves in Southampton County, Virginia, that resulted in the death of 58 whites. Although the revolt was quickly suppressed and Turner and his supporters were executed, the incident spread fear throughout the South. Governor John B. Floyd of Virginia turned an accusatory finger toward the abolitionists when he concluded that the Turner uprising was "undoubtedly designed and matured by unrestrained fanatics in some of the neighboring states."

One such abolitionist was John Brown who became a martyr in the antislavery pantheon when he was executed following his unsuccessful raid on the federal arsenal in Harpers Ferry, Virginia, in 1859. In this issue, the late noted historian of the American South, C. Vann Woodward, explains that John Brown, who may very well have been insane, had no qualms about using terrorist tactics to conduct his fanatical war on slavery, even to the point of committing treason to realize his goal.

In the second selection, biographer David S. Reynolds agrees that Brown's actions represent an antebellum version of terrorism but that it would be misleading to associate him with modern terrorists such as Timothy McVeigh or Osama bin Laden. Brown's violent assaults, Reynolds concludes, marked an understandable attack on a uniquely immoral institution whose existence contradicted the goals of a democratic society that presumed to assign full rights to all.

YES 

C. Vann Woodward

John Brown's Private War

The figure of John Brown is still wrapped in obscurity and myth. . . . His fifty-nine years were divided sharply into two periods. The obscurity of his first fifty-five years was of the sort natural to a humble life unassociated with events of importance. The obscurity of his last four years, filled with conspiratorial activities, was in large part the deliberate work of Brown, his fellow conspirators, and their admirers. . . .

After 1855 John Brown abandoned his unprofitable business career when he was almost penniless and for the rest of his life was without remunerative employment. He depended for support upon donations from people whom he convinced of his integrity and reliability. Here and elsewhere there is strong evidence that Brown was somehow able to inspire confidence and intense personal loyalty.

The Kansas phase of Brown's guerrilla warfare has given rise to the "Legend of Fifty-six," a fabric of myth that has been subjected to a more rigorous examination than any other phase of Brown's life has ever received. [James C.] Malin establishes beyond question that "John Brown did not appear to have had much influence either in making or marring Kansas history," that his exploits "brought tragedy to innocent settlers," but that "in no place did he appear as a major factor." He also establishes a close correlation between the struggle over freedom and slavery and local clashes over conflicting land titles on the Kansas frontier, and he points out that "the business of stealing horses under the cloak of fighting for freedom and running them off to the Nebraska-Iowa border for sale" is a neglected aspect of the struggle for "Bleeding Kansas." John Brown and his men engaged freely and profitably in this business and justified their plunder as the spoils of war. Two covenants that Brown drew up for his followers contained a clause specifically providing for the division of captured property among the members of his guerrilla band.

It would be a gross distortion, however, to dismiss John Brown as a frontier horse thief. He was much too passionately and fanatically in earnest about his war on slavery to permit of any such oversimplification. His utter fearlessness, courage, and devotion to the cause were greatly admired by respectable antislavery men who saw in the old Puritan an ideal revolutionary leader.

One exploit of Brown in Kansas, however, would seem to have put him forever beyond the pale of association with intelligent opponents of slavery. This was the famous Pottawatomie massacre of May 24, 1856. John Brown, leading four of his sons, a son-in-law, and two other men, descended by night upon an unsuspecting settlement of four proslavery families. Proceeding from one home to another the raiders took five men out, murdered them, and left their bodies horribly mutilated. None of the victims was a slaveholder, and two of them were born in Germany and had no contact with the South. By way of explanation Brown said the murders had been "decreed by Almighty God, ordained from Eternity." He later denied responsibility for the act, and some of the Eastern capitalists and intellectuals who supported him refused to believe him guilty. In view of the report of the murders that was laid before the country on July 11, 1856, in the form of a committee report in the House of Representatives, it is somewhat difficult to excuse such ignorance among intelligent men. . . .

In the spring of 1858 plans for a raid on Virginia began to take definite shape. To a convention of fellow conspirators in Chatham, Canada, in May, John Brown presented his remarkable "Provisional Constitution and Ordinances for the People of the United States." It represented the form of government he proposed to establish by force of arms with a handful of conspirators and an armed insurrection of slaves. Complete with legislative, executive, and judicial branches, Brown's revolutionary government was in effect a military dictatorship, since all acts of his congress had to be approved by the commander-in-chief of the army in order to become valid. Needless to say, John Brown was elected commander-in-chief.

By July, 1859, Commander-in-Chief Brown had established himself at a farm on the Maryland side of the Potomac River, four miles north of Harpers Ferry. There he assembled twenty-one followers and accumulated ammunition and other supplies, including 200 revolvers, 200 rifles, and 950 pikes specially manufactured for the slaves he expected to rise up in insurrection. On Sunday night, October 16, after posting a guard of three men at the farm, he set forth with eighteen followers, five of them Negroes, and all of them young men, to start his war of liberation and found his abolitionist republic. Brown's first objective, to capture the United States arsenal at Harpers Ferry, was easily accomplished since it was without military guard. In the Federal armory and the rifle works, also captured, were sufficient arms to start the bloodiest slave insurrection in history.

The commander-in-chief appears to have launched his invasion without any definite plan of campaign and then proceeded to violate every military principle in the book. He cut himself off from his base of supplies, failed to keep open his only avenues of retreat, dispersed his small force, and bottled the bulk of them up in a trap where defeat was inevitable. "In fact, it was so absurd," remarked Abraham Lincoln, "that the slaves, with all their ignorance, saw plainly enough it could not succeed." Not one of them joined Brown voluntarily, and those he impressed quickly departed. The insurrectionists killed one United States Marine and four inhabitants of Harpers Ferry, including the mayor and a Negro freeman. Ten of their own number, including two of Brown's sons, were killed, five were taken prisoner by a small force of Marines commanded by Robert E. Lee, and seven escaped, though two of them were later arrested. John Brown's insurrection ended in a tragic and dismal failure.

When news of the invasion was first flashed across the country, the most common reaction was that this was obviously the act of a madman, that John Brown was insane. This explanation was particularly attractive to Republican politicians and editors, whose party suffered the keenest embarrassment from the incident. Fall elections were on, and the new Congress was about to convene. Democrats immediately charged that John Brown's raid was the inevitable consequence of the "irresistible-conflict" and "higher-law" abolitionism preached by Republican leaders William H. Seward and Salmon P. Chase. "Brown's invasion," wrote Senator Henry Wilson of Massachusetts, "has thrown us, who were in a splendid position, into a defensive position. . . . If we are defeated next year we shall owe it to that foolish and insane movement of Brown's." The emphasis on insanity was taken up widely by Wilson's contemporaries and later adopted by historians.

It seems best to deal with the insanity question promptly, for it is likely to confuse the issue and cause us to miss the meaning of Harpers Ferry. In dealing with the problem it is important not to blink, as many of his biographers have done, at the evidence of John Brown's close association with insanity in both his heredity and his environment. In the Brown Papers at the Library of Congress are nineteen affidavits signed by relatives and friends attesting the record of insanity in the Brown family. John Brown's maternal grandmother and his mother both died insane. His three aunts and two uncles, sisters and brothers of his mother, were intermittently insane, and so was his only sister, her daughter, and one of his brothers. Of six first cousins, all more or less mad, two were deranged from time to time, two had been repeatedly committed to the state insane asylum, and two were still confined at the time. Of John Brown's immediate family, his first wife and one of his sons died insane, and a second son was insane at intervals. On these matters the affidavits, signers of which include Brown's uncle, a half brother, a brother-in-law, and three first cousins, are in substantial agreement. On the sanity of John Brown himself, however, opinion varied. Several believed that he was a "monomaniac," one that he was insane on subjects of religion and slavery, and an uncle thought his nephew had been "subject to periods of insanity" for twenty years. . . .

"John Brown may be a lunatic," observed the Boston *Post,* but if so, "then one-fourth of the people of Massachusetts are madmen," and perhaps three-fourths of the ministers of religion. Begging that Brown's life be spared, Amos A. Lawrence wrote Governor Wise: "Brown is a Puritan whose mind has become disordered by hardship and illness. He has the qualities to endear him to our people." The association of ideas was doubtless unintentional, but to the Virginian it must have seemed that Lawrence was saying that in New England a disordered mind was an endearing quality. The Reverend J. M. Manning of Old South Church, Boston, pronounced Harpers Ferry "an unlawful, a foolhardy, a suicidal act" and declared, "I stand before it wondering and admiring." Horace Greeley called it "the work of a madman" for which he had not "one reproachful word," and for the "grandeur and nobility" of which he was "reverently grateful." And the New York *Independent* declared that while "Harpers Ferry was insane, the controlling motive of this demonstration was sublime." It was both foolhardy and godly, insane and sublime, treasonous and admirable.

The prestige and character of the men who lent John Brown active, if sometimes secret, support likewise suggest caution in dismissing Harpers Ferry as merely the work of a madman. Among Brown's fellow conspirators the most notable were the so-called Secret Six. Far from being horse thieves and petty traders, the Secret Six came from the cream of Northern society. Capitalist, philanthropist, philosopher, surgeon, professor, minister—they were men of reputability and learning, four of them with Harvard degrees.

With a Harvard Divinity School degree, a knowledge of twenty languages, and a library of sixteen thousand volumes, Theodore Parker was perhaps the most prodigiously learned American of his time. In constant correspondence with the leading Republican politicians, he has been called "the Conscience of a Party." What Gerrit Smith, the very wealthy philanthropist and one-time congressman of Peterboro, New York, lacked in mental endowments he made up in good works—earnest efforts to improve the habits of his fellow men. These included not only crusades against alcohol and tobacco in all forms, but also coffee, tea, meat, and spices—"almost everything which gave pleasure," according to his biographer. Generous with donations to dietary reform, dress reform, woman's rights, educational and "non-resistance" movements, Smith took no interest whatever in factory and labor reform, but he was passionately absorbed in the antislavery movement and a liberal contributor to John Brown. Dr. Samuel G. Howe of Boston, husband of the famous Julia Ward Howe, was justly renowned for his humanitarian work for the blind and mentally defective. In his youth he had gone on a Byronic crusade in Greece against the Turk. These experiences contributed greatly to his moral prestige, if little to his political sophistication. The most generous man of wealth among the conspirators was George L. Stearns of Boston, a prosperous manufacturer of lead pipe. In the opinion of this revolutionary capitalist, John Brown was "the representative man of this century, as Washington was of the last." Finally there were two younger men, fledgling conspirators. The son of a prosperous Boston merchant who was bursar of Harvard, Thomas Wentworth Higginson became pastor of a church in Worcester after taking his divinity degree at Harvard. Young Franklin B. Sanborn was an apostle of Parker and a protégé of Emerson, who persuaded Sanborn to take charge of a school in Concord.

The most tangible service the Secret Six rendered the conspiracy lay in secretly diverting to John Brown, for use at Harpers Ferry, money and arms that had been contributed to the Massachusetts-Kansas Aid Committee for use in "Bleeding Kansas." . . . By this means the Kansas Committee was converted into a respectable front for subversive purposes, and thousands of innocent contributors to what appeared to be a patriotic organization discovered later that they had furnished rifles for a treasonous attack on a Federal arsenal. . . .

The Secret Six appear to have been fascinated by the drama of conspiratorial activity. There were assumed names, coded messages, furtive committee meetings, dissembling of motives, and secret caches of arms. And over all the romance and glamor of a noble cause—the liberation of man. Although they knew perfectly well the general purpose of Brown, the Secret Six were careful to request him not to tell them the precise time and place of the invasion. The wily old revolutionist could have told them much that they did not know about the psychology of fellow travelers. Brown had earlier laid down this strategy for conspirators who were hard pressed: "Go into the houses of your most prominent and influential white friends with your wives; and that will effectually fasten upon them the suspicion of being connected with you, and will compel them to make a common cause with you, whether they would otherwise live up to their professions or not." The same strategy is suggested by Brown's leaving behind, in the Maryland farmhouse where they would inevitably be captured, all his private papers, hundreds of letters of himself and followers, implicating nobody knew how many respectable fellow travelers. . . .

The assistance that the Secret Six conspirators were able to give John Brown and his Legend was as nothing compared with that rendered by other Northern intellectuals. Among them was the cultural and moral aristocracy of America in the period that has been called a "Renaissance." Some of these men, Ralph Waldo Emerson and Henry Thoreau among them, had met and admired Brown and even made small contributions to his cause. But they were safely beyond reproach of the law and were never taken into his confidence in the way that the Secret Six were. Their service was rendered after the event in justifying and glorifying Brown and his invasion.

In this work the intellectuals were ably assisted by a genius, a genius at self-justification—John Brown himself. From his prison cell he poured out a stream of letters, serene and restrained, filled with Biblical language and fired with overpowering conviction that his will and God's were one and the same. These letters and his famous speech at the trial constructed for the hero a new set of motives and plans and a new role. For Brown had changed roles. In October he invaded Virginia as a conqueror armed for conquest, carrying with him guns and pikes for the army he expected to rally to his standard and a new constitution to replace the one he overthrew. In that role he was a miserable failure. Then in November he declared at his trial: "I never did intend murder, or treason, or the destruction of property, or to excite or incite slaves to rebellion, or to make an insurrection." He only intended to liberate slaves without bloodshed, as he falsely declared he had done in Missouri the year before. How these statements can be reconciled with the hundreds of pikes, revolvers, and rifles, the capture of an armory, the taking of hostages, the killing of unarmed civilians, the destruction of government property, and the arming of slaves is difficult to see. Nor is it possible to believe that Brown thought he could seize a Federal arsenal, shoot down United States Marines, and overthrow a government without committing treason. . . .

Emerson seemed hesitant in his first private reactions to Harpers Ferry. Thoreau, on the other hand, never hesitated a moment. On the day after Brown's capture he compared the hero's inevitable execution with the crucifixion of Christ. Harpers Ferry was "the best news that America ever had"; Brown, "the bravest and humanest man in all the country," "a Transcendentalist above all," and he declared: "I rejoice that I live in this age, that I was his contemporary." Emerson quickly fell into line with Thoreau, and in his November 8 lecture on "Courage" described Brown as "the saint, whose fate yet hangs in suspense, but whose martyrdom, if it shall be perfected, will make the gallows as glorious as the cross." Within a few weeks Emerson gave three important lectures, in all of which he glorified John Brown.

With the Sage of Concord and his major prophet in accord on the martyr, the majority of the transcendental hierarchy sooner or later joined in—William E. Channing, Bronson and Louisa May Alcott, Longfellow, Bryant, and Lowell, and of course Wendell Phillips and Theodore Parker. Parker pronounced Brown "not only a martyr . . . but also a SAINT." Thoreau and Henry Ward Beecher frankly admitted they hoped Brown would hang. To spare a life would be to spoil a martyr. They were interested in him not as a man but as a symbol, a moral ideal, and a saint for a crusade. In the rituals of canonization the gallows replaced the cross as a symbol. . . .

The task to which the intellectuals of the cult dedicated themselves was the idealizing of John Brown as a symbol of the moral order and the social purpose of the Northern cause. Wendell Phillips expressed this best when he declared in the Boston Music Hall: "'Law' and 'order' are only means for the halting ignorance of the last generation. John Brown is the impersonation of God's order and God's law, moulding a better future, and setting for it an example." In substituting the new revolutionary law and order for traditional law and order, the intellectuals encountered some tough problems in morals and values. It was essential for them to justify a code of political methods and morals that was at odds with the Anglo-American tradition.

John Brown's own solution to this problem was quite simple. It is set forth in the preamble of his Provisional Constitution of the United States, which declares that in reality slavery is an "unjustifiable War of one portion of its citizens upon another." War, in which all is fair, amounted to a suspension of ethical restraints. This type of reasoning is identical with that of the revolutionaries who hold that class struggle is in reality a class war. The assumption naturally facilitates the justification of deeds otherwise indefensible. These might include the dissembling of motives, systematic deception, theft, murder, or the liquidation of an enemy class. . . .

The crisis of Harpers Ferry was a crisis of means, not of ends. John Brown did not raise the question of whether slavery should be abolished or tolerated. That question had been raised in scores of ways and debated for a generation. Millions held strong convictions on the subject. Upon abolition, as an *end,* there was no difference between John Brown and the American and Foreign Anti-Slavery Society. But as to the *means* of attaining abolition, there was as much difference between them, so far as the record goes, as there is between the modern British Labour Party and the government of Soviet Russia on the means of abolishing capitalism. The Anti-Slavery Society was solemnly committed to the position of nonviolent means. In the very petition that Lewis Tappan, secretary of the society, addressed to Governor Wise in behalf of Brown he repeated the rubric about "the use of all carnal weapons for deliverance from bondage." But in their rapture over Brown as martyr and saint the abolitionists lost sight of their differences with him over the point of means and ended by totally compromising their creed of nonviolence.

But what of those who clung to the democratic principle that differences should be settled by ballots and that the will of the majority should prevail? Phillips pointed out: "In God's world there are no majorities, no minorities; one, on God's side, is a majority." And Thoreau asked, "When were the good and the brave ever in a majority?" So much for majority rule. What of the issue of treason? The Reverend Fales H. Newhall of Roxbury declared that the word "treason" had been "made holy in the American language"; and the Reverend Edwin M. Wheelock of Boston blessed "the sacred, and the radiant 'treason' of John Brown."

No aversion to bloodshed seemed to impede the spread of the Brown cult. William Lloyd Garrison thought that "every slaveholder has forfeited his right to live" if he impeded emancipation. The Reverend Theodore Parker predicted a slave insurrection in which "The Fire of Vengeance" would run "from man to man, from town to town" through the South. "What shall put it out?" he asked. "The White Man's blood." The Reverend Mr. Wheelock thought Brown's "mission was to inaugurate slave insurrection as the divine weapon of the antislavery cause." He asked: "Do we shrink from the bloodshed that would follow?" and answered, "No such wrong [as slavery] was ever cleansed by rose-water." Rather than see slavery continued the Reverend George B. Cheever of New York declared: "It were infinitely better that three hundred thousand slaveholders were abolished, struck out of existence." In these pronouncements the doctrine that the end justifies the means had arrived pretty close to justifying the liquidation of an enemy class.

The reactions of the extremists have been stressed in part because it was the extremist view that eventually prevailed in the apotheosis of John Brown and, in part, because by this stage of the crisis each section tended to judge the other by the excesses of a few. "Republicans were all John Browns to the Southerners," as Professor Dwight L. Dumond has observed, "and slaveholders were all Simon Legrees to the Northerners." As a matter of fact Northern conservatives and unionists staged huge anti-Brown demonstrations that equaled or outdid those staged by the Brown partisans. Nathan Appleton wrote a Virginian: "I have never in my long life seen a fuller or more enthusiastic demonstration" than the anti-Brown meeting in Faneuil Hall in Boston. The Republican press described a similar meeting in New York as "the largest and most enthusiastic" ever held in that city. Northern politicians of high rank, including Lincoln, Douglas, Seward, Edward Everett, and Henry Wilson, spoke out against John Brown and his methods. The Republican party registered its official position by a plank in the 1860 platform denouncing the Harpers Ferry raid. Lincoln approved of Brown's execution, "even though he agreed with us in thinking slavery wrong." Agreement on ends did not mean agreement on means. "That cannot excuse violence, bloodshed, and treason," said Lincoln. . . .

Among the Brown partisans not one has been found but who believed that Harpers Ferry had resulted in great gain for the extremist cause. So profoundly were they convinced of this that they worried little over the conservative dissent. "How vast the change in men's hearts!" exclaimed Phillips. "Insurrection was a harsh, horrid word to millions a month ago." Now it was "the lesson of the hour." Garrison rejoiced that thousands who could not listen to his gentlest rebuke ten years before "now easily swallow John Brown whole, and his rifle in the bargain." "They all called him crazy then," wrote Thoreau; "Who calls him crazy now?" To the poet it seemed that "the North is suddenly all Transcendentalist." On the day John Brown was hanged church bells were tolled in commemoration in New England towns, out along the Mohawk Valley, in Cleveland and the Western Reserve, in Chicago and northern Illinois. In Albany one hundred rounds were fired from a cannon. Writing to his daughter the following day, Joshua Giddings of Ohio said, "I find the hatred of slavery greatly intensified by the fate of Brown and men are ready to march to Virginia and dispose of her despotism at once." It was not long before they *were* marching to Virginia, and marching to the tune of "John Brown's Body." . . .

David S. Reynolds  NO

John Brown, Abolitionist: The Man Who Killed Slavery, Sparked the Civil War, and Seeded Civil Rights

One of the most symbolic events of the Civil War occurred in a mansion. The event was the reception held on January 1, 1863, at the Medford, Massachusetts, estate of the businessman George L. Stearns to celebrate the Emancipation Proclamation, which had been issued that afternoon by President Lincoln.

Stearns called the affair "the John Brown Party." The highlight of the evening was the unveiling of a marble bust of John Brown, the antislavery martyr who had died on a scaffold three years earlier after his doomed, heroic effort to free the slaves by leading a twenty-two-man raid on Harpers Ferry, Virginia.

Brown's presence was felt elsewhere in America that day. The Union general Robert H. Milroy, stationed near Harpers Ferry, read Lincoln's proclamation aloud to his regiment, which spontaneously thundered forth the war song "John Brown's Body," with its heady chorus about Brown "mouldering in the grave" while "his soul keeps marching on." The Emancipation Proclamation made General Milroy feel as though John Brown's spirit had merged with his. "That hand-bill order," he said, "gave Freedom to the slaves through and around the region where Old John Brown was hung. I felt then that I was on duty, in the most righteous cause that man ever drew sword in."

In Boston, a tense wait had ended in midafternoon when the news came over the wires that the proclamation had been put into effect. At a Jubilee Concert in the Music Hall, Ralph Waldo Emerson read his Abolitionist poem "Boston Hymn" and was followed by performances of Handel's Hallelujah Chorus, Beethoven's Fifth Symphony, and Mendelssohn's "Hymn of Praise." That evening at Tremont Temple a huge crowd cheered as the proclamation was read aloud and exploded into song when Frederick Douglass led in singing "Blow Ye the Trumpet, Blow!," the joyous hymn that had been Brown's favorite and had been sung at his funeral.

A number of people missed the Boston celebration because they had gone to George Stearns's twenty-six-acre estate in nearby Medford for the John Brown Party. The party was, in its own way, as meaningful as Lincoln's proclamation. It celebrated the man who had sparked the war that led to this historic day. Lincoln's proclamation, freeing millions of enslaved blacks, sped the process that led eventually to civil rights. John Brown's personal war against slavery had set this process in motion.

Gathered in Stearns's elegant home was a motley group. Stearns himself, long-bearded and earnest, had made a fortune manufacturing lead pipes. His guests included the bald, spectacled William Lloyd Garrison and the volatile Wendell Phillips, pioneers of Abolitionism; the stately, reserved philosopher Ralph Waldo Emerson, magus of Transcendentalism; his idealistic cohort Amos Bronson Alcott, who was there with his daughter, Louisa May, soon to captivate young readers with *Little Women;* Franklin Sanborn, the Concord schoolteacher whose students included children of Emerson, John Brown, and Henry James, Sr.; and the red-haired, vivacious Julia Ward Howe, writer of "The Battle Hymn of the Republic." They represented cultural threads that had once been aimed in various directions but were now unified in their devotion to the memory of John Brown. . . .

Perhaps the most significant meaning of the John Brown Party was that everyone present was joined by an idealistic vision of a man who, in other circles, was branded as a murderer, a thief, and an insane fanatic. The pristine purity of Brackett's bust was as distant from John Brown's real looks as the starry-eyed hero worship of Stearns's guests was from a true appraisal of his achievements.

The fact is that during his life and after it Brown gave rise to significant misreadings that shaped the course of American history. Brown himself had misread the slaves and sympathetic whites among the locals, whom he expected to rally in masses to his side as soon as his raid on Harpers Ferry began. The blacks he liberated misread him, since, by most reports, few of them voluntarily joined him in the battle against the Virginia troops—a fact that may have contributed to the fatal delay on the part of Brown, who had expected "the bees to hive" as soon as his liberation plan became known among the slaves.

Most important, Brown himself became the subject of crucial misreadings. Although after the raid he was at first denounced by most Northerners, a few influential individuals, especially the Transcendentalists, salvaged his reputation by placing him on the level of Christ—a notable misreading of a man who, despite his remarkable virtues, had violent excesses, as evidenced by the nighttime slaughter of five proslavery residents he had directed in Pottawatomie, Kansas. The Transcendentalist image of Brown spread throughout the North and was fanned by books, melodramas, poems, and music—culminating in "John Brown's Body," the inspiring song chanted by tens of thousands of Union troops as they marched south.

At the same time that this misreading swept North, an opposite one was pervading the South. The South's initial grudging admiration for Brown's courage was quickly overwhelmed by a paranoid fear that he was a malicious aggressor who represented the entire North—a tremendous and tragic misreading, since virtually everyone in the Northern-led Republican Party, from Lincoln to Seward, actually disapproved of his violent tactics. The South's misreading was fanned by Democratic Party propaganda that unjustifiably smeared the Republicans with responsibility for Harpers Ferry. In this view, "Black Republicanism" meant not only "niggerworship" but also deep alliance with John Brown, whom the Democrats Characterized as a villain of the blackest dye.

These dual misreadings, positive and negative, were perpetuated in biographies of Brown. The early biographers were mainly people who had known Brown personally and who idolized him—they therefore twisted facts to make him seem heroic, at times godlike. In reaction, there arose a school of biographers intent upon exploding this saintly image. They swung to the other extreme of portraying him as little more than a cold-blooded murderer, house thief, inflexible egotist, fanatical visionary, and shady businessman.

These extremes of hagiography and vilification were in time answered by scholarly objectivity. Several biographers—most notably Oswald Garrison Villard and Stephen B. Oates—present information about Brown's life factually, unfiltered by partisan bias. Villard and Oates pitilessly expose Brown's savagery at Pottawatomie and question the wisdom of his provisional constitution and his attack on Harpers Ferry, even as they praise his humanitarian aims.

Still, there is a danger to an overstrict insistence on impartiality. One reviewer's comment on Villard—i.e., that he "holds a position of impartiality, and almost of aloofness"—speaks for the best modern biographies. For example, biographers have waffled on the issue of Brown's sanity, leaving it as an unsolved problem. One can be objective without remaining impartial about the crucial moral, political, and human issues that Brown's life poses.

My stand on some key issues is: (a) Brown was not insane; instead, he was a deeply religious, flawed, yet ultimately noble reformer; (b) the Pottawatomie affair was indeed a crime, but it was a war crime committed against proslavery settlers by a man who saw slavery itself as an unprovoked war of one race against another; and (c) neither Brown's provisional constitution nor the Harpers Ferry raid were wild-eyed, erratic schemes doomed to failure: instead, they reflect Brown's overconfidence in whites' ability to rise above racism and in blacks' willingness to rise up in armed insurrection against their masters. . . .

[H]istorians—and Americans in general—are not completely comfortable with Brown, who remains an elusive, marginal figure. A 1996 collection of essays by modern historians titled *Why the Civil War Came* makes no mention of Brown, focusing instead on Lincoln and the Republicans. The discomfort many feel about John Brown has been expressed even by knowledgeable authorities such as the Kansas-based historian Jonathan Early, who said in an interview of 2003: "If I were going to write a biography, one of the last people I'd want to write a biography about is John Brown. He's really interesting, but we've had 150 years of people in my business trying to 'get inside his head,' and I don't think we've done a very good job at all."

A key difficulty modern Americans have with Brown is that his goal—the abolition of slavery—was undeniably good, but his violent methods are hard to swallow. Indeed, John Brown's legacy is complicated by the fact that ever since his death he has been championed by fringe revolutionaries and agitators. . . .

Complicating Brown's legacy even further is the terrorism of recent times. The historian David W. Blight asks, "Can John Brown remain an authentic

American hero in an age of Timothy McVeigh, Usama Bin Laden, and the Bombers of abortion clinics?"

How can America, which regards terrorism as its greatest threat, admit to the fact that it was shaped by a terrorist of its own?

The question is a vital one, especially since a number of terrorists insist they acted in the tradition of John Brown. Violent right-to-lifers like Matthew J. Goldsby, John Burt, and Paul Hill venerated the memory of John Brown and claimed to act in his name. After bombing an abortion clinic in Pensacola Florida, Burt said: "Maybe like Harpers Ferry, where John Brown used violence to bring the evils of slavery into focus, these bombings may do the same thing on the abortion issue." As if echoing Brown's militancy, Burt added, "When the history of this period is written, it won't be the pickets or the letter-writers who will be the heroes. It's going to be the bombers." Hill, who received the death sentence for murdering an abortion doctor, wrote that Brown's "example has and continues to serve as a source of encouragement to me," and "the political impact of Brown's actions continues to serve as a powerful paradigm in my understanding of the potential effects of the use of defensive force may have for the unborn.

Timothy McVeigh, who killed 168 people by bombing a federal building in Oklahoma City, was also a devotee of John Brown. As the journalist Dan Herbeck reported, "One of his big heroes was John Brown, who committed some very violent acts during the 1800s in the effort to eliminate slavery in our country." Similarly, the author Gore Vidal noted, "McVeigh saw himself as John Brown of Kansas."

The connection between McVeigh and Brown has been hotly argued. For instance, a debate was posted online, titled "Was Timothy McVeigh Our John Brown?" between the historians Clayton Cramer and Paul Finkelman. Cramer took the affirmative side, arguing that both Brown and McVeigh responded with brutality against systems they regarded as brutal—one against the slave system, the other against the intrusive federal government whose tyranny, McVeigh felt, was exhibited at Waco and Ruby Ridge. Finkelman argued for the negative, saying that Brown attacked proslavery forces in a time when the political debate was stifled, whereas McVeigh slaughtered innocent people in an era when he could have made his point peacefully.

Other modern terrorists who have been compared to John Brown are Ted Kaczynski (the so-called Unabomber) and Osama bin Laden. The legal scholar Michael Mello compares the Unabomber's single-handed assault on technological industrialism with Brown's attack on slavery, suggesting that Kaczynski sparked a new environmentalism the way Brown spelled the end of slavery. Those who see Brown-like elements in bin Laden point to the latter's murderous campaign against a social system perceived as corrupt, launched by a charismatic fanatic in the name of God.

What are we to make of these comparisons between Brown and modern terrorism? To some degree they are valid. Terrorism, or murder to make a political point, is utilized by groups or individuals who feel that social change cannot be achieved through normal channels. Just as John Brown saw that decades of what he called "talk, talk, talk" had done nothing to halt slavery, so some modern terrorists stand opposed to social institutions or governmental systems that they feel have become overwhelming and impossible to challenge in any way other than through violence.

The idea that "one man's terrorist is another man's freedom fighter" is no less true now than it was in Brown's day. For some ardent foes of abortion, Paul Hill, who claimed to follow Brown, was a hero. Others thought that Timothy McVeigh carried out justice—Gore Vidal, for instance, disgusted by what he saw as an oppressive American government, compared McVeigh not only to Brown but also to Paul Revere, spreading the alarm that "The Feds are coming, the Feds are coming." Some militant Muslims, appalled by what they regarded as the decadence and corrupt imperialism of the United States, applauded bin Laden's destruction of the World Trade Center. In this sense, contemporary terrorists are no different from Brown, deified by some and demonized by others.

Still, it is misleading to identify Brown with modern terrorists. Actually, Brown would have disapproved of the use of violence by most of those who have proclaimed themselves as his heirs. It is important to recognize that many of the social ills that later bred radical violence plagued the nation in his time, but he went to war only over the issue of slavery.

Brown saw many things wrong with American society. In some respects social conditions were even worse then than in recent times. Americans were caught in the dizzying throes of a boom-and-bust economy, unregulated by federal programs, that left millions of poor people utterly without relief during times of economic decline, particularly between 1839 and 1842. Widening divisions between the pampered "upper ten" and the oppressed "lower millions" gave rise to labor groups and angry protest novels by George Lippard, J. H. Ingraham, and others. Native Americans, cruelly forced off their land by rapacious whites, journeyed west on the so-called Trail of Tears. Women were caught between the impulse to advance, signaled by the women's rights movement, and the reality of their political disenfranchisement and their entrapment in the home as a result of the "separate spheres" doctrine of capitalism. Incapacitated economically, city women were forced to turn in astounding numbers to the most lucrative job, prostitution. Because birth control was primitive, unwanted pregnancies abounded, and abortion was a vexed issue. In the absence of safe medical procedures, women seeking abortions risked their lives when helped on the sly by unprofessional people like New York's notorious Ann Lohman (aka "Madame Restell"), who was known as "the wickedest woman in New York" for operating a "house built on babies' skulls" on Fifth Avenue.

Political corruption was rife, as was noted by many observers, including Walt Whitman, who impugned the "swarms of cringers, suckers, doughfaces, lice of politics, planners of sly involutions for their own preferment to city offices or state legislatures or the judiciary or congress or the presidency." In America's cities the environment was a serious concern. Most city streets, still unpaved, turned to swampy muck in the winter and dust bowls in the summer. In an age before public sanitation, garbage was tossed into the city streets, where it rotted amid the feces of the animals. Not only horses but also pigs, cows, and sheep roamed through the cities. The lack of organized police and fire departments added to the precariousness of daily life.

In other words, there was plenty for John Brown to protest against. He *did* protest, as evidenced by remarks about corruption, women, Native Americans, and economic inequality in his writings. But slavery was the one thing that drove him to violence.

Why? Because slavery was a uniquely immoral institution that seemed cemented in place by law, custom, and prejudice. Bad economic times came and went. The status of women promised to change. Native Americans, although horribly maltreated, still had a measure of freedom. City conditions were improving as technology progressed. But slavery, the "sum of all evils," was there to stay, at least for the foreseeable future. And slavery was qualitatively different from all other social issues, since it deprived millions of their rights as Americans and their dignity as human beings. No other social phenomenon approached its wickedness. No other problem, Brown believed, called for the use of arms.

Brown had a breadth of vision that modern terrorists lack. He was an *American* terrorist in the amplest sense of the word. He was every bit as religious as Osama bin Laden—but was the Muslim bin Laden able to enlist Christians, atheists, or Jews among his followers? The Calvinistic Brown, reflecting the religious toleration of his nation, counted Jews, liberal Christians, spiritualists, and agnostics among his most devoted soldiers. Bin Laden's ultimate goal was the creation of a Muslim theocracy in which opposing views, especially Western ones, were banned. Brown's goal was a democratic society that assigned full rights to all, irrespective of religion, race, or gender.

Also, Brown possessed an eloquence unique among terrorists. When Thoreau said that Brown's words were more powerful than his rifles or when Emerson ranked his court speech with the Gettysburg Address, they were highlighting the power of his language. Perhaps Ted Kaczynski would have won more people to his side if he had published something more forceful than the meandering, garbled manifesto against leftism that he sent to newspapers. Similarly, Timothy McVeigh's final written statement, a handwritten copy of William Ernest Henley's poem "Invictus"—a work of self-serving machismo asserting one's power to survive in a harsh world (e.g., "My head is bloody but unbowed./ . . . I am the master of my fate;/ I am the captain of my soul")—was on the opposite side of the rhetorical spectrum from the generous, other-oriented letters Brown wrote in prison. And Kaczynski and McVeigh are Shakespeares when compared with other modern terrorists, many of whom are anonymous suicide bombers, exploited devotees, or the like—faceless tools of a cause, not original interpreters of one.

John Brown alone wielded both the sword and the sword-pen. His words sprang from deep wells of compassion for a race whose suffering he felt on his very nerve-endings.

The African American view of Brown as the selfless herald of emancipation was memorably expressed in the 1964 book *The Negro Mood and Other Essays* by Lerone Bennett, Jr., a senior editor at *Ebony* magazine. Bennett wrote: "It is to John Brown that we must go, finally, if we want to understand the limitations and possibilities of our situation. He was of no color, John Brown, of no race or age. He was pure passion, pure transcendence. He was an elemental force like wind, rain and fire."

John Brown as "pure transcendence," as "an elemental force." This was Thoreau and Emerson again, but with a key difference. As an African American, Bennett prized Brown's racial program with an intensity the Concord philosophers lacked. Brown's violence, Bennett argued, retaliated for centuries of violence inflicted on American blacks:

> There was in John Brown a complete identification with the oppressed. It was his child that a slaveowner was selling; his sister who was being whipped in the field; his wife who was being raped in the gin house. It was not happening to Negroes; it was happening to him. Thus it was said that he could not bear to hear the word slave spoken. At the sound of the word, his body vibrated like the strings of a sensitive violin. John Brown *was* a Negro, and it was in this aspect that he suffered.

The statement "John Brown *was* a Negro," coming as it did from an African American, was one Brown himself would have singled out for praise. Brown's violent actions seem aberrant and insane if torn from their racial referents. Without the racial factor, Pottawatomie seems like heartless butchery and Harpers Ferry appears inane and quixotic. With the racial factor, both make sense. At Pottawatomie, Brown was responding to proslavery outrages: not only the sack of Lawrence and the caning of Sumner but the whole bloody history of America's cruelty toward blacks. At Harpers Ferry, he was tapping into Southern whites' deepest fear—slave insurrection—and protesting against the proslavery federal government in the process.

Brown's violence resulted from America's egregious failure to live up to one of its most cherished ideals—human equality. To expose his failure, Brown exercised the right of the individual to challenge the mass. In doing so he kept alive the revolutionary spirit that ran from Puritan antinomianism through the founding fathers' resistance to tyranny to the self-reliant nonconformity of the Transcendentalists.

It is this individualistic spirit that seems most threatened today. Lerone Bennett, in the same piece in which he announced that "John Brown *was* a Negro," posed the trenchant question: What happened to the America that produced Brown and other forceful rebels, such as Thomas Jefferson, Thomas Paine, and Wendell Phillips? Bennett wrote in alarm: "It may be that America can no longer produce such men. If so, all is lost. Cursed is the nation, cursed is the people, who can no longer breed indigenous radicals when it needs them." "What happened to that America?" Bennett asked. "Who killed it?"

These questions are even more urgent today than when Bennett asked them. America has become a vast network of institutions that tend to stifle vigorous challenges from individuals. Such challenges are needed if the nation is to remain healthy. There must be modern Americans who identify with the oppressed with such passion that they are willing to die for them, as Brown did. And America must be large enough to allow for meaningful protest, instead of remaining satisfied with patriotic bromides and a capitalist mass culture that fosters homogenized complacency. Unless America is ready at every moment to see its own failings, it is one step closer to becoming the tyrannical monster it pretends not to be.

Had John Brown and a few other forceful antislavery persons not been able to bring about the fall of slavery, one can only speculate about the terrible results. What would have happened if Brown had not violently disrupted the racist juggernaut that was America? As we have seen, even emancipation and manhood suffrage did not ensure the security of African Americans. It took nine decades of struggle for America to approach John Brown's goal of civil rights for all ethnic minorities. Even today the goal is not fully realized.

W. E. B. Du Bois's startling pronouncement thunders through American history. Indeed, "John Brown was right."

POSTSCRIPT

Was John Brown an Irrational Terrorist?

One of the weaknesses of most studies of abolitionism, which is reflected in both of the preceding essays, is that they generally are written from a monochromatic perspective. In other words, historians typically discuss whites within the abolitionist crusade and give little, if any, attention to the roles African Americans played in the movement. Whites are portrayed as the active agents of reform, whereas blacks are the passive recipients of humanitarian efforts to eliminate the scourge of slavery. Students should be aware that African Americans, slave and free, also rebelled against the institution of slavery both directly and indirectly, although very few rallied to the call of John Brown.

Benjamin Quarles in *Black Abolitionists* (Oxford University Press, 1969) describes a wide range of roles played by blacks in the abolitionist movement. The African American challenge to the slave system is also evident in the network known as the "underground railroad." Larry Gara, in *The Liberty Line: The Legend of the Underground Railroad* (University of Kentucky Press, 1961), concludes that the real heroes of the underground railroad were not white abolitionists but the slaves themselves who depended primarily upon their own resources or assistance they received from other African Americans, slave and free.

Other studies treating the role of black abolitionists in the antislavery movement include James M. McPherson, *The Struggle for Equality: Abolitionists and the Negro in the Civil War and Reconstruction* (Princeton University Press, 1964); Jane H. and William H. Pease, *They Who Would Be Free: Blacks' Search for Freedom, 1830–1861* (Atheneum, 1974); R. J. M. Blackett, *Building an Antislavery Wall: Black Americans in the Atlantic Abolitionist Movement, 1830–1860* (Louisiana State University Press, 1983) and *Beating Against the Barriers: The Lives of Six Nineteenth-Century Afro-Americans* (Louisiana State University Press, 1986); Ronald K. Burke, *Samuel Ringgold Ward: Christian Abolitionist* (Garland, 1995); Nell Irvin Painter, *Sojourner Truth: A Life, A Symbol* (W. W. Norton, 1997); and Catherine Clinton, *Harriet Tubman: The Road to Freedom* (2004). Frederick Douglass's contributions are evaluated in Benjamin Quarles, *Frederick Douglass* (Atheneum, 1968; originally published 1948); Nathan Irvin Huggins, *Slave and Citizen: The Life of Frederick Douglass* (Little, Brown, 1980); Waldo E. Martin, Jr., *The Mind of Frederick Douglass* (University of North Carolina Press, 1984); and William S. McFeely, *Frederick Douglass* (W. W. Norton, 1991).

Conflicting views of the abolitionists are presented in Richard O. Curry, ed., *The Abolitionists: Reformers or Fanatics?* (Holt, Rinehart and Winston, 1965). For general discussions of the abolitionist movement, see Gerald Sorin, *Abolitionism: A New Perspective* (Praeger, 1972); Lewis Perry, *Radical Abolitionism:*

Anarchy and the Government of God in Antislavery Thought (Cornell University Press, 1973); James Brewer Stewart, *Holy Warriors: The Abolitionists and American Slavery* (Hill and Wang, 1976); Lawrence J. Friedman, *Gregarious Saints: Self and Community in American Abolitionism, 1830–1870* (Cambridge University Press, 1982); Stanley Harrold, *The Abolitionists in the South, 1831–1861* (University Press of Kentucky, 1995); Richard S. Newman, *The Transformation of American Abolitionism: Fighting Slavery in the Early Republic* (University of North Carolina Press, 2002); and John Stauffer, *The Black Hearts of Men: Radical Abolitionists and the Transformation of Race* (Harvard University Press, 2002). The lives of individual participants in the abolitionist movement are discussed in Henry Mayer, *All on Fire: William Lloyd Garrison and the Abolition of Slavery* (St. Martin's, 1998); Gerda Lerner, *The Grimké Sisters from South Carolina: Pioneers for Woman's Rights and Abolition* (Schocken Books, 1967); and Irving H. Bartlett, *Wendell and Ann Phillips: The Community of Reform, 1840–1880* (Harvard University Press, 1979).

John Brown's controversial role in the movement is evaluated in W. E. B. DuBois, *John Brown* (G. W. Jacobs, 1909); Oswald Garrison Villard, *John Brown, 1800–1859: A Biography Fifty Years After* (Houghton Mifflin, 1910); Herbert Aptheker, *John Brown: American Martyr* (New Century, 1960); Stephen B. Oates, *To Purge This Land With Blood: A Biography of John Brown* (Harper and Row, 1970); Benjamin Quarles, *Allies for Freedom: Blacks and John Brown* (Oxford University Press, 1974); Paul Finkleman, ed., *His Soul Goes Marching On: Responses to John Brown and the Harper's Ferry Raid* (University of Virginia Press, 1995); Louis A. DeCaro, Jr., *"Fire From the Midst of You": A Religious Life of John Brown* (New York University Press, 2002); and Merrill D. Peterson, *John Brown: The Legend Revisited* (University of Virginia Press, 2002); and Jonathan Earle, ed., *John Brown's Raid on Harpers Ferry: A Brief History with Documents* (Bedford/St. Martin's, 2008).

Internet References . . .

AmericanCivilWar.com

The goal of this site is to provide a comprehensive source of Civil War information from the public domain or works published with the authors' permission. The sources are directed at students and Civil War buffs of all ages.

http://americancivilwar.com/index.html

The Valley of the Shadow Project

Developed under the direction of Edward Ayers and his graduate students at the University of Virginia, this site includes digital archives of thousands of primary source materials related to life in the Civil War era communities in Augusta County, Virginia, and Franklin County, Pennsylvania.

http://valley.vcdh.virginia.edu/

Abraham Lincoln Online

Dedicated to the sixteenth president of the United States, this site offers educational links, Lincoln's speeches and writings, information on historic places, and much more.

http://www.netins.net/showcase/creative/lincoln.html

Reconstruction Era Documents

This page includes links to various Reconstruction era documents by such authors as Frederick Douglass, Booker T. Washington, and W. E. B. DuBois.

http://www.libraries.rutgers.edu/rul/rr_gateway/research_guides/history/civwar.shtml

UNIT 4

Conflict and Resolution

The changing nature of the United States and the demands of its own principles finally erupted into violent conflict. Perhaps it was an inevitable step in the process of building a coherent nation from a number of distinct and diverse groups. The leaders, attitudes, and resources that were available to the North and the South were to determine the course of the war itself, as well as the national healing process that followed.

- Was Slavery the Key Issue in the Sectional Conflict Leading to the Civil War?
- Did Abraham Lincoln Free the Slaves?
- Did Reconstruction Fail as a Result of Racism?

ISSUE 14

Was Slavery the Key Issue in the Sectional Conflict Leading to the Civil War?

YES: Charles B. Dew, from *Apostles of Disunion: Southern Secession Commissioners and the Causes of the Civil War* (University of Virginia Press, 2001)

NO: Joel H. Silbey, from *The Partisan Imperative: The Dynamics of American Politics Before the Civil War* (Oxford University Press, 1985)

ISSUE SUMMARY

YES: Charles B. Dew uses the speeches and public letters of 41 white southerners who, as commissioners in 1860 and 1861, attempted to secure support for secession by appealing to their audiences' commitment to the preservation of slavery and the doctrine of white supremacy.

NO: Joel H. Silbey argues that historians have overemphasized the sectional conflict over slavery and have neglected to analyze local ethnocultural issues among the events leading to the Civil War.

In April 1861, less than a month after his inauguration, President Abraham Lincoln attempted to send provisions to Fort Sumter, a federal military installation nestled in the harbor of Charleston, South Carolina, part of the newly formed Confederate States of America. Southern troops under the command of General P. G. T. Beauregard opened fire on the fort, forcing its surrender on April 14. The American Civil War had begun.

Numerous explanations have been offered for the cause of this "war between the states." Many contemporaries and some historians saw the conflict as the product of a conspiracy housed either in the North or South, depending upon one's regional perspective. For many in the northern states, the chief culprits were the planters and their political allies who were willing to defend southern institutions at all costs. South of the Mason-Dixon line, blame was laid at the feet of the fanatical abolitionists, like John Brown (see Issue 13) and the free-soil architects of the Republican Party. Some viewed secession and war as the consequence of a constitutional struggle between states-rights advocates and defenders of the federal government, whereas others focused upon the economic rivalries or the cultural differences between North and South. Embedded in each of these interpretations, however, is the powerful influence of the institution of slavery.

In the 85 years between the start of the American Revolution and the coming of the Civil War, Americans made the necessary political compromises on the slavery issue in order not to split the nation apart. The Northwest Ordinance of 1787 forbade slavery from spreading into those designated territories under its control, and the new Constitution written in the same year held out the possibility that the Atlantic slave trade would be prohibited after 1808.

There was some hope in the early nineteenth century that slavery might die from natural causes. The Revolutionary generation was well aware of the contradiction between the values of an egalitarian society and the practices of a slaveholding aristocracy. Philosophically, slavery was viewed as a necessary evil, not a positive good. The northern states were well on their way to abolishing slavery by 1800, and the erosion of the tobacco lands in Virginia and Maryland contributed to the lessening importance of a slave labor system.

Unfortunately, two factors—territorial expansion and the market economy—made slavery the key to the South's wealth in the 35 years before the Civil War. First, new slave states were created out of a population expanding into lands ceded to the United States as a result of the Treaty of Paris of 1783 and the Louisiana Purchase of 1803. Second, slaves were sold from the upper to the lower regions of the South because the cotton gin (invented by Eli Whitney in 1793) made it possible to harvest large quantities of cotton, ship it to the textile mills in New England and the British Isles, and turn it into cloth and finished clothing as part of the new, specialized market economy.

The slavery issue came to the forefront in 1819 when some northern congressmen proposed that slavery be banned from the states being carved out of the Louisiana Purchase. A heated debate ensued, but the Missouri Compromise drew a line that preserved the balance between free and slave states and that (with the exception of Missouri) prohibited slavery north of the 36°30′ latitude.

The annexation of Texas in 1845 and the acquisition of New Mexico, Utah, and California, as a result of the Mexican-American War (see Issue 12), reopened the slavery question. Attempts at compromises in 1850 and 1854 only accelerated the conflict. The Kansas-Nebraska Act of 1854, which repealed the Missouri Compromise, allowed citizens in the new territories to decide whether or not they wanted slavery on the basis of the doctrine of popular sovereignty. As the second party system of Whigs and Democrats fell apart, the Republican party, whose unifying principle was to confine slavery to states where it already existed but not to allow it to spread to any new territories, mounted a successful challenge against the Democrats and in 1860 elected Abraham Lincoln as president of the United States, a result that 11 slaveholding states in the South refused to accept.

In the following essays, Charles B. Dew challenges the neo-Confederate arguments of this and the last century that insists that the decision to secede was driven by the federal government's abuse of states' rights. Joel H. Silbey, on the other hand, argues that historians have overemphasized the conflict over slavery and have neglected to analyze local ethnocultural issues as causes for the Civil War.

YES 

Charles B. Dew

Apostles of Disunion: Southern Secession Commissioners and the Causes of the Civil War

Slavery, States' Rights, and Secession Commissioners

"The Civil War was fought over what important issue?" So reads one of twenty questions on an exam administered by the Immigration and Naturalization Service to prospective American citizens. According to the INS, you are correct if you offer either one of the following answers: "Slavery or states rights."

It is reassuring to know that the INS has a flexible approach to one of the critical questions in American history, but one might ask how the single "issue" raised in the question can have an either/or answer in this instance—the only time such an option occurs on the test. Beyond that, some might want to know whether "slavery" or "states rights" is the more correct answer. But it is probably unfair to chide the test preparers at the INS for trying to fudge the issue. Their uncertainty reflects the deep division and profound ambivalence in contemporary American culture over the origins of the Civil War. One hundred and forty years after the beginning of that fratricidal conflict, neither the public nor the scholarly community has reached anything approaching a consensus as to what caused the bloodiest four years in this country's history. . . .

There is, however, a remarkably clear window into the secessionist mind that has been largely ignored by students of this era. If we want to know what role slavery may or may not have played in the coming of the Civil War, there is no better place to look than in the speeches and letters of the men who served their states as secession commissioners on the eve of the conflict.

As sectional tension mounted in late 1860 and early 1861, five states of the lower South—Mississippi, Alabama, South Carolina, Georgia, and Louisiana—appointed commissioners to other slave states and instructed them to spread the secessionist message across the entire region. These commissioners often explained in detail why their states were exiting the Union, and they did everything in their power to persuade laggard slave states to join the secessionist cause. From December 1860 to April 1861, they carried the *gospel of disunion to* the far corners of the South.

The overwhelming majority of the commissioners came from the four Deep South states of Mississippi, Alabama, South Carolina, and Georgia. In Mississippi and Alabama the commissioners were appointed by the governor and thus took the field first. In South Carolina, Georgia, and Louisiana, the secession conventions chose the commissioners.

The number of men sent on this vital mission varied from state to state. Mississippi and Alabama named commissioners to every one of the fourteen other slave states. South Carolina, however, only appointed commissioners to those states which had announced they were calling secession conventions, so only nine representatives eventually went out from the cradle of the secession movement—to Alabama, Mississippi, Georgia, Florida, Louisiana, Texas, Arkansas, Virginia, and North Carolina. Georgia dispatched commissioners to six of these same states—Alabama, Louisiana, Texas, Arkansas, North Carolina, and Virginia—and added the border slave states of Maryland, Delaware, Kentucky, and Missouri to the list. The Louisiana Convention appointed a single commissioner, to neighboring Texas, and he did not arrive in Austin until well after the Texas Convention had passed its ordinance of secession.

In all, some fifty-two men served as secession commissioners in the critical weeks just before the Civil War. These individuals were not, by and large, the famous names of antebellum Southern politics. They were often relatively obscure figures—judges, lawyers, doctors, newspaper editors, planters, and farmers—who had had modest political careers but who possessed a reputation for oratory. Sometimes they were better known—ex-governors or state attorneys general or members of Congress. Often they had been born in the states to which they were sent; place of birth was clearly an important factor in the choice of a number of commissioners.

The commissioners appeared in a host of different venues. They addressed state legislatures, they spoke before state conventions called to consider the question of secession, they took the platform before crowds in meeting halls and in the streets, and they wrote letters to governors whose legislatures were not in session. To a man, what they had to say was, and remains, exceedingly instructive and highly illuminating.

Despite their enormous value, the commissioners' speeches and letters have been almost completely overlooked by historians and, as a consequence, by the public at large. This scholarly neglect is difficult to understand. Contemporaries in both North and South paid close attention to the commissioners' movements and what they had to say. Many of their speeches were reprinted in full in newspapers and official state publications, and several appeared in pamphlet form and apparently gained wide circulation. Accounts of the secession crisis published during and just after the war also devoted considerable space to their activities. In the late nineteenth century when editors at the War Department were assembling a documentary record of the Civil War, they included extensive coverage of the commissioners in the volume dealing with the onset of the conflict—a clear indication that they considered these men to be key players in the sequence of events leading up to the war.

Dwight Lowell Dumond highlighted the importance of the commissioners in his 1931 study of the secession movement, a book that remains the most detailed scholarly treatment of this subject. He described the commissioners' words as extraordinarily important and revealing. "From the speeches and writings of the commissioners, as nowhere else, one may realize the depth of feeling and the lack of sympathy between the two sections of the country," Dumond wrote. "Vividly denunciatory of a party pledged to the destruction of Southern institutions, almost tragic in their prophetic tone, and pleading for a unity of allied interests, they constitute one of the most interesting series of documents in American history," he went on to say.

Yet Professor Dumond's book provides little detailed coverage of what these men actually said, and that pattern has persisted in the torrent of literature on the Civil War that has appeared in subsequent decades. As Jon L. Wakelyn notes in his recent *Southern Pamphlets on Secession,* "No adequate study of the Lower South delegates sent to the Upper South exists," and that same observation could be made about the commissioners who addressed their remarks to fellow Southerners in the states of the Deep South as well. Indeed, Professor Wakelyn does not include the full text of a single commissioner's speech in his otherwise superb collection of pamphlet literature, even though, in my opinion, several of the addresses published in pamphlet form are among the most powerful and revealing expressions of the secessionist persuasion put to paper on the eve of the war.

I have managed to locate the full texts or detailed synopses of forty-one of the commissioners' speeches and public letters. It is, as Professor Dumond suggested, a truly remarkable set of documents. What is most striking about them is their amazing openness and frankness. The commissioners' words convey an unmistakable impression of candor, of white Southerners talking to fellow Southerners with no need to hold back out of deference to outside sensibilities. These men infused their speeches and letters with emotion, with passion, and with a powerful "Let's cut to the chase" analysis that reveals, better than any other sources I know, what was really driving the Deep South states toward disunion.

The explanations the commissioners offered and the arguments the commissioners made, in short, provide us with extraordinary insight into the secession of the lower South in 1860–61. And by helping us to understand the "why" of secession, these apostles of disunion have gone a long way toward answering that all-important question, "The Civil War was fought over what important issue?" . . .

John Smith Preston spent the war years in uniform. After serving in a number of different staff positions in the army, he found a home in the Confederate Bureau of Conscription. He took over that agency in 1863, was promoted to the rank of brigadier general in 1864, and headed the Conscript Bureau until the South went down to defeat. Preston lived for a time in England after the war, but in 1868 he went back to South Carolina. His reputation as an orator still intact, Preston was invited to return to his native state in 1868 to address the Washington and Jefferson Societies of the University of Virginia. On June 30 of that year, Preston spoke in Charlottesville to the young Virginians.

Much of his address was an eloquent tribute to the Founding Fathers and their principal handiwork—the Revolution, the state constitutions, and the

Constitution of the United States. Through their efforts "your fathers achieved that liberty which comes of a free government, founded on justice, order and peace," Preston said. In order to preserve the principles and the constitutional forms established by the Revolutionary generation, "you, the immediate offspring of the founders, went forth to that death grapple which has prevailed against you," he continued. It was the North, "the victors," who rejected "the principles," destroyed "the forms," and defeated "the promised destiny of America," Preston charged. "The Constitution you fought for"—the Confederate Constitution—"embodied every principle of the Constitution of the United States, and guaranteed the free Constitution of Virginia. It did not omit one essential for liberty and the public welfare," he claimed. The Confederacy was in ashes, however, and so was true constitutional liberty. "That liberty was lost, and now the loud hosanna is shouted over land and sea—'Liberty may be dead, but the Union is preserved. Glory, glory, glory to Massachusetts and her Hessian and Milesian mercenaries,'" Preston declaimed. Yet all was not lost. Even though "cruel, bloody, remorseless tyrants may rule at Fort Sumter and at Richmond . . . they cannot crush that immortal hope, which rises from the blood soaked earth of Virginia," Preston believed. "I see the sacred image of regenerate Virginia, and cry aloud, in the hearing of a God of Right, and in the hearing of all the nations of the earth—ALL HAIL OUR MOTHER."

Passionate, unregenerate, unapologetic, unreconstructed—all these and more apply to Preston's remarks on this occasion. But so do words like "conveniently forgetful," "strongly revisionist," and "purposely misleading." Nowhere to be found are references to many of the arguments and descriptions he had used over and over again before the Virginia Convention in February 1861—things like "the subject race . . . rising and murdering their masters" or "the conflict between slavery and non-slavery is a conflict for life and death," or his insistence that "the South cannot exist without African slavery," or his portrait of the "fermenting millions" of the North as "canting, fanatics, festering in the licentiousness of abolition and amalgamation." All this was swept aside as Preston sought to paint the Civil War as a mighty struggle over differing concepts of constitutional liberty. Like Jefferson Davis and Alexander H. Stephens in their postwar writings, Preston was trying to reframe the causes of the conflict in terms that would be much more favorable to the South.

Preston was not the only former secession commissioner to launch such an effort after the war. Jabez L. M. Curry, who had served as Alabama's commissioner to Maryland in December 1860, became a leading figure in the drive to improve primary and secondary education in the postwar South. As agent for both the Peabody and Slater Funds and as supervising director of the Southern Education Board, Curry worked tirelessly to establish public schools and teacher training for both races in the states of the former Confederacy. Curry also worked diligently to justify the Lost Cause of the Confederacy. In his *Civil History of the Government of the Confederate States, with Some Personal Reminiscences,* published in Richmond in 1901, Curry offered an analysis of the coming of the war that closely paralleled the argument used by John S. Preston in 1868. "The object in quitting the Union was not to destroy, but to save the principles of the Constitution," Curry wrote. "The Southern States from the beginning of the government had striven to keep it within the orbit prescribed by the Constitution and failed." The Curry of 1901 would hardly have recognized the Curry of 1860, who told the governor of Maryland that secession meant "deliverance from Abolition domination," and who predicted that under Republican rule the South's slave-based social system would "be assaulted, humbled, dwarfed, degraded, and finally crushed out."

In 1860 and 1861 Preston, Curry, and the other commissioners had seen a horrific future facing their region within the confines of Abraham Lincoln's Union. When they used words like "submission" and "degradation," when they referred to "final subjugation" and "annihilation," they were not talking about constitutional differences or political arguments. They were talking about the dawning of an abominable new world in the South, a world created by the Republican destruction of the institution of slavery.

The secession commissioners knew what this new and hateful world would look like. Over and over again they called up three stark images that, taken together, constituted the white South's worst nightmare.

The first threat was the looming specter of racial equality. The commissioners insisted almost to a man that Republican ascendancy in Washington placed white supremacy in the South in mortal peril. Mississippi commissioner William L. Harris made this point clearly and unambiguously in his speech to the Georgia legislature in December 1860. "Our fathers made this a government for the white man," Harris told the Georgians, "rejecting the negro, as an ignorant, inferior, barbarian race, incapable of self-government, and not, therefore, entitled to be associated with the white man upon terms of civil, political, or social equality." But the Republicans intended "to overturn and strike down this great feature of our Union . . . and to substitute in its stead their new theory of the universal equality of the black and white races." Alabama's commissioners to North Carolina, Isham W. Garrott and Robert H. Smith, predicted that the white children of their state would "be compelled to flee from the land of their birth, and from the slaves their parents have toiled to acquire as an inheritance for them, or to submit to the degradation of being reduced to an equality with them, and all its attendant horrors." South Carolina's John McQueen warned the Texas Convention that Lincoln and the Republicans were bent upon "the abolition of slavery upon this continent and the elevation of our own slaves to an equality with ourselves and our children." And so it went, as commissioner after commissioner—Leonidas Spratt of South Carolina, David Clopton and Arthur F. Hopkins of Alabama, Henry L. Benning of Georgia—hammered home this same point.

The impending imposition of racial equality informed the speeches of other commissioners as well. Thomas J. Wharton, Mississippi's attorney general and that state's commissioner to Tennessee, said in Nashville on January 8, 1861, that the Republican Party would, "at no distant day, inaugurate the reign of equality of all races and colors, and the universality of the elective franchise." Commissioner Samuel L. Hall of Georgia told the North Carolina legislature on February 13, 1861, that only a people "dead to all sense of virtue and dignity" would embrace the Republican doctrine of "the social and political equality of the black and white races." Another Georgia commissioner,

Luther J. Glenn of Atlanta, made the same point to the Missouri legislature on March 2, 1861. The Republican platform, press, and principal spokesmen had made their "purposes, objects, and motives" crystal clear, Glenn insisted: "hostility to the South, the extinction of slavery, and the ultimate elevation of the negro to civil, political and social equality with the white man." These reasons and these reasons alone had prompted his state "to dissolve her connexion with the General Government," Glenn insisted.

The second element in the commissioners' prophecy was the prospect of a race war. Mississippi commissioner Alexander H. Handy raised this threat in his Baltimore speech in December 1860—Republican agents infiltrating the South "to excite the slave to cut the throat of his master." Alabamians Garrott and Smith told their Raleigh audience that Republican policies would force the South either to abandon slavery "or be doomed to a servile war." William Cooper, Alabama's commissioner to Missouri, delivered a similar message in Jefferson City. "Under the policy of the Republican party, the time would arrive when the scenes of San Domingo and Hayti, with all their attendant horrors, would be enacted in the slaveholding States," he told the Missourians. David Clopton of Alabama wrote the governor of Delaware that Republican ascendancy "endangers instead of insuring domestic tranquility by the possession of channels through which to circulate insurrectionary documents and disseminate insurrectionary sentiments among a hitherto contented servile population." Wharton of Mississippi told the Tennessee legislature that Southerners "will not, cannot surrender our institutions," and that Republican attempts to subvert slavery "will drench the country in blood, and extirpate one or other of the races." In their speeches to the Virginia Convention, Fulton Anderson, Henry L. Benning, and John S. Preston all forecast a Republican-inspired race war that would, as Benning put it, "break out everywhere like hidden fire from the earth."

The third prospect in the commissioners' doomsday vision was, in many ways, the most dire: racial amalgamation. Judge Harris of Mississippi sounded this note in Georgia in December 1860 when he spoke of Republican insistence on "equality in the rights of matrimony." Other commissioners repeated this warning in the weeks that followed. In Virginia, Henry Benning insisted that under Republican-led abolition "our women" would suffer "horrors . . . we cannot contemplate in imagination." There was not an adult present who could not imagine exactly what Benning was talking about. Leroy Pope Walker, Alabama's commissioner to Tennessee and subsequently the first Confederate secretary of war, predicted that in the absence of secession all would be lost—first, "our property," and "then our liberties," and finally the South's greatest treasure, "the sacred purity of our daughters."

No commissioner articulated the racial fears of the secessionists better, or more graphically, than Alabama's Stephen F. Hale. When he wrote of a South facing "amalgamation or extermination," when he referred to "all the horrors of a San Domingo servile insurrection," when he described every white Southerner "degraded to a position of equality with free negroes," when he foresaw the "sons and daughters" of the South "associating with free negroes upon terms of political and social equality," when he spoke of the Lincoln administration consigning the citizens of the South "to assassinations and her wives and daughters to pollution and violation to gratify the lust of half-civilized Africans," he was giving voice to the night terrors of the secessionist South. States' rights, historic political abuses, territorial questions, economic differences, constitutional arguments—all these and more paled into insignificance when placed alongside this vision of the South's future under Republican domination.

The choice was absolutely clear. The slave states could secede and establish their independence, or they could submit to "Black Republican" rule with its inevitable consequences: Armageddon or amalgamation. Whites forced to endure racial equality, race war, a staining of the blood—who could tolerate such things?

The commissioners sent out to spread the secessionist gospel in late 1860 and early 1861 clearly believed that the racial fate of their region was hanging in the balance in the wake of Lincoln's election. Only through disunion could the South be saved from the disastrous effects of Republican principles and Republican malevolence. Hesitation, submission—any course other than immediate secession—would place both slavery and white supremacy on the road to certain extinction. The commissioners were arguing that disunion, even if it meant risking war, was the only way to save the white race.

Did these men really believe these things? Did they honestly think that secession was necessary in order to stay the frenzied hand of the Republican abolitionist, preserve racial purity and racial supremacy, and save their women and children from rape and slaughter at the hands of "half-civilized Africans"? They made these statements, and used the appropriate code words, too many times in too many places with too much fervor and raw emotion to leave much room for doubt. They knew these things in the marrow of their bones, and they destroyed a political union because of what they believed and what they foresaw.

But, we might ask, could they not see the illogicality, indeed the absurdity, of their insistence that Lincoln's election meant that the white South faced the sure prospect of either massive miscegenation or a race war to the finish? They seem to have been totally untroubled by logical inconsistencies of this sort. Indeed, the capacity for compartmentalization among this generation of white Southerners appears to have been practically boundless. How else can we explain Judge William L. Harris's comments before the Mississippi State Agricultural Society in November 1858? "It has been said by an eminent statesman," Harris observed on this occasion, "'that nothing can advance the mass of society in prosperity and happiness, nothing can uphold the substantial interest and steadily improve the general condition and character of the whole, but this one thing—compensating rewards for labor.'" It apparently never occurred to Harris that this observation might apply to the hundreds of thousands of slaves working in Mississippi in 1858 as well as to the white farmers and mechanics of his adopted state. His mind could not even comprehend the possibility that slaves, too, were human beings who, if given the opportunity, might well respond to "compensating rewards" for their labor.

In setting out to explain secession to their fellow Southerners, the commissioners have explained a very great deal to us as well. By illuminating so clearly the racial content of the secession persuasion, the commissioners would seem to have laid to rest, once and for all, any notion that slavery had nothing to do with the coming of the Civil War. To put it quite simply, slavery and race were absolutely critical elements in the coming of the war. Neo-Confederate groups may have "a problem" with this interpretation, as the leader of the Virginia Heritage Preservation Association put it. But these defenders of the Lost Cause need only read the speeches and letters of the secession commissioners to learn what was really driving the Deep South to the brink of war in 1860–61.

Joel H. Silbey

NO

The Civil War Synthesis in American Political History

The Civil War has dominated our studies of the period between the Age of Jackson and 1861. Most historians of the era have devoted their principal attention to investigating and analyzing the reasons for differences between the North and South, the resulting sectional conflict, and the degeneration of this strife into a complete breakdown of our political system in war. Because of this focus, most scholars have accepted, without question, that differences between the North and the South were the major political influences at work among the American people in the years between the mid-1840s and the war. Despite occasional warnings about the dangers of overemphasizing sectional influences, the sectional interpretation holds an honored and secure place in the historiography of the antebellum years. We now possess a formidable number of works which, in one way or another, center attention on the politics of sectionalism and clearly demonstrate how much the Civil War dominates our study of American political history before 1861.

Obviously nothing is wrong in such emphasis if sectionalism was indeed the dominant political influence in the antebellum era. However, there is the danger in such emphasis of claiming too much, that in centering attention on the war and its causes we may ignore or play down other contemporary political influences and fail to weigh adequately the importance of nonsectional forces in antebellum politics. And, in fact, several recent studies of American political behavior have raised serious doubts about the importance of sectional differences as far as most Americans were concerned. These have even suggested that the sectional emphasis has created a false synthesis in our study of history which increases the importance of one factor, ignores the significance of other factors, and ultimately distorts the reality of American political life between 1844 and 1861.

Scholars long have used the presidential election of 1844 as one of their major starting points for the sectional analysis of American political history. In a general sense they have considered American expansion into Texas to be the most important issue of that campaign. The issue stemmed from the fact that

From *Civil War History*, vol. 10, no. 2, June 1964. Copyright © 1964 by Kent State University Press. Reprinted by permission.

Texas was a slave area and many articulate Northerners attacked the movement to annex Texas as a slave plot designed to enhance Southern influence within the Union. Allegedly because of these attacks, and the Southerners' defending themselves, many people in both North and South found themselves caught up in such sectional bitterness that the United States took a major step toward civil war. Part of this bitterness can be seen, it is pointed out, in the popular vote in New York State where the Whig candidate for the presidency, Henry Clay, lost votes to the abolitionist Liberty party because he was a slaveholder. The loss of these votes cost him New York and ultimately the election. As a result of Clay's defeat, historians have concluded that as early as 1844 the problem of slavery extension was important enough to arouse people to act primarily in sectional terms and thus for this episode to be a milestone on the road to war.

Recently Professor Lee Benson published a study of New York State politics in the Jacksonian era. Although Benson mainly concerned himself with other problems, some of his findings directly challenge the conception that slavery and sectional matters were of major importance in New York in 1844. In his analysis Benson utilized a more systematic statistical compilation of data than have previous workers in the field of political history. Observing that scholars traditionally have looked at what people said they did rather than at what they actually did, Benson compiled a great number of election returns for New York State in this period. His purpose was to see who actually voted for whom and to place the election in historical perspective by pinpointing changes in voting over time and thus identifying the basic trends of political behavior. Through such analysis Benson arrived at a major revision of the nature of New York State voting in 1844.

Benson pointed out, first of all, that the abolitionist, anti-Texas Liberty party whose vote total should have increased if the New York population wanted to strike against a slave plot in Texas, actually lost votes over what it had received in the most immediate previous election, that of 1843. Further analysis indicated that there was no widespread reaction to the Texas issue in New York State on the part of any large group of voters, although a high degree of anti-Texas feeling indeed existed among certain limited groups in the population. Such sentiment, however, did not affect voting margins in New York State. Finally, Benson concluded that mass voting in New York in 1844 pivoted not on the sectional issue but rather on more traditional divisions between ethnic and religious groups whose voting was a reaction to matters closer to home. These proved of a more personal and psychological nature than that of Texas and its related issue of slavery extension. Sectional bitterness, contrary to previous historical conceptions, neither dominated nor seriously influenced the 1844 vote in New York. Although Benson confined his study to one state, his conclusions introduce doubts about the influence of sectionalism in other supposedly less pivotal states.

Another aspect of the sectional interpretation of American politics in the pre-Civil War era involves Congress. Political historians have considered that body to be both a forum wherein leaders personally expressed attitudes that intensified sectional bitterness, as well as an arena which reflected the general pattern of influences operative in the country at large. Therefore, writers on the period have considered the behavior of congressmen to have been more and more dominated by sectionalism, particularly after David Wilmot introduced his antislavery extension proviso into the House of Representatives in 1846. Although there may have been other issues and influences present, it is accepted that these were almost completely overborne in the late 1840s and 1850s in favor of a widespread reaction to sectional differences.

In a recently completed study, I have analyzed congressional voting in the allegedly crucial pivotal decade 1841–52, the period which historians identify as embodying the transition from nationalism to sectionalism in congressional behavior. This examination indicates that a picture of the decade as one in which sectional influences steadily grew stronger, overwhelmed all other bases of divisions, and became a permanent feature of the voting behavior of a majority of congressmen, is grossly oversimplified and a distortion of reality. In brief, although sectional influences, issues, and voting did exist, particularly between 1846 and 1850, sectional matters were not the only problems confronting congressmen. In the period before the introduction of the Wilmot Proviso in 1846, national issues such as the tariff, financial policy, foreign affairs, and land policy divided congressmen along political, not sectional, lines. Furthermore, in this earlier period issues which many believed to have shown a high degree of sectional content, such as admittance of Texas and Oregon, reveal highly partisan national divisions and little sectional voting.

Even after the rise of the slavery-extension issue, other questions of a national character remained important. Slavery was but one of several issues before Congress and it was quite possible for congressmen to vote against one another as Northern and Southern sectionalists on an issue and then to join together, regardless of section, against other Northerners and Southerners on another matter. Certainly some men from both geographic areas were primarily influenced by sectional considerations at all times on all issues, but they were a minority of all congressmen in the period. The majority of congressmen were not so overwhelmingly influenced by their being Northerners or Southerners, but continued to think and act in national terms, and even resisted attempts by several sectionally minded congressmen to forge coalitions, regardless of party, against the other section.

A careful study of congressional voting in these years also demonstrates that another assumption of historians about the nature of politics is oversimplified: the period around 1846 did *not* begin the steady forward movement of congressional politics toward sectionalism and war. Rather, it was quite possible in the period between 1846 and 1852 for congressmen to assail one another bitterly in sectional terms, physically attack one another, and even threaten secession, and still for the majority of them to return in the following session to a different approach—that of nonsectional political differences with a concomitant restoration of nonsectional coalitions. For example, it was possible in 1850, after several years of sectional fighting, for a national coalition of Senators and Representatives to join together and settle in compromise terms the differences between North and South over expansion. And they were able to do this despite the simultaneous existence of a great deal of sectional maneuvering by some congressmen in an attempt to prevent any such compromise. Furthermore, during this same session Congress also dealt with matters of railroad land grants in a way that eschewed sectional biases. Obviously the usual picture of an inexorable growth of sectional partisanship after 1846 is quite overdone. And lest these examples appeared to be isolated phenomena, preliminary research both by Gerald Wolff and by myself demonstrates that as late as 1854 there was still no complete or overwhelming sectional voting even on such an issue as the Kansas-Nebraska Act.

Such analyses of congressional behavior in an alleged transition period reinforce what Lee Benson's work on New York politics demonstrated: many varieties and many complexities existed with respect to political behavior in the antebellum period, so that even slavery failed to be a dominating influence among all people at all times—or even among most people at most times—during the 1840s and early 1850s. Again, our previous image of American politics in this period must be reconsidered in light of this fact and despite the emergence of a Civil War in 1861.

Perhaps no aspect of antebellum politics should demonstrate more fully the overpowering importance of sectional influences than the presidential election of 1860. In the preliminaries to that contest the Democratic party split on the rock of slavery, the Republican party emerged as a power in the Northern states with a good chance of winning the presidency, and loud voices in the Southern states called for secession because of Northern attacks on their institutions. In dealing with these events, historians, as in their treatment of other aspects of antebellum politics, have devoted their primary attention to sectional bickering and maneuvering among party leaders, because they considered this activity to be the most important facet of the campaign and the key to explaining the election. Although such a focus obviously has merit if one is thinking in terms of the armed conflict which broke out only five months after the election, once again, as in the earlier cases considered here, recent research has raised pertinent questions about the political realities of the situation. We may indeed ask what were the issues of the campaign as seen by the majority of voters.

Earlier studies of the 1860 election, in concerning themselves primarily with the responses and activities of political leaders, have taken popular voting behavior for granted. This aspect has either been ignored or else characterized as reflecting the same influences and attitudes as that of the leadership. Therefore, the mass of men, it is alleged, voted in response to sectional influences in 1860. For instance, several scholars concerned with the Germans in the Middle West in this period have characterized the attitudes of that group as overwhelmingly antislavery. Thus the Republican party attracted the mass of the German vote because the liberal "Forty-Eighters" saw casting a Lincoln vote as a way to strike a blow against slavery in the United States. Going beyond this, some historians have reached similar conclusions about other Middle Western immigrant groups.

As a result, according to most historians, although narrowly divided, the area went for Lincoln thanks in large part to its newest citizens, who were Northern sectionalists in their political behavior. Such conclusions obviously reinforce the apparent importance of geographic partisanship in 1860.

Testing this hypothesis, two recent scholars systematically studied and analyzed election returns in Iowa during 1860. Such examinations are important because they should reveal, if the sectional theory is correct, preoccupation among Iowa voters—especially immigrants—with the slavery question and the increasingly bitter differences between North and South. Only one of these studies, that of Professor George H. Daniels of Northwestern University, has appeared in print. But Daniels's findings shatter earlier interpretations which pinpointed sectional concerns as the central theme of the 1860 election.

Briefly stated, Daniels isolated the predominantly German townships in Iowa and, following Lee Benson's methodological lead, analyzed their vote. He found that, far from being solidly Republican voters, or moved primarily by the slavery question, the Germans of Iowa voted overwhelmingly in favor of the Democratic party. And Daniels discovered that the primary issue motivating the Germans in 1860 was an ethnic one. They were conscious of the anti-alien Know-Nothing movement which had been so strong in the United States during the 1850s and they identified the Republican party as the heir and last refuge of Know-Nothingism. If the Germans of Iowa were attracted to the Republicans by the latter's antislavery attitudes, such attraction was more than overcome by the Republicans' aura of antiforeignism. Furthermore, the Republicans were also identified in the minds of the Iowa Germans as the party of prohibitionism, a social view strongly opposed by most Germans. Thus, as Daniels concludes, ". . . The rank and file Germans who did the bulk of the voting considered their own liberty to be of paramount importance. Apparently ignoring the advice of their leaders, they cast their ballots for the party which consistently promised them liberty from prohibition and native-American legislation." As a result, the Germans of Iowa voted Democratic, not Republican, in 1860.

Lest this appear to be an isolated case, the research of Robert Swierenga on Dutch voting behavior in Iowa in 1860 confirms Daniels's findings. Swierenga demonstrated that the Dutch also voted Democratic despite their vaunted antislavery attitudes; again, revulsion from certain Republican ideals overpowered any attraction toward that party on the slavery issue.

Such research into the election of 1860, as in the earlier cases of the election of 1844 and congressional voting behavior in the 1840s and early 1850s, suggests how far the sectional and slavery preconceptions of American historians have distorted reality. Many nonsectional issues were apparently more immediately important to the groups involved than any imminent concern with Northern-Southern differences. Once again, the Civil War synthesis appears to be historically inaccurate and in need of serious revision.

Several other provocative studies recently have appeared which, while dealing with nonpolitical subjects, support the conclusion that sectional problems, the slavery issue, and increasing bitterness between North and South were not always uppermost concerns to most Americans in the fifteen years before the outbreak of the war. Building upon the work of Leon Litwack, which emphasizes the general Northern antagonism toward the Negro before 1860, and that of Larry Gara demonstrating the fallacy of the idea that a well-organized and widespread underground railroad existed in the North, Professor C. Vann Woodward has cautioned students against an easy acceptance of a "North-Star" image—a picture of a universally militant Northern population determined to ease the burden of the slave in America. Rather, as Woodward points out, a great many Northerners remained indifferent to the plight of the slave and hostile to the would-be antislavery reformer in their midst.

In this same tenor, Milton Powell of Michigan State University has challenged long-held assumptions that the Northern Methodist church was a bulwark of antislavery sentiment after splitting with its Southern branch in 1844. As Powell makes clear, Northern Methodists were concerned about many other problems in which slavery played no part, as well as being beset by conditions which served to tone down any antislavery attitudes they may have held. More importantly, this led many of them to ignore slavery as an issue because of its latent tendency to divide the organization to which they belonged. Thus, even in areas outside of the political realm, the actual conditions of antebellum society challenge the validity of the sectional concept in its most general and far-reaching form.

This review of recent research indicates that much of our previous work on the prewar period should be reexamined free from the bias caused by looking first at the fact of the Civil War and then turning back to view the events of the previous decade in relation only to that fact. Although it is true that the studies discussed here are few in number and by no means include the entire realm of American politics in the antebellum era, their diversity in time and their revisionist conclusions do strongly suggest the fallacy of many previous assumptions. No longer should any historian blithely accept the traditional concept of a universal preoccupation with the sectional issue.

But a larger matter is also pointed up by this recent research and the destruction of this particular myth about political sectionalism. For a question immediately arises as to how historians generally could have accepted so readily and for so long such oversimplifications and inaccuracies. Fortunately for future research, answers to this question have been implicitly given by the scholars under review, and involve methodological problems concerning evidence and a certain naïveté about the political process.

Historians generally have utilized as evidence the writings and commentaries of contemporary observers of, and participants in, the events being examined. But, as both Benson and Daniels emphasize, this can endanger our understanding of reality. For instance, not enough attention has been paid to who actually said what, or of the motives of a given reporter or the position he was in to know and understand what was going on around him.

Most particularly, scholars have not always been properly skeptical about whether the observer's comments truly reflected actuality. As Daniels pointed out in his article on German voting behavior, "contemporary opinion, including that of newspapers, is a poor guide."

If such is true, and the evidence presented by these studies indicates that it is, a question is raised as to how a historian is to discover contemporary opinion if newspapers are not always reliable as sources. The work of Benson, Daniels, and myself suggests an answer: the wider use of statistics. When we talk of public opinion (that is, how the mass of men acted or thought) we are talking in terms of aggregate numbers, of majorities. One way of determining what the public thought is by measuring majority opinion in certain circumstances—elections, for example, or the voting of congressmen—and then analyzing the content and breakdown of the figures derived. If, for example, 80 percent of the Germans in Iowa voted Democratic in 1860, this tells us more about German public opinion in 1860 than does a sprightly quote from one of the Germans in the other 20 percent who voted Republican "to uphold freedom." Historians are making much more use of statistics than formerly and are utilizing more sophisticated techniques of quantitative analysis. And such usage seems to be prelude to, judging by the works discussed here, a fuller and more accurate understanding of our past.

There are also other ways of approaching the problems posed by the 1850s. Not enough attention has been paid, it seems to me, to the fact that there are many different levels of political behavior—mass voting, legislative activity, leadership manipulation, for example—and that what is influential and important on one level of politics may not be on another. Certainly the Germans and Dutch of Iowa in 1860 were not paying much attention to the desires of their leaders. They were responding to influences deemed more important than those influences shaping the responses of their leaders. As Swierenga pointed out in his analysis of Dutch voting:

> While Scholte [a leader of the Dutch community] fulminated against Democrats as slave mongers, as opponents of the Pacific Railroad and Homestead Bills, and as destroyers of the Constitution, the Dutch citizens blithely ignored him and the national issues he propounded and voted their personal prejudices against Republican nativists and prohibitionists.

Obviously, when historians generalize about the nature of political behavior they must also be sure which group and level of political activity they mean, and so identify it, and not confuse different levels or assume positive correlations between the actions of people on one level with those on another level. Such precision will contribute greatly to accuracy and overcome tendencies toward distortion.

Finally, based on the work under discussion here, it is clear that historians must become more aware of the complexities of human behavior. All people, even of the same stratum of society or living in the same geographic area, do not respond with the same intensity to the same social or political stimuli. Not everyone perceives his best interests in the same way, or considers the same things to be the most important problems confronting him. Depending upon time and circumstances, one man may respond primarily to economic influences; another one, at the same time and place, to religious influences; and so on. Sometimes most people in a given community will respond to the same influences equally, but we must be careful to observe *when* this is true and not generalize from it that this is *always* true. Single-factor explanations for human behavior do not seem to work, and we must remain aware of that fact.

With improved methodological tools and concepts historians may begin to engage in more systematic and complete analyses of popular voting, legislative voting, and the motivations and actions of political leaders. They will be able to weigh the relative influence of sectional problems against other items of interest and concern on all levels of political behavior. Until this is done, however, we do know on the basis of what already has been suggested that we cannot really accept glib explanations about the antebellum period. The Civil War has had a pernicious influence on the study of American political development that preceded it—pernicious because it has distorted the reality of political behavior in the era and has caused an overemphasis on sectionalism. It has led us to look not for what was occurring in American politics in those years, but rather for what was occurring in American politics that tended toward sectional breakdown and civil war—a quite different matter.

POSTSCRIPT

Was Slavery the Key Issue in the Sectional Conflict Leading to the Civil War?

Charles B. Dew makes a very powerful argument regarding the influence of the slavery question on the decision by 11 southern slaveholding states to secede and to join the Confederate States of America. Whose attitudes would provide a better window into the thinking of white southerners on the eve of the Civil War than those individuals commissioned to travel throughout the region to drum up support for secession? Dew, however, by no means stands alone as a proponent of the view that slavery was the main cause of the war. In *America in 1857: A Nation on the Brink* (Oxford University Press, 1990), Kenneth M. Stampp argues that conflict became inevitable after the election of James Buchanan (not Lincoln) to the presidency, the continuing firestorm in Kansas, and the Supreme Court's decision in the Dred Scott case. Eric Foner, who has written extensively on the influence of the free-soil ideology and its impact on the coming of the Civil War in such works as *Free Soil, Free Labor, Free Men: The Ideology of the Republican Party Before the Civil War* (Oxford University Press, 1970), also points out that the argument for states' rights as an explanation for the cause of the war is largely a product of the post–Civil War era and, hence, more or less an afterthought on the part of southerners who hoped to distance themselves from the institution of slavery that dominated their region in the antebellum period.

Silbey's selection represents the first sustained attack on the sectional interpretation of the events leading to the Civil War. Historians, he contends, have created a false "Civil War synthesis" that positions slavery as the major issue that divided the United States, thereby distorting "the reality of American political life between 1844 and 1861."

Silbey is one of the "new political historians" who have applied the techniques of modern-day political scientists in analyzing the election returns and voting patterns of Americans' nineteenth- and early- twentieth-century predecessors. These historians use computers and regression analysis of voting patterns, they favor a quantitative analysis of past behavior, and they reject the traditional sources of quotes from partisan newspapers and major politicians because these sources provide anecdotal and often misleading portraits of our past. Silbey and other new political historians maintain that all politics are local. Therefore, the primary issues for voters and their politicians in the 1860 election were ethnic and cultural, and party loyalty was more important than sectional considerations.

Another approach is presented by Michael F. Holt in *The Political Crisis of the 1850s* (John Wiley & Sons, 1978). Holt also is interested in analyzing the struggles for power at the state and local levels by the major political parties, but he is critical of the ethnocultural school represented by Silbey. In Holt's view, Silbey's emphasis on voter analysis does not explain why the Whig Party disappeared nor why the Republican Party became the majority party in the northern and western states in the 1850s. Holt also rejects the more traditional view that the Civil War resulted from the "intensifying sectional disagreements over slavery." Instead, he promotes a more complicated picture of the events leading to the Civil War. Between 1845 and 1860, he maintains, three important things happened: (1) the breakdown of the Whig Party; (2) the realignment of voters; and (3) "a shift from a nationally balanced party system where both major parties competed on fairly even terms in all parts of the nation to a sectionalized polarized one with Republicans dominant in the North and Democrats in the South."

The list of books about the causes of the Civil War is extensive. Kenneth M. Stampp, ed., *The Causes of the Civil War* (Prentice-Hall, 1965) provides a collection of primary documents and historical interpretations by leading scholars. Other edited volumes of scholarly interpretations can be found in William R. Brock, ed., *The Civil War* (Harper & Row, 1969); Hans L. Trefousse, ed., *The Causes of the Civil War: Institutional Failure or Human Blunder?* (Holt, Rinehart and Watson, 1971); and Michael Perman, ed., *The Coming of the American Civil War* (3d ed.; D. C. Heath, 1993). John Niven's *The Coming of the Civil War, 1837–1861* (Harlan Davidson, 1990) is a brief narrative, but readers seeking a compelling narrative cannot do much better than David Potter, *The Impending Crisis, 1848–1861* (Harper & Row, 1976), one of the best volumes in the prestigious New American Nation Series.

ISSUE 15

Did Abraham Lincoln Free the Slaves?

YES: Stephen B. Oates, from *Abraham Lincoln: The Man Behind the Myths* (Harper & Row, 1984)

NO: Vincent Harding, from *There Is a River: The Black Struggle for Freedom in America* (Harcourt Brace Jovanovich, 1981)

ISSUE SUMMARY

YES: Stephen B. Oates argues that Abraham Lincoln, in his capacity as president of the United States, was the individual most responsible for sanctioning an unprecedented use of military power against state institutions in the form of the Emancipation Proclamation, which further encouraged slaves to abandon the farms and plantations of their rebel masters.

NO: Vincent Harding credits slaves themselves for engaging in a dramatic movement of self-liberation while Abraham Lincoln initially refused to declare the destruction of slavery as a war aim and then issued the Emancipation Proclamation, which failed to free any slaves in areas over which he had any authority.

Abraham Lincoln fully understood the role slavery had played in the outbreak of the Civil War. In March 1865, as the war was nearing its end, he presented the following analysis: "One eighth of the whole population (in 1861) was colored slaves, not distributed generally over the Union, but localized in the southern part of it. These slaves constituted a peculiar and powerful interest. All knew that this interest was somehow the cause of the war. To strengthen, perpetuate, and extend this interest was the object (of the South) . . . , while the (North) . . . claimed no right to do more than to restrict the territorial enlargement of it."

In light of Lincoln's recognition of the role slavery played in the clash between North and South, none should find it surprising that the Emancipation Proclamation, which the president issued, established a policy to end slavery. Hence, the demise of slavery became a war aim, and Lincoln seemed to have earned his place in history as "the Great Emancipator." Upon learning of the president's announcement, the fugitive slave and abolitionist Frederick Douglass was ecstatic. "We shout for joy," Douglass declared, "that we live to record this righteous decree."

But Douglass had not always been so certain of Lincoln's commitment to freedom. Lincoln was not an abolitionist by any stretch of the imagination, but Douglass was convinced that the Republican victory in the presidential election of 1860 had brought to the White House a leader with a deserved reputation as an antislavery man. That confidence declined, however, in the early months of Lincoln's presidency as Douglass and other abolitionists lobbied for emancipation during the secession crisis and, when the war began, as a military necessity only to have their demands fall on deaf ears. Lincoln consistently avoided any public pronouncements that would suggest his desire to end slavery as a war aim. The priority was preserving the Union, and Lincoln did not view emancipation as essential to that goal.

Until the president changed his course, it appeared that the slaves would have to free themselves. This is precisely what some scholars insist happened. Southern slaves, they argue, became the key agents for their own liberation through a variety of actions. Black northerners pitched in as well by enlisting in the United States Army and risking their lives to defeat the Confederacy and end slavery. In Cleveland, Ohio, for example, a meeting of local African Americans adopted a resolution proclaiming that "as colored citizens of Cleveland, desiring to prove our loyalty to the Government, feel that we should adopt measures to put ourselves in a position to defend the Government of which we claim protection. Resolved, That to-day, as in the times of '76, and the days of 1812, we are ready to go forth and do battle in the common cause of the country."

The question "Who freed the slaves?" is the focus of the following essays. Stephen B. Oates certainly recognizes that slaves did not sit idly by, waiting for someone to emancipate them. He also understands that President Lincoln, an antislavery man, was reluctant to take a forward position on emancipation that ran counter to the majority will of the American people, including those residing in the North and West. He first tried a voluntary program of gradual, compensated emancipation followed by colonization of the former slaves outside the boundaries of the United States. Once he was able to link emancipation with the nation's war aims, however, Lincoln went further than anything Congress had attempted with regard to the slavery question and issued his famous proclamation, which Oates characterizes as "the most revolutionary measure to come from an American President up to that time."

For Vincent Harding, credit for the end of slavery belongs to the masses of slaves who sought self-liberation by running away from their masters, undermining plantation operations, engaging in local insurrections, and offering their services to the Union army and navy. Rather than waiting for assistance from a distant central authority, slaves became the agents of their own freedom.

YES 

Stephen B. Oates

Abraham Lincoln: The Man Behind the Myths

Death Warrant for Slavery

The pressure on [President Abraham] Lincoln to strike at slavery was unrelenting. In between abolitionist delegations came [Charles] Sumner and his stern colleagues again, with Vice-President Hannibal Hamlin and Congressman Owen Lovejoy, also advanced Republicans, often with them. As the war progressed, they raised still another argument for emancipation, an argument [Frederick] Douglass and members of Lincoln's own Cabinet were also making. In 1862, his armies suffered from manpower shortages on every front. Thanks to repeated Union military failures and to a growing war weariness across the North, volunteering had fallen off sharply; and Union generals bombarded Washington with shrill complaints, insisting that they faced an overwhelming southern foe and must have reinforcements before they could win battles or even fight. While Union commanders often exaggerated rebel strength, Union forces did need reinforcements to carry out a successful offensive war. As Sumner reminded Lincoln, the slaves were an untapped reservoir of strength. "You need more men," Sumner said, "not only at the North, but at the South. You need the slaves." If Lincoln freed them, he could recruit black men into his armed forces, thus helping to solve his manpower woes.

On that score, the slaves themselves were contributing to the pressures on Lincoln to emancipate them. Far from being passive recipients of freedom, as Vincent Harding has rightly reminded us, the slaves *were* engaged in self-liberation, abandoning rebel farms and plantations and escaping to Union lines by the thousands. This in turn created a tangled legal problem that bedeviled the Lincoln administration. What was the status of such "contraband of war," as Union General Benjamin F. Butler designated them? Were they still slaves? Were they free? Were they somewhere in between? The administration tended to follow a look-the-other-way policy, allowing field commanders to solve the contraband problem any way they wished. Some officers sent the fugitives back to the Confederacy, others turned them over to refugee camps, where benevolent organizations attempted to care for them. But with more and more slaves streaming into Union lines, Sumner, several of Lincoln's Cabinet members, Douglass, and many others urged him to grant them freedom and enlist the able-bodied men in the army. "Let the slaves and free colored people be called into service

From *Abraham Lincoln: The Man Behind the Myths* by Stephen B. Oates (Harper & Row, 1984).

and formed into a liberating army," Douglass exhorted the President, "to march into the South and raise the banner of Emancipation among the slaves."

At first, Lincoln rejected a presidential move against slavery. "I think Sumner and the rest of you would upset our applecart altogether if you had your way," he told some advanced Republicans one day. "We didn't go into the war to put down slavery, but to put the flag back; and to act differently at this moment would, I have no doubt, not only weaken our cause, but smack of bad faith. . . . This thunderbolt will keep."

In short, as President he was accountable to the entire country, or what remained of it in the North and West, and the vast majority of whites there remained adamantly opposed to emancipation

Still, Lincoln was sympathetic to the entire range of arguments Sumner and his associates rehearsed for him. Personally, Lincoln hated slavery as much as they did, and many of their points had already occurred to him. On certain days he could be seen like them in the lecture hall of the Smithsonian Institution, listening quietly and intently as antislavery orators damned slavery for the evil that it was. Under the combined and incessant demands that he act, Lincoln began wavering in his hands-off policy about slavery; as early as November and December, 1861, he began searching about for some compromise—something short of a sweeping emancipation decree, which he still regarded as "too big a lick." Again he seemed caught in an impossible dilemma: how to remove the cause of the war, keep Britain out of the conflict, solve the refugee problem, cripple the Confederacy, and suppress the rebellion, and yet retain the allegiance of northern Democrats and the critical border.

In March, 1862, he proposed a plan to Congress he thought might work: a gradual, compensated emancipation program to commence in the loyal border states. According to Lincoln's plan, the border states would gradually abolish slavery themselves over the next thirty years, and the federal government would compensate slaveowners for their loss. The whole program was to be voluntary; the states would adopt their own emancipation laws without federal coercion. This was consistent with Lincoln's old hope that when slavery was no longer workable southerners would get rid of it themselves. That moment had arrived.

At the same time, the federal government would sponsor a colonization program, which was also to be entirely voluntary. Lincoln was not going to make Negroes leave America anymore than he was going to coerce the states into liberating them. The idea of forcing people out of the country violated his very conception of what it was about.

Lincoln had good reason to attach colonization to his federal-state emancipation plan. Without a promise of colonization, he understood only too well, most northern whites would never accept emancipation, even if it was carried out by the states. From now on, every time he contemplated some new antislavery move, he made a great fuss about colonization: he embarked on a resettlement project in central America and another in Haiti, and he held an interview about colonization with Washington's black leaders, an interview he published in the press. In part, the ritual of colonization was designed to calm white racial fears.

If his gradual, state-guided plan was adopted, Lincoln contended that a presidential decree—federally enforced emancipation—would never be necessary.

Abolition would begin on the local level in the loyal border and then be extended into the rebel states as they were conquered. Thus by a slow and salubrious process would the cause of the rebellion be removed and the future of the American experiment guaranteed.

On Capitol Hill, Congressman Thaddeus Stevens of Pennsylvania belittled Lincoln's scheme as "diluted milk-and-water gruel." But Sumner and other advanced Republicans, noting that Lincoln's was the first emancipation proposal ever offered by an American President, acclaimed it as an excellent step. On April 10, 1862, the Republican-controlled Congress endorsed Lincoln's plan. But the border-state representatives, for whom it was intended, rejected the scheme emphatically. "I utterly spit at it and despise it," said one Kentucky congressman. "Emancipation in the cotton States is simply an absurdity. . . . There is not enough power in the world to compel it to be done." . . .

On July 22, 1862, Lincoln summoned his Cabinet members and read them a draft of a preliminary Emancipation Proclamation. Come January 1, 1863, in his capacity as Commander-in-Chief of the armed forces in time of war, Lincoln would free all the slaves everywhere in the rebel states. He would thus make it a Union objective to annihilate slavery as an institution in the Confederate South.

Contrary to what many historians have said, Lincoln's projected Proclamation went further than anything Congress had done. True, Congress had just enacted (and Lincoln had just signed) the second confiscation act, which provided for the seizure and liberation of all slaves of people who supported or participated in the rebellion. Still, most slaves would be freed only after protracted case-by-case litigation in the federal courts. Another section of the act did liberate certain categories of slaves without court action, but the bill exempted loyal slaveowners in the rebel South, allowing them to keep their slaves and other property. Far short of a genuine emancipation measure, the act was about as far as Congress could go in attacking slavery, for most Republicans still acknowledged that Congress had no constitutional authority to remove bondage as a state institution. Only the President with his war powers—or a constitutional amendment—could do that. Nevertheless, the measure seemed a clear invitation for the President to exercise his constitutional powers and abolish slavery in the rebellious states. And Stevens, Sumner, and others repeatedly told Lincoln that most congressional Republicans now favored this.

In contrast to the confiscation act, Lincoln's Proclamation was a sweeping blow against slavery as an institution in the rebel states, a blow that would free *all* slaves there—those of secessionists and loyalists alike. Thus Lincoln would handle emancipation himself (as congressional Republicans wanted him to do), avoid judicial red tape, and use the military to vanquish the cornerstone of the Confederacy. Again, he justified this as a military necessity to save the Union—and with it America's experiment in popular government. . . .

The Man of Our Redemption

Lincoln's Proclamation was not "of minor importance," as one historian maintained several years ago. On the contrary, it was the most revolutionary measure ever to come from an American President up to that time. This "momentous decree," as Martin Luther King, Jr., later described it, was an unprecedented use of federal military power against a state institution. It was an unprecedented federal assault against the very foundation of the South's ruling planter class and economic and social order. As Union armies punched into rebel territory, they would tear slavery out root and branch, automatically freeing all slaves in the areas and states they conquered. In this respect (as Lincoln said), the war brought on changes more fundamental and profound than either side had expected when the conflict began. Now slavery would perish as the Confederacy perished, would die by degrees with every Union advance, every Union victory.

Moreover, word of the Proclamation hummed across the slave grapevine in the Confederacy; and as Union armies drew near, more slaves than ever abandoned rebel farms and plantations and (as one said) "demonstrated with their feet" their desire for freedom. In short, slaves like these did not sit back and wait for their liberty: they went out and got it for themselves.

The Proclamation was not some anemic document that in effect freed no slaves. By November, 1864, the Philadelphia *North American* estimated that more than 1,300,000 Negroes had been liberated by Lincoln's Proclamation or "the events of the war." By war's end, all three and a half million slaves in the defeated Confederacy could claim freedom under Lincoln's Proclamation and the victorious Union flag.

What is more, the Proclamation did something for Lincoln personally that has never been stressed enough. In truth, the story of emancipation could well be called the liberation of Abraham Lincoln. For in the process of granting freedom to the slaves, Lincoln also emancipated himself from his old dilemma. His Proclamation now brought the private and the public Lincoln together: now the public statesman could obliterate a wicked thing the private citizen had always hated, a thing that had long had "the power of making me miserable." Now the public statesman could destroy what he regarded as "a cruel wrong" that had always besmirched America's experiment in popular government, had always impeded her historic mission in the progress of human liberty in the world.

The Proclamation also opened the army to black volunteers, and northern free Negroes and southern ex-slaves now enlisted as Union soldiers. As Lincoln said, "the colored population is the great *available* and yet unavailed of, force for restoring the Union." And he now availed himself of that force. In occupied northern Alabama, a Union recruiter "of salty temper" put up a large poster with the legend: "**ALL SLAVES WERE MADE FREEMEN BY ABRAHAM LINCOLN, PRESIDENT OF THE UNITED STATES.** Come, then, able-bodied **COLORED MEN,** to the nearest United States Camp, and fight for the **STARS AND STRIPES.**" And fight they did. In all, some 186,000 Negro troops—most of them emancipated slaves—served in Union forces on every major battle front, helping to liberate their brothers and sisters in bondage and to save the American experiment. As Lincoln observed, the blacks added enormous and indispensable strength to the Union war machine. Without them, it is doubtful that he could have won the war.

Unhappily, the blacks fought in segregated units under white officers, and until late in the war received less pay than whites did. In 1863 Lincoln told Frederick Douglass that he disliked the practice of unequal pay, but that the government had to make some concessions to white prejudices, noting that a great many northern whites opposed the use of black soldiers altogether. But he promised that they would eventually get equal pay—and they did. Moreover, Lincoln was proud of the performance of his black soldiers: he publicly praised them for fighting "with clenched teeth, and steady eye, and well poised bayonet" to save the Union, while certain whites strove "with malignant heart" to hinder it.

As one historian has noted, the use of black troops had potent social and psychological overtones. A black soldier, dressed in Union blue and armed with a rifle and bayonet, posed a radically different picture from the obsequious "Sambo" image cultivated and cherished by southern whites. Fighting as soldiers not only gave black men a new sense of manhood, as the Reverend Turner had predicted, but undermined the whole nineteenth-century notion of innate Negro inferiority.

With blacks now fighting in his armies, Lincoln abandoned colonization as a solution to racial adjustment in Dixie. His colonization schemes had all floundered, and in any case black people adamantly refused to participate in the President's voluntary program. Across the North, free Negroes denounced Lincoln's highly publicized colonization efforts—this was their country too!—and they petitioned him to deport slaveholders instead. And Lincoln seemed in sympathy with that. Later, as the war drew to a close, he told his Cabinet that he would like to frighten rebel leaders out of the country. He waved his arms as though he were shooing chickens.

After he issued the Emancipation Proclamation, Lincoln never again urged colonization in public—an eloquent silence, indicating that he had concluded that Dixie's whites and liberated Negroes must somehow learn to live together. How, then, could Lerone Bennett and others maintain that Lincoln to the end of his life was a champion of colonization? That argument rests exclusively on the 1892 autobiography of Union political general Benjamin F. Butler. In it, Butler claimed that in April, 1865, Lincoln feared a race war in the South and still wanted to ship the blacks abroad. Not only is Butler a highly dubious witness, but there is not a scintilla of corroborative evidence to support his story, which one Lincoln scholar has recently exposed as "entirely a fantasy." There is not a single other source that quotes the President, in public or in private, as stating that he still favored colonization.

In any case, such a stance would have been glaringly inconsistent with Lincoln's Gettysburg Address, which called for a new birth of freedom in America for blacks and whites alike (here, in fact, is the eloquent defense of liberty that critics have found lacking in the Proclamation itself). And a colonization stance would have been inconsistent, too, with Lincoln's appreciation of the indispensable role his black soldiers played in subduing the rebellion. No man of Lincoln's honesty and sense of fair play would enlist 186,000 black troops to save the Union and then advocate throwing them out of the country. He simply did not advocate that.

Still, he needed some device during the war, some program that would pacify white northerners and convince them that southern freedmen would not flock into their communities, but would remain in the South instead. What

Lincoln worked out was a refugee system, installed by his adjutant general in occupied Dixie, which utilized blacks there in a variety of military and civilian pursuits. Then Republican propaganda went to work selling northern whites on the system and the Emancipation Proclamation: *See, liberated Negroes will not invade the North, but will stay in Dixie as free wage earners, learning to help themselves and our Union cause.*

Even so, emancipation remained the most explosive and unpopular act of Lincoln's presidency. By mid-1863, thousands of Democrats were in open revolt against his administration, denouncing Lincoln as an abolitionist dictator who had surrendered to radicalism. In the Midwest, dissident Democrats launched a peace movement to throw "the shrieking abolitionist faction" out of office and negotiate a peace with the Confederacy that would somehow restore the Union with slavery unmolested. There were large antiwar rallies against Lincoln's war for slave liberation. Race and draft riots flared in several northern cities.

With all the public unrest behind the lines, conservative Republicans beseeched Lincoln to abandon emancipation and rescue his country "from the brink of ruin." But Lincoln seemed intractable. He had made up his mind to smash the slave society of the rebel South and eliminate the moral wrong of Negro bondage, and no amount of public discontent, he indicated, was going to change his mind. He had deemed his Proclamation "an act of justice" and contended in any case that blacks who had tasted freedom would never consent to be slaves again. "To use a coarse, but an expressive figure," he wrote an aggravated Democrat, "broken eggs cannot be mended. I have issued the Proclamation, and I cannot retract it."

On Capitol Hill, the advanced Republicans were overjoyed. "He is stubborn as a mule when he gets his back up," Chandler said of Lincoln, "*& it is up* now on the Proclamation." "His mind acts slowly," said Owen Lovejoy, "but when he moves, it is *forward*."

He wavered once—in August, 1864, a time of unrelenting gloom for Lincoln, when his popularity had sunk to an all-time low and it seemed he could not be reelected. He confessed that maybe the country would no longer sustain a war for slave emancipation, that maybe he shouldn't pull the nation down a road it did not want to travel. On August 24 he decided to offer Jefferson Davis peace terms that excluded emancipation as a condition, vaguely suggesting that slavery would be adjusted later "by peaceful means." But the next day Lincoln changed his mind. With awakened resolution, he vowed to fight the war through to unconditional surrender and to stick by emancipation come what may. He had made his promise of freedom to the slaves, and he meant to keep it as long as he was in office.

When he won the election of 1864, Lincoln interpreted it as a popular mandate for him and his emancipation policy. But in reality the election provided no clear referendum on slavery, since Republican campaigners had played down emancipation and concentrated on the folly of the Democrats in running General George McClellan on a peace plank in the midst of civil war. Nevertheless, Lincoln used his reelection to promote a constitutional amendment that would guarantee the freedom of all slaves, those in the loyal border states as well as those in the rebel South. Even before issuing his Proclamation, Lincoln had worried that it might be nullified in the courts or thrown out by a later Congress or a subsequent administration. Consequently he wanted a constitutional amendment that would safeguard his Proclamation and prevent emancipation from ever being overturned.

Back in December, 1862, Lincoln himself had called on Congress to adopt an emancipation amendment, and advanced Republicans had introduced one in the Senate and guided it through, reminding their colleagues that nobody could deny that all the death and destruction of the war stemmed from slavery and that it was their duty to support this amendment. In April, 1864, the Senate adopted it by a vote of thirty-eight to six, but it failed to muster the required two-thirds majority in the House.

After that Lincoln had insisted that the Republican platform endorse the measure. And now, over the winter of 1864 and 1865, he put tremendous pressure on the House to approve the amendment, using all his powers of persuasion and patronage to get it through. He buttonholed conservative Republicans and opposition Democrats and exhorted them to support the amendment. He singled out "sinners" among the Democrats who were "on praying ground," and informed them that they had a lot better chance for the federal jobs they desired if they voted for the measure. Soon two Democrats swung over in favor of it. In the House debates, meanwhile, Republican James Ashley quoted Lincoln himself that "*if slavery is not wrong, nothing is wrong,*" and Thaddeus Stevens, still tall and imposing at seventy-two, asserted that he had never hesitated, even when threatened with violence, "to stand here and denounce this infamous institution." With the outcome much in doubt, Lincoln and congressional Republicans participated in secret negotiations never made public—negotiations that allegedly involved patronage, a New Jersey railroad monopoly, and the release of rebels related to congressional Democrats—to bring wavering opponents into line. "The greatest measure of the nineteenth century," Stevens claimed, "was passed by corruption, aided and abetted by the purest man in America."

On January 31, 1865, the House adopted the present Thirteenth Amendment by just three votes more than the required two-thirds majority. At once a storm of cheers broke over House Republicans, who danced around, embraced one another, and waved their hats and canes. "It seemed to me I had been born into a new life," recalled one advanced Republican, "and that the world was overflowing with beauty and joy."

Lincoln, too, pronounced the amendment "a great moral victory" and "a King's cure" for the evils of slavery. When ratified by the states, the amendment would end human bondage everywhere in America.* Lincoln pointed across the Potomac. "If the people over the river had behaved themselves, I could not have done what I have."

Lincoln conceded, though, that he had not controlled the events of the war, but that events had controlled him instead, that God had controlled him.

---

*The amendment was finally ratified in December, 1865. Until then, the freedom of most southern blacks rested on Lincoln's Proclamation.

He thought about this a good deal, especially at night when he couldn't sleep, trying to understand the meaning of the war, to understand why it had begun and grown into such a massive revolutionary struggle, consuming hundreds of thousands of lives (the final casualties would come to 620,000 on both sides). By his second inaugural, he had reached an apocalyptic conclusion about the nature of the war—had come to see it as divine punishment for the "great offense" of slavery, as a terrible retribution God had visited on a guilty people, in North as well as South. Lincoln's vision was close to that of old John Brown, who had prophesied on the day he was hanged, on that balmy December day back in 1859, that the crime of slavery could not be purged from this guilty land except by blood. Lincoln's vision was close to that of the deeply religious slaves, to the self-liberating forebears of historian Vincent Harding, who saw the hand of God in this terrible war and the inexorable approach of Judgment Day. Now, in his Second Inaugural Address, Lincoln too contended that God perhaps had willed this "mighty scourge of War" on the United States, "until all the wealth piled by the bondman's two hundred and fifty years of unrequited toil shall be sunk, and until every drop of blood drawn with the lash, shall be paid by another drawn from the sword."

He had come a long distance from the harassed political candidate of 1858, opposed to emancipation lest his political career be jeopardized, convinced that only the distant future could remove slavery from his troubled land, certain that only colonization could solve the ensuing problem of racial adjustment. He had also come a long way in the matter of Negro social and political rights, as we shall see. The Proclamation had indeed liberated Abraham Lincoln, enabling him to act more consistently with his moral convictions.

He had none of the racial prejudice that infected so many whites of that time, even advanced Republicans like Benjamin Wade. Frederick Douglass, who interviewed Lincoln in 1863, said he was "the first great man that I talked with in the United States freely who in no single instance reminded me of the difference between himself and myself, of the difference of color." Other blacks also testified that the President treated them as they wanted to be treated—as human beings with feelings. He did not tell dialect jokes in their presence, did not condescend to them, did not spell out his thoughts in imbecilic one-syllable language, as did many other whites when speaking to Negroes. He opened the White House doors to black visitors as no other President had ever done before and as few would do after. At his New Year's reception in 1865, he shook hands with a parade of Negro men and women, some in their Sunday finest, others in patched overalls, who had come to pay their respects to the man who signed "the Freedom bill."

During his inaugural reception that March, the President learned that Frederick Douglass was at the front door of the executive mansion, but was having trouble getting past the police because he was a Negro. Lincoln had him shown in at once, hailed him as "my friend Douglass," and asked what he thought of the Inaugural Address. "There is no man in the country whose opinion I value more than yours," Lincoln said. Douglass replied that he was impressed, that he thought it "a sacred effort." "I am glad you liked it!" Lincoln said. In truth, he strongly identified with this proud black man, referring to "the similarity with which I had fought my way up, we both starting off at the lowest round of the ladder."

Douglass, reflecting back on Lincoln's presidency, recalled how in the first year and a half of the war, Lincoln "was ready and willing" to sacrifice black people for the benefit and welfare of whites. But since the preliminary Emancipation Proclamation, Douglass said, American blacks had taken Lincoln's measure and had come to admire and some to love this complicated man. Though Lincoln had taxed Negroes to the limit, they had decided, in the roll and tumble of events, that "the how and the man of our redemption had somehow met in the person of Abraham Lincoln."

Vincent Harding

NO

The Blood-Red Ironies of God

Although the destruction of the oppressors God may not effect by the oppressed, yet the Lord our God will surely bring other destructions upon them—for not infrequently will he cause them to rise up against one another, to be split and divided, and to oppress each other, and sometimes to open hostilities with sword in hand.

— David Walker, 1829

On certain stark and bloody levels, a terrible irony seemed to be at work. For those who interpreted the events of their own times through the wisdom and anguish of the past, the guns of Charleston certainly sounded like the signal for the fulfillment of David Walker's radical prophecies. Here at last was the coming of the righteous God in judgment, preparing to bring "destructions" upon America. Here was the divine culmination of the struggle toward freedom and justice long waged by the oppressed black people. From such a vantage point, the conflict now bursting out was the ultimate justification of the costly freedom movement, a welcome vindication of the trust in Providence. And yet the war was not simply an ally. Like all wars, it brought with it a train of demoralizing, destructive elements, deeply affecting even those persons and causes which seemed to be its chief beneficiaries. In the case of black people, the guns broke in upon their freedom struggle at many levels, diverted and diffused certain of its significant radical elements, and became a source of profound confusion and disarray among its most committed forces. This was especially the case where independent radical black struggle for justice and self-determination was concerned. . . .

When the war broke out, black men and women were convinced that it had to destroy slavery. Especially in the North, this inner certainty flooded their consciousness, buoyed up their hopes. Now it appeared that God was providing a way out of the darkness of slavery and degradation, a way which would release some of the frightening tension of the previous decade. Because they wanted a way out so desperately, because it was hard to be driven by a fierce urgency, fearsome to experience the personal honing in spite of one's own softer and blunter ways, the children of Africa in America clutched at a solution which would not cause them to be driven into the depths of radicalism. For they must have realized that the chances were good that they might not survive without

From *There Is a River: The Black Struggle for Freedom in America* by Vincent Harding (Vintage Books, 1981).

being seriously, unpredictably transformed. Therefore, when the guns began, black people shunted aside the knowledge of certain fierce realities.

In that mood their men surged forward to volunteer for service in the Union cause, repressing bitter memories. In spite of their misgivings, disregarding the fact that it was not the North which had initiated this righteous war, they offered their bodies for the Northern cause, believing that it was—or would be—the cause of black freedom. If the excited, forgetful young volunteers sought justification, they could find it in the *Anglo-African:* "Talk as we may, we are concerned in this fight and our fate hangs upon its issues. The South must be subjugated, or we shall be enslaved. In aiding the Federal government in whatever way we can, we are aiding to secure our own liberty; for this war can end only in the subjugation of the North or the South." When hard pressed, the journal, like the young men it encouraged, knew very well the nature of the "liberty" they had found so far in the unsubjugated North, and the writer admitted that the North was not consciously fighting for black rights. However, the *Anglo-African* chose to see a power beyond the councils of the North: "Circumstances have been so arranged by the decrees of Providence, that in struggling for their own nationality they are forced to defend our rights." . . .

And what of the South? What of those sometimes God-obsessed black believers who had long lifted their cries for deliverance in songs and shouts, in poetry filled with rich and vibrant images? Did they sense the coming of Moses now? Was this finally the day of the delivering God, when he would set his people free? Did they hear Nat Turner's spirit speaking in the guns? Did they believe he was calling them to freedom through all the lines of skirmishers who left their blood upon the leaves? Did they have any difficulty knowing which of the white armies was Pharaoh's?

The answers were as complex as life itself. In many parts of the nation and the world there had been predictions that secession, disunion, and war would lead to a massive black insurrection which would finally vindicate Turner and Walker, and drown the South in blood. Such predictions were made without knowledge of the profound racism and fear which pervaded the white North, and certainly without awareness of the keen perceptions of black people in the South. For most of the enslaved people knew their oppressors, and certainly realized that such a black uprising would expose the presence of Pharaoh's armies everywhere. To choose that path to freedom would surely unite the white North and South more quickly than any other single development, making black men, women, and children the enemy—the isolated, unprepared enemy. For anyone who needed concrete evidence, Gen. George B. McClellan, the commander of the Union's Army of the Ohio, had supplied it in his "Proclamation to the people of Western Virginia" on May 26, 1861: "Not only will we abstain from all interferences with your slaves, but we will, with an iron hand, crush any attempt at insurrection on their part."

So, heeding their own intuitive political wisdom, the black masses confirmed in their actions certain words which had recently appeared in the *Anglo-African.* Thomas Hamilton, the editor, had heard of Lincoln's decision to countermand an emancipation order issued by one of his most fervent Republican generals, John C. Fremont, in Missouri. Hamilton predicted: "The forlorn hope of insurrection among the slaves may as well be abandoned. They are too well informed and too *wise* to court destruction at the hands of the combined Northern and Southern armies—for the man who had reduced back to slavery the slaves of rebels in Missouri would order the army of the United States to put down a slave insurrection in Virginia or Georgia." He was right, of course, and the enslaved population was also right. Therefore, instead of mass insurrection, the Civil War created the context for a vast broadening and intensifying of the self-liberating black movement which had developed prior to the war. Central to this black freedom action, as always, was the continuing series of breaks with the system of slavery, the denials of the system's power, the self-emancipation of steadily increasing thousands of fugitives. Thus, wherever possible, black people avoided the deadly prospects of massive, sustained confrontation, for their ultimate objective was freedom, not martyrdom.

As the guns resounded across the Southern lands, the movement of black folk out of slavery began to build. Quickly it approached and surpassed every level of force previously known. Eventually the flood of fugitives amazed all observers and dismayed not a few, as it sent waves of men, women, and children rushing into the camps of the Northern armies. In this overwhelming human movement, black people of the South offered their own responses to the war, to its conundrums and mysteries. Their action testified to their belief that deliverance was indeed coming through the war, but for thousands of them it was not a deliverance to be bestowed by others. Rather it was to be independently seized and transformed through all the courage, wisdom, and strength of their waiting black lives.

This rapidly increasing movement of black runaways had been noted as soon as the reality of Southern secession had been clearly established. Shortly after the guns of April began to sound in Charleston harbor, large companies of fugitives broke loose from Virginia and the Carolinas and moved toward Richmond. Again, one day in Virginia in the spring of 1861, a black fugitive appeared at the Union-held Fortress Monroe. Two days later eight more arrived, the next day more than fifty, soon hundreds. The word spread throughout the area: there was a "freedom fort," as the fugitives called it, and within a short time thousands were flooding toward it. Similarly, in Louisiana two families waded six miles across a swamp, "spending two days and nights in mud and water to their waists, their children clinging to their backs, and with nothing to eat." In Georgia, a woman with her twenty-two children and grandchildren floated down the river on "a dilapidated flatboat" until she made contact with the Union armies. In South Carolina, black folk floated to freedom on "basket boats made out of reeds," thus reviving an ancient African craft. A contemporary source said of the black surge toward freedom in those first two years of the war: "Many thousands of blacks of all ages, ragged, with no possessions, except the bundles which they carried, had assembled at Norfolk, Hampton, Alexandria and Washington. Others . . . in multitudes . . . flocked north from Tennessee, Kentucky, Arkansas, and Missouri."

This was black struggle in the South as the guns roared, coming out of loyal and disloyal states, creating their own liberty. This was the black movement toward a new history, a new life, a new beginning. W. E. B. Du Bois later said,

"The whole move was not dramatic or hysterical, rather it was like the great unbroken swell of the ocean before it dashes on the reefs." Yet there was great drama as that flowing movement of courageous black men and women and children sensed the movement of history, heard the voice of God, created and signed their own emancipation proclamations, and seized the time. Their God was moving and they moved with him.

And wherever this moving army of self-free men and women and children went, wherever they stopped to wait and rest and eat and work, and watch the movement of the armies in the fields and forests—in all these unlikely sanctuaries, they sent up their poetry of freedom. Some of them were old songs, taking on new meaning:

> Thus said the Lord, Bold Moses said
> Let my people go
> If not I'll smite your first-born dead
> Let my people go.
> No more shall they in bondage toil
> Let my people go.

But now there was no need to hide behind the stories of thousands of years gone by, now it was clearly a song of black struggle, of deliverance for their own time of need. Now the singers themselves understood more fully what they meant when they sang again:

> One of dese mornings, five o'clock
> Dis ole world gonna reel and rock,
> Pharaoh's Army got drownded
> Oh, Mary, don't you weep.

They were part of the drowning river. Out there, overlooking the battlefields of the South, they were the witnesses to the terrible truth of their own sons, to the this-worldliness of their prayers and aspirations. Remembering that morning in Charleston harbor, who could say they were wrong? "Dis ole world gonna reel and rock . . ."

Every day they came into the Northern lines, in every condition, in every season of the year, in every state of health. Children came wandering, set in the right direction by falling, dying parents who finally knew why they had lived until then. Women came, stumbling and screaming, their wombs bursting with the promise of new and free black life. Old folks who had lost all track of their age, who knew only that they had once heard of a war against "the Redcoats," also came, some blind, some deaf, yet no less eager to taste a bit of that long-anticipated freedom of their dreams. No more auction block, no more driver's lash, many thousands gone.

This was the river of black struggle in the South, waiting for no one to declare freedom for them, hearing only the declarations of God in the sound of the guns, and moving.

By land, by river, creating their own pilgrim armies and their own modes of travel, they moved south as well as north, heading down to the captured areas of the coast of South Carolina. *Frederick Douglass's Monthly* of February 1862 quoted the report of a *New York Times* correspondent in Port Royal: "Everywhere I find the same state of things existing; everywhere the blacks hurry in droves to our lines; they crowd in small boats around our ships; they swarm upon our decks; they hurry to our officers from the cotton houses of their masters, in an hour or two after our guns are fired. . . . I mean each statement I make to be taken literally; it is not garnished for rhetorical effect." As usual, black people were prepared to take advantage of every disruption in the life of the oppressing white community. When they heard the guns, they were ready, grasping freedom with their own hands, walking to it, swimming to it, sailing to it—determined that it should be theirs. By all these ways, defying masters, patrols, Confederate soldiers, slowly, surely, they pressed themselves into the central reality of the war.

. . . By the end of the spring of 1862, tens of thousands [of self-liberated fugitives] were camped out in whatever areas the Northern armies had occupied, thereby making themselves an unavoidable military and political issue. In Washington, D.C., the commander-in-chief of the Union armies had developed no serious plans for the channeling of the black river. Consequently, in the confusion which all war engenders, his generals in the field made and carried out their own plans. They were badly strapped for manpower, and the black fugitives provided some answers to whatever prayers generals pray. The blacks could relieve white fighting men from garrison duties. They could serve as spies, scouts, and couriers in the countryside they knew so well. They could work the familiar land, growing crops for the food and profit of the Union armies. But as the war dragged on and Northern whites lost some of their early enthusiasm, many Union commanders saw the black men among them primarily as potential soldiers. Many of the black men were eager to fight, but Lincoln was still not prepared to go that far.

Nevertheless, some Union commanders like Gen. David Hunter in South Carolina were again issuing their own emancipation proclamations and beginning to recruit black soldiers. In places like occupied New Orleans it was the unmanageable and threatening movement of the blacks themselves which placed additional pressures on the Union's leader. Reports were pouring into Washington which told not only of the flood of fugitives, but of black unrest everywhere. Black men were literally fighting their way past the local police forces to get themselves and their families into the Union encampments. There was word of agricultural workers killing or otherwise getting rid of their overseers, and taking over entire plantations. Commanders like Gen. Ben Butler warned that only Union bayonets prevented widespread black insurrection. (In August 1862, to preserve order and satisfy his need for manpower, Butler himself had begun to recruit black troups in New Orleans, beginning with the well-known Louisiana Native Guards.) The dark presence at the center of the national conflict could no longer be denied. Lincoln's armies were in the midst of a surging movement of black people who were in effect freeing themselves from slavery. His generals were at once desperate for the military resources represented by the so-called contrabands, and convinced that only through military discipline could this volatile, potentially revolutionary black element be contained. As a result, before 1862 was over, black troops were being enlisted to fight for their own freedom in both South Carolina and Louisiana.

In Washington, Congress was discussing its own plans for emancipation, primarily as a weapon against the South, hoping to deprive the Confederacy of a major source of human power and transfer it into Union hands. Their debates and imminent action represented another critical focus of pressure on the President. While Lincoln continued to hesitate about the legal, constitutional, moral, and military aspects of the matter, he was also being constantly attacked in the North for his conduct of the war. The whites were weary and wanted far better news from the fronts. The blacks were angry about his continued refusal to speak clearly to the issue of their people's freedom and the black right to military service. In the summer of 1862 Frederick Douglass declared in his newspaper: "Abraham Lincoln is no more fit for the place he holds than was James Buchanan. . . . The country is destined to become sick of both [Gen. George B.] McClellan and Lincoln, and the sooner the better. The one plays lawyer for the benefit of the rebels, and the other handles the army for the benefit of the traitors. We should not be surprised if both should be hurled from their places before this rebellion is ended. . . . The signs of the times indicate that the people will have to take this war into their own hands." But Frederick Douglass was not one to dwell on such revolutionary options. (Besides, had he considered what would happen to the black cause, if the white "people" really did take the war into their own hands?) Fortunately, by the time Douglass's words were published, he had seen new and far more hopeful signs of the times.

In September 1862 Abraham Lincoln, in a double-minded attempt both to bargain with and weaken the South while replying to the pressures of the North, finally made public his proposed Emancipation Proclamation. Under its ambiguous terms, the states in rebellion would be given until the close of the year to end their rebellious action. If any did so, their captive black people would not be affected; otherwise, the Emancipation Proclamation would go into effect on January 1, 1863, theoretically freeing all the enslaved population of the Confederate states and promising federal power to maintain that freedom.

What actually was involved was quite another matter. Of great import was the fact that the proclamation excluded from its provisions the "loyal" slave states of Missouri, Kentucky, Delaware, and Maryland, the anti-Confederate West Virginia Territory, and loyal areas in certain other Confederate states. Legally, then, nearly one million black people whose masters were "loyal" to the Union had no part of the emancipation offered. In effect, Lincoln was announcing freedom to the captives over whom he had least control, while allowing those in states clearly under the rule of his government to remain in slavery. However, on another more legalistic level, Lincoln was justifying his armies' use of the Confederates' black "property," and preparing the way for an even more extensive use of black power by the military forces of the

Union. Here, the logic of his move was clear, providing an executive confirmation and extension of Congress's Second Confiscation Act of 1862: once the Emancipation Proclamation went into effect, the tens of thousands of black people who were creating their own freedom, and making themselves available as workers in the Union camps, could be used by the North without legal qualms. Technically, they would no longer be private property, no longer cause problems for a President concerned about property rights.

It was indeed a strange vessel that the Lord had chosen, but black folk in the South were not waiting on such legal niceties. Not long after the preliminary proclamation, an insurrectionary plot was uncovered among a group of blacks in Culpepper County, Virginia. Some were slaves and some free, and the message of their action carried a special resonance for South and North alike, and perhaps for the President himself. For a copy of Lincoln's preliminary proclamation was reportedly found among the possessions of one of the conspirators. Though at least seventeen of the group were executed, their death could not expunge the fact that they had attempted to seize the time, to wrest their emancipation out of the hands of an uncertain President. On Nat's old "gaining ground" they had perhaps heard the voice of his God and, forming their own small army, were once again searching for Jerusalem.

Such action symbolized a major difference in the movement of the Southern and Northern branches of the struggle. In the South, though most of the self-liberating black people eventually entered the camps, or came otherwise under the aegis of the Northern armies, they were undoubtedly acting on significant, independent initiatives. During the first years of the war, the mainstream of the struggle in the South continued to bear this independent, self-authenticating character, refusing to wait for an official emancipation.

In such settings black hope blossomed, fed by its own activity. Even in the ambiguous context of the contraband communities the signs were there. In 1862–63, in Corinth, Mississippi, newly free blacks in one of the best of the contraband camps organized themselves under federal oversight, and created the beginnings of an impressive, cohesive community of work, education, family life, and worship. They built their own modest homes, planted and grew their crops (creating thousands of dollars of profit for the Union), supported their own schools, and eventually developed their own military company to fight with the Union armies. It was not surprising, then, that black fugitives flocked there from as far away as Georgia. Nor was it unexpected that, in 1863, federal military plans demanded the dismantling of the model facility. Nevertheless, the self-reliant black thrust toward the future had been initiated, and Corinth was only one among many hopeful contraband communities.

Such movement, and the vision which impelled it, were integral aspects of the freedom struggle in the South. Meanwhile, to aid that struggle, by 1863 Harriet Tubman had entered the South Carolina war zone. Working on behalf of the Union forces, she organized a corps of black contrabands and traveled with them through the countryside to collect information for army raids, and to urge the still-enslaved blacks to leave their masters. Apparently the intrepid leader and her scouts were successful at both tasks, though Tubman complained that her long dresses sometimes impeded her radical activities.

In the North the situation was somewhat different. Word of Lincoln's anticipated proclamation had an electrifying effect on the black community there, but at the same time further removed the focus from the black freedom-seizing movement in the South. The promised proclamation now gave the Northerners more reason than ever to look to others for release, to invest their hope in the Union cause. Now it seemed as if they would not need to be isolated opponents of an antagonistic federal government. Again, because they wanted to believe, needed to hope, yearned to prove themselves worthy, they thought they saw ever more clearly the glory of the coming; before long, in their eyes the proclamation was clothed in what appeared to be almost angelic light. As such, it became an essentially religious rallying point for the development of a new, confusing mainstream struggle: one which, nervous and excited, approached and embraced the central government and the Republican Party as agents of deliverance. Doubts from the past were now cast aside, for their struggle was unquestionably in the hands of Providence and the Grand Army of the Republic. The voice of God was joined to that of Abraham Lincoln.

. . . [F]rom a certain legal point of view it could be argued that the Emancipation Proclamation set free no enslaved black people at all. Since by December 31, 1862, no Confederate state had accepted Lincoln's invitation to return to the fold with their slaves unthreatened, and since Lincoln acknowledged that he had no real way of enforcing such a proclamation within the rebellious states, the proclamation's power to set anyone free was dubious at best. (Rather, it confirmed and gave ambiguous legal standing to the freedom which black people had already claimed through their own surging, living proclamations.)

Indeed, in his annual address to Congress on December 1, 1862, Lincoln had not seemed primarily concerned with the proclamation. Instead, he had taken that crucial opportunity to propose three constitutional amendments which reaffirmed his long-standing approach to national slavery. The proposed amendments included provisions for gradual emancipation (with a deadline as late as 1900), financial compensation to the owners, and colonization for the freed people. In other words, given the opportunity to place his impending proclamation of limited, immediate emancipation into the firmer context of a constitutional amendment demanding freedom for all enslaved blacks, Lincoln chose another path, one far more in keeping with his own history.

But none of this could dampen the joy of the black North. Within that community, it was the Emancipation Proclamation of January 1, 1863, which especially symbolized all that the people so deeply longed to experience, and its formal announcement sent a storm of long-pent-up emotion surging through the churches and meeting halls. It was almost as if the Northern and Southern struggles had again been joined, this time not through wilderness flights, armed resistance, and civil disobedience, but by a nationwide, centuries-long cord of boundless ecstasy. In spite of its limitations, the proclamation was taken as the greatest sign yet provided by the hand of Providence. The river had burst its boundaries, had shattered slavery's dam. It appeared as if the theodicy of the Northern black experience was finally prevailing. For the freedom struggle, especially in the South, had begun to overwhelm the white man's war, and had forced the President and the nation officially to turn their faces toward the moving black masses. Wherever black people could assemble, by themselves or with whites, they came together to lift joyful voices of thanksgiving, to sing songs of faith, to proclaim, "Jehovah hath triumphed, his people are free." For them, a new year and a new era had been joined in one.

On the evening of December 31, 1862, Frederick Douglass was in Boston attending one of the hundreds of freedom-watch-night services being held across the North in anticipation of the proclamation. That night, a line of messengers had been set up between the telegraph office and the platform of the Tremont Temple, where the Boston meeting was being held. After waiting more than two hours in agonized hope, the crowd was finally rewarded as word of the official proclamation reached them. Douglass said: "The effect of this announcement was startling beyond description, and the scene was wild and grand. Joy and gladness exhausted all forms of expression, from shouts of praise to sobs and tears . . . a Negro preacher, a man of wonderful vocal power, expressed the heartfelt emotion of the hour, when he led all voices in the anthem, 'Sound the loud timbrel o'er Egypt's dark sea, Jehovah hath triumphed, his people are free.'"

Such rapture was understandable, but like all ecstatic experiences, it carried its own enigmatic penalties. Out of it was born the mythology of Abraham Lincoln as Emancipator, a myth less important in its detail than in its larger meaning and consequences for black struggle. The heart of the matter was this: while the concrete historical realities of the time testified to the costly, daring, courageous activities of hundreds of thousands of black people breaking loose from slavery and setting themselves free, the myth gave the credit for this freedom to a white Republican president. In those same times when black men and women saw visions of a new society of equals, and heard voices pressing them against the American Union of white supremacy, Abraham Lincoln was unable to see beyond the limits of his own race, class, and time, and dreamed of a Haitian island and of Central American colonies to rid the country of the constantly accusing, constantly challenging black presence. Yet in the mythology of blacks and whites alike, it was the independent, radical action of the black movement toward freedom which was diminished, and the coerced, ambiguous role of a white deliverer which gained pre-eminence.

POSTSCRIPT

Did Abraham Lincoln Free the Slaves?

Abraham Lincoln's reputation as "the Great Emancipator" traditionally has been based upon his decision in 1862 to issue the Emancipation Proclamation. Although Harding stresses that Lincoln was forced to act by the large number of slaves who already had engaged in a process of self-liberation, he and other scholars point out the limited impact of Lincoln's emancipation policy. Announced in September of 1862, the measure would not go into effect until January 1, 1863, and it would apply only to those slave states still in rebellion against the Union. In other words, emancipation would become law in states where the federal government was in no position to enforce the measure. Also, the status of slaves residing in states that had not seceded (Missouri, Kentucky, Maryland, and Delaware) would not be altered by this fiat. Theoretically, then, the Proclamation would have few benefits for those held in bondage in the Confederacy.

Critics of Lincoln's gradualist approach to ending slavery in particular and to the rights of African Americans, slave and free, in general also cite a number of other examples that draw Lincoln's commitment to freedom into question. During the presidential election campaign of 1860, candidate Lincoln had insisted that he had no desire to abolish slavery where the institution already existed. There was, of course, the president's statement that he would be willing to keep slavery intact if that was the best means of preserving the Union. His alternative claim that he would be willing to free all the slaves to maintain the sanctity of the Union appeared as just so much rhetoric when compared to his policies as president. For example, Lincoln initially opposed arming black citizens for military service, he countermanded several of his field generals' emancipation orders, and he consistently expressed doubts that blacks and whites would be able to live in the United States as equal citizens. Then, in December 1862, between his announcement of the preliminary emancipation proclamation and the time that the order was to go into effect, the president proposed a constitutional amendment that would provide for gradual emancipation, with compensation to the slave owners followed by colonization of the liberated blacks to a site outside the boundaries of the United States.

In assessing Lincoln's racial attitudes and policies, care should be taken not to read this historical record solely from a twenty-first century perspective. Lincoln may not have been the embodiment of the unblemished racial egalitarian that some might hope for, but few whites were, including most of the abolitionists. Still, as historian Benjamin Quarles has written, Lincoln "treated Negroes as they wanted to be treated—as human beings." Unlike most white Americans of his day, Lincoln opposed slavery, developed a policy that held out hope for emancipation, and supported the Thirteenth Amendment.

Lincoln is the most written-about president. Students should consult Carl Sandburg, *Abraham Lincoln*, 6 vols. (Harcourt, Brace & World, 1926–1939), a poetic panorama that focuses upon the mythic Lincoln. Benjamin Thomas, *Abraham Lincoln: A Biography* (Alfred A. Knopf, 1952); Stephen B. Oates, *With Malice Toward None: The Life of Abraham Lincoln* (Harper & Row, 1977); Philip Shaw Paludan, *The Presidency of Abraham Lincoln* (University Press of Kansas, 1994); and David Donald, *Lincoln* (1995) are excellent one-volume biographies. David Donald, *Lincoln Reconsidered: Essays on the Civil War Era* (Alfred A. Knopf, 1956) and Richard N. Current, *The Lincoln Nobody Knows* (McGraw-Hill, 1958) offer incisive interpretations of many aspects of Lincoln's political career and philosophy. George B. Forgie, in *Patricide in the House Divided: A Psychological Interpretation* (W. W. Norton, 1979), and Dwight G. Anderson, in *Abraham Lincoln: The Quest for Immortality* (Alfred A. Knopf, 1982), offer psychoanalytical approaches to Lincoln. Lincoln's responsibility for the precipitating event of the Civil War is explored in Richard N. Current, *Lincoln and the First Shot* (Lippincott, 1963). T. Harry Williams, in *Lincoln and His Generals* (Alfred A. Knopf, 1952), looks at Lincoln as commander-in-chief and remains one of the best Lincoln studies. *The Historian's Lincoln: Pseudohistory, Psychohistory, and History,* edited by Gabor S. Boritt (University of Illinois Press, 1988), is a valuable collection. For Lincoln's role as "the Great Emancipator" and his attitudes toward race and slavery, see Benjamin Quarles, *Lincoln and the Negro* (Oxford University Press, 1962); James M. McPherson, *Abraham Lincoln and the Second American Revolution* (Oxford University Press, 1990); and Mark E. Neely, Jr., *The Fate of Liberty: Abraham Lincoln and Civil Liberties* (Oxford University Press, 1991). John Hope Franklin, *The Emancipation Proclamation* (Anchor, 1965) and Allen C. Guelzo, *Lincoln's Emancipation Proclamation: The End of Slavery in America* (Simon & Schuster, 2004) view Lincoln's policy from different perspectives and with different conclusions.

In addition to the work of Vincent Harding, the self-emancipation thesis is developed in Ira Berlin, Barbara J. Fields, Thavolia Glymph, Joseph P. Reidy, and Leslie S. Rowland, eds., *Freedom: A Documentary History of Emancipation, 1861–1867*, 4 vols. (Cambridge University Press, 1982–1993). Lerone Bennett's *Forced Into Glory: Abraham Lincoln's White Dream* (Johnson Publishing Company, 2000) is highly critical of Lincoln's racial attitudes and commitment to emancipation. The role of African Americans in the Civil War is the subject of James McPherson, ed., *The Negro's Civil War* (Pantheon, 1965). Black military experience is treated in Benjamin Quarles, *The Negro in the Civil War* (Little, Brown, 1969); Dudley Cornish, *The Sable Arm: Black Troops in the Union Army, 1861–1865* (Longmans, 1956); Joseph Glatthaar, *Forged in Battle: The Civil War Alliance of Black Soldiers and White Officers* (Free Press, 1990); Ervin L. Jordan, Jr., *Black Confederates and Afro-Yankees in Civil War Virginia* (University Press of Virginia, 1995); and James G. Hollandsworth, Jr., *The Louisiana Native Guards: The Black Military Experience During the Civil War* (Louisiana State University Press, 1995).

ISSUE 16

Did Reconstruction Fail as a Result of Racism?

YES: George M. Fredrickson, from *The Black Image in the White Mind: The Debate on Afro-American Character and Destiny, 1817-1914* (Harper & Row, 1971)

NO: Heather Cox Richardson, from *The Death of Reconstruction: Race, Labor, and Politics in the Post-Civil War North, 1865-1901* (Harvard University Press, 2001)

ISSUE SUMMARY

YES: George M. Fredrickson concludes that racism, in the form of the doctrine of white supremacy, colored the thinking not only of southern whites but of most white northerners as well and produced only half-hearted efforts by the Radical Republicans in the postwar period to sustain a commitment to black equality.

NO: Heather Cox Richardson argues that the failure of Radical Reconstruction was primarily a consequence of a national commitment to a free-labor ideology that opposed an expanding central government that legislated rights to African Americans that other citizens had acquired through hard work.

Given the complex issues of the post-Civil War years, it is not surprising that the era of Reconstruction (1865–1877) is shrouded in controversy. For the better part of a century following the war, historians typically characterized Reconstruction as a total failure that had proved detrimental to all Americans—northerners and southerners, whites and blacks. According to this traditional interpretation, a vengeful Congress, dominated by radical Republicans, imposed military rule upon the southern states. Carpetbaggers from the North, along with traitorous white scalawags and their black accomplices in the South, established coalition governments that rewrote state constitutions, raised taxes, looted state treasuries, and disenfranchised former Confederates while extending the ballot to the freedmen. This era finally ended in 1877 when courageous southern white Democrats successfully "redeemed" their region from "Negro rule" by toppling the Republican state governments.

This portrait of Reconstruction dominated the historical profession until the 1960s. One reason for this is that white historians (both northerners and southerners) who wrote about this period operated from two basic assumptions:

(1) the South was capable of solving its own problems without federal government interference; and (2) the former slaves were intellectually inferior to whites and incapable of running a government (much less one in which some whites would be their subordinates). African American historians, such as W. E. B. DuBois, wrote several essays and books that challenged this negative portrayal of Reconstruction, but their works seldom were taken seriously in the academic world and rarely were read by the general public. Still, these black historians foreshadowed the acceptance of revisionist interpretations of Reconstruction, which coincided with the successes of the civil rights movement (or "Second Reconstruction") in the 1960s.

Without ignoring obvious problems and limitations connected with this period, revisionist historians identified a number of accomplishments of the Republican state governments in the South and their supporters in Washington, D.C. For example, revisionists argued that the state constitutions that were written during Reconstruction were the most democratic documents that the South had seen up to that time. Also, while taxes increased in the southern states, the revenues generated by these levies financed the rebuilding and expansion of the South's railroad network, the creation of a number of social service institutions, and the establishment of a public school system that benefited African Americans as well as whites. At the federal level, Reconstruction achieved the ratification of the Fourteenth and Fifteenth Amendments, which extended significant privileges of citizenship (including the right to vote) to African Americans, both North and South. Revisionists also placed the charges of corruption leveled by traditionalists against the Republican regimes in the South in a more appropriate context by insisting that political corruption was a *national* malady. Although the leaders of the Republican state governments in the South engaged in a number of corrupt activities, they were no more guilty than several federal officeholders in the Grant administration, or the members of New York City's notorious Tweed Ring (a Democratic urban political machine), or even the southern white Democrats (the Redeemers) who replaced the radical Republicans in positions of power in the former Confederate states. Finally, revisionist historians sharply attacked the notion that African Americans dominated the reconstructed governments of the South.

In the essays that follow, George M. Fredrickson and Heather Cox Richardson present thought-provoking analyses of the influence racism played in the failure of Reconstruction. In the first selection, Fredrickson contends that the doctrine of white supremacy that galvanized southern opposition to the political, economic, and social empowerment of African Americans after the war also dominated the thinking of white northerners, including many Radical Republicans. As a consequence, racism prevented the success of efforts to incorporate African Americans fully into American society on an equitable basis.

Heather Cox Richardson offers a post-revisionist interpretation of the failure of Reconstruction and contends that the key barrier to postwar assistance for African Americans was the nation's commitment to a free-labor ideology. Believing that social equality derived from economic success, most Americans opposed legislation, such as the Civil Rights Act of 1875, which appeared to provide special interest legislation solely for the benefit of the former slaves.

YES 

George M. Fredrickson

The Black Image in the White Mind: The Debate on Afro-American Character and Destiny, 1817–1914

Race and Reconstruction

Once freed, the black population of the South constituted a new element that had to be incorporated somehow into the American social and political structure, Some Radical Republicans and veterans of the antislavery crusade regarded justice and equality for the freedmen as a fulfillment of national ideals and a desirable end in itself. For a larger number of loyal Northerners the question of Negro rights was, from first to last, clearly subordinate to the more fundamental aim of ensuring national hegemony for Northern political, social, and economic institutions. But even those who lacked an ideological commitment to black equality could not avoid the necessity of shaping a new status for the Southern blacks; for there they were in large numbers, capable of being either a help or a hindrance to the North's effort to restore the Union and secure the fruits of victory.

Before 1863 and 1864, Northern leaders had been able to discuss with full seriousness the possibility of abolishing slavery while at the same time avoiding the perplexing and politically dangerous task of incorporating the freed blacks into the life of the nation. President Lincoln and other moderate or conservative Republicans, feeling the pulse of a racist public opinion, had looked to the reduction or elimination of the black population through colonization or emigration as a way of approaching the racial homogeneity which they associated with guaranteed national unity and progress. By itself the Emancipation Proclamation had not destroyed such hopes, but events soon made the colonization schemes irrelevant and inappropriate. . . .

Whatever the motivation of Radical Reconstruction and however inadequate its programs, it was a serious effort, the first in American history, to incorporate Negroes into the body politic. As such, it inevitably called forth bitter opposition from hardcore racists, who attempted to discredit radical measures by using many of the same arguments developed as part of the proslavery argument in the prewar period.

The new cause was defined as "white supremacy"—which in practice allowed Southern whites to reduce the freedmen to an inferior caste, as they had attempted to do by enacting the "Black Codes" of 1865. To further this cause in 1868, [John] Van Evrie simply reissued his book *Negroes and Negro "Slavery"* with a topical introduction and under the new title *White Supremacy and Negro Subordination.* [Josiah] Nott also entered the Reconstruction controversy. In an 1866 pamphlet he reasserted the "scientific" case for inherent black inferiority as part of an attack on the Freedmen's Bureau and other Northern efforts to deal with the Southern race question. "If the whites and blacks be left alone face to face," he wrote, "they will soon learn to understand each other, and come to proper terms under the law of necessity."

Edward A. Pollard, a Richmond journalist and prewar fire-eater, also attacked Northern Reconstruction proposals on racial grounds. His book *The Lost Cause Regained,* published in 1868, contended that "the permanent, natural inferiority of the Negro was the true and *only* defense of slavery" and lamented the fact that the South had wasted its intellectual energy on other arguments. Before the war, Pollard had advocated a revival of the slave trade because it would deflate the pretensions of uppity house servants and town Negroes by submerging them in a flood of humble primitives; he now endorsed Van Evrie's thesis that white democracy depended on absolute black subordination, and concluded his discussion of Negro racial characteristics by asserting that the established "fact" of inferiority dictated "the true *status* of the Negro." Other propagandists of white supremacy, North and South, joined the fray. A writer named Lindley Spring attacked Radical Reconstruction in 1868 with a lengthy discourse on the benighted and savage record of blacks in Africa; and a Dr. J. R. Hayes excoriated the proposed Fifteenth Amendment in 1869 with a rehash of all the biological "evidence" for Negro incapacity.

Inevitably, the pre-Adamite theory of Dr. Samuel A. Cartwright and Jefferson Davis was trotted out. In 1866 Governor Benjamin F. Perry of South Carolina made it the basis of a defense of white supremacy; and in 1867 a Nashville publisher named Buckner Payne, writing under the pseudonym "Ariel," revived a controversy among racists by expounding the doctrine at some length in a pamphlet entitled *The Negro: What Is His Ethnological Status?* Payne not only asserted that the Negro was "created before Adam and Eve" as "a *separate* and *distinct* species of the *genus homo,*" but also argued that it was because some of the sons of Adam intermarried with this inferior species, related, as it was, to the "higher orders of the monkey," that God had sent the flood as a punishment for human wrongdoing. Like almost all the racist respondents to Reconstruction, he contended that Negro equality would lead inevitably to amalgamation, and that miscegenation, in addition to resulting in the debasement of the white race, would bring on catastrophic divine intervention: "The states and people that favor this equality and amalgamation of the white and black races, *God will exterminate.* . . . A man can not commit so great an offense against his race, against his country, against his God, . . . as to give his daughter in marriage to a negro—a *beast.* . . ."

Most of the propagandists who attacked Radical measures on extreme racist grounds had a prewar record as apologists for slavery, but Hinton Rowan Helper attracted the greatest attention because of his fame or notoriety as an antebellum critic of slavery, As we have seen, Helper had never concealed his anti-Negro sentiments. A letter of 1861 summed up his philosophy: "A trio of unmitigated and demoralizing nuisances, constituting in the aggregate, a most foul and formidable obstacle to our high and mighty civilization in America are Negroes, Slavery, and Slaveholders. . . .

> Death to Slavery!
> Down with the Slaveholders!
> Away with the Negroes!"

Having done justice to the first two imperatives in *The Impending Crisis,* Helper turned after the war to the third. His *Nojoque,* published in 1867, may have been the most virulent racist diatribe ever published in the United States. It contemplated with relish the time when "the negroes, and all the other swarthy races of mankind," have been "completely fossilized." To speed up the divinely ordained process of racial extermination, Helper proposed as immediate steps the denial of all rights to Negroes and their complete separation from the whites. All this of course went in the teeth of the emerging Reconstruction policies of what had been Helper's own party, and throughout the book he excoriated "the Black Republicans" for departing from the attitudes of the prewar period, a time when Republicans had billed themselves as "the white man's party." His heroes were "White Republicans" like Secretary of State Seward and those few Republicans in the House and Senate who had remained loyal to President Johnson and joined the Democrats in efforts to prevent Federal action on behalf of Negro equality.

The active politicians—mostly Democrats—who opposed Radical Reconstruction were quite willing to resort to racist demagoguery, although they generally avoided the excesses of polemicists like Payne and Helper. President Johnson, for example, played subtly but unmistakably on racial fears in his veto messages of 1866; and later, in his third annual message to Congress, he put his views squarely on the line: ". . . it must be acknowledged that in the progress of nations negroes have shown less capacity for self-government than any other race of people. No independent government of any form has ever been successful in their hands. On the contrary whenever they have been left to their own devices they have shown an instant tendency to relapse into barbarism. . . . The great difference between the two races in physical, mental, and moral characteristics will prevent an amalgamation or fusion of them together in one homogeneous mass. . . . Of all the dangers which our nation has yet encountered, none are equal to those which must result from the success of the effort now making to Africanize the [Southern] half of our country." Equally blatant were the Northern Democratic Congressmen who made speeches against Radical measures which appealed directly to the prejudices of white workingmen. As Representative John W. Chanler of New York put it, in attacking an 1866 proposal to give the vote to Negroes in the District of Columbia: "White democracy makes war on every class, caste, and race which assails its sovereignty or would undermine the mastery of the white working man, be he ignorant or learned, strong or weak. Black democracy does not exist. The black race have never asserted and maintained their inalienable right to be a people, anywhere, or at any time."

In addition to such crude appeals to "white democracy," Democratic spokesmen in Congress provided detailed and pretentious discourses on the "ethnological" status of the Negro, drawn from writers like Nott and Van Evrie. The most notable of such efforts was the speech Representative James Brooks of New York delivered on December 18, 1867, in opposition to the First Reconstruction Act. "You have deliberately framed a bill," he accused the Radicals, "to overthrow this white man's government of our fathers and to erect an African Government in its stead. . . . The negro is not the equal of the white man, much less his master; and this I can demonstrate anatomically, physiologically and psychologically too, if necessary. Volumes of scientific authority establish the fact. . . ." Brooks then proceeded "in the fewest words possible to set forth scientific facts." He discoursed at length on "the hair or wool of the negro," on "the skull, the brain, the neck, the foot, etc.," and on the perils of miscegenation. In considering the last topic, he conceded that "the mulatto with white blood in his veins often has the intelligence and capacity of a white man," but added that he could not consent to suffrage for mulattoes because to do so would violate the divine decree "that all are to be punished who indulge in a criminal admixture of races, so that beyond the third or fourth generation there could be no further mulatto progeny." Having covered black and brown physiology, Brooks went on in standard racist fashion to portray Negro history as a great emptiness.

In general such anti-Negro arguments were simply ignored by the proponents of Radical Reconstruction, who, by and large, tried to avoid the whole question of basic racial characteristics. But Brook's speech, perhaps the most thorough presentation of the racist creed ever offered in Congress, could not go unanswered. In a brief reply, Thaddeus Stevens dismissed Brook's views as contradicting the Biblical doctrine of the unity of mankind. Resorting to sarcasm and impugning Brook's loyalty, Stevens agreed that Negroes were indeed "barbarians," because they had "with their own right hands, in defense of liberty, stricken down thousands of the friends of the gentleman who has been enlightening us today." Disregarding Brooks's point about the "intelligence and capacity of mulattoes," Stevens proposed to match Frederick Douglass against Brooks in an oratorical contest. A more serious and extended reply to Brooks was made from the Republican side of the aisle by John D. Baldwin of Massachusetts. Baldwin's speech is significant because it clearly reveals both the strengths and weaknesses of the Radical position on race as a factor in Reconstruction.

In the first place, Baldwin contended, Brooks's argument was largely a *non sequitur;* for "the question presented in these discussions is not a question concerning the equality or the inequality of human races . . . it is a question concerning human rights. It calls on us to decide whether men shall be equal before the law and have equality in their relations to the Government of their country." Races, like individuals, might indeed differ in their capacities, but this should not affect their fundamental rights. In reply to Brooks's claim that miscegenation would result from equality, Baldwin suggested that it was much more likely to result from degradation such as had occurred under slavery, a system which provided a "fatal facility" for "the mixture of races." As for Brooks's position on political rights, it meant in effect that all Negroes should be excluded from suffrage while "even the most ignorant and brutal white man" should be allowed to vote: "If he should propose to guard the ballot by some exclusion of ignorance or baseness, made without regard to race or class, candid men would listen to him and discuss that proposition." But Brooks was propounding, according to Baldwin, a concept of white privilege and "divine right" completely incompatible with the American egalitarian philosophy. Eventually Baldwin touched gingerly on the question of inherent racial differences and conceded the point that the races were not alike, but argued that "it is quite possible that we shall find it necessary to revise our conception of what constitutes the superiority of race." The prevailing conception, he noted, had resulted from an admiration for the ability to conquer and dominate; but were such aggressive qualities "really the highest, the most admirable development of human nature?" Pointing to the recent rise of a higher regard for the gentler, more peaceable virtues, Baldwin suggested "that each race and each distinct family of mankind has some peculiar gift of its own in which it is superior to others; and that an all-wise Creator may have designed that each race and family shall bring its own peculiar contribution to the final completeness of civilization. . . ." Although he did not discuss directly how the racial character of whites and Negroes differed, he was clearly invoking the romantic racialist conceptions that had long been popular among Radicals and abolitionists.

At first glance it would appear that Baldwin's speech constituted an adequate response to the racist critique of Radical Reconstruction, despite his avoidance of Brooks's specific physiological, anatomical, and historical arguments. It was indeed "rights" that the Radicals were attempting to legislate and not the identity of the races. But if, as Baldwin conceded, the races had differing "gifts"—with the whites holding a monopoly of the kind of qualities that led to dominance and conquest—then the competitive "test" of racial capabilities that the Radicals envisioned as resulting from their program would, to follow their own logic, lead inevitably to white domination, even without the support of discriminatory laws. Furthermore, their tendency to accept the concept of innate racial differences and their apparent repulsion to intermarriage were invitations to prejudice and discrimination on the part of those whites—presumably the overwhelming majority of Americans—who were less likely to respond to romantic appeals to racial benevolence than to draw traditional white-supremacist conclusions from any Radical admissions that blacks were "different" and, in some sense, unassimilable.

A few Radicals and abolitionists had early and serious doubts about the efficacy and underlying assumptions of the Reconstruction Acts of 1867 and 1868. They suspected that quick readmission of Southern states into the Union under constitutions providing for Negro suffrage and the disfranchisement of prominent ex-Confederates would not by itself give blacks a reasonable opportunity to develop their full capacities and establish a position of genuine equality. Some understanding of this problem had been reflected in the land confiscation proposals of men like Thaddeus Stevens and Wendell Phillips. But it was the Radicals who worked for extended periods among the freedmen in the South who gained the fullest awareness of what needed to be done beyond what most Congressional proponents of Radical Reconstruction thought was necessary. Charles Stearns, an abolitionist who attempted to establish a co-operative plantation in Georgia as a step toward Negro landownership, attacked the notion that legal and political rights were all that was required to give the black man a fair, competitive position. In *The Black Man of the South and the Rebels,* published in 1872, Stearns denounced Greeley's philosophy of "root hog or die," arguing that even a hog could not root without a snout. In his view, provisions for land and education, far beyond anything that was then available to the blacks, were absolutely essential. Arguing that "the black man possesses all the natural powers that we possess," he pointed out that the blacks had not yet recovered from the degrading effects of slavery and were unable, even under Radical Reconstruction, to compete successfully or maintain their rights in the face of a bitterly hostile Southern white population.

Albion W. Tourgée, an idealistic "carpetbagger" who settled in North Carolina and became a judge under its Radical regime, was an eloquent and persistent spokesman for the same point of view. Tourgée, who eventually made his experiences and perceptions the basis of a series of novels, sensed from the beginning that the Radical program, as it finally emerged from Congress, constituted a halfhearted commitment to Negro equality which was doomed to fail in the long run. In a letter to the *National Anti-Slavery Standard* in October, 1867, he announced his opposition to the "Plan of Congress" that was taking shape. "No law, no constitution, no matter how cunningly framed," he wrote, "can shield the poor man of the South from the domination of that very aristocracy from which rebellion sprang, when once states are established here. Anarchy or oligarchy are the inevitable results of reconstruction. Serfdom or bloodshed must necessarily follow. The 'Plan of Congress,' so called, if adopted, would deliver the free men of the South, bound hand and foot to their old-time, natural enemies." The Southern Republican Party, Tourgée was saying, was composed largely of impoverished blacks and lower-class whites. Even if assured of temporary political dominance by the disfranchisement of ex-Confederates, these men would soon find themselves at the mercy of the large landowners, who were in a position to apply economic pressure and undo the reforms of Reconstruction. With rare realism, Tourgée argued in effect that political power could not be maintained on the basis of suffrage alone but must be bolstered by adequate economic and social power—and this was precisely what Southern Republicans lacked.

Tourgée's predictions of course came true. As the North looked on, manifesting an increasing reluctance to interfere—a growing desire to wash its hands of the whole matter—Southern white "redeemers" toppled one Radical government after another between 1870 and 1877 and established white-supremacist regimes. Southern Radicalism, supported largely by black votes and ruling through shifting and unstable alliances of Northern "carpetbaggers," Southern white "scalawags," and emergent black spokesmen, had no chance of withstanding the economic, political, and paramilitary opposition of the white majority. In his 1879 Reconstruction novel, *A Fool's Errand,* Tourgée provided an acute assessment of what the Northern leadership had done and why it failed to achieve its original objectives:

> After having forced a proud people to yield what they had for more than two centuries considered a right,—the right to hold the African race in bondage,—they proceeded to outrage a feeling as deep and fervent as the zeal of Islam or the exclusiveness of the Hindoo caste, by giving the ignorant, the unskilled and dependent race—a race which could not have lived a week without the support or charity of the dominant one—equality of political right. Not content with this, they went farther, and by erecting the rebellious territory into self-regulating and sovereign states, they abandoned these parties to fight out the question of predominance without the possibility of national interference, they said to the colored man in the language of one of the pseudo-philosophers of that day, 'Root, hog, or die!'

The Negro never had a chance in this struggle, as the entire novel makes clear. His ignorance and poverty made him no match for the white conservative forces.

What Tourgée and a few others—notably Representative George W. Julian of Indiana—would have preferred as a plan of reconstruction was a comparatively long-term military occupation or territorial rule of the South, which would have guaranteed "Regeneration before Reconstruction." This "territorial tutelage" would have lasted for an indeterminate period, perhaps as long as twenty or thirty years—long enough to give the North a chance to prepare the freedmen for citizenship through extensive programs of education and guidance, presumably including some form of economic assistance, while at the same time working for a diminution of the racial prejudice and "disloyalty" of the whites. But such an approach was rendered impossible both by pressures which impelled Republican politicians to seek readmission of loyalist-dominated Southern states to the Union in time for the election of 1868 and by the underlying social and racial attitudes that have been described. According to the dominant "self-help" ideology, no one, regardless of his antecedents, had a claim on society for economic security or special protection, or was entitled to a social status that he had not earned through independent struggle and hard work; the just penalty for laziness, inefficiency, or vice was severe social and economic deprivation, and it was becoming an open question at this time whether society's most abysmal "failures" should even retain their full right to participate in the political process. Having been provided with Federal laws and Constitutional amendments which supposedly guaranteed his legal equality, the black man was expected to make his own way and find his "true level" with a minimum of interference and direct assistance. When the Reconstruction governments foundered, many in the North were quick to say that the blacks had had their fair chance, had demonstrated their present incapacity for self-government, and could justifiably be relegated, for the time being at least, to an inferior status.

Tourgée probably understood better than anyone how tenuous and conditional the Northern commitment to Negro equality had been. His book *An Appeal to Caesar,* published in 1884, contended that the Northern people "have always reflected the Southern idea of the negro in everything except as to his natural right to be free and to exercise the rights of the freedman. From the first [the North] seems to have been animated by the sneaking notion that after having used the negro to fight its battles, freed him as the natural result of a rebellion based on slavery, and enfranchised him to constitute a political foil to the ambition and disloyalty of his former master, it could at any time unload him upon the states where he chanced to dwell, wash its hands of all further responsibility in the matter, and leave him to live or die as chance might determine."

Heather Cox Richardson

The Death of Reconstruction: Race, Labor, and Politics in the Post–Civil War North, 1865–1901

Civil Rights and the Growth of the National Government, 1870–1883

Northern Republican disillusionment with African-American attitudes toward social issues compounded the Northern association of Southern freedmen with labor radicals who advocated confiscation of wealth. Taking place during and immediately after the South Carolina tax crisis, the civil rights debates of the 1870s seemed to confirm that African-Americans were turning increasingly to legislation to afford them the privileges for which other Americans had worked individually. Civil rights agitation did more than simply flesh out an existing sketch of disaffected black workers, however; it suggested that advocates of African-American rights were actively working to expand the national government to cater to those who rejected the free labor ideal.

"Civil rights," in the immediate aftermath of the war, meant something different than it gradually came to mean over the next several years. *Harper's Weekly* distinguished between "natural rights" to life, liberty, and "the fruits of . . . honest labor," and "civil rights," which were critical to a freedperson's ability to function as a free worker. Civil rights, it explained, were "such rights as to sue, to give evidence, to inherit, buy, lease, sell, convey, and hold property, and others. Few intelligent persons in this country would now deny or forbid equality of natural and civil rights," it asserted in 1867. The 1866 Civil Rights Act, written by the man who had drafted the Thirteenth Amendment, Illinois senator Lyman Trumbull, was intended to secure to African-Americans "full and equal benefit of all laws and proceedings for the security of person and property as is enjoyed by white citizens." It guaranteed only that the legal playing field would be level for all citizens; state legislatures could not enact legislation endangering a black person's right to his life or his land. By 1867, hoping to woo conservative Republican voters into the Democratic camp and to undercut the justification for black suffrage, even moderate Democrats claimed to be willing to back civil rights for African-Americans "with every token of sincerity . . . from a free and spontaneous sense of justice."

"Social" equality was a different thing—it was a result of a person's economic success rather than a condition for it. It was something to be earned by whites and blacks alike. Directly related to economic standing, a man's social standing rose as he prospered. A good social position also required that a person possess other attributes that the community valued. A place in upwardly mobile American society required religious observance and apparently moral behavior, as well as the habits of thrift and economy dictated by a plan for economic success. This gradual social elevation became a mirror of gradual economic elevation through hard work as a traditional free laborer.

Immediately after the Civil War, as Democrats insisted that black freedom would usher in social mixing between races and intermarriage, almost all Northern Republicans emphatically denied that emancipation was intended to have any effect on social issues and reiterated that African-Americans must rise in society only through the same hard effort that had brought other Americans to prominence. In 1867, a correspondent to the radical *Cincinnati Daily Gazette* from Louisiana painted a complimentary portrait of Louisiana African-Americans, then concluded that they had neither the expectation nor the desire for "social equality, that favorite bugbear." They would ridicule any attempt to break down social distinctions by legislation, knowing that the government could give them only political equality, the writer claimed, quoting his informants as saying, "Our own brains, our own conduct, is what we must depend upon for our future elevation; each one of us striving for himself and laboring to improve his mental and moral condition." Adding credence to the correspondent's representations, the Georgia Freedmen's Convention of 1866 resolved, "We do not in any respect desire social equality beyond the transactions of the ordinary business of life, inasmuch as we deem our own race, equal to all our wants of purely social enjoyment."

As the Republicans enacted legislation promoting the interests of African-Americans, however, racist Democrats insisted they were forcing social interaction to promote African-Americans artificially, at the expense of whites. When the Civil Rights Act of 1866 took effect, Democrats charged that the Republican concept of black equality before the law meant Republicans believed that blacks and whites were entirely equal. The *New York World* predicted interracial marriages; the *Columbus (Ohio) Crisis* insisted that a black orator in Richmond had told his black audience to "vote for the man who will bring you into his parlor, who will eat dinner with you, and who, if you want her, will let you marry his daughter." In 1868, *De Bow's Review* argued that negro suffrage meant that African-Americans would "next meet us at the marriage altar and in the burial vault," where they would "order the white ancestors' bones to be disinterred and removed elsewhere, and their own transferred into these hitherto held sacred white family sepulchers."

In response to Democratic attacks, in 1868 the *New York Times* reiterated that Republicans planned only for African-Americans to share the rights and opportunities of typical free laborers. It maintained that "reconstruction did not fly in the face of nature by attempting to impose social . . . equality," it simply established political and legal equality. These rights would eventually "obliterate" social prejudices as white men sought black votes. The next year the *Times* approvingly reported that abolitionist agitator Wendell Phillips had said that "the social equality of the black race will have to be worked out by their own exertion." Frederick Douglass put out the best idea, it continued later, namely: "Let the negro alone."

Republican insistence that social equality would work itself out as freedpeople worked their way up to prosperity could not provide an answer for the overwhelming discrimination African-Americans faced. While many black and white Southerners accepted the established patterns of segregation, those practices meant that African-Americans' public life was inferior to that of their white counterparts. Black people could not sit on juries in most of the South, they could not be certain of transportation on railroads or accommodation at inns, their schools were poor copies of white schools. In addition to creating a climate of constant harassment for African-Americans, discrimination, especially discrimination in schooling, seemed to hamper their ability to rise economically. The Fourteenth and Fifteenth Amendments had made all Americans equal before the law, but they could not guarantee equal access to transportation, accommodations, or schools, and while many ex-slaves accepted conditions as an improvement on the past and dismissed civil rights bills as impractical, those African-Americans who had worked hard to become members of the "better classes" deeply resented their exclusion from public facilities. "Education amounts to nothing, good behavior counts for nothing, even money cannot buy for a colored man or woman decent treatment and the comforts that white people claim and can obtain," complained Mississippi Sheriff John M. Brown. Prominent African-Americans called for legislation to counter the constant discrimination they faced.

African-American proponents of a new civil rights law to enforce nondiscrimination in public services had a champion in the former abolitionist Senator Charles Sumner of Massachusetts. An exceedingly prominent man, the tall, aloof Sumner was the nation's leading champion of African-American rights after the war and had advocated a civil rights measure supplementary to the Civil Rights Act of 1866 since May 1870, when he introduced to the Senate a bill (S. 916) making the federal government responsible for the enforcement of equal rights in public transportation, hotels, theaters, schools, churches, public cemeteries, and juries.

But Sumner's sponsorship of a civil rights bill immediately made more moderate congressmen wary of it; his enthusiasm for black rights frequently made him advocate measures that seemed to remove African-Americans from the free labor system and make them favored wards of a government that was expanding to serve them. Only two months after the ratification of the fifteenth Amendment had reassured moderate Republicans and Democrats alike that they had done everything possible to make all men equal in America, Sumner told the Senate that black men were not actually equal enough, but that his new bill would do the trick. When it passes, he said, "I [will] know nothing further to be done in the way of legislation for the security of equal rights in this Republic." . . .

By 1874, most Republicans were ready to cut the freedpeople's ties to the government in order to force African-Americans to fall back on their own resources and to protect the government from the machinations of demagogues pushing special-interest legislation. When Mississippi Republicans asked President Grant in January 1874 to use the administration to shore up their state organization, the *Philadelphia Inquirer* enthusiastically reported his refusal. Grant "remove[d] his segar from his mouth and enunciate[d] a great truth with startling emphasis," according to a writer for the newspaper. The president said it was "time for the Republican party to unload." The party could not continue to carry the "dead weight" of intrastate quarrels. Grant was sick and tired of it, he told listeners. "This nursing of monstrosities has nearly exhausted the life of the party. I am done with them, and they will have to take care of themselves." The *Philadelphia Inquirer* agreed that the federal government had to cease to support the Southern Republican organizations of freedpeople and their demagogic leaders. The *New York Daily Tribune* approved Grant's similar hands-off policy in Texas, thrilled that "there [was] no longer any cause to apprehend that another State Government will be overturned by Federal bayonets."

Benjamin Butler's role as the House manager of the civil rights bill only hurt its chances, for he embodied the connection between freedpeople and a government in thrall to special interests. The symbol of the "corruption" of American government, Butler was popularly credited with strong-arming the House into recognizing the Louisiana representatives backed by the Kellogg government, which was generally believed to be an illegal creation of Louisiana's largely black Republican party, supported not by the people of the state but by federal officers. Honest men wanted to destroy "the principle which Mr. Butler and his followers represent," wrote the *New York Daily Tribune* and others. "The force in our politics of which he is the recognized exponent, and of which thousands of our politicians of less prominence are the creatures." "Butlerism" meant gaining power by promising an uneducated public patronage or legislation in their favor, and all but the stalwart Republicans and Democratic machine politicians hoped for the downfall of both Butler and what he represented.

Despite the fact that it was prosperous African-Americans who advocated the bill, it appeared to opponents that the civil rights bill was an extraordinary piece of unconstitutional legislation by which demagogues hoped to hold on to power in the South, and thus in the nation, by catering to the whims of disaffected African-Americans who were unwilling to work. The proposed law seemed to offer nothing to the nation but a trampled constitution, lazy freedpeople, and a growing government corrupted into a vehicle for catering to the undeserving.

The civil rights bill would probably never have passed the Senate had it not been for the sudden death of Charles Sumner on March 11, 1874. Before he died, Sumner charged fellow Massachusetts senator George F. Hoar to "take care of the civil-rights bill,—my bill, the civil-rights bill, don't let it fail." Even Republican enemies of the bill eulogized the "great man"; the *Chicago Tribune* reflected that "there is no man, friend or enemy, who does not pause to pay respect to the memory of Charles Sumner." African-Americans across the country mourned Sumner's death and called for the passage of his "last and grandest work," and on April 14, 1874, from the Committee on the Judiciary Senator Frederick T. Frelinghuysen reported Sumner's civil rights bill protecting African-Americans from discrimination in public facilities, schools, and juries. The committee's amendments placed firmly in the national legal apparatus responsibility for overseeing violations of the proposed law. In caucus on May 8, some Republican senators objected to "certain features" of the bill but expressed a desire to act "harmoniously" on the measure. In the next caucus, the Republicans decided to support the bill without amendments.

After an all-night session of the Senate, a handful of African-American men in the galleries applauded as the Senate passed the bill on May 23, 1874, by a vote of twenty-nine to sixteen. Rumors circulated that the president had "some doubts about signing it" if it should pass the House, and many Republicans indicated they would not mind the loss of the bill. "Respect for the dead is incumbent on us all," snarled the *New York Times*, "—but legislation should be based on a careful and wise regard for the welfare of the living, not upon 'mandates,' real or fictitious, of the dead." Referring to the apparent African-American control of Southern governments, the *Times* asked whether the freedman "stands in need of protection from the white man, or the white man stands in need of protection from him." The House Judiciary Committee could not agree on its own civil rights measure and decided to replace its bill with the Senate's. The House then tabled the bill for the rest of the session, despite the continued urging of "leading colored men" that Benjamin Butler get it taken up and passed. . . .

The civil rights bill was rescued from oblivion only by Democratic wins in the 1874 elections. Republican congressmen's desire to consolidate Reconstruction before the Democrats arrived barely outweighed party members' fears that the measure was an attempt of corrupt politicians to harness the black vote by offering African-Americans extraordinary benefits that would undermine their willingness to work. When the lame-duck Congress reconvened in December 1874, House Republican leader Benjamin Butler tried to pass a bill protecting freedmen at the polls and an army appropriations bill to shore up stalwart Republicans in the South. Democrats filibustered. Butler was unable to get a suspension of the rules to maneuver around them as fifteen Republicans joined the opposition, worried that Butler's attempt to suspend the rules was simply a means "to get through a lot of jobbing measures under cover of Civil Rights and protection of the South." With his reputation as a special-interest broker, Butler had a terrible time getting the civil rights bill off the Speaker's table. Finally Republicans agreed to let Butler take it to the floor in late January.

The galleries were full as the House discussed the bill in early February. After omitting provisions for integrated schools, churches, and cemeteries, the

House passed the bill on February 5 by a vote of 162 to 100. While African-Americans in favor of a civil rights bill were horrified at the sacrifice of the school clause, all but the most radical Republicans approved the omission. "The bill . . . is worthy [of] the support of every congressman who wishes to deal equitably with the citizens of the United States, white and black," wrote even the *Boston Evening Transcript*. "This measure simply provides for the education of the blacks, and does not force their children into association with white scholars," at the same time demanding that the schools be equal. "The Republicans can stand upon such a platform as that," the *Transcript* chided unwilling party members. "The great desire and solicitude of the people are to support 'civil rights' and so execute in good faith the constitutional pledges of the nation." After initial reluctance, the Senate passed the school amendment by a vote of 38 to 62, and despite Democratic plans to talk the bill to death, the Senate repassed the civil rights bill without further amendment on February 27, 1875, with Democrats in the opposition. Grant signed the civil rights bill into law on March 1, 1875.

While some radical papers like the *Boston Evening Transcript* defended the bill—wondering "[i]f the blacks and whites cannot shave and drink together . . . how can they remain tolerably peaceful in the same community?"—its passage drew fire from conservative and moderate Northern Republicans who still read into the measure a larger political story of the corruption of a growing government by those determined to advance through government support rather than through productive labor. The *New York Times* noted that Nothern African-Americans were "quiet, inoffensive people who live for and to themselves, and have no desire to intrude where they are not welcome." In the South, however, it continued, "there are many colored men and women who delight in 'scenes' and cheap notoriety." It was these people, the "negro politician, . . . the ignorant field hand, who, by his very brutality has forced his way into, and disgraces, public positions of honor and trust—men . . . who have no feeling and no sensibility," who would "take every opportunity of inflicting petty annoyances upon their former masters." The author concluded that the law would not be enforceable, and that "it is a great mistake to seek to impose new social customs on a people by act of Congress." Noticing the immediate efforts of Southerners to circumvent the law by giving up public licenses and legislating against public disturbances, the *San Francisco Daily Alta California* agreed that the act was likely to produce more trouble than equality, and reiterated that social equality must be earned rather than enforced by law.

The true way for African-Americans to achieve equality, Republicans argued, was to work. The *New York Times* approvingly quoted an African-American minister in the South who reiterated the idea that laborers must rise socially only as they acquired wealth and standing. The *Times* recorded his warning that "character, education, and wealth will determine their position, and all the laws in the world cannot give them a high position if they are not worthy of it." Even a correspondent for the staunchly Republican *Cincinnati Daily Gazette* reflected that "Sambo . . . can go to the hotels, ride in first-class cars, and enjoy a box in the theater. To what good is all this? . . . He needs now, to be let alone, and let work out his own destiny, aided only as his wants make him an object of charity. . . .

In 1883, the U.S. Supreme Court considered five civil rights cases, one each from Tennessee, New York, Kansas, Missouri, and California. On October 15, 1883, the court decided that the Civil Rights Act of 1875 was unconstitutional because federal authority could overrule only state institutional discrimination, not private actions; Justice John Marshall Harlan of Kentucky cast the only dissenting vote. With the decision, Northern Republicans stated that they had never liked the law, because it removed African-Americans from the tenets of a free labor society, using the government to give them benefits for which others had to work. The *New York Times* declared that African-Americans "should be treated on their merits as individuals precisely as other citizens are treated in like circumstances" and admitted that there was, indeed, "a good deal of unjust prejudice against" them. But the *Times* remained skeptical that legislation could resolve the problem. Even newspapers like the *Hartford Courant*, which supported the law, said it did so only because it proved that Americans were sincere in their quest for equal rights. Three days later that newspaper mused that the law had been necessary only for "the reorganization of a disordered society," and that freedpeople no longer needed its protection. The *Philadelphia Daily Evening Bulletin* agreed that public sentiment had changed so dramatically that the law was now unnecessary. Even the radical African-American *Cleveland Gazette*, which mourned the court's decision, agreed that the law was a dead letter anyway. The *New York Times* welcomed the decision, going so far as to charge the law with keeping "alive a prejudice against the negroes . . . which without it would have gradually died out."

Instead of supporting the Civil Rights Act, Republicans reiterated the idea that right-thinking African-Americans wanted to succeed on their own. The *New York Times* applauded the public address of the Louisville, Kentucky, National Convention of Colored Men that concentrated largely on the needs of Southern agricultural labor and referred not at all to civil rights. That the convention had pointedly rejected chairman Frederick Douglass's draft address, which had included support for civil rights legislation, made the *Times* conclude that most attendees were "opposed to the extreme views uttered by Mr. Douglass," and that the great African-American leader should retire, since his "role as a leader of his race is about played out."

Despite the *Times*'s conclusion, African-Americans across the country protested the decision both as individuals and in mass meetings, reflecting, "It is a mercy that Charles Sumner is not alive to mourn for his cherished Civil Rights bill." At a mass meeting in Washington, D.C., Frederick Douglass admonished that the decision "had inflicted a heavy calamity on the 7,000,000 of colored people of this country, and had left them naked and defenceless against the action of a malignant, vulgar and pitiless prejudice." When the African Methodist Episcopal (AME) Church Conference of Western States, in session in Denver, discussed the decision, delegates made "incendiary" speeches and "[a] Bishop declared that if the negroes' rights were thus trampled upon a revolution would be the result." . . .

Republicans and Democrats agreed that the only way for African-Americans to garner more rights was to work to deserve them, as all others did in America's free labor system. The *Philadelphia Daily Evening Bulletin* repeated this view:

> [F]urther advancement depends chiefly upon themselves, on their earnest pursuit of education, on their progress in morality and religion, on their thoughtful exercise of their duties as citizens, on their persistent practice of industry, on their self-reliance, and on their determination to exalt themselves, not as proscribed or despised Africans, but as American men clothed with the privileges of citizenship in the one great republic of the earth. They have it in their power to secure for themselves, by their own conduct, more really important "rights" than can be given to them by any formal legislation of Congress.

The Democratic *Hartford Weekly Times* agreed, and asserted that true black leaders, "not men like Fred. Douglass, who are 'professional' colored men, and who have been agitating something and been paid for it all of their lives," approved of the decision. "They say there is no such thing as social equality among white men, and that the colored man cannot get it by law, but by the way he conducts himself."

Republican and Democratic newspapers highlighted those African-Americans who cheerfully told their neighbors "to acquire knowledge and wealth as the surest way of obtaining our rights." From Baltimore came the news that "Mr. John F. Cook, a colored man of character, who deservedly enjoys the respect of this entire community, who has held and administered with marked ability for years the responsible office of Collector of Taxes for the District of Columbia," told a reporter that he had no fears of white reprisals after the decision, expecting whites to accord to African-Americans "what legislation could never accomplish." "These are golden words, and if all men of his race were like Mr. Cook there would never be any trouble on this subject," concluded the Republican *Philadelphia Daily Evening Bulletin.*

Even many Northern Democrats painted their own picture of an egalitarian free labor society that had no need of a civil rights law. First they restated the idea that Republican efforts for African-Americans had simply been a ploy to control the government by marshalling the black vote. Trying to make new ties to African-American voters, the Democratic *San Francisco Examiner* emphasized that Republicans had only wanted to use the black vote to create a Republican empire and that the reversal showed that Republicanism no longer offered advantages to black citizens. A reporter noted that members of the black community had said that "it was about time to shake off the Republican yoke and act in politics as American citizens, not as chattels of a party who cared but for their votes."

While the rhetoric of the *San Francisco Examiner* repeated long-standing Democratic arguments, it also reinforced the idea that some hardworking African-Americans had indeed prospered in America, and that these upwardly mobile blacks were fully accepted even in Democratic circles. In San Francisco, the paper noted, "there are . . . many intelligent and educated men and women of African descent." Using the Republican pattern of according prosperous African-Americans names, descriptions, and their own words, it interviewed the Reverend Alexander Walters, whom it described respectfully as an educated and well-traveled young man, and happily printed both his assertion that in cities across the nation and "in the West . . . race prejudice has died out," and his prediction that the court's decision would drive black voters from the Republican party. Similarly, it quoted P. A. Bell, "the veteran editor of the *Elevator*, the organ of the colored people," as saying that in California—a Democratic state—"we people are treated just as well as if there were fifty Civil Rights bills."

With the overturning of the 1875 Civil Rights Act, mainstream Republicans and Democrats, black and white, agreed that there must be no extraordinary legislation on behalf of African-Americans, who had to work their way up in society like everyone else. Stalwart Republicans who advocated additional protection for black citizens were seen as either political demagogues who wanted the black vote to maintain their power or misguided reformers duped by stories of white atrocities against freedpeople. Northern black citizens who advocated civil rights legislation, like Frederick Douglass, were either scheming politicians who, like their white counterparts, needed the votes of uneducated African-Americans, or they were disaffected workers who believed in class struggle and wanted to control the government in order to destroy capital.

Southern blacks seemed to be the worst of all these types. They appeared to want to increase the government's power solely in order to be given what others had earned, and to do so, they were corrupting government by keeping scheming Republican politicos in office.

POSTSCRIPT

Did Reconstruction Fail as a Result of Racism?

There can be little doubt that racism played some role in the failure of the Radical Republicans to realize their most ambitious goals for integrating African Americans into the mainstream of American society in the years following the Civil War. After all, white supremacy was a powerful doctrine. At the same time, we should not so cavalierly dismiss some of the more positive conclusions reached by that first generation of revisionist historians who built upon W. E. B. DuBois's characterization of Reconstruction as a "splendid failure." For example, Kenneth Stampp's *The Era of Reconstruction, 1865–1877* (Alfred A. Knopf, 1965) ends with the following statement: "The Fourteenth and Fifteenth Amendments, which could have been adopted only under the conditions of radical reconstruction, make the blunders of that era, tragic though they were, dwindle into insignificance. For if it was worth a few years of civil war to save the Union, it was worth a few years of radical reconstruction to give the American Negro the ultimate promise of equal civil and political rights." Eric Foner, too, recognizes something of a silver lining in the nation's post–Civil War reconstruction process. In *Reconstruction: America's Unfinished Revolution, 1863–1877* (Harper & Row, 1988), Foner claims that Reconstruction, though perhaps not all that radical, offered African Americans at least a temporary vision of a free society. Similarly, in *Nothing But Freedom: Emancipation and Its Legacy* (Louisiana State University Press, 1984), Foner advances his interpretation by comparing the treatment of ex-slaves in the United States with that of newly emancipated slaves in Haiti and the British West Indies. Only in the United States, he contends, were the freedmen given voting and economic rights. Although these rights had been stripped away from the majority of black southerners by 1900, Reconstruction had, nevertheless, created a legacy of freedom that inspired succeeding generations of African Americans.

On the other hand, C. Vann Woodward, in "Reconstruction: A Counterfactual Playback," an essay in his thought-provoking *The Future of the Past* (Oxford University Press, 1988), shares Fredrickson's pessimism about the outcome of Reconstruction. For all the successes listed by the revisionists, he argues that the experiment failed. He challenges Foner's conclusions by insisting that former slaves were as poorly treated in the United States as they were in other countries. He also maintains that the confiscation of former plantations and the redistribution of land to the former slaves would have failed in the same way that the Homestead Act of 1862 failed to generate equal distribution of government lands to poor white settlers.

Thomas Holt's *Black Over White: Negro Political Leadership in South Carolina During Reconstruction* (University of Illinois Press, 1977) is representative of state and local studies that employ modern social science methodology to yield new perspectives. Although critical of white Republican leaders, Holt (who is African American) also blames the failure of Reconstruction in South Carolina on free-born mulatto politicians, whose background distanced them economically, socially, and culturally from the masses of freedmen. Consequently, these political leaders failed to develop a clear and unifying ideology to challenge white South Carolinians who wanted to restore white supremacy.

The study of the Reconstruction period benefits from an extensive bibliography. Traditional accounts of Reconstruction include William Archibald Dunning's *Reconstruction, Political and Economic, 1865–1877* (Harper & Brothers, 1907); Claude Bowers's *The Tragic Era: The Revolution after Lincoln* (Riverside Press, 1929); and E. Merton Coulter's, *The South During Reconstruction, 1865–1877* (Louisiana State University Press, 1947), the last major work written from the Dunning (or traditional) point of view. Some of the earliest revisionist views appeared in the scholarly works of African American historians such as W. E. B. DuBois, *Black Reconstruction in America: An Essay Toward a History of the Part Which Black Folk Played in the Attempt to Reconstruct Democracy in America, 1860–1880* (Harcourt, Brace, 1935), a Marxist analysis, and John Hope Franklin, *Reconstruction: After the Civil War* (University of Chicago Press, 1961); and Kenneth M. Stampp, *The Era of Reconstruction, 1865–1877* (Alfred A. Knopf, 1965). Briefer overviews are available in Forrest G. Wood, *The Era of Reconstruction, 1863–1877* (Harlan Davidson, 1975) and Michael Perman, *Emancipation and Reconstruction, 1862-1879* (Harlan Davidson, 1987). One of the best-written studies of a specific episode during the Reconstruction years is Willie Lee Rose's *Rehearsal for Reconstruction: The Port Royal Experiment* (Bobbs-Merrill, 1964), which describes the failed effort at land reform in the sea islands of South Carolina. Richard Nelson Current's *Those Terrible Carpetbaggers: A Reinterpretation* (Oxford University Press, 1988) is a superb challenge to the traditional view of these much-maligned Reconstruction participants. Finally, for collections of interpretive essays on various aspects of the Reconstruction experience, see Staughton Lynd, ed., *Reconstruction* (Harper & Row, 1967); Seth M. Scheiner, ed., *Reconstruction: A Tragic Era?* (Holt, Rinehart and Winston, 1968); and Edwin C. Rozwenc, ed., *Reconstruction in the South* (2d ed., Heath, 1972).

Contributors to This Volume

EDITORS

LARRY MADARAS is professor of history emeritus at Howard Community College in Columbia, Maryland. He received a B.A. from the College of Holy Cross in 1959 and an M.A. and Ph.D. from New York University in 1961 and 1964, respectively. He has also taught at Spring Hill College, the University of South Alabama, and the University of Maryland at College Park. He has been a Fulbright Fellow and has held two fellowships from the National Endowment for the Humanities. He is the author of dozens of journal articles and book reviews.

JAMES M. SoRELLE is a professor of history and former chair of the Department of History at Baylor University in Waco, Texas. He received a B.A. and M.A. from the University of Houston in 1972 and 1974, respectively, and a Ph.D. from Kent State University in 1980. In addition to introductory courses in United States and world history, he teaches advanced undergraduate classes in African American history, the American civil rights movement, and the 1960s, as well as a graduate seminar on the civil rights movement. His scholarly articles have appeared in *Houston Review, Southwestern Historical Quarterly,* and *Black Dixie: Essays in Afro-Texan History and Culture in Houston* (Texas A & M University Press, 1992), edited by Howard Beeth and Cary D. Wintz. He also has contributed entries to *The New Handbook of Texas, The Oxford Companion to Politics of the World, Encyclopedia of African American Culture and History,* the *Encyclopedia of the Confederacy,* and the *Encyclopedia of African American History.*

AUTHORS

JON BUTLER is the Howard R. Lamar Professor of American History and Dean of the Graduate School of Arts and Sciences at Yale University. He is the author of *Awash in a Sea of Faith: Christianizing the American People* (Harvard University Press, 1990) and is currently writing a book on religion in modern New York City.

COLIN G. CALLOWAY is professor of history and Samson Occom Professor of Native American Studies at Dartmouth where he chairs the Native American Studies Program. He recently published *The Scratch of a Pen: 1763 and the Transformation of North America* (Oxford University Press, 2006).

CHARLES B. DEW is the Ephraim Williams Professor of American History at Williams College. Two of his books, *Apostles of Disunion* and *Ironmaker to the Confederacy: Joseph R. Anderson and the Tredegar Iron Works* (Yale University Press, 1966), received the Fletcher Pratt Award presented by the Civil War Round Table of New York for the best nonfiction book on the American Civil War. He is also the author of *Bond of Iron: Master and Slave at Buffalo Forge* (W. W. Norton, 1994), which received the Elliott Rudwick Prize from the Organization of American Historians.

THOMAS DUBLIN is professor of history and codirector of the Center for the Historical Study of Women and Gender at The State University of New York at Binghamton. He is the author of *Women at Work: The Transformation of Work and Community in Lowell, Massachusetts, 1826–1860* (Columbia University Press, 1979) and *Transforming Women's Work: New England Lives in the Industrial Revolution* (Cornell University Press, 1994).

WILMA A. DUNAWAY is associate professor of sociology at Virginia Polytechnic Institute and State University. Her first book, *The First American Frontier: Transition to Capitalism in Southern Appalachia, 1700–1860* (University of North Carolina Press, 1996) won the 1996 Weatherford Award for the best book about Southern Appalachia.

GEORGE M. FREDRICKSON is the Edgar E. Robinson Professor of U. S. History Emeritus at Stanford University and the preeminent American scholar on the history of race. He is the author of *The Inner Civil War: Northern Intellectuals and the Crisis of the Union* (Harper & Row, 1965), *White Supremacy: A Comparative Study of American and South African History* (Oxford University Press, 1981), and *Black Liberation: A Comparative History of Black Ideologies in the United States and South Africa* (Oxford University Press, 1995).

EUGENE D. GENOVESE, a prominent Marxist historian and Civil War scholar, is president of the Historical Society, a professional organization of historians, and a former president of the Organization of American Historians. His many publications include *A Consuming Fire: The Fall of the Confederacy in the Mind of the White Christian South* (University of Georgia Press, 1998) and *The Southern Front: History and Politics in the Cultural War* (University of Missouri Press, 1995).

JOHN STEELE GORDON is a specialist in business and financial history whose articles have appeared in numerous prominent magazines and newspapers for the past 20 years. He is a contributing editor to *American Heritage* and since 1989 has written the "Business of America" column. His other books include *Hamilton's Blessing: The Extraordinary Life and Times of Our National Debt* (Walker, 1997), *The Great Game: The Emergence of Wall Street as a World Power: 1653–2000* (1999), and *A Thread across the Ocean: the Heroic Story of the Transatlantic Cable* (Walker, 2002).

NORMAN A. GRAEBNER is the Randolph P. Compton Professor Emeritus of History at the University of Virginia in Charlottesville, Virginia. He has held a number of other academic appointments and has received distinguished teacher awards at every campus at which he has taught. He has edited and written numerous books, articles, and texts on American history, including *Foundations of American Foreign Policy: A Realist Appraisal From Franklin to McKinley* (Scholarly Resources Press, 1985) and *Empire on the Pacific: A Study in American Continental Expansion,* 2d ed. (Regina Books, 1983).

OSCAR HANDLIN is professor emeritus of history at Harvard University. He is the author of numerous books, including *The Uprooted: The Epic Story of the Great Migrations That Made the American People* (Little, Brown, 1951), *Boston's Immigrants, 1790–1880: A Study in Acculturation* (rev. and enl. ed., Belknap Press, 1991), and with Lilian Handlin, *Liberty in America,* 4 vols. (Harper & Row, 1986–1994).

VINCENT HARDING is a professor of religion and social transformation at the Iliff School of Theology in Denver, Colorado, and has long been involved in domestic and international movements for peace and justice. He is the author of *Hope and History: Why We Must Share the Story of the Movement* (Orbis Books, 1990) and coauthor, with Robin D. G. Kelley and Earl Lewis, of *We Changed the World: African Americans, 1945–1970* (Oxford University Press, 1997).

NATHAN O. HATCH currently serves as president of Wake Forest University following a distinguished teaching and administrative career at Notre Dame University. A specialist in American religious history, he is the author of *The Sacred Cause of Liberty: Republican Thought and the Millennium in Revolutionary New England* (Yale University Press, 1977), *The Search for Christian America* (Helmers and Howard, 1983), and *The Democratization of American Christianity* (Yale University Press, 1989).

DONALD R. HICKEY is professor of history at Wayne State College in Nebraska. He is also the author of *Nebraska Moments: Glimpses of Nebraska's Past* (University of Nebraska Press, 1992).

DAVID S. JONES is an assistant professor in the History and Culture of Science and Technology at MIT. He also works as a staff psychiatrist in the Psychiatric Emergency Center at Cambridge Hospital. He is the author of *Rationalizing Epidemics: Meanings and Uses of American Indian Mortality since 1600* (Harvard University Press, 2004).

CAROL F. KARLSEN is professor of history and women's studies at the University of Michigan. She also has published *The Salem Witchcraft Trials: A History in Documents* (Oxford University Press, 2005) and *The Journal of Esther Edwards Burr, 1754–1757* (Yale University Press, 1986).

KAREN ORDAHL KUPPERMAN is the Silver Professor of History at New York University. Her other books include *Settling With the Indians: The Meeting of English and Indian Cultures in America, 1580–1640* (Rowman & Littlefield, 1980), *Providence Island, 1630–1641: The Other Puritan Colony* (Cambridge University Press, 1993), which won the Albert Beveridge Prize from the American Historical Association, and *Indians and English: Facing Off in Early America* (Cornell University Press, 2000), winner of the AHA Prize in Atlantic History.

GERDA LERNER is Robinson-Edwards Professor of History Emerita at the University of Wisconsin at Madison. One of the foremost historians of women in America, she is the author of numerous books, including *The Grimké Sisters from South Carolina* (Houghton Mifflin, 1967) and *The Creation of Patriarchy* (Oxford University Press, 1986).

RICHARD P. McCORMICK (1916–2006) was professor emeritus of history at Rutgers University at the time of his death. He was the author of several influential works on American political history, including *The Second American Party System* (W. W. Norton, 1966) and *The Presidential Game: The Origin of American Presidential Politics* (Oxford University Press, 1982).

DREW R. McCOY is the Jacob and Frances Hiatt Professor of History and chair of the Department of History at Clark University. A specialist in American political and intellectual history, he also is the author of *The Elusive Republic: Political Economy in Jeffersonian America* (University of North Carolina Press, 1980).

WILLIAM H. McNEILL is professor emeritus of history at the University of Chicago where he was the Robert A. Milliken Distinguished Service Professor prior to his retirement. He is the author of *The Rise of the West: A History of the Human Community* (University of Chicago, 1970), which received the National Book Award, *Plagues and Peoples* (Anchor Press, 1976), and *A World History* (4th ed., Oxford University Press, 1998).

JAMES M. McPHERSON is the George Henry Davis '86 Professor Emeritus of United States History at Princeton University. The author of 17 books, his major works include *The Struggle for Equality: Abolitionists and the Negro in the Civil War and Reconstruction* (Princeton University Press, 1964), *The Negro's Civil War: How American Negroes Felt and Acted During the War for the Union* (Pantheon Books, 1965), *Ordeal by Fire: The Civil War and Reconstruction* (3d ed.; McGraw-Hill, 2001), and *Battle Cry of Freedom: The Civil War Era* (Oxford University Press, 1988), for which he won the Pulitzer Prize.

EDMUND S. MORGAN is the Sterling Professor Emeritus of History at Yale University and the author of 16 books on the American colonial period. These works include *The Puritan Family: Religion and Domestic Relations in*

Seventeenth-Century New England (Harper & Row, 1966), *The Puritan Dilemma: The Story of John Winthrop* (2d ed., Longman, 1998), and *Benjamin Franklin* (Yale University Press, 2002). His most recent book, *The Genuine Article: A Historian Looks at Early America* (W. W. Norton, 2004), is a collection of his review essays that appeared in *The New York Review of Books*. In 2000, he received the National Humanities Medal.

MARK E. NEELY, JR. is the McCabe Greer Professor in the American Civil War Era at Penn State University. He is the author of several books on Abraham Lincoln and the Civil War period, including *The Fate of Liberty: Abraham Lincoln and Civil Liberties* (Oxford University Press, 1991), which won the Pulitzer Prize for History and the Bell I. Wiley Prize, *The Last Best Hope of Earth: Abraham Lincoln and the Promise of America* (Harvard University Press, 1993), and *The Boundaries of American Political Culture in the Civil War Era* (University of North Carolina Press, 2005).

MARY BETH NORTON is the Mary Donlon Alger Professor of American History at Cornell University. She is the author of *Liberty's Daughters: The Revolutionary Experience of American Women, 1750–1800, The British-Americans: The Loyalist Exiles in England, 1774–1789* (Cornell University Press, 1980), *Founding Mothers and Fathers: Gendered Power and the Forming of American Society* (1996), and coauthor of the popular college text *A People and a Nation* (7th ed.; Houghton Mifflin, 2004).

STEPHEN B. OATES is a former professor of history at the University of Massachusetts, Amherst. The author of 16 books, he has written several critically acclaimed biographies, including *To Purge This Land with Blood: A Biography of John Brown* (Harper & Row, 1970), *With Malice Toward None: The Life of Abraham Lincoln* (Harper & Row, 1977), *Let the Trumpet Sound: The Life of Martin Luther King, Jr.* (HarperCollins, 1982), and *Woman of Valor: Clara Barton and the Civil War* (The Free Press, 1994). He received the Nevins-Freeman Award of the Chicago Civil War Round Table for his scholarly work on the American Civil War.

DAVID S. REYNOLDS is Distinguished Professor of English and American Studies at the Graduate Center and Baruch College of the City University of New York. His book *Walt Whitman's America: A Cultural Biography* (Alfred A. Knopf, 1985) won the Bancroft Prize, and he also is the author of the award-winning *Beneath the American Renaissance: The Subversive Imagination in the Age of Emerson and Melville* (Alfred A. Knopf, 1988).

HEATHER COX RICHARDSON is professor of history at the University of Massachusetts, Amherst. Her other books include *The Greatest Nation of the Earth: Republican Economic Policies during the Civil War* (Harvard University Press, 1997) and *West from Appomattox: The Reconstruction of America after the Civil War* (Yale University Press, 2007).

CAREY ROBERTS is assistant professor of history at Arkansas Tech University. He has presented papers and written articles on eighteenth- and nineteenth-century American history. His particular interests are northern conservatism and conflicting patterns of early nationalism.

JOHN P. ROCHE (1923–1993) was the Olin Distinguished Professor of American Civilization and Foreign Affairs at the Fletcher School of Law and Diplomacy in Medford, Massachusetts, and director of the Fletcher Media Institute. His many publications include *Shadow and Substance: Essays on the Theory and Structure of Politics* (Macmillan, 1964).

RAMÓN EDUARDO RUIZ is professor emeritus of Latin American history at the University of California–San Diego. He is the author of *Triumphs and Tragedy: A History of the Mexican People* (W. W. Norton, 1993).

JOEL H. SILBEY is the President White Professor of History Emeritus at Cornell University. He has written several books and many important articles on the political parties during the Civil War. Among his publications are *Respectable Minority: The Democratic Party in the Civil War Era, 1860–1868* (W. W. Norton, 1977), *The American Political Nation, 1838–1893* (Stanford University Press, 1991), and *Martin Van Buren and the Emergence of American Popular Politics* (Rowman & Littlefield, 2002).

SEAN WILENTZ is Dayton-Stockton Professor of History and director of the Program in American Studies at Princeton University. His book *Chants Democratic: New York City and the Rise of the American Working Class, 1788–1850* (Oxford University Press, 1984) won the prestigious Frederick Jackson Turner Award and the Albert J. Beveridge Award.

C. VANN WOODWARD (1908–1999), considered the dean of historians of the American South prior to his death, was Sterling Professor of History at Yale University. He won the Pulitzer Prize in 1982 for *Mary Chesnut's Civil War* (Yale University Press, 1981). His other distinguished books include *Origins of the New South, 1877–1913* (Louisiana University Press, 1951), *The Strange Career of Jim Crow* (3d rev. ed., Oxford University Press, 1979), *The Future of the Past* (Oxford University Press, 1989), and *Reunion and Reaction: The Compromise of 1877 and the End of Reconstruction* (rev. ed., Oxford University Press, 1991).

HOWARD ZINN is professor emeritus of political science at Boston University. A political activist and prolific writer, he is the author of *SNCC: The New Abolitionists* (Beacon Press, 1964), *Postwar America: 1945–1971* (MacMillan, 1973), and *A People's History of the United States* (Harper & Row, 1980).